On Thin Ice

On Thin Ice

The Inuit, the State, and the Challenge of Arctic Sovereignty

Barry Scott Zellen

LEXINGTON BOOKS
A division of
ROWMAN & LITTLEFIELD PUBLISHERS, INC.
Lanham • Boulder • New York • Toronto • Plymouth, UK

Published by Lexington Books
A division of Rowman & Littlefield Publishers, Inc.
A wholly owned subsidiary of The Rowman & Littlefield Publishing Group, Inc.
4501 Forbes Boulevard, Suite 200, Lanham, Maryland 20706
http://www.lexingtonbooks.com

Estover Road, Plymouth PL6 7PY, United Kingdom

British Library Cataloguing in Publication Information Available

Library of Congress Cataloging-in-Publication Data
Zellen, Barry Scott, 1963–
  On thin ice : the Inuit, the state, and the challenge of Arctic sovereignty / Barry Scott
Zellen.
      p. cm.
  Includes bibliographical references and index.
  ISBN 978-0-7391-3278-4 (cloth : alk. paper)
  eISBN: 978-0-7391-3280-7
  1. Inuit—Land tenure. 2. Inuit—Government relations. 3. Inuit—Politics and
government. 4. Sovereignty. 5. Self-determination, National—Alaska. 6. Self-
determination, National—Canada, Northern. 7. Alaska—Race relations. 8. Alaska—
Politics and government. 9. Canada, Northern—Race relations. 10. Canada, Northern—
Politics and government. I. Title.
  E99.E7Z45 2009
  979.8004'9712—dc22

                                                                            2009033031

Printed in the United States of America

Contents

Foreword by Rob Huebert
Inuit Endurance and the Arctic Transformation

Dr. Rob Huebert is an associate professor in the Department of Political Science at the University of Calgary. He is also the associate director of the Centre for Military and Strategic Studies. He was the recipient of the 2008 Robert I. Hendy Award for Maritime Affairs, which recognizes Canadians who have accomplished feats or achievements of national or international significance in the area of maritime affairs.

The Arctic is undergoing fundamental change. The forces of climate change, technological developments, resource development, and geopolitical changes are opening up the Arctic to the world. Many now see the Arctic as the last undeveloped region of the world. As the Arctic melts many global and regional actors are now beginning to position themselves for the anticipated new opportunities.

The five Arctic states that have continental shelf claims have had a meeting amongst themselves to prepare for the division of the Arctic Ocean. Non-Arctic states such as Japan, South Korea, and China are undertaking substantial preparations for becoming involved in the region. At the heart of this activity is a common view that the Arctic is an open and formidable no-man's land that is now becoming "ripe for the picking." But nothing could be farther from the truth.

The Arctic is not a "no-man's land." Men, women, and children did—and still do—live there. In fact they have been living there now for thousands of years. There were people living in the Arctic long before southerners could approach the region, let alone function there. These people were the Inuit. They have called the Arctic home for a very long time. Their ability to both survive and thrive in this formidable region is the stuff of legends. The Arctic is opening up. This means that the world will soon be coming to them.

The Inuit learned how to read the land for its bounty. They learnt how to read its moods. Their classroom was the entire Arctic. And if they failed their lessons, they died. But most did not. They discovered what foods were necessary to survive in a region where they could eat almost only meat. They adopted dietary practices that confounded our modern understanding of nutrition. It is understood by nearly all that our diet must include fruits and vegetables to prevent diseases like scurvy. Many explorers could not understand how the Inuit, with almost no vegetables or fruits in their diet, could survive. Western science only later found out that the whale blubber eaten raw was their main source of vitamin C. If cooked, the vitamin C was lost. Thus, by eating *muktuk*, the Inuit did not have to worry about the ravages of scurvy that killed so many European sailors.

When the Europeans first encountered the Inuit, they tended to consider them barely more than savages. As a result, many explorers treated the superb adaptation by the Inuit to their homeland with disdain. They refused to accept the Inuit knowledge of the region. Thus many of the first explorers died from the cold, from starvation, and from diseases. Had individuals such as John Franklin, who famously perished on his quest for the Northwest Passage in the nineteenth century, incorporated the practices that the Inuit had learned to employ in the Arctic to survive and even flourish, then the history of European exploration of the North would have been quite different. Of course even this statement betrays a biased view of the Arctic. For the Inuit, there was no need of discovery, because they were already there—and already knew where everything was! It was only those from the South that needed to "discover" the region. Ultimately, most southerners realized by the end of the 1800s that the riches and transportation routes that the Arctic seemed to promise existed in theory, but were simply beyond the technology of the day. Thus when explorers such as Amundsen did at last find the fabled Northwest Passage, it took him so long to get through that it rendered any use of the passage totally impracticable.

It was only at the end of the Second World War that the southern world was able to begin to make inroads into the Arctic on a sustained basis. In part this was due to improvements in ship and aircraft construction. But the technology that truly opened up the Arctic was the development of nuclear power and weapons. Given the geopolitical tensions that quickly escalated between the Soviet Union and the western powers, the new weapons systems meant that the Arctic had become one of the most important strategic locations in the world. If a war was to break out, bombers and intercontinental ballistic missiles would overfly the Arctic, while at the same time nuclear-powered submarines would sail under the ice to launch their own missiles and to attack the other side's submarines. At the same time, as both sides ultimately began to recognize the futility of war, they developed policies of mutual deterrence. These policies required early warning systems built across the Arctic to ensure that neither side could hope to launch a successful surprise nuclear attack of the other.

The Soviet Union, United States, Canada, and Denmark all began massive projects in their respective northern territories to meet these strategic requirements. The Soviets built huge cities in their North, mainly populated by citizens who were often forcibly moved from more southern locations. For the three northern members of NATO, the Distant Early Warning Line (DEW Line) was built from the western-most tip of Alaska to the eastern-most section of Greenland. The impact of these radar sites on the Inuit was tremendous. In the Soviet Union, there was little if any consideration given to such impacts on the lives of the indigenous peoples on its side of the Arctic, as new Soviet cities, towns, military bases, and research centers completely disrupted (and often destroyed) their traditional way of life.

On the other side of the Arctic, the Inuit were introduced to an entirely new economic order. Many were hired to work on the new construction. These left, at least temporarily, their subsistence way of life. They also began to find themselves living around the new radar sites in order to be close to the economic opportunities that now existed. In effect their traditional lifestyles were fundamentally altered. The Cold War also divided families and communities. Traditionally, families had moved without concern about borders across the Bering Strait. Once the Cold War began, these communities were completely divided as the "Ice Curtain" extended the Iron Curtain into the North.

Only with the end of the Cold War were the Inuit able to begin to fully reassert their role in the international system. This was first done through the creation of the Inuit Circumpolar Conference in 1977. While the Inuit from the Soviet side of the Ice Curtain would have to wait until the collapse of that state before they could participate, the Inuit from Canada, Greenland, and the United States were able to start to develop an international voice. When the Cold War ended, and new international bodies and agreements began to be formed in the region, the ICC became an important player. Included as a permanent participant in first the Arctic Environmental Protection Strategy (AEPS) and then the Arctic Council, the ICC found itself an important member of the global effort to understand and protect the Arctic environment. Individual Inuit leaders such as Mary Simon and Sheila Watt-Cloutier also gave a human face to the impact of climate change on the Arctic.

However, despite these important steps forward, the Inuit now find themselves facing new pressures. The Arctic is being fundamentally altered. The forces of climate change are literally changing the very face of the North in ways that are only now beginning to be understood. At the same time, new technologies are allowing for the search for and exploitation of the treasure trove of natural resources that are found throughout the region. The technologies now exist to allow for interested parties to go to the North Pole and drill for oil. To further complicate these forces, there are also emergent geopolitical concerns developing as the coastal Arctic states attempt to determine their Arctic maritime boundaries under international law. At the same time, many of the Arctic states are also beginning to redevelop their northern military capabilities.

It is clear that there is a critical need for understanding the international role played by the Inuit in the Arctic region. It is often forgotten that the north has never been an empty wasteland. It has been the home of the Inuit. The changing nature of the region does not negate the fact that they intend to stay and have every right to do so. Thus a study of their role in the new Arctic is needed if the full story of the Arctic transformation is to be properly understood. That is the objective of this book. This is why Barry Zellen's *On Thin Ice: The Inuit, the State, and the Challenge of Arctic Sovereignty* is an essential read for anyone attempting to understand the Arctic and the role played by those who call it home.

Preface

Ambiguities of Arctic Sovereignty: Beyond the Ice Fog

Across the polar region there is a unique meteorological phenomenon known as ice fog, which can turn the Arctic landscape into a "fuzzy dream world pierced only by bright lights."[1] Ice fog is created when water vapor meets Arctic air that's so cold it is unable to absorb any more water: the result is the formation of tiny ice crystals that can blanket the ground with "cotton candy-like clouds."[2] Generally man-made, commonly produced by car and truck exhaust as well as by the breath of man, ice fog is an apt metaphor for the fundamental ambiguity present in claims of Arctic sovereignty. And it is suggestive of another concept borne of the study of war and strategy, "the fog" of war, made famous by Clausewitz with his colorful, and metaphorical, description of fog in his famous tome, *On War*. As Clausewitz described it: "war is the realm of uncertainty; three quarters of the factors on which action is based are wrapped in a fog of greater or lesser uncertainty," and "all action takes place, so to speak, in a kind of twilight, which, like fog or moonlight, often tends to makes things seem grotesque and larger than they really are."[3] Like all elements of friction encountered in war, the metaphor of fog reflects armed conflict's many inherent incalculables, particularly the inescapable assertion of uncertainty, and probability, on the course of human events, confounding the plans of the commander. Thus "ice fog" becomes an even more apt metaphor for our inquiry in the nature of Arctic sovereignty and security, describing that fuzzy interface where tribe and state both assert their distinct and overlapping claims to the region.

Efforts by the Arctic rim states to assert their sovereignty along their icy periphery confront a humbling reality check; the further north they reach, the more difficult it becomes to project their power. Navies have been readily turned back by the massive ice pack of the polar sea; and permafrost confounds the efforts to build air strips, or to construct military facilities. As a result, the Arctic remains largely under-developed and only lightly colonized, and this has enabled its original inhabitants to remain in the majority across the North American Arctic. And while the Arctic rim states struggle to assert their sovereignty over this forbidding land, the Inuit stand their ground, hunting on the sea ice and in the brief Arctic summer, on the liquid sea.

The Arctic has long been the homeland of the Inuit, but as former B.C. Supreme Court Justice Thomas R. Berger described in his report on the Mackenzie Valley Pipeline Inquiry, it is also the frontier region of the modern state. Two distinct visions of sovereignty overlap here, representations of the aspirations of two peoples, North and South. Much of Canadian history has concerned the evolution of this relationship, from early RCMP expeditions to assert the first national presence, to the creation of Nunavut to firmly embed the Inuit homeland into the constitutional and political structure of Canada. While never easy, the relationship has borne much fruit, resulting in much innovation as new structures of co-management and self-government provide the Inuit with greater control over their lives, more tightly integrating the fates of the two peoples, under one constitutional umbrella. As the Inuit became more closely bound to the rest of Canada, Ottawa's sovereign assertions became more legitimate in the eyes of the world as well as those of its first peoples, increasing the credibility of Ottawa's sovereign claim to its northern frontier, with the Inuit becoming the front line in Canada's territorial defense during World War II, the Cold War, and now at the start of an Arctic thaw. Their enthusiastic participation in the Canadian Rangers program has demonstrated how effective they can be as partners, and how a shared commitment to mutual sovereignty is the most viable path to a secure northland. And yet the relationship between Ottawa and the Inuit remains troubled, with distrust growing over their frustrating experience implementing the historic Nunavut land claim and the persistence of deep social challenges across the Inuit homeland. Some call for an historic apology to the Inuit, and in particular the "exiles" of the High Arctic exodus in the early Cold War period. Others call for a program of Arctic investment and development akin to a domestic Marshall Plan, much like that called for by Justice Berger, or the advocates for jump-starting the long-stalled Kelowna Accord.

With climate change fast transforming the Arctic's geophysical features, from a land of snow and ice to what might soon become a maritime crossroads of the world, and Canada's neighbors racing to lay claim to as much of the Arctic seabed as they can, in order for Ottawa to meaningfully assert sovereignty over its Arctic territories, it must ensure the internal political stability of its northern frontier. And this requires that its partnership with Nunavut succeed, and that the promise of Nunavut be fulfilled. The challenges faced by the Inuit, and by Ottawa, are huge. Social and economic conditions in the Arctic are amongst the nation's most challenging, and with global warming causing greater uncertainty in the near-term, it is imperative that Ottawa address and, to the best of its ability, resolve these issues, and ensure that the social peace is maintained.

A conversation has been taking place on Arctic sovereignty and security in recent months, part of a longer dialogue that has been taking place for many decades over the relationship between Canada and the Inuit. Ottawa has largely focused on the strategic challenges of a thawing Arctic, and has made bold plans to assert a military presence in the region and thus be better able to defend its northern frontier from external challenges. But it has largely overlooked the increasing social tensions found across the Arctic, and as these tensions rise, the internal dimension of its Arctic security challenge become ever more critical. The purpose of this book is to examine this conversation, and its historical roots, and to develop an analytical framework to help clarify the distinct voices in this conversation, in the hope that by so doing, the gap between North and South can be narrowed. For as this gap narrows, Ottawa's ability to assert its sovereignty across the Arctic, and to secure its northern frontier, will increase, along with the hopes of all Canadians, North and South.

A similar conversation has been taking place across the border in Alaska in recent years, and over this same period efforts to narrow the gap between Washington, Juneau, and Alaska Natives have been ongoing—with increased economic and political participation by Alaska Natives evidence of steady progress since the early days of the Alaska land claims movement. With an Arctic thaw becoming more likely, Alaskan eyes increasingly look north to the Arctic, and at the opportunities and challenges that lie ahead. As in Canada, the Inuit communities that dot the Arctic coast find themselves the subject of increased attention, as America re-awakens to the fact that it is not just an Atlantic or a Pacific power, but an Arctic one as well. A new sea is emerging, one connecting east and west, with Alaska as the gateway.

As many scholars of international relations know, Kenneth Waltz's classic *Man, the State, and War* was published in 1959—a half century ago as of the year this book was written. In no small part, this book is a tribute to his ideas. Waltz's artful presentation of the levels of analysis continues to engage students around the world, as it has for generations and as it no doubt will for many generations to come—providing them with a valuable framework for understanding the complex world of international politics. I had the great privilege of studying with professor Waltz as a graduate student at Berkeley many years ago, and the additional privilege of having him serve as my advisor. When my Arctic research began in earnest in the early 1990s, as the Cold War came to its swift and quiet end, I found Waltz's framework especially valuable for understanding the dynamic transformation underway there. Living along the outer frontier of the modern state, I quickly recognized the continued vitality of the indigenous tribes who have long called the Arctic home, and their perseverance in the face of colonization, modernization, globalization, and now climatological transformation taught me that in addition to the individual, the state, and the international system there is, in many remote regions where the modern state has yet to fully assert its sovereignty, a tribal level of analysis, and understanding this often-forgotten level is essential for gaining a complete picture of the Arctic transformation underway. So inspired, the work that follows is my own humble effort to apply the levels of analysis to the Arctic region, and to bring back from this application my strong belief that this important yet oft-neglected "fourth image" remains with us still—not just in the Arctic, but elsewhere in the world where tribal sovereignty still reigns, and where the power of the modern state has yet to make its presence fully felt.

As with my earlier book *Breaking the Ice*, this work is dedicated to the first peoples of the Far North, whose spirit, tenacity, and endurance have transformed the very way we conceptualize sovereignty, and who have not only earned a seat at the table in matters of national and international security, but who have shown us a way forward toward the resolution of many of our age's most pressing issues and concerns. They have earned a heartfelt thanks from those of us whose presence in this still new world is by all historical measures quite recent.

I also want to thank my parents, Bill and Paula Zellen, and my sister Jody Zellen, for their encouragement and patience as I endeavored to complete this project in recent months. My thanks as well to my colleagues at the Center for Contemporary Conflict, the Program for Culture and Conflict Studies, and the Department of National Security Affairs at the Naval Postgraduate School for their continuous encouragement, without which this project would likely have remained just an aspiration; and to professor Rob Huebert and author Ed Struzik for kindly contributing their words and ideas to these pages. In closing, I want to express my gratitude to my partner Sunfa Kim, whose spirit, tenacity and endurance—and a Herculean work ethic that surpasses any I have ever before encountered—inspires me in ways that words can not adequately describe: my appreciation knows no bounds.

Chapter One

Northern Perspectives on Arctic Sovereignty and Security

While the Arctic has long been associated with Canadian national identity, attention to the Arctic region from the majority of Canadians who reside south of sixty has ebbed and flowed since an independent, sovereign Canada was born in 1867. In recent years, southern interest in the Arctic has begun to flow again. As has often been the case, this renewed southern interest in the Arctic was stimulated by external events that reveal a new vulnerability to Canada's northern frontier, such as happened during World War II and the Cold War when the region came under external threat. For the people of the North, the recurring ebb in national attention to the region has been both frustrating and a blessing. Frustrating, since for them Arctic sovereignty and security are always front and center. A blessing in that southern neglect meant continued northern insularity, such as the expression "out of sight, out of mind" suggests. But over the years, northern leaders have sought to engage their southern counterparts in a conversation, hoping to foster a re-imagination of Arctic sovereignty and security that better balances southerners' concerns with external security, and northerners' concerns with internal security, in an effort to end the neglect, but to moderate the influence of the south, and thereby preserve northern cultures from a southern onslaught of assimilating forces. Both northerners and southerners seek a stable and secure northern frontier; but the distinct difference in their geographical perspectives has led to the articulation of two very different conceptions of Arctic sovereignty and security.

One might expect, with the passage of time and the longevity of the conversation between leaders from both parts of Canada, that this conversation would lead to a narrowing of the gap in perception and the divergence in conceptualization of Arctic sovereignty and security. But as seen most recently in Ottawa's effort to implement a new "use it or lose it" policy with a strong military dimension but virtually no civil component, it appears the long effort of northerners to educate their southern counterparts has not yet borne fruit. Things looked very different during the 1990s, when northern and Aboriginal leaders had the ear of the country's top leadership, earning them seats at the constitutional negotiating table at Charlottetown in 1992, helping to secure the political will required to make the Nunavut dream into reality by the decade's end. But with the change in leadership in 2006, those old lessons have not yet carried over, and a new effort appears to be needed to ensure that leaders North and South understand one another, the needs of their constituents, and each other's role in achieving the hope shared by all Canadians that Canada's Arctic sovereignty and security are ensured.

In recent years, issues relating to Canada's Arctic sovereignty and security have leapt from the back pages to the front page, from a story rarely if ever reported to the lead story. A prime driver of this renewal of interest, of course, has been the rapid manifestation of global warming in the Arctic region, resulting in longer summers, milder temperatures, and record ice melts—leading in 2007 to, for the very first time in recorded history, the opening of the Northwest Passage. The impassability of the Passage has been an indelible fixture on Canada's northern landscape, perhaps its defining feature, and as such it has become a metaphor for Canada's Arctic sovereignty and security. So long as the Passage remained frozen, blocked by ice, and only navigable at great effort and cost with the aid of heavy icebreakers, it generally contributed to Canada's security; on the rare occasion when the Passage was transited, most infamously by the supertanker Manhattan in 1969 and the Polar Sea icebreaker in 1985, both U.S. vessels, it precipitated brief sovereignty crises, resulting in a flurry of policy commitments to defend Canada's Arctic sovereignty and secure its vulnerable northern flank, and the enactment of legislation designed to strengthen Ottawa's hand. But for most of the time, the Passage was not breached, and Canada's virginal Arctic sovereignty remained untouched. During these times, most Canadians slept soundly at night knowing they were protected by a blanket of snow and ice that rendered their northern frontier largely inviolable.

All this would change in 2007, when the convergence of melting ice, warming temperatures, and rising commodity prices led to a "race for the Arctic," as receding ice opened up vast stretches of the undersea Arctic to exploration, resource development, and potentially transpolar shipping. Canada, like its Arctic neighbors, sensed the opportunity ahead, but also the risks as new interest in a region long ignored and long inaccessible rapidly grew. When Russia laid claim to a huge portion of the undersea Arctic and placed a titanium flag on the seafloor at the North Pole, it precipitated a reaction that was similar to that which took place when the Passage was breached in 1969 and 1985. Action was required to reassure the public that Canada's Arctic sovereignty and security would be protected. University of Calgary Political Scientist and preeminent Arctic security expert Robert Huebert noted, "everything has changed quite dramatically" in the Arctic, and how after Russia's polar claims were asserted in the Summer of 2007, the "Canadian response was, 'Oh my God! We have to do something!'"[1] Huebert recalled how past crises concerning Arctic sovereignty tended to be resolved fairly quickly, including those sparked by the 1969 transit of the oil tanker, the SS Manhattan, through the Northwest Passage; and the 1985 transit of the U.S. Coast Guard icebreaker, Polar Sea.[2] But Huebert is concerned this latest Arctic sovereignty crisis is unlikely to be quickly resolved, owing to three issues transforming the Arctic: climate change, which has increased accessibility to the Arctic; high energy and commodity prices, which encourage further claims to Arctic resources; and growing international environmental awareness, and the development of means to resolve disputes in the Arctic as reflected by the Convention on the Law of the Sea. "All three of these issues are coming together, and that means the time of the Arctic is now."[3] The "use it or lose it" doctrine was borne in response to these issues, and Ottawa redoubled its military presence in the Arctic, reversing years of declining interest and commitment to a northern military presence.

But Ottawa's new northern efforts seemed to ignore one essential component: the people of the North. It was as if the Arctic was an empty, barren frontier region, and not the homeland of the Inuit and the northern Dene peoples. Indeed, Ottawa's assertion of a bolder, more visible, more activist Arctic sovereignty and security policy seemed oblivious to all the advances in north-south relations since Justice Berger chaired the Mackenzie Valley Pipeline Inquiry thirty years earlier, and which had begun the process of reconciliation between North and South, and the two competing mindsets of what a secure and sovereign Arctic really was: homeland or frontier. After Berger, it became clear that it was both, and a truly sovereign and secure Canada required not just attention to external security, but to internal security as well. The process of internal political and constitutional development, and greater inclusion and participation of the people of the North, was the focus of my earlier volume, *Breaking the Ice.* This volume will consider the conversation on Arctic sovereignty and security that has been taking place, applying a "levels of analysis" framework to help identify the different perspectives represented. The "levels of analysis" has been a popular tool in the international relations literature, enabling scholars to separate the individual, national, and international levels from one another, and by clarifying the analytical units, helping to elucidate cause and effect from the fog of international politics.

Kenneth Waltz's *Man, the State, and War* famously explained these three levels as distinct "images," and in his later work, *Theory of International Politics,* he postulated that the third image, the international system, had an overarching causal effect over the first and second. Accordingly, a Waltzian or neorealist interpretation of the Arctic sovereignty and security conversation would suggest that the international environment would drive behavior at the national and subnational level, and in many ways, Ottawa's response to Russia's Arctic ambitions reflects this classic top-down cause and effect sequence. And yet, the local and regional contribution to this conversation, about the aspirations of the people of the North for greater political and economic participation, and their aspiration to preserve their cultural traditions that played such an important role in the land claims and self-government movements, suggest that the first and second images are not just responding to external, international causal influences, but are interacting among themselves as a bottom-up causal sequence incrementally transforms the national conception of Arctic sovereignty and security. In short, just as neorealism posits the causal primacy of the third image, the first image has had a persistent, and cumulative, causal impact as well, especially during the 1990s when national policies increasingly reflected the aspirations of the peoples of the North. While in more recent years, external events appear to have superseded internal stimuli, it is interesting to note that the causal mosaic appears to be more complex in reality than neorealist theory would suggest.

As such, this work will examine in greater detail the articulation of policy aspirations at both the national and subnational levels with regard to Arctic sovereignty and security, not to definitively determine the nuanced details of cause and effect so much as to understand the multiple dimensions involved in the conversation, and to come to better appreciate the full complexity inherent in asserting Arctic sovereignty, and enjoying a more secure Arctic frontier. In the pages ahead, we will explore the way sovereignty and security in the Arctic has been defined at the tribal, territorial, and national levels, and their respective efforts to integrate the Arctic frontier into the economic, military, and political structure of the modern state. We will consider how these issues have unfolded—and continue to unfold—across the top of the world, and in so doing, we will better understand how subnational, transnational, national, and international forces dynamically interact within the Arctic region, and how Arctic sovereignty and security have evolved over the years to reflect a broadening, and diversifying, mosaic of participants in the conceptualization, definition, and articulation of Arctic issues, interests, and policies.

Importantly, we will come to understand how issues central to the indigenous peoples of the Arctic, such as their desire to preserve the Arctic environment and its ecosystems, have, over time, influenced the policies of the regional and national governments that govern the Arctic, and in recent years, have become increasingly adopted as an emergent global value, moderating the traditional, systemic values borne of the anarchy of international politics that feature so prominently in realist, neorealist, and strategic theories. At the substate, and trans-state level, concepts of Arctic sovereignty and security that originated as tribal values have withstood the test of time, and the encroachment of the modern state and all its power—redefining the way much of the world defines Arctic sovereignty, enhances Arctic security, and constructs a more balanced, and stable, Arctic future.

We will thus turn to levels of analysis as a framework for understanding the Arctic and the debate over Arctic sovereignty and security. By examining northern perspectives of Arctic sovereignty and security, we can better understand the response by the people of the Arctic to the many changes experienced since the Cold War's end and the dialogue that has been going on for many years between northern and southern leaders, and see how at times the gap that once dominated this dialogue has narrowed as tribal and regional conceptions of Arctic sovereignty and security converge with national and international conceptions.

Numerous works of scholarship have explored how systemic forces have exerted a top-down causal influence on subsystemic outcomes in the Arctic region, and how changes in the external, international political environment have influenced subsequent internal policies pertaining to the defense, security, and development of the Arctic region.[4] Their examination of the interrelationship of domestic and international politics in the Arctic region suggests a primary causal flow that is top-down, from the systemic to the subsystemic, or in terms of the classic "levels of analysis" as defined by Kenneth Waltz in his classic *Man, the State, and War*, from the overarching third image down to the second and first. Other works, such as the fascinating contributions to the regime theory literature made by Oran Young with his studies of the Arctic, have considered a bottom-up causal flow, examining how subsystemic causal forces have shaped the evolution of the Arctic's international environment, exerting an upward influence on the systemic level, as substate and trans-state values and interests permeate their way to the international agenda, becoming embedded in the policies of the Arctic rim states, and the objectives of various international organizations like the United Nations.

While most subsystemic analyses of the Arctic—such as the bountiful legal and comparative analytical literature concerning Native land claims, the ongoing processes of political devolution from center to periphery and the continuing constitutional evolution of Canada and Alaska, and the emergence of new institutions of Aboriginal self-government—have focused on domestic policy issues and processes, they are often distinct from the study of the international security issues that have, upon a close historical analysis, been so fundamental to the Arctic's political evolution, defining the very stage upon which existing northern political, economic, and legal structures have evolved. There are of course exceptions to this, most notably the pioneering work of Oran Young, co-founder of the Center for Northern Studies, long-time Dartmouth professor, now on the faculty of the University of California, Santa Barbara, and the governing board of the University of the Arctic. Over several decades, he has worked tirelessly in his analysis of Arctic politics, the interplay of domestic and international forces, and the fascinating and unique substate and trans-state political processes that have resulted in the formation of a unique constellation of regimes and "regime-like" entities to govern the circumpolar Arctic. His application of regime theory and regional subsystems theory to the Arctic has broken new ground, setting the stage for an analysis of the substate and trans-state dynamics of the Arctic, and their causal role in the making of Arctic history.[5]

Young was one of the first scholars to describe the unique Beringian region as a distinct international subsystem spanning the East-West frontier. The Arctic's unique, resource management structures, and their sub- and trans-state nature, reflect complex, underlying political contours that can be easily obscured by state boundaries, and officially recognized international frontiers. Young's probing analysis, and his theoretical insights, wed the study of the Arctic with the methodology of international relations theory, looking beyond lines on maps to the more complex, political topologies that can and do exist beneath the surface, particularly along frontiers where state power is often weakest and where trans-state and substate tribal entities have survived into the modern era. Such a sub- and trans-state perspective has been similarly reflected in the policy prescriptions promoted by the Aboriginal peoples of the Arctic and their many advocacy organizations, including the Inuit Circumpolar Council, inspired by their unique trans-boundary existence with cultural, linguistic, and kinship ties on nearly all sides of the Arctic's international frontiers. As Young recently wrote: "During the years since the waning of the Cold War, the Arctic has experienced a dramatic shift from the status of sensitive theater of operations for the deployment of strategic weapons systems to that of focal point for a range of initiatives involving transnational cooperation. These initiatives take a variety of forms."[6] They range from "intergovernment agreements" including the 1991 Arctic Environmental Strategy (1991) and the formation of the Arctic Council in 1996, and "leagues of subnational actors drawn together in pursuit of common interests that differ from those of national governments," such as the Northern Forum, which was formed in 1991. Additionally, there are "nongovernmental arrangements designed to address specific Arctic issues" such as the Inuit Circumpolar Conference, which formed in 1977, to the University of the Arctic, created in 2001.[7]

Young explores "this flurry of regional initiatives in a world increasingly dominated by global processes," shows how this "mosaic of cooperative arrangements emerging in the Arctic differs from what mainstream accounts characterize as international regimes," and demonstrates "the importance of regional responses to global issues."[8] As he explains, "The Arctic differs fundamentally from more familiar regions" and "is a region of peripheries in the sense that it comprises more or less remote portions of seven countries: Canada, Denmark, Finland, Norway, Russia, Sweden, and the United States."[9] Young continues:

> Although the area generally included within the boundaries of the Arctic is vast, covering some 40 million square kilometers, or 8 percent of the Earth's surface, the human population of the region includes only about 4 million people. Because the region is large and relatively remote, matters of policy relating to the Arctic have traditionally involved interactions between northern peripheries and the metropoles of states located far to the south. On the one hand, the pattern of interaction underlying this north/south axis looms as a barrier to be overcome for those seeking to foster a distinct identity for the Arctic as an international region. On the other hand, the shared experiences that accompany

peripheral status constitute one of the starting points for cooperation among those concerned with issues of importance to the Arctic and its peoples.[10]

In my preceding volume, *Breaking the Ice: From Land Claims to Tribal Sovereignty in the Arctic*, I explored the political history along this periphery, and how a dialectical process began when Alaska Natives, the state of Alaska, and the U.S. federal government transformed the way Alaska was governed with the enactment of the Alaska Native Claims Settlement Act (ANCSA); as the land claims paradigm permeated its way across the Arctic, it evolved to increasingly reflect the values, interests, and perspective of the people along the periphery, moderating the modernizing and assimilating pressures of the southern metropoles. This work was less concerned with resource-management issues per se, as is the case in many publications—such as *Northern Ecology and Resource Management*, edited by Olson, Geddes, and Hastings, and *Oil Age Eskimos*, by Joseph G. Jorgensen—and more with the underlying decision-making structures that were first established by land claims settlements for the purposes of resource management, land access, and environmental protection but which evolved into more sophisticated and farther-reaching institutions of Aboriginal self-governance, ultimately redefining our understanding of Arctic sovereignty and security. These structures, designed in part to protect tribal and community values, have interfaced with the national security programs and policies of the southern governments, contributing to a new, dynamic political environment in which the concept of northern security has been (and continues to be) redefined to reflect not just the national interest, but the local and regional interest as well, including a trans-state component that is inherently predisposed to resolve problems collaboratively. In short, a sub- and trans-state idealism borne of enduring tribal values has intermingled with the realism of the modern state, creating a fascinating and unique international experience. Rather than focus on a specific issue area, such as resource management or oil and gas development, which would inevitably lure us away from the all-important task of theorizing and disentangling regional structures from their political effects, I will instead apply and adapt the traditional "levels of analysis" to the study of Arctic sovereignty and security, how they are defined, and how they have evolved as international, national, subnational, and transnational forces interplay.

Breaking the Ice looked closely at the new structures of decision-making created by the land claims process, and how these structures were utilized creatively by the Aboriginal people of the Arctic to reclaim elements of their lost (or unrecognized) sovereignty, fostering the emergence of a hybrid loyalty to both tribe and state, not unlike the medieval dual allegiance to churchly and princely rule. I dubbed this "sovereign duality," with a balancing of the interests of the modern state, and the pre-modern tribal entities that had not been assimilated, exterminated, or otherwise conquered by the superior power of the state. In this work, rather than focus on the decision-making structures, we will examine how, at each level of analysis, the sovereignty of the Arctic is conceived, and how over time, tribal conceptions of Arctic sovereignty and security have held strong, against the superior power of the state, balancing the economic and military imperatives of the modern state to fully develop, economically exploit, and militarily occupy a frontier region with its own distinct logic, to preserve the Arctic environment, its fragile ecosystems, and unique cultures and wildlife. Just as land claims enabled the Native peoples of the Arctic to balance development with the preservation of their traditions to some degree, their persistence, and insistence, to fulfill their obligations as stewards of the land, and to counterbalance the external and potentially calamitous influences of the modern state, has similarly helped to redefine how much of the world defines the security of the Arctic, and how best to assert sovereignty over the Arctic. Ultimately, ascertaining the nuanced detail of cause and effect, and eliciting the ultimate impact of regional, subsystemic structures on issues of international and strategic importance—such as the sovereignty and security of the Arctic—requires a broad application of the levels of analysis framework in order to understand the causal impulses from the substate, national, and international levels.

In the pages that follow, we will examine northern perspectives of Arctic sovereignty and security, and their interplay with national perspectives of these concepts, to better understand the response by the people of the Arctic to the many changes experienced since the modern state first reached into the North, and their continuing dialogue with the Arctic rim states that have tried so hard to assert their sovereignty over their traditional homeland. We will examine the perspective of the peoples of the North, and how they define the security of the Arctic region, and how they conceptualize Arctic sovereignty. As the era of colonialism continues to recede into the past, and efforts to restore sovereignty, increase democratization, and foster the renewal of self-governance continue worldwide, the way sovereignty and security are defined at the national and international level increasingly incorporates concepts that have long been enunciated at the subnational level, including values long associated with Aboriginal organizations such as environmental security and human security. This became especially apparent in the immediate post–Cold War period, as Balkanization and state failure revealed the dangers of substate forces to international security, and again after 9/11 when these dangers were shown to be no longer hypothetical possibilities. Thereafter, the fields of international, strategic, and security studies adopted viewpoints that had been largely consigned to domestic policy studies until then. Issues that concerned domestic, internal, and substate dynamics took on an increasingly international profile, such as decolonization, sovereign independence, sectarianism and fundamentalism, insurgency and revolution, balkanization, tribalism, state collapse, environmental protection and pollution prevention, and the gradual processes of devolution of decision-making and increased local and regional autonomy.

These phenomena are prominent worldwide, having come to center stage during the anti-colonial struggles at the end of World War II, and reappearing during the democratic revolutions that erupted near the end of the Cold War, and again during the current struggles for democracy in the Global War on Terror.

They also emerge in the discussions with the indigenous people in the Arctic about their values and their hopes for the future, and in the speeches and policy statements of the indigenous political elites of the Arctic, who speak more abstractly, more theoretically, and in some cases more ideologically about the interests and aspirations of their people. For instance, Inuit leaders have long worked to demilitarize their homeland and to promote efforts at arms control and disarmament, while local, grassroots people from the smaller villages have focused their attention on issues like the preservation of hunting rights, land access, and the protection of their ecosystem, all vital components of their subsistence economy and culture. While they were fighting to protect their right to hunt, their leadership were vocally advocating nuclear weapons free zones (NWFZs), and mitigating the risks of nuclear war through reciprocal confidence-building measures (CBMs). Intriguingly from a theoretical perspective, the local hunters and trappers, whose interests are now represented by local hunters and trappers committees or associations (HTCs or HTAs), are primarily concerned with an issue defined by their distinct level of analysis, which can be described as tribal in its reflection of local or regional geographic dimensions and its internal ethnocultural characteristics; whereas their leaders, who operate at a national and international level and directly engage national governments and international organizations, were concerned with issues of salience to the international/systemic realm, also manifesting the conceptual taxonomy indigenous to their level of analysis. The national Inuit leaders were also eager to preserve their subsistence traditions, but because they were themselves partly assimilating into their new, globalizing realm, they proved most effective operating in their new global milieu. This should be construed as a criticism, even though politically, within the Aboriginal community, the national leaders have often been rebuked, and sometimes voted out of office, for spending too much time far from home, even though their success required them to spend this time traveling to centers of national decision-making like Ottawa and international diplomacy like the United Nations headquarters in New York and Geneva. Time and again, successful leaders who helped bring Native issues to national and international prominence were rebuked by their constituents, showing the gulf that existed between these two levels of analysis, and the challenges inherent in bridging this gap.

The conceptualization and articulation of Arctic sovereignty and security becomes increasingly sophisticated as one moves from the grassroots level to the regional political level—but this does not mean that Arctic security should be defined more by the latter than the former, since it's local issues that are paramount to the Inuit of the Arctic communities, such as the preservation of subsistence harvesting of wildlife. Rather, tying local values to the global, and rooting global values in the local, would help unite these otherwise disparate levels of analysis. Sometimes simplicity is of itself quite sophisticated, albeit elegantly presented. This has been true through history, especially in revolutionary settings, where simplistic elegance can build a stronger ideological consensus than a more artificial sophistication as articulated by leaders who might otherwise be perceived as out of touch with their populace. We've seen this all around the world. For instance, Mao's simple dicta made sense to peasants, soldiers, and workers alike, and ultimately his ruling coalition was built upon a rural power base of which peasants and soldiers were the two primary pillars but which required urban support to succeed. The Crusades, which restructured the medieval international system, were about loyalty to God and the physical conquest of the infidel and liberation of the Holy Land—ideas that made sense to religious ideologues, but perhaps not to more sophisticated theorists and philosophers, especially those who were more secular in their mindset. (Current efforts by the West to prosecute the war on terror would benefit from a greater understanding of the spiritual motivations of its opponent, and to address those motivations at their root.) The failure of communism, too, which collapsed as a worldwide movement at the end of the 1980s, can be attributed at least in part to popular rejection of a highly developed ideology fueled by simple and oftentimes selfish ideas about choice, opportunity, and the desire to fulfill consumer appetites, but which proved powerful—even though the ideals of communism, concerning the welfare of the worker and the equity of all citizens, were theoretically quite elegant and uniquely inclusive.

That's why, when defining Arctic sovereignty and security, it is essential to remember the perspective of the Arctic hunter, and his perspective on the world. It is this perspective that fits most organically, most naturally, with the tribal level of analysis. Arctic security is thus, to the Inuit hunter, more about hunting, trapping, and the preservation of an Aboriginal subsistence economy than with more global and more modern phenomena, whether economic modernization and corporate development, the promotion of CBMs, or the establishment of NWFZs. These other, more sophisticated ideas were a big part of Inuit policies with regard to Arctic security, reflecting the aspirations of the Inuit leadership to reach beyond the local and regional context, and engage directly with national and international decision-makers. This reflects a bifurcation of the conversation taking place on Arctic sovereignty and security, with the meaning of Arctic sovereignty and security varying greatly from one level of analysis to the other, and with the Inuit leadership dedicated to building a bridge from one level to the next, in order to deliver effective change to their people.

Levels of Analysis and Arctic Security

Students of international relations are generally introduced to Kenneth Waltz's *Man, the State, and War* early on. It is a fascinating work, with an unusual methodology derived from political philosophy. Using philosophy as a lens for how theorists see the world, he presents three distinct levels of analysis that have come to dominate the field—often unequally. J. David Singer has analyzed the implications of the "level of analysis" problem that still causes methodological and theoretical ambiguity within the field of international politics, which spawned an endless debate over cause and effect similar to the old chicken and egg question, with no single root of causal certainty. Singer focuses on the national level (within the state) and the international level (i.e., the international system). But Waltz elaborates on Singer's two levels, and within his own historical context, concludes at the end of his classic text that the third level of analysis—the systemic level—is overriding and of most importance to international affairs: "The third image describes the framework of world politics, but without the first and second images there can be no knowledge of the forces that determine policy; the first and second images describe the forces in world politics, but without the third image it is impossible to assess their importance or predict their results."[11]

In *Theory of International Politics*, Waltz later moved away from a philosophical analysis of world images (individual, state, and international) to a more scientific and properly theoretical analysis of international politics. The elegance of his work is testimony to his skills as a theorist and his understanding of mathematics as an ingredient of good theorizing. In his work he pits reductionist theories against systemic, clarifying the levels of analysis problem in international theory far more effectively than any predecessor. Essential to a systems theory of international politics, argued Waltz, are "the structure of the system and its interacting units."[12] So simple a point, observed Waltz, is yet a major milestone in international relations theory: "In doing so, I have broken sharply away from common approaches. As we have seen, some scholars who attempt systems approaches to international politics conceive of a system as being the product of its interacting parts, but they fail to consider whether anything at the systems level affects those parts."[13]

From the viewpoint of most students of international relations, internal forces produce the external effects that states wield in their international affairs. This interaction is fueled by internal forces, though the effects are clearly visible in world politics. Such a view, however, is clearly not a systemic theory. Rather it is a "reductionist" theory, rooting cause at the level of the nation-state (either its bureaucracy, decision-making processes, or political culture in general). Waltz instead conceptualizes a different relationship between cause and effect. In his theory, the structure of the international system affects "both the interactions of states and their attributes." Similar in theoretical elegance to geopolitics, which attributes causal force to geographical systems, Waltz attributes cause to international political, military, and economic structures: "Structure is the concept that makes it possible to say what the expected organizational effects are and how structures and units interact and affect each other."[14] The difficulty, of course, is distinguishing "changes of systems from changes within them," which Waltz aids with the following advice: that structures "are defined, first, according to the principle by which a system is ordered" (anarchy vs. hierarchy); secondly, "by the specification of functions of differentiated units"; and thirdly, "by the distribution of capabilities across units," whereby changes in this distribution "are changes of system" regardless of the ordering principle of the system.[15]

Moving directly to an application of a systemic theory to the Arctic, we can understand how changes unleashed by international systemic change and structural modification affect the relationship between decision-making centers and their farthest flung, Arctic frontiers—and how at those frontiers, the local actors who administer their "homelands" can utilize the present structural modifications to assert their own regional, subsystemic aspirations, possibly molding new structures at the regional level, and potentially building new international units at a tribal level to replace the disappearing international structures of the Cold War era. An especially helpful set of analytical tools for understanding Arctic international dynamics can be found in the field of geopolitics, which asserts an inexorable link between the land—and its resources—and the destiny or historical potential of modern states. The field's pioneering theorist, Sir Halford John Mackinder, focused on Eurasia, from which he helped conceptualize such basic building blocks of the geopolitical order as Heartland, Rimland, and the isolated realm of Lenaland, cut off from much of world history by north-flowing rivers, the frozen sea, and vast inland waters and deserts to the south. The peculiarities of Lenaland, itself cut off from the demographic and industrial potential of the Heartland, are similar to the Arctic basin in today's world system. Geography and climate are the overriding constraints—physical structures, but not political structures. Land claims, northern development, and historical efforts at colonization and settlement sought to reorder things and more tightly integrate the isolated region with the world along a largely north-south axis, introducing modern political structures to a realm that had hitherto been constrained and limited by only that of the land and sea. Lenaland today, as well as the Chukotkan extremis to its east, is a land marked by the scars of exploration and industrial development. Diseases like cancer and tuberculosis are much higher there than elsewhere in the North. But greater political autonomy is gradually arriving, with unprecedented gains in self-governance having been won through Native land claims, as illustrated by the historical achievement of Nunavut. But across the North, harsh conditions endure. Poverty, shorter life expectancy, and an absence of many of life's comforts remain regionwide realities.

Geopolitics captures one essential pillar of the Arctic's structural constraints, though these structures are distinctly pre-political or apolitical. The other side of the coin, however, is reflected in the growing regional political structures, which are increasingly interacting with the pre-existing state structures in place since the region first came under colonial dominion. Neorealism—political science's most elegant theoretical manifestation of structural realism in international politics—focuses on the structural constraints of world politics, and the underlying economic and military realities, as opposed to the underlying geophysical realities, though the geophysical attributes of any region do directly effect its economic and military capabilities. In the anarchy of international politics, most structures exist to ensure the autonomy of the states as essential units. Autonomy, rather than sovereignty—which is often freely and voluntarily weakened through international arrangements, as discussed by Keohane and others—is essential here. As Waltz writes, sovereignty is indeed "a bothersome concept."[16] He further explained: "Many believe, as the anthropologist M. G. Smith has said, that 'in a system of sovereign states no state is sovereign.' The error lies in identifying the sovereignty of states with their ability to do as they wish."[17] That's because to "say that states are sovereign is not to say that they can do as they please, that they are free of others' influence, that they are able to get what they want. Sovereign states may be hard-pressed all around, constrained to act in ways they would like to avoid, and able to do hardly anything just as they would like to. The sovereignty of states has never entailed their insulation from the effects of other states' actions. To be sovereign and to be dependent are not contradictory conditions."[18] And so it is in the Arctic—where the state's sovereignty overlaps with, and thus depends upon, the continued sovereign expression of its indigenous Natives, and where the Natives, who have always been there and will hopefully always be there, have learned that sovereignty and dependence are likewise not contradictory. As Waltz writes:

> What then is sovereignty? To say that a state is sovereign means that it decides for itself how it will cope with its internal and external problems, including whether or not to seek assistance from others and in doing so to limit its freedom by making commitments to them. States develop their own strategies, chart their own courses, make their own decisions about how to meet whatever needs they experience and whatever desires they develop. It is no more contradictory to say that sovereign states are always constrained and often tightly so than it is to say that free individuals often make decisions under the heavy pressure of events.[19]

This "heavy pressure of events," in geopolitical terms, is borne of land and sea and climate. In the Arctic, geopolitics is heavy-handed indeed. But the "heavy pressure" of external political events on the Arctic, up until the age of air power—and submarine power as well—had barely reached into the Arctic. There the geopolitics of the last ice age prevented the intrusion of the structure of modern world politics, preventing the indigenous people of the North from being overrun or routed, banished to reservations, or exterminated by force of arms like their counterparts in so many other parts of the world. International structures only worked their way into the Arctic at an age when technology and world politics witnessed the diffusion of power away from the Rimland powers of Europe. As Germany's military ambitions were crushed and Russia found itself heir to the spoils of the Eurasian Heartland—something that was enhanced when U.S. sea power crushed the other great Rimland power, Japan, in the Pacific, enabling American sea power and Russian land power to essentially divide control between Eurasia's Rimland and Heartland—an uneasy balance that Mackinder did not entirely foresee, but that later geopolitical theorists did understand to be the natural outcome of the tug-of-war between Rimland and Heartland.

Europe and Asia were thus the two primary "theaters" of world competition between Soviet and American power, with the vast and (seemingly) empty stretches of the Arctic between the superpowers. Air power had a global reach and Cold War targets placed the Arctic in the pathway of bombardment—during both the bomber and missile age. The Arctic was also the only route by which submarine forces could be quickly rotated from the Asian to European theaters, and in the nuclear age's dangerous game of deterrence and survival, the Arctic became a safe haven for nuclear armed submarines from which they could effectively hide from ASW forces and launch their deadly payload at targets to the south. Two Heartlands thus emerged—a North American Heartland and a Eurasian Heartland, vast regions of riches protected by the inaccessible Arctic frontier of the Arctic littoral and archipelago. So a coincidence of history—borne of technology and political change—brought external political structures into the Arctic region, and precepts borne of the Cold War led to an effort to stabilize the Arctic frontier through varying processes including the creation of permanent settlements, mandatory schools, and a variety of social programs that forced a people of the land, free for so long from what Waltz described as the "heavy pressures of events," into the fabric of political and economic society.

National integration, and assimilation into national society, became policy, with internal relocations including the infamous, and tragic, relocation of the "High Arctic Exile" to the communities of Grise Fjord and Resolute in the far northern Elizabeth Islands that resulted from the perceived need in the South to centralize and stabilize and assert the presence, and reinforce the sovereignty, of the center, of the modern state, in the farthest reaches of Arctic frontier. Hence the colonial legacy in the Arctic, which inspired the Inuit to aspire to restore their own traditional sovereignty over their land and to escape from the assimilating forces brought to bear by external "heavy pressures" of world politics. The resolution of Native land claims were thus the first step away from these forces—with one foot moving forward, toward greater centralization and assimilation and the other moving backward, to preserve ancient traditions, with a balance between the two hoped for; with later efforts to restore more traditional institutions of self-governance, culminating in the ambitious creation of the Nunavut territory, being the next step along the path toward a reconciliation of Inuit and national conceptions of sovereignty and security in the Arctic.

In international affairs, causal ambiguity has long been a problem for theorists unable to say precisely why things happen. To help their analysis, they try to break the world into smaller parts and to elucidate distinct analytical perspectives and levels. This has resulted in international relations theory fissioning into subfields that orient themselves around distinct levels of analysis. Psychological explanations and decision-making studies are consigned to the first image or individual level; and foreign policy, bureaucratic, and strategic studies are relegated to the second image, or national level. Neorealism and other systems-level theories are much broader and exist in another plane of thought altogether, an international or global realm. Of course, there are those regime theorists and specialists of regional subsystems who hover at the interface of level two and three. As some states in Europe began to fragment at the end of the Cold War, revealing an underlying complexity overlooked by many Cold War–era scholars that burst forth with a fury when communism collapsed, and whose echoes still reverberate today, a new substate, trans-state, and tribal level of analysis emerged. It is this new, tribal level that seems to define so well the Arctic. It is obvious, upon reflection, that the very concept of "security" has the same problem with causal ambiguity, and suffers from the very same "levels of analysis problem," as we find in international relations theory in general, with all its riddles and ambiguities.

Indeed, when we use the term, we must clarify whether we are talking about subnational, national, international, or global security—and sometimes, as became popular during the immediate post–Cold War period, human security, affecting personal and community security.[20] Indeed, the concept of human security bears many similarities to the notions of tribal security articulated by the Inuit, including the security of the environment, and the preservation of the subsistence culture. Erika Simpson, an international relations professor at the University of Western Ontario, authored an insightful article in the first volume of the *McNaughton Papers* in 1991, titled "Redefining Security," that examines the concept of security using a levels-of-analysis framework.[21] In addition to developing the concept of the "levels of security," analogous to the perennial levels of analysis problem in international relations, Simpson explained that the word security is quite vague and "has come to mean so many different things to different people that it may have no precise meaning at all. In a seminal conceptual piece on security, Arnold Wolfers characterizes security as an 'ambiguous symbol' and draws attention to the potential mischief which ambiguity of the symbol can cause."[22] Simpson concludes if "security is potentially a deceptive symbol, then our options are either to avoid using the concept entirely or begin chipping away at the analytical problems underlying the way the concept of security has been conceived of."[23] And to help "chip away" at the term's ambiguity, Simpson proposes to examine the "levels of security"[24] in a manner similar to the levels of analysis examined by Waltz in *Man, the State, and War.*

Simpson writes that "what is seen to be a threat to security at the individual level might not be significant at the national level of analysis," and that "threats to security which occur at various levels, both state and individual, may be responded to at multiple levels of analysis," as we have seen with the bifurcation of the Inuit articulation of Arctic security principles, which diverge along a spectrum defined by the levels of analysis.[25] Simpson draws on several sources in the literature such as Ronald H. Linden's June 1982 *International Studies Quarterly* article, "The Security Bind in East Europe," and Thomas C. Schelling's 1978 classic *Micromotives and Macrobehavior*, noting Schelling argues that micromotives do not necessarily correspond to macrobehavior, and that the pursuit of national security does not necessarily enhance the individual security of those involved. Interestingly, Simpson's reflections on this potential conflict between individual security and the pursuit of national security predates the emergence of the field of "Human Security" that emerged during the immediate post–Cold War years, culminating with the publication in 1994 of the United Nations Development Programme's *Human Development Report*. And like many prominent theorists of international relations, Simpson draws upon the great political philosopher, Thomas Hobbes, who grapples with the conflicting loyalties of self-preservation and the national interest in his classic *Leviathan*.

Simpson distinguishes "subjective" security from "objective" security, the latter being "physical security" and the former a result of perception (and misperception).[26] She argues that "any attempt to ameliorate insecurity will necessitate that we try to understand the physical, psychological, and social realities of those who are experiencing insecurity."[27] Applying her ideas to the Arctic, we can imagine how tribal values, community needs, and the psychological devastation of assimilation (often forced, induced through physical and psychological abuse) affect how northerners define security, and their relationship to national society as a whole. Subjective and objective aspects of security in the Arctic are both of importance—and the achievement of Aboriginal land claims in the Canadian Arctic, helping to forestall the complete assimilation of the indigenous peoples of the Arctic, has addressed both the objective and subjective, the physical and the spiritual, in a way that was not experienced in Alaska with its earlier land claims model bent on fully assimilating Alaska Natives. As we have seen, however, even on the Canadian side, land claims fostered continued economic integration with its corporate model, and this in turn contributed to further social assimilation, and this came into conflict with the elements of the land claims model that aim to preserve indigenous cultures and traditions; the physical can, in this case, predominate over the spiritual, fostered by the resource and power inequality of the land claims structure in Canada, where the new Native land claims corporations and their relative preponderance of wealth have become more influential than the hunters and trappers committees created to manage subsistence, and the weakly funded social development programs, that appear to be important on paper but which are endowed with fewer resources and thus less efficacy during implementation. The result of this imperfect model was that it implemented only half a solution, and the endurance of a major problem of human security in the Arctic as physical security supersedes the psychological and cultural dimensions of security—in spite of the notable transfers of wealth and devolution of political power that take place upon conclusion of a land claims accord. When it comes to fostering cultural identity, money and power are not just powerless, but in fact can be counterproductive, further eroding traditions in favor of a corporate modernity. What is also needed is the reinforcement of tradition, the revitalization of language, and the preservation of culture, much as Thomas Berger has concluded in Nunavut, with his call for a grand recommitment to the Nunavut Project.

We will next look at the northern and indigenous perspectives on the security of the Arctic, including those presented by Inuit leaders at the end of the Cold War when systemic forces were in retreat and tribal and regional aspirations to reshape the conception of Arctic sovereignty and security achieved an unprecedented degree of influence over the formulation of national policy. These perspectives will include the ideas articulated by then-president of the

Inuit Circumpolar Conference (ICC), now called the Inuit Circumpolar Council, Mary Simon at *The Arctic: Choices for Peace and Security* conference in 1989 as well as the official policy statement of the ICC as presented in its 1992 *Principles and Elements for a Comprehensive Arctic Policy* that defined Inuit post–Cold War policies and priorities, and illustrated Inuit conceptions of Arctic sovereignty and security as they adapted to the post–Cold War world. In addition, we will examine the ideas presented by the northern governments and their representatives, such as the November 1990 Government of the Northwest Territories' (GNWT) *Discussion Paper on Military Activity in the North*. Then, we will examine the national perspective as well, in particular the evolution of Canada's northern defense and security policy after the Cold War period, when it began to embrace concepts that had long topped the northern and Aboriginal agenda. And lastly, we will consider how the national and subnational levels interact, and in so doing, engage in a dialectic as policy evolves to balance these two perspectives. While somewhat uneven, the influence of subnational values on the evolution of national policy is evident in the transformation of Canada's policies with regard to Arctic sovereignty and security, suggesting that the neorealist presumption of a top-down causal sequence so prominent in the Cold War is not an accurate description of the post–Cold War Arctic. The enormous influence of external, international forces on the Arctic should not be overlooked or understated, but the energetic pushback by the Inuit and their tireless effort to change the terms of the discussion, and to redefine how people in the South conceptualize the sovereignty and security of the Arctic, in a manner more compatible with northern ideals and values should also be noted. Their ambition is laudable; and their apparent success quite extraordinary, suggesting the tremendous efficacy in linking local and regional values, aspirations, and policies to their national and international counterparts, and thereby literally changing the world.

Inuit Perspectives on Arctic Sovereignty and Security

In 1989, ICC president Mary Simon presented the Inuit concept of security at *The Arctic: Choices for Peace and Security* conference, interconnecting issues of war and peace with those of the land and culture of the Inuit, stating that, "the ICC believes that there is a profound relationship between peace, human rights and development," and that none "of these objectives can be realized in isolation from the others. For Inuit of the North, each of these key elements is linked to our environment and to the lands, waters, sea ice and resources upon which we as a distinct people depend. Any measurement of security in the Arctic must take into account all of these factors."[28] Simon noted that as "ICC president and as an Inuk from northern Québec, I will be speaking from an Inuit perspective."[29] She explained that the "choices for peace and security in the Arctic are being limited unnecessarily by states in the Arctic, to the detriment of our common objectives. Moreover, if Inuit and other Aboriginal peoples in the Arctic continue to be effectively excluded from policy and decision-making processes relevant to the North, it is highly unlikely that lasting peace and real security—as we perceive it—will be achieved."[30] She added that it was "vital to recognize that vast regions in northern Canada, Alaska, Greenland and eastern Siberia constitute, first and foremost, the Inuit homeland," and that as Inuit, "We do not wish our traditional territories to be treated as a strategic military and combat zone between Eastern and Western alliances. For thousands of years, Inuit have used and continue to use the lands, waters and sea ice in circumpolar regions. As Aboriginal people, we are the Arctic's legitimate spokespersons."[31] And as a prominent Inuit leader, she presented the Inuit policy in international peace and security issues:

> Since our northern lands and communities transcend the boundaries of four countries, we are in a unique position to promote peace, security and arms control objectives among states of the Arctic Rim. Any excessive military buildup in the North, whether by the Soviet Union or the United States, only serves to divide the Arctic, perpetuate East-West tensions and the arms race, and put our people on opposing sides. For these and other reasons, militarization of the Arctic is not in the interests of Inuit who live in Canada, the Soviet Union, Alaska and Greenland. Nor do such military preparations further security or world peace.[32]

Inuit opposition to the region's militarization, and advocacy of arms control measures and other efforts to ameliorate East-West tensions, emerged logically from the unique geostrategic position of the Inuit at the top of the world, where East and West literally come together at a single point. While clearly influenced by the arms control and disarmament community, and which waged a bottom-up campaign throughout the Cold War to restrain the superpower competition and reverse the arms race, the rejection by Inuit leaders of the Arctic militarization was not universally accepted at the village level, and in parts of the Arctic, particularly in Alaska but in Canada as well, the Inuit and the military had a long and close relationship dating back to World War II, when Muktuk Marston formed the Alaska Eskimo Scouts to help defend the country from Japanese attack, and which contributed to the national defense during the Cold War period. Indeed, the Inuit are among the most widely armed people in the world due to the strength of their hunting culture and warmly embraced then—as they do today—membership in the Canadian Rangers Program, just as Alaska's Inuit enthusiastically joined Muktuk Marston's famed Tundra Army during World War II.

Inuit opposition to Arctic militarization at the leadership level thus appears somewhat at odds with a significant plurality of the local Inuit of the villages, and dissonant with the broader strategic integration of the Arctic region during World War II and the Cold War, which enjoyed significant Inuit participation in coastal surveillance, defense, search and rescue, and military training exercises.

The Natives of Alaska also have a long and proud military tradition, having experienced war on their own soil during World War II, and having participated in the protracted hostilities of the Cold War up close—with some Native leaders fondly recalling how they benefited both politically and culturally from their military participation, finding it to be a healthy alternative to the strict and doctrinaire ideals brought into the North by missionaries intent on religious conversion and cultural assimilation. Indeed, the military in Alaska has been a progressive agent of civil rights, helping to narrow the gulf between Native and non-Native just as the Canadian Rangers program is, offering a neutral meeting point between tribe and state where a shared love of the land, a respect for the culture of arms, and a commitment to defend the homeland forged a close and lasting bond. Nonetheless, the Inuit advocated a "gradual, balanced and fair" demilitarization of the Arctic—and noted that the ICC felt "encouraged by the signing of the Intermediate-range Nuclear Forces (INF) Treaty in December 1987," which was the first step in a series of deep strategic weapons cuts that would be negotiated between the East and West toward the end of the Cold War period.[33] The Inuit leadership thus believed that "in order to strengthen security in the North, increase militarization is hardly the path to a lasting solution."[34]

As ICC president Simon counseled, the governments of the Arctic countries: "must look beyond geographical and political borders and alliances. Like Inuit, they must begin to perceive and value the Arctic as an integral whole that not only sustains our Inuit way of life but also determines the Earth's future in many ways. It is in this context that Inuit support the idea of working towards the formal establishment of the Arctic as a zone of peace. Consistent with such a zone must be the reduction and eventual elimination of nuclear weapons in ever-increasing parts of the North."[35] The Arctic as a zone of peace was a popular concept during the latter days of the Cold War, one eventually endorsed by reformist Soviet Premier Mikhail Gorbachev but long advocated by the Inuit leadership. As a frontier shared by both the Soviet Union and the West, and with its unique geophysical characteristics serving as a natural buffer to help limit the East-West conflict, the Arctic made an ideal arena for conflict de-escalation and for the introduction of confidence-building measures (CBMs), the Inuit embrace of the zone of peace concept is logical, even compelling. But the logic had a soft underbelly: those who believed most in the idea were not necessarily the ones with the power to transform the Arctic into a zone of peace—such as the armed forces of the United States, which had been active in the region since World War II, or their Soviet counterpart, where the impetus to demilitarize the Arctic really gained traction. Of course, local people on both sides of the Arctic divide did want to see Inuit from each side of the "Ice Curtain" that had separated them since 1948 reunited, and to lower those artificial boundaries that had divided them for over a generation, and thus likely agreed with the ICC that the conflict between East and West should be transcended by an Arctic that was "an integral whole," thus presenting a path to world peace. But while the East-West divide was artificial to the Inuit, it was very real to the people of Europe whose continent was divided by the more menacing Iron Curtain, along which a million men of arms stood prepared for war for an entire generation.

Wishful thinking, alone, will not make peace; but understanding the root causes of conflict can help. Ignoring the heart of the Cold War conflict—reflected by the division of Europe in the aftermath of World War II, and the advanced strategic position of the Soviet Union, which now stood in control of the Baltic states, Eastern and Central Europe, and stood poised in a menacing fashion at the very threshold of Western Europe—was a real and present danger to the fragile post-war democracies. Peace was maintained in Europe at high cost and with high risk, and part of the reason was deterrence—and a big part of the reason deterrence succeeded for two generations in the dangerous post-World War II world was its credible linkage of the security of Western Europe to North America through the nuclear umbrella, which evolved into an integrated triad of land, sea, and air forces that came to include the Arctic. With peace thus maintained by the stability of nuclear deterrence, perhaps the ICC's solution, a demilitarized Arctic, would have inadvertently led to a disaster in the Arctic, akin to the opening shots of World War I when seemingly peripheral events led to uncontrolled escalation, and ultimately to world conflict. Had the Arctic been demilitarized, its DEW Line radar sites shuttered, nuclear submarine patrols curtailed, it is plausible that nuclear warfare may have become more likely, not less; and deterrence less stable, not more—with a heightened risk that Arctic targets like the Alaska Pipeline may have been destroyed preemptively in the event of armed conflict.

Indeed, were it not for the mutual and extreme scale of destruction threatened by the specter of nuclear warfare, the very logic of Mutual Assured Destruction (MAD) might have failed, and with it the peace. And the forward presence of the Soviet ballistic submarine fleet was, toward the end of the Cold War, a critical component of Moscow's deterrent. The entire logic of assured destruction, with the prospects of peace enhanced by the sheer terror of total war, was full of contradictions. As a consequence, the pursuit of a disarmament agenda, even in the Arctic, may well have been a destabilizing factor and thus a precursor to war—or at the very least, may have contributed to the continued existence and potential strengthening of the Soviet Union, and its enforcement of tyranny in so many countries under its domination. Oddly enough, the accelerated pace of militarization, of the Arctic, and later of space, placed increasing budgetary pressure on Moscow, some believe contributing to the eventual collapse, resulting in the eventual dissolution of the Soviet Union and the liberation of dozens of countries and hundreds of millions of people around the world, including the Inuit of eastern Siberia. An Arctic zone of peace may have delayed or forestalled this transformative liberation, and instead of having contributed to the wave of democratic revolutions that began in 1989, the Arctic might have unwittingly contributed to the continuation of the Cold War. As both George Orwell and Tracy Chapman have observed satirically, "War is peace," suggesting that a peaceful intent could unknowingly, and unintentionally, increase the risk of war.

In contrast, the Inuit hunter or trapper, with an intuitive respect for the armed forces and their mutual love of the land, a spartan lifestyle, and respect for arms, presented a contrast to the official position of the ICC with regard to war and peace issues, and very likely better understood the essence of realism, and how being armed, and prepared to defend one's homeland, could contribute to a more stable and lasting peace than arms reductions and demilitarization. Thus, the idealism of the ICC's position on war and peace issues conflicts with the grassroots realism that has been omnipresent in the Arctic villages since long before the Tundra Army was first assembled.

The ICC leadership did argue effectively, and innovatively, that "states in the Arctic must not continue to narrow the discussion" of security "to just national, continental or Western security in military terms,"[36] and introduced some concepts such as "environmental security" as well as precursors to what became known as "human security" to the discussion—ideas that, five years later, would be formally included in Canada's official Department of National Defence (DND) policy. On environmental security, the ICC president urged that:

> Immediate steps must be taken cooperatively by nations in the Arctic and by other nations to counter transboundary pollution effectively. Polychlorinated biphenyls (PCBs) and other persistent chemicals are seriously jeopardizing the health of Inuit, our northern environment and our wildlife. In addition, the Arctic and other regions of the world are being threatened by the continuing destruction of the ozone layer by chlorofluorocarbons (CFCs). While some positive steps are being taken by governments, increased measures are still needed. At this point, threats to the Arctic and global environments, not military threats, pose the greatest dangers to the security of the North and other regions of the world.[37]

Simon called upon the non-nuclear Arctic countries (Canada, Norway, Denmark) to urge that nuclear powers prevent the "concentration of weapons systems in the Arctic."[38] The sustained military presence in the Arctic, especially on the Soviet side, had profound environmental consequences, and a lasting legacy of toxicity. As reported by Patrick E. Tyler in a May 4, 1992, article in the *New York Times*, "For three decades the nuclear-powered Soviet Navy and icebreaking fleet have dumped much of their radioactive waste in the Arctic, the Russian authorities now acknowledge. The dumping, in the shallow waters of the Barents and Kara Seas, has potentially serious consequences for the Arctic environment."[39] And *BBC* reporter Alex Kirby described the port of Murmansk, in his March 3, 1999, report, "Russia's Growing Nuclear Dustbin," as "Chernobyl 2," and a "nuclear disaster waiting to happen," as it was "one of the parts of the world at greatest risk of a nuclear accident, largely because of the number of reactors and other debris dumped haphazardly from obsolete Soviet submarines."[40]

Lastly, Simon took issue with a 1988 statement on the Arctic that former External Affairs Minister, and briefly Prime Minister, Joe Clark made at Carleton University in which he affirmed that NATO allies, "including Denmark and

Norway, agree that security in the Arctic cannot be dealt with in isolation—it's a NATO issue and not a northern issue."[41] As Simon explained, the ICC could accept the broad perspective "that Arctic security need not be addressed in isolation," but she differed in her belief that "Arctic-specific measures may still be needed in order to avoid a weapons buildup in the circumpolar regions," and as a consequence, "To describe security in the Arctic as a NATO issue and not a northern issue restricts this crucial notion to military terms," and "minimizes the role and responsibilities of Canada as an independent and sovereign Arctic state with its own particular northern interests. Equally, it serves to ignore the rights, concerns and priorities of Inuit in the Arctic and to deprive us of a meaningful role."[42] Simon's parsing of Clark's statement, and her concern with its de-emphasis of the northern perspective, reflects the regional and one might argue sovereign perspective of the Inuit, and their aspiration to have greater control over their own destiny as a people and resistance to continued external domination.

As such, it is contextualized by the distinct substate, and in some respects, trans-state, Inuit level of analysis. Clark's statement reflects Canada's state-level perspective, and reflected Ottawa's desire for alliance solidarity to enhance the collective interests of the Western powers, and the security of each NATO member, whose environmental stewardship and commitment to civil rights, human rights, and indigenous minority rights were far and away more tolerant and respectful than the Soviet Union's approach to the rights of minority peoples. With Soviet power then a very real threat to the freedom of the peoples of the West and the sovereignty and survival of the states of the Atlantic Alliance, Clark's perspective that Arctic issues were best addressed as NATO issues was both logical and prudent. Arctic security in the Cold War was directly tied to the fate of Europe, and the military infrastructure built in the Inuit homeland was built to help preserve the peace, and to prevent external attacks such as those delivered by Japan during World War II. It is understandable why the Inuit leadership felt this linkage somehow made the Inuit seem less important, reinforced by their exclusion from NATO decision-making on matters of supreme importance to the Inuit homeland—but all over the world, global systemic structures had a similar effect on peripheral regions and peoples. For instance, the Korean War was waged as if a battle in a larger world war, to roll back Communist expansion from the Korean peninsula, just as was the war in Indochina was later waged. In both situations, the countries affected by war were divided between the East and West along a north/south axis, causing much regional dislocation, with families separated for a generation or longer, and resulting in millions of deaths and untold destruction. Much of the Cold War was waged by regional proxy wars, with client states fitting into a grand strategic calculus. The Arctic was not alone in this regard, but the Arctic was relatively benignly treated when compared to the millions of victims of Cold War–armed clashes around the world. There, protracted wars were fought and the environment was often seriously degraded in the pursuit of military victory, as the continued legacy of the

77 million liters of "Agent Orange" and other defoliants sprayed between 1962 and 1971 over Vietnam attests to.

In the Canadian Arctic, most Cold War military activities involved surveillance and efforts to maintain the strategic balance. Military forces would largely transit the region as part of surveillance missions or sovereignty patrols, or while conducting field exercises and training ranger militia members, activities with a relatively light and largely transitory footprint. The Inuit leadership is correct to point out that the Inuit in Canada have their own perspective and their own values distinct from national concerns. But this does not negate or undermine the larger strategic relationships borne of the bipolar structure of world politics during the Cold War, or the formation of alliances like NATO for the broader defense of the West, or NORAD for continental defense. Ottawa's intentions were not offensive in their orientation, but rather defensive; their aim was not colonial, but rather survival. It just so happened that the frontier Ottawa was defending was also the homeland of the Inuit, and to the Inuit leadership, these activities did not appear to be benevolent, nor necessarily in the interest of the Inuit, though members of the Canadian Rangers no doubt had a different view of this. It's just two realities overlapping in one region—and not for the first time.

The "Two Solitudes" of English and French Canada, or the protracted clash between Israel and the Palestinians, each claiming Jerusalem as their national capital, face a similar predicament: two peoples, one land. The ICC must be lauded for promoting Inuit participation, and for defending Inuit values, with such commitment, standing up to states with far greater resources and tools of power. Indeed, ICC president Simon persuasively argued that: "Without effective and ongoing Inuit involvement, we feel that the full range of Arctic concerns and options for peace and security will likely be neither identified nor appropriately addressed."[43] Indeed, her tireless and valiant efforts helped to give the Inuit a voice, and thus to elucidate the subnational level of analysis in a forceful, and effective way. It is no surprise that only a few years later she would be appointed Ottawa's first Arctic Ambassador, becoming part of the global community of statesmen and diplomats she had so effectively communicated with, and in her person unifying the two levels of analysis she had fought so hard to interconnect. Her eloquence, and her stamina, illuminated a level of analysis long hidden and often ignored, the tribal and substate dimensions of a modern, multi-ethnic state, and in so illuminating it, she helped to moderate the causal impacts of the international and national levels, finding a common language with her national counterparts, and introducing into their conceptual taxonomy a suite of concepts and ideas borne of the Inuit homeland, redefining the way Ottawa understood Arctic sovereignty and security.

Simon presented a visionary look at the future, articulating a goal to which Inuit continue to aspire: "Inuit are hopeful that Arctic Rim nations will not remain submerged in the policies of the past. Now is the time to shape new visions and prepare fresh blueprints for circumpolar cooperation. Collectively, we can breathe new life into the concept of security. Only together can we ensure that the Arctic will be in the future what it was to our Inuit ancestors—a land of sustenance and a land of peace."[44] History would show these words to be prophetic, as the very concept of security was in fact redefined. The end of the Cold War surely paved the way for this definitional transformation, but the efforts of the Inuit, over so many years, helped to condition the national landscape, introducing the necessary vocabulary to greet the new, post–Cold War world. Through her efforts, and the efforts of other trailblazing Aboriginal leaders across the Arctic, the national leadership would gain valuable insight into the realities of Arctic and Aboriginal life, and the aspirations of the peoples of the North. This understanding would enable them to make structural changes to the Canadian and Alaskan polities, through constitutional and political reform efforts. The end result, of course, was evident in the achievement of Nunavut, and more recent innovations such as the restoration of traditional Inuit self-governance in Labrador, with many stops along the way. And with the re-formulation of Canadian defense policy after the Cold War, when Ottawa would also embrace concepts that were embraced early on by the Inuit, and reflect to a large measure the Inuit perspective, demonstrating how the efforts of the Inuit leadership to bridge the tribal level of analysis with that of the nation were in the end successful, in numerous ways.

In 1992, the ICC released its *Principles and Elements for a Comprehensive Arctic* Policy, a detailed statement of Inuit rights and their hope for more effective involvement in decision-making in a wide variety of issues areas affecting the Arctic, and in many ways the lasting testament of Simon's leadership of this Inuit international organization. One can consider the *ICC Principles* to be a blueprint of Inuit values but not necessarily a handbook for the restoration of Inuit independence, since the members of the ICC have agreed to work to promote reform within their various countries rather than to break away from those countries and embark upon a path toward independence. Indeed, when reading the *ICC Principles*, they seem to be more of a declaration of continued dependence on the Arctic states that have come to rule over the North—a statement of compromise, of negotiating more power but not winning back Inuit sovereignty. They are practical, pragmatic principles and not pie-in-the-sky ideals. But the Inuit, borne of a cruel, harsh landscape, have generally been realists when it comes to political power, and their dreams have always been constrained by a pragmatism borne of necessity.

The 1992 *ICC Principles* contain in chapter 2 of the policy on "Inuit Rights, Peace and Security Issues," subsections on the following: "The Affirmation of Inuit Rights at the National Level," "The Affirmation of Rights at the International Level," "Self-Government," "Arctic and Global Security and Disarmament," "Peaceful and Safe Uses of the Arctic," "The Emerging Rights of Peace and Development," and "Circumpolar Regional Cooperation." The inclusion of these issues suggests that to the Inuit, security is something that has as much to do with the local political aspirations of Inuit as with national policy or international diplomacy, and indicates an Inuit awareness of the levels of analysis and an understanding that security exists at the levels of community, region, nation, and international system, suggesting a granularity of analysis on par with the philosophical framework articulated by famed international relations theorist Kenneth Waltz in his classic *Man, the State, and War*. In sophistication, the *ICC Principles* far exceed earlier declarations of ICC policy on peace and security issues and reflect a maturation of Inuit policy. It is also interesting to note that environmental issues are discussed in its third chapter—including issues of environmental protection, the tension between conservation and development, the management of renewable and non-renewable resources, water and marine use in the Arctic, transportation in the Arctic and transboundary pollution—all concerns that can be considered central to the "Inuit interest," whether defined as a national interest proper, or a tribal interest that exists within and between sovereign nation-states.

One could argue this placement in chapter 3 suggests that environmental issues, which are of such vital importance to Inuit hunters and trappers in the communities, are not considered by the political elites to be as important to Inuit security as the meta-concepts that deal with political power at the local, regional, national, and international level. But one might also attribute this to the need to organize the *ICC Principles* thematically: after all, the *ICC Principles* are a wide set of ideas pertaining to the whole of Inuit existence. At the outset, the *ICC Principles* identify "nuclear and other weapons of mass destruction and the arms race" as an "unprecedented threat to the survival of the world's nations and humanity";[45] and while acknowledging that foreign and defense policy "are traditionally the domain of state governments," the ICC affirms that they are too "crucial to exclude northern communities and should not be left solely to experts within the military and government."[46] The ICC believes that "new concepts of common security are urgently needed that incorporate environmental, social, cultural and economic aspects," and that security no longer be defined "in military terms." Bringing "security" into regional focus, the ICC believes that "respect for the rights, values and perspectives of the Arctic's indigenous peoples is vital."[47] The ICC further advocates arms control, and making "the transition to disarmament."[48] But apart from their stated belief that such policies are in the interest of world security, they do not demonstrate the means or capability for inducing this shift toward disarmament. They did not possess nuclear weapons so they could not coerce the major powers into disarming. They have not asserted much of a threat in terms of terrorism or sabotage or even broader economic non-cooperation in order to compel their national governments to change course. They lacked artillery to defend their homeland; and had no ground-to-air missiles to control their air space such as the Afghani freedom fighters had to deny the Soviet invader access to their airspace; indeed, a few stingers left over from the Afghanis' anti-Soviet jihad might go farther toward inducing the withdrawal of state military power from the Arctic than a thousand international conferences ever could. After all, Islamist and tribal Jihadists eventually ejected the Red Army from Afghanistan, and fifteen years later knocked down America's Twin Towers and attacked the Pentagon using jet aircraft as battering rams, symbols of the ferocity of their will and their tactical innovation in pursuit of the liberation of the Holy Land and an end to a foreign military presence. Being a non-militant transnational group, the ICC chose instead to rely upon moral persuasion in its efforts to get the world to disarm. But are words enough? The ICC, while stating that Arctic security policies must incorporate regional Inuit values, adopts policies that are consonant with "disarmament" school of thought—a group inspired by idealism and that believes a disarmed world is inherently more pacific than an armed one. The ICC advocates the need for peace education, "to teach students of different ages the values of disarmament, non-violent resolution of conflicts, and world peace."[49] These values were shared throughout the Cold War with a global community of allies whose concerns were not necessarily with the root political causes of international conflict so much as its military symptoms, and who believed, as their slogan went, that "arms are for hugging." As experienced with idealism elsewhere around the world, good and even noble intentions are not the same as effective means of change. Even Gandhi knew that to oust the British from India without the use of armed force, he would have to make British India ungovernable, and to paralyze the interconnected, globalized system of economic interdependence that sustained the British economy, and through economic coercion bargain for a British withdrawal. The Zapatista movement and its army, the EZLN, pursued a similar agenda within Mexico as the Inuit pursued across the circumpolar Arctic, using armed force to bring their long-overlooked issues to the top of that country's agenda in 1994, and in the long process of negotiating in the years since, contributing to a movement of democratization, political inclusion, and indigenous rights. But the Inuit calculated that militancy would backfire, when determined pragmatism, and a refusal to give up, would be respected by the political culture of North America, and generate a climate of good will to advance their cause. Their success is evidence that their calculation, and patience, showed foresight.

However, while advocating peace education and promoting disarmament as a path to peace, the reality in the Inuit communities was far more Hobbesian in nature, as they were torn asunder by deep, and painful, social problems, with youth turning to substance and solvent abuse as well as suicide far more often than their southern counterparts. Peace education is fine and good—but to a people faced with the loss of their language, and the loss of their culture, and the loss of so much hope, such a recommendation may seem naïve, and potentially partisan, particularly in light of the popularity at the community level of the Canadian Rangers program. With so many important values at stake—many of central importance to Inuit cultural survival—peace education may look to be something of a distraction from the troubling problems within Inuit society, where the fabric of social peace had long been unraveling, as chronicled by the moving journalism of *Nunatsiaq News*. One could speculate that the *ICC Principles* are thus more a reflection of the sentiment of its leaders and policy advisors, and less a reflection of the more hard-nosed pragmatism and inherent realism of the grassroots Inuit where the daily struggle to survive was paramount. After all, Inuit society is highly armed and it was its expert marksmanship that turned Muktuk Marston's Tundra Army into a formidable coastal defense force during World War II when Alaska was under external threat from Japanese forces. All across the Inuit homeland, hunting is essential. Survival on the land and excellent marksmanship are important skills. These skills are compatible with the goals of the military, and its commitment to a strong defense, and not necessarily aligned with the sentiment, often anti-military, espoused by the peace community.

Indeed, the military history of the Arctic is quite a bit more complex, and inclusive of the Inuit, than that suggested by the *ICC Principles*. The promotion of the Arctic zone of peace by the ICC presumes a commitment to the demilitarization of the Arctic by the Inuit—yet the ICC did not demonstrate consensus on this point, and no polling data or referendum backs up this policy objective. And, more importantly, it ignores the important work of the Canadian Rangers and the Alaska Territorial Guard and the ebullient enthusiasm that these programs have sustained for decades from grassroots Inuit, and which have enjoyed enduring, and enthusiastic, community support for over half a century. Curiously, when outlining the idea for the zone of peace, such familiar values as a respect for, and expertise using, arms are excluded from the ICC's posture. Recalling the standard bifurcation of classical international relations theory into "idealist" and "realist" schools of thought, one wonders if at the level of international policy development, the Inuit were predominantly influenced by the idealist school, and thus overlooked the views of the realists who more fully represented the community perspective where the hunting culture, its closeness to the land, and its respect for arms created a natural synergy with the armed forces, and which sustained a multigenerational connection to the armed forces through active participation in the Rangers or Scouts programs. Based on my observations living in the Arctic during the 1990s, this seemed to be very much the case, as the Inuit leadership seemed strongly influenced by an articulate segment of the non-Inuit intelligentsia closely aligned with the arms control and disarmament movements, and who viewed the Inuit leadership as a natural, and in many ways powerful, ally in their efforts. Many of the speeches, white papers and policy documents put forth at international fora thus appear to be at least in part a reflection of the ideals and values of these non-Inuit policy advisors and consultants, who were not just important allies but kindred spirits of the Inuit leadership. So while idealism became closely identified with Inuit values, realism remained every bit as much a part of the Inuit perspective, one that was at times overlooked by the leadership, but never fully silenced.

In addition to denuclearizing the region, environmental concerns were reflected in the ICC's call to prevent nuclear testing in the Arctic, and to make certain that "the safeguarding of the Arctic environment must take precedence over military exercises and activities."[50] This policy seems more in tune with the sentiments of grassroots Inuit, and less an artifice of social construction imagined by non-Inuit consultants, though one could argue that the pragmatism and survival instincts of the Inuit would more likely lead toward a balancing of military necessity and environmental protection, and not a prioritization of the latter over the former. But the importance of the environment as a central pillar of Inuit identity can not be overstated. The ICC insisted that military activity that "disrupts" or "undermines" traditional activities of northerners should be prohibited—including "low-level and supersonic flight testing and training," placing cultural survival first and foremost in the hierarchy of principles.[51] As such, the ICC is asserting the moral primacy of Inuit values above these other defense-related national interests of the circumpolar states. Of course, lacking the means to assert their sovereignty, it was unrealistic for the ICC to expect that the Arctic rim states would voluntarily surrender, or diminish, their own sovereignty or subsume it to a substate or trans-state minority for idealistic reasons—and there is no mention of sanctions to encourage international cooperation, or threats of non-cooperation or resistance.

The 1992 *ICC Principles* were not intended to be a blueprint for resistance or militant action, or even for reclaiming Inuit independence, but rather reflected an expression of hope, an aspiration for moral influence upon the policies of the Arctic rim states. ICC's faith seems to be in the development of sustained, multilateral, international pressure, very much the role of a non-governmental organization operating at the sub- and trans-state level. Yet very different tactics and strategies for political change at this time during the immediate post–Cold War period would be reflected by the assertion of sovereignty by Serbia, which used force and violence in its effort to carve out a Greater Serbia from the remnants of the Yugoslavian state after its collapse, nearly succeeding in its effort. Push-back by its Croatian and Bosniak neighbors and their allies in the international community thwarted the Serbian vision, and the audacity and brutality of its methods. The Zapatista movement, more akin to the Inuit in its struggle for indigenous rights within the Mexican state, likewise sought to assert their indigenous sovereignty through arms but within an existing constitutional framework, working for reform of a system and not its overthrow or dissolution. The Inuit, no doubt sensing that militancy against militarily and economically superior national-level actors, united in a mutual defense pact, would be futile, chose a different and more practical path to achieve their vision, working with the national governments of the circumpolar states, negotiating for increased political power, while engaging at the international level with organizations like the United Nations. Realists might argue that the ICC seems to overvalue the power of the UN and the efficacy of international opinion, and undervalues the importance of force to achieve effective results. But given their small population and limited resources, the path of idealism in this case seems to be more prudent than the realism that powered more militant aspirations for indigenous rights in this period. In the absence of any hard-power advantages, soft-power seemed a logical path for the Inuit to achieve their aspirations for greater autonomy and increased sovereignty. Even the more powerful, better armed, and strategically innovative Serbians, despite their many advantages, failed to successfully use force to carve out their own ethnically homogenous state at that same point in history.

Even today, a generation later, the Inuit interest, and that of the sovereign Arctic rim states continue to come into conflict, and at the Ilulissat Summit in Greenland in May 2008, the Arctic rim states asserted their sovereign predominance, and only addressed Inuit concerns as a subordinate set of interests. The Inuit noted their exclusion with displeasure, and countered by formulating their own declaration on sovereignty reaffirming their intent to play a central role in future discussions of Arctic sovereignty. As ICC vice-chair Duane Smith observed, "Our Canadian land claims and self-government processes makes it mandatory for the Federal Government to include us," and yet the Ilulissat Declaration "that Minister Lunn signed on behalf of Canada ignores the role we should be playing."[52] Smith added that the Inuit "understand that foreign ministers of the five Arctic nations that have jurisdiction over the Arctic Ocean would want to meet on this issue. But the next time, I call for Inuit to have a separate seat at the negotiating table."[53] Greenlandic ICC representative Aqqaluk Lynge told the ministers at Ilulissat, whom he was invited to address, that "while Inuit do not formally recognize the borders that have been created among us, we are nevertheless practical and believe in compromise."[54]

The Inuit, with far fewer tools of national power, were wise to follow the path of peaceful coexistence. Indeed, even as the ICC promoted an Arctic nuclear weapons free zone (NWFZ), it adopted a pragmatic view toward existing strategic systems: "Due consideration must be given to existing strategic deterrents within each of the states involved, and the NWFZ boundaries recommended must not have the potential effect of threatening regional security interests."[55] As such, their idealism accommodated the realism of the circumpolar states, reflecting an underlying pragmatism that appears to be, at heart, the Inuit way. The ICC hoped that local Inuit communities would endorse the idea of the NWFZ, and declare their municipalities to be nuclear weapons free zones.[56]

The nuclear history in the North was certainly worrisome to the Inuit, and for good reason. In Alaska, the U.S. government secretly installed strontium-cored atomic batteries to run a seismic station between the Yukon River and the Brooks Range, and buried nuclear waste near a community along the Northwest Arctic coast. In the 1950s, the Atomic Energy Commission had planned to detonate a thermonuclear device along the Alaskan coast to create a deepwater harbor during Project Chariot, as chronicled by Dan O'Neill in his 1995 book *The Firecracker Boys*, without regard to the health of the environment or the Inuit of the region, but local resistance blocked the project from proceeding. Even in the post–Cold War era, the United States has not demonstrated any intent to denuclearize the Arctic, and in addition to using nuclear power at its base in Greenland, and nuclear subs beneath the Arctic Ocean, and nuclear batteries and atomic waste in rural Alaska, it placed one of its two Ballistic Missile Defense sites at Fort Greeley, Alaska. To be fair, the Soviet Union's nuclear legacy in the Arctic was even less environmentally and culturally sensitive; it dumped untreated nuclear waste, including whole nuclear reactor cores, into the Arctic Ocean—causing immeasurable harm to the Arctic food chain and ecosystem, and the Murmansk Port on the Kola Peninsula continues to be something of a time bomb, with its large number of nuclear fuel components literally rusting away.

Given the Arctic's troubling nuclear legacy and the specific irresponsibility of the Russians with regard to nuclear security and environmental protection, the desire for an Arctic NWFZ is natural. A realist, or more aptly a neorealist, might counsel that the Inuit would do better to commandeer some nuclear weapons, with which they could better persuade the Arctic rim states to accede to their will—as power does, in the end, come more readily from the barrel of a gun, as Mao once wrote. Indeed, consider for a moment the potential persuasive power of a nuclear armed Inuit nation, reclaiming its full sovereignty knowing that it could deliver its urbanized, industrialized neighbors a more costly blow than they could inflict back upon the largely uninhabited, unimaginably vast, pre-industrial, demographically dispersed, and seemingly indestructible Arctic? The Inuit homeland is somewhat similar to the highly tribalized, demographically dispersed, economically underdeveloped, and pre-industrial country of Afghanistan, which presented the American military with few aerial targets at the start of Operation Enduring Freedom in 2001, and which a generation earlier withstood the full might of the Soviet Red Army. This suggests the potential for developing an effective defense doctrine to ensure an Inuit republic remains unconquerable, much as Afghanistan proved to the surprise of many invaders from Alexander to Brezhnev—should the Inuit pursue formal independence once day.

But the ICC instead sought to moderate the behavior of the states that had incorporated their homeland, hoping its ideals would influence their choices in matters of peace and security. The ICC thus promoted the formulation of an Arctic foreign policy that promoted a comprehensive nuclear test ban, an anti-satellite weapons treaty, a nuclear freeze, a no first-use policy, controls on nuclear and weapons technology, prevention of horizontal nuclear proliferation, and nuclear disarmament as well as the illegalization of nuclear weapons and other means of mass destruction, policies that after 9/11 would be adopted by nearly the entire world, as the risk of WMD-terror to all the world was made crystal clear that day.[57] Meanwhile, as the ICC presented its vision for a more secure world, most of the rest of the world continued strengthening its defenses—small nations were arming themselves so that they could again assert, and defend, their own sovereignty, in the wake of the Soviet collapse. Numerous states and substate entities began seeking nuclear weapons technology through illicit networks at this time. Small, dirty wars became commonplace and soon international terrorism would become a salient threat to world order as state and substate forces collided on September 11, 2001. The international system, though no longer bipolar, has become even less inclined toward disarmament, and even pariah states like North Korea felt compelled to develop an atomic capacity to ensure their own survival. The authors of the *ICC Principles* saw beyond the chaos of the "New World Disorder" of the immediate post–Cold War period, and resisted the temptation to pursue policies of self-help and self-defense as the starting point for the self-expression of sovereignty. Perhaps this is why the Inuit achieved their dream of Nunavut, while at nearly the same moment in history, the Mexican government walked away from the negotiating table, leaving the EZLN without a partner to negotiate a lasting peace. But even as the ICC promoted the prohibition from the Arctic of weapons systems like tactical nuclear short-range attack missiles, bombers, and cruise missiles,[58] it recognized the need for "a proper defense system" that includes passive detection systems like radar and sea-bed sonar detection systems to "cover land, sea and air"—though not as part of a ballistic missile defense system, which they opposed.[59] The ICC explained that NGOs "have a specifically recognized role to play in furthering disarmament and peace objectives,"[60] and that negotiations and treaties can be counted on to ensure international compliance with their policy objectives.[61]

In *ICC Principles,* II.21, the ICC reiterates its synthesis of environmental concerns with security issues—integrating the two into a regional set of values for redefining security, providing an important lens through which to understand Arctic security as distinct from other perspectives on national and international security. It believes that "environmental and social impact assessment procedures must be mandatory for proposed defense-related projects or activities, which may cause adverse environmental or social impacts within the Inuit circumpolar regions. In particular, the siting, construction, and operation of military bases, installations, and facilities must be subject to impact assessment. Such assessments must take place at the earliest practicable point in time, prior to the approval of an activity or project."[62] In Canada, both federal environmental assessment policy and the co-management structures of Aboriginal land claims accords support these processes—and they have shown tremendous potential to bring Inuit and national values into balance.

Macro-development projects, and their threat, had long-catalyzed political change in the North, from Project Ramparts and Project Chariot in Alaska to the oil strike at Prudhoe Bay and subsequent exploration rush across the border in the NWT. The new ethos that followed Justice Berger's recommendations after the Mackenzie Valley Pipeline Inquiry led, over several years, to the establishment of new rules enabling Inuit to not only demand environmental impact assessments and reviews, but to participate in them as well. By controlling, to a large degree, the environmental impact of external development activities in their homeland, Inuit have gained one possible "hammer" with which to assert their values. Of course, co-management is not controlled by political elites as much as they would like the public to think, and as such is not completely effective as a method of Inuit control in their homeland given the continued role of the national government as the final arbiter of decisions. But it has enabled Native communities to take a big step forward toward the realization of the principles articulated by the ICC at the dawn of the post–Cold War era.

The importance of the land to Inuit culture, and the land's fragility and vulnerability to pollution and climate change, ensures that participation in the environmental assessment and review process is an important starting point for the Inuit re-assertion of sovereignty in the Arctic. Though not emphasized within the *ICC Principles*, Inuit participation in environmental assessments has become extremely important, allowing Inuit to stand at the crossroads of the ongoing debate between development and conservation. Sometimes the Inuit community is divided, but this division only emphasizes the fact that Inuit are major participants—and that this participation enables Inuit to begin to govern themselves once again. As *ICC Principles*, 11.20 states, "Inuit and other northern peoples must be assured timely access to relevant information and full participation in the impact assessment process." Land claims have helped to bring this about, and new and emerging structures of Aboriginal self-government promises to do so even more.

The Environment and Arctic Security

In addition to the geostrategic conditions of the Arctic shaped in large measure by the Cold War, there is also the central importance of the environment to the Inuit conception of Arctic sovereignty and security. The Arctic environment is and has been central to Inuit identity and their survival as a distinct culture, and it is this continued importance that leads us to next consider environmental security as a pillar of Arctic security in the post–Cold War world. While not a traditional component of national security, the environment is increasingly recognized to be important to regional, national, and international security concerns—and has led to revisions in military strategy over the last few decades as military policies have inexorably greened along with the societies they protect, resulting in the emergence of environmental security as a core component of the national security of modern states.

Indeed, it was European concerns about the extreme risks to their environment of nuclear warfare on their continent that led to mass demonstrations against the installation of intermediate-range nuclear missiles in the 1980s—and which, at least indirectly, led to a bilateral East-West consensus on INF talks and eventually an accord to withdraw such forces from the European theater. Similarly, French concerns with the physical devastation of nuclear weapons, particular to a small or medium-sized country with limited geographic breadth and depth, led to their development of the highly focused neutron bomb—which, while no gift to the peace movement, demonstrated a willingness to minimize physical explosive damage and the spread of nuclear fallout and pollution. A concentrated neutron emission, while highly lethal in a localized area, was a major improvement in overall environmental impact—and a major step toward developing "clean" nuclear weapons, as opposed to "dirty" nuclear bombs.

The 1989 Exxon Valdez oil spill shocked much of the world, as the pristine Prince William Sound and its delicate ecosystem were nearly destroyed by a major, and long foreseen, oil spill. The lesson of the Valdez was not lost on northerners—as evident in the decision of the Inuvialuit to prevent Gulf Canada from drilling offshore in the winter of 1990. But when the winds of war blew toward the Persian Gulf later that year, it became apparent that environmental degradation was not yet a primary concern of military planners. Indeed, some argue that allied bombing of oil terminals created intentional Valdez-sized oil slicks in the Persian Gulf, turning an ugly industrial accident into a military tactic. Much of the world watched in shock as sea and bird life washed to the shores of Kuwait, dead from oil spills brought to the Persian Gulf by war. After the war, it became clear that Saddam Hussein's "exit strategy" from Kuwait included the intentional destruction of the marine environment surrounding Kuwait, from which it drew water into its desalinization plants—and though it was too late for that conflict, it did provide insight useful for the next military engagement between Saddam and the United States in Operation Iraqi Freedom in 2003, when a similar environmental tragedy was avoided.

Elsewhere, the idea emerged that the health of the environment was a concern to regional, national and international security—from the Chernobyl explosion that awakened Europe to the danger of nuclear energy plants to the post–Cold War revelations of nuclear dumping in the Arctic ocean by the former Soviet Union—poisoning the fragile Arctic food chain. Around the same time, University of Alaska researchers discovered that the U.S. military had placed strontium nuclear batteries on Gwich'in land in central Alaska to power a seismic observatory that listened to underground Soviet nuclear tests. In addition, a nuclear dumpsite was found in Northwest Alaska, whose existence had been kept from nearby Inuit residents—not far from where the U.S. military had proposed to detonate an above-ground nuclear explosion as part of Project Chariot, to create a deep water port along the Arctic coast.[63] That proposal had been defeated, and was one of the catalysts that drove the movement to settle the Alaska Native land claim in 1971. Northerners quickly understood that their local and regional security depended upon the health of their environment and their ability to prevent its degradation. Canadian land claims built into their structure the primacy of the environment and its security, though the Alaska claim did not. In Alaska, big business was a major player in the development of the land claim; in Canada, the compact was between Aboriginal people and the government, with industry held at bay pending their resolution, as recommended by Thomas Berger in his report on the Mackenzie Valley Pipeline Inquiry.

Interestingly, when the United States challenged Canadian sovereignty over the Northwest Passage with its transit of the supertanker Manhattan in 1969, Ottawa's response was very much in sync with the values of its indigenous peoples as articulated at the Mackenzie Valley Pipeline Inquiry hearings; it asserted its right to protect the Arctic marine environment, and thereby regulate maritime traffic in its Arctic waters, embracing environmental security as a fundamental sovereign right, thereby integrating environmental security with its overall national security values. As D. M. McRae explained in *Politics of the Northwest Passage*, the environment was the cornerstone to Ottawa's response to the 1969 transit of the Manhattan through the Northwest Passage. The consequent passage on April 8, 1970, of the Arctic Waters Pollution Prevention Act "extended Canadian jurisdiction for the prevention of pollution in waters north of 60 degrees North to a zone 100 miles from the baseline from which the territorial sea is measured"—within which Ottawa "would have the authority to regulate all shipping, including the authority to prohibit shipping from the whole or part of the area, and to prescribe standards on such matters as design, construction, and manning for ships entering the zone," enforced with "powers of arrest and prosecution."[64] This "represented something novel in international law," and is described by McRae as "radical as it was novel. It was novel because it put environmental considerations to the forefront as a justification for the exercise by the coastal state of jurisdiction over adjacent maritime areas. It was radical because it rested on a philosophy that called for a rethinking of the traditional doctrine of the law of the sea"—challenging its principle of "unfettered freedom of navigation on the high seas," and justified "not on a traditional basis of sovereignty but rather in the concepts of 'self-defence' and 'self-preservation.' A state is entitled to defend its environmental integrity, the argument, just as traditional doctrine allows it to defend its territorial and political integrity."[65] As John Kirton and Don Munton explained, "at the outer 100-mile perimeter the government asserted jurisdiction for the specific purpose of pollution control. Within the archipelago formed by the Arctic islands, it strengthened its ability to secure jurisdiction for further purposes in the future. And in the vital core of the Northwest Passage, it enlarged Canadian control over the critical eastern and western gateways at Barrow and Prince of Wales straits, where the channels were less than 24 miles wide."[66] Kirton and Munton added, "With these moves the Canadian government effectively protected its fragile Arctic maritime environment," and noted this "constituted one of the largest geographic extensions of the Canadian state's jurisdiction in the country's history."[67]

Environmental imperatives increasingly determined the political agenda, at not just the regional level but the national and international as well. During the 1970s, concerns about the erosion of the ozone layer by CFCs gradually led to a global consensus on the need to minimize CFC output and to limit the acceleration of global warming. While a direct result of industrial and transportation policies and not military policy, the consensus that gradually emerged by the time of the Second Earth Summit in 1992 was that short- and immediate-term economic security could not be allowed to overshadow longer-term issues of environmental security. As reported on the "Warming Earth" section of the Woods Hole Research Center website, in 1992, the Second Earth Summit was convened in Rio de Janeiro, where the United Nations Framework Convention on Climate Change was finalized for ratification. In December 1997, the countries which met in Rio in 1992 reconvened in Kyoto where they developed a set of legally binding agreements on the reduction of greenhouse gas emissions.

The Kyoto Protocol calls for the reduction of greenhouse gas emissions for several industrialized nations below 1990 levels by 2008–2012, and the United States agreed to a 7-percent reduction, while the European Union agreed to an 8-percent reduction, and Japan agreed to 6 percent. Twenty-one other industrialized nations agreed to similar binding targets. The Kyoto Protocol allows for the trading of emissions quotas among industrialized nations, a significant victory for the United States, but nonetheless, the George W. Bush administration withdrew the United States from the Kyoto Protocol in 2001, claiming that its science was unsound, and that adherence to its provisions would be harmful to the U.S. economy. Russia made similar arguments but eventually was persuaded to sign on for the benefits of emissions trading coupled with pressure from the EU in return for its support of Russia's admission to the WTO. As of February 16, 2005, 141 nations had ratified the Kyoto Protocol, accounting for 61.6 percent of 1990 greenhouse gas emission and entering into force three months after ratification by Russia. But even if the Protocol were implemented by all parties to the Kyoto conference, it would result in a just a 5.2 percent reduction of greenhouse gas emissions below 1990 levels—reducing anthropogenic emissions from around 7.2 billion tons per year to about 6.8 billion tons per year, well short of that needed to prevent the warming of the Earth, which scientists believe would require emissions reductions closer to 50 percent of 1990 levels, and the cessation of wide scale deforestation, also a contributor to greenhouse gas accumulation. Nonetheless, the Kyoto Protocol is seen by environmentalists as a small step in the right direction.

In December 2007, the 2007 United Nations Climate Change Conference took place in Bali, Indonesia, with representatives from over 180 countries attending, where they agreed upon a road-map to reaching an agreement by 2009.[68] In an effort to rejoin the collective of international opinion, the Bush Administration finally agreed to join the Bali Roadmap negotiated in December 2007. As Chad Bouchard reported on *Voice of America*: "The road map does call for global man-made emissions to peak in the next 15 years, and for emission levels recorded in 2000 to be cut in half by 2050. It also promotes a plan enabling wealthy countries to pay poor countries to keep remaining forests intact. Deforestation accounts for at least 20 percent of the world's carbon emissions, according to the U.N. . . . Further conferences to discuss the new climate pact are scheduled for Warsaw next year, and Copenhagen in 2009."[69] Interestingly, among the 10,000 delegates from around the world was a delegation of Inuit leaders. According to a press release from the national Inuit organization, Inuit Tapiriit Kanatami (ITK), "Inuit leaders representing National Canadian Inuit organizations, and the International Inuit Circumpolar Council are heading to Bali, Indonesia to participate in the United Nations Climate Change Conference," including Mary Simon, now president of ITK, and vice president of the ICC (Canada); Patricia Cochran, chair of the ICC; Violet Ford, vice president, ICC (Canada); Aqqaluk Lynge, president, ICC (Greenland); Carl Christian Olsen, vice president, ICC (Greenland); and Jonathan Epoo, president, National Inuit Youth Council (Canada), vice president, Inuit Circumpolar Youth Council.[70]

By the start of the 1990s, alternative views of security perceived a direct link between the environment on one hand, and national and international security on the other; but in military circles, strategic thought still only paid lip service to the environment—largely in recognition of the new political attitudes that colored most government activities increasingly green, and consequently the growing demands for the military to engage in environmentally sensitive activities. Canada's *1992 Defence Policy Statement* recognized the place of the environment in its first post–Cold War revision of defense strategy. But the way the first Gulf War was fought reveals that traditional views of security had not yet disappeared from the world of military planning. Indeed, a later agreement between Canada and the United States to allow nuclear submarines to pass through Dixon Entrance between the Queen Charlotte Islands and Alaska's Prince of Wales Island showed how concerns about the risk to the environment could still be overlooked by Ottawa when an issue of military security, and in particular the U.S.-Canada defense relationship, came into conflict with an environmental issue. A similar phenomenon was described during the Cold War, as Ottawa pursued what Canadian Peace Alliance coordinator Robert Penner described as Canada's status as a "silent nuclear power," opposing the nuclear arms race rhetorically while enabling it through its actions.[71]

The Inuit have long been champions of the environment, and in many ways led the rest of the world toward understanding how environmental security was a critical dimension of our security. As explained in the 1992 *ICC Principles*, "It is a fundamental objective of the Arctic policy to protect the delicate environment, including the marine and other resources on which Inuit depend. The right to a safe and healthy environment is an emerging human right and is especially important to Inuit."[72] Further, "Within the vast Inuit homeland, Inuit have the right and responsibility to ensure the integrity of the circumpolar environment and its resources, as a continuing source of life, livelihood and well-being for present and future generations."[73] Consequently, "Neither development nor conservation objectives should be considered in isolation from each other; rather, both should be developed in harmony."[74]

The *ICC Principles* advocate a "holistic approach" to dealing with the environment, "where the analysis of different but related elements could be combined."[75] Through such an approach, "inter-relationships and consequences of actions and phenomena in different sectors of the environment could receive proper consideration," and at the "same time, specialized analysis of specific aspects would still be vital. Primary emphasis should be placed more on 'prevention' than 'cure,' and on 'cause' more than 'effect.'"[76] As noted in the *ICC Principles*, the ICC seeks to promote the protection and management of the Arctic environment "at international, national and regional levels,"[77] and, as noted in III:7: "When undertaking developmental or other activities of any nature, planners and decision-makers must not simply view the Arctic as an exploitable frontier. Foremost, respect must be accorded to circumpolar regions on the basis that they constitute the ancestral Inuit homeland. Moreover, it must be recognized that, in many instances, detrimental impacts on the Arctic environment can have serious adverse consequences beyond northern limits and significantly affect the world environment."[78]

Furthermore, III:18 pointed out that: "There is an essential relationship between conservation and development. Unless northern development applies conservation principles, it will not be sustainable and Arctic eco-systems and resources may be severely damaged. As a result, care of the natural environment should be an integral part of development at all stages." Along the same line of reasoning, III:19 explained that: "In order to promote developmental activity which is compatible with the Arctic environment and its northern peoples, the Arctic policy should encourage 'eco-development.' Northern development must refer to more than economic growth. It must allow for and facilitate spiritual, social, and cultural development." Eco-development is defined by the ICC to: "operate within the limits of the biosphere and local ecosystems in the North. Such development would also address basic local needs and encourage self-reliance" and to "benefit Inuit and other northern peoples and improve their quality of life." The ICC observed the continued importance of Inuit "subsistence practices," and argued they are "an important element of northern ecosystems." In addition, the ICC argues that "Inuit have the right to meaningfully participate in policy and decision-making processes affecting any aspect of the Arctic environment."

Shelagh Grant explains that this holistic approach taken by the Inuit when dealing with the environment is a reflection of their unique relationship to the Arctic landscape, which is one rooted in a realism quite distinct from the idealist conception of the Arctic environment by outsiders who have long romanticized the region, and in a fusion with their landscape that is inconceivable to those who only imagine the Arctic: "Many Canadians still conceive the Arctic as a vast area of pristine wilderness, a concept not shared by its indigenous peoples, the Inuit. The eco-tourism industry promotes the vision of an unspoiled natural world to attract thousands of visitors northward by air or cruise ships. Environmentalists argue that this wilderness must be protected against roads, mineral exploitation, trapping and hunting."[79] However, Grant points out that "The Inuit, who for centuries have relied upon their environment for sustenance and survival, argue the right to decide how best to utilize their lands and waters to sustain them, culturally and economically, through the next millennium." The gap between the Euro-Canadian image of the Arctic, and the Inuit experience, is reminiscent of the divide within the field of classical international relations theory that separated idealism from realism. Idealists view the world through the lens of hope, focusing on what the world could be, while realists view the world through the lens of fear, focusing on the world as it is, warts and all:

> From the time of Pythias the Greek through to the mid-twentieth century, Europeans envisioned the Arctic as a wilderness, a place of the unknown—cold, mysterious, forbidding, inhabited by wild beasts, yet magnificent in its grandeur—bereft of Western civilization. Although this image has moderated over time, many southern Canadians still think of the Arctic as wilderness. Inuit, meanwhile, have held and continue to hold a much different view of their homelands. They do not set themselves apart from the natural world, but see

the Arctic as a single entity encompassing land, sea, sky, as well as Inuit, birds, animals, marine life, vegetation, weather and even the spirits who once guided the destiny of their ancestors. The environment is the very essence of their being, a concept at odds with the anthropocentric views of the Western world that set humans apart from, and dominant over, nature.[80]

In addition to the "Arctic Wilderness Myth," Grant finds the Inuit are "equally suspect" of the "Myth of the North" that so many southerners believe in. How, asks Grant, "could their homeland affect the collective identity of Canadians, when the vast majority have never visited the Arctic, let alone lived there?"[81] Indeed, Grant adds that "the Myth of the North cannot play a role in defining national identity unless they and other northern Native peoples were central to that myth. Even today, they are not. In this sense, the two myths—the Arctic Wilderness Myth and the Myth of the North—are interconnected in that they have both ignored a vital Inuit presence when appropriating the Arctic landscape into a southern vision."[82]

As Grant observes, "Predictably, these perceptual differences have led to political tensions, initially between Inuit and governments over exploitation of resources, but more recently with environmentalists who have campaigned to make vast wilderness areas into national parks to prevent future development."[83] Indeed, Grant notes that "Particularly contentious is the idea that preservation of Arctic wildlife must include a ban on Inuit hunting and fishing, as proposed at a recent wilderness symposium. Inuit leaders believe that the Arctic resources, which have sustained their people for more than a thousand years, must be responsibly utilized to ensure cultural and economic survival into the next millennium. At issue is the question of ownership and control over the Arctic lands and their resources."[84] That's why, Grant explains, the Inuit "refer to their ancestral lands as Nunavut or Nunavik, meaning 'our land,' in response to those who would call them Crown lands."[85] With environment so important to Inuit culture and identity, one might think the Inuit would be well advised to team up with the park and nature preserve planners and create new parks to protect their environment for perpetuity. But the interests of the state, and its concept of conservation, differ from Inuit interests on and perspective of the land. Indeed, in Alaska, the state has been locked in a protracted conflict with Native subsistence hunters and trappers. There, pro-development interests favoring natural resource exploration and development fear the restrictions placed on park lands by federal lands administrators, which could effectively strangle the emerging economies of the North, preferring the state, which over time has been sympathetic toward their interests. As Grant observes, "Most environmental activists thought their efforts to halt further development in the Arctic would be welcomed, failing to understand that a pristine wilderness could not provide a viable economy sufficient to sustain the Inuit people. Nor could national parks and game preserves solve the problems of air and water pollution. Inuit are committed to protecting the integrity of their environment against degradation, but at the same time are searching for new economic opportunities that do not deny or compete with cultural traditions."[86] She added that the "freedom to hunt and fish is central to their cultural identity and tied to an age-old belief in the co-dependence of 'the hunter and the hunted,' described by Hugh Brody as a 'contract between partners, in which it is not always clear who is the prey.' This principle also places the Inuit in opposition to 'animal rights' activists."[87]

In Canada, however, the relationship between park administrators and Natives has evolved to be quite collaborative. Park creation has been pursued vigorously in conjunction with the settlement of northern land claims, enabling a larger quantum of land to be protected from future development, complementing the objectives of the land claim (and in particular the environmental and wildlife provisions). As a consequence, new and vast parks have been created that further protect Inuit heritage across northern Canada, accommodating traditional subsistence activities and embracing the principle of co-management in a manner not seen in Alaska, which has had a more troubled relationship with regard to park creation inside traditionally Native areas, owing to a far less mutual and reciprocal embrace of the primacy of subsistence rights inside land claims settlement regions. In contrast, inside the Inuvialuit Settlement Region, Ivvavik National Park became the very first national park in Canada to be created by a land claim agreement, followed by Aulavik National Park on Banks Island, and Tuktut Nogait National Parks outside of Paulatuk.[88]

Clearly, a central tenet to the *ICC Principles*, and a foundation of the Inuit concept of Arctic security, is the protection of the environment, and preservation of its ecosystems. These are essential to the cultural, and nutritional, needs of the Inuit, and reflect in many ways the highest and most sacred of values to Inuit life. More modern and conventionally western notions of private property, economic participation and development, and even democratic structures of decision-making are in comparison artifices grafted onto the modern Arctic. As Grant described it: "For Inuit people, their homelands had no borders or boundaries, nor were they limited to physical space. Their traditional concept of land, or *nuna*, did not admit ownership or possession. Even today, there are no fences separating Inuit homes from their neighbours. Land is considered communal and Inuit collectively accept responsibility for its protection."[89] She added:

> Although Inuit hunting territory may comprise a relatively small portion of the Arctic, the distant lands and the seas beyond are of equal importance, as they provide sustenance for the wildlife upon which they were once dependant for survival. As such, the Arctic in its entirety is considered to be as much a part of their environment as their communities and surrounding hunting grounds. Rooted in the distant past, this belief is still held today, as depicted in a poster designed by the Inuit Youth Council. At the centre, an Inuk hunter stands tall atop an *inuksuk*, his harpoon held to the skies, surrounded by polar bears, seal and walrus, with water, ice floes and snow-clad mountains in the background. The title is explicit—Land, Inuit and Wildlife are One—the symbolism is electrifying.[90]

Or, as Alootook Ipellie described in "Thirsty for Life: A Nomad Learns to Write and Draw," in John Moss, ed., *Echoing Silence: Essays on Arctic Narrative*: "Each day was a struggle full of hope that bounty awaited for us in one of those seal breathing holes on the vast sea ice. Our dogged determination to survive will never be understood by those who did not keep company with us when our stomachs yearned for their latest salvation. Not even the greatest of Arctic narrators, I believe, will ever come close to interpreting the anguish we nomads felt when each day dawned and darkness fell at the end of the day. Our only saving grace was to keep dreaming about the feast that had once again eluded us."[91]

But it is the physical environment itself that lays the foundation of Inuit culture and identity, and it is the preservation of this environment that runs like a golden thread throughout the *ICC Principles*, rooting the various policies and programs articulated by the ICC. While their terminology may at times drift toward abstraction, and appear to reflect a more modern or western mindset, the *ICC Principles* are embedded firmly in what we may think of as a tribal, or ethnographically defined regional, level of analysis, more fundamental than the modern state itself, suggesting a tangibility and causal import to the substate dynamics of the Arctic region. This informs us of the necessity to appreciate the Inuit conception of Arctic security and how it has evolved historically and is being re-imagined today, at the threshold of a new era marked by warming climates, open waters, and manifold changes to the Arctic as we have come to know it.

Self-Government, Sovereignty, and Security in the Arctic

The 1992 *ICC Principles* discussed in detail the Inuit aspiration for self-government, but its sections devoted to peace and security refer only tangentially to self-government. As with the discussion of the environment, which earns its very own chapter (due to its extraordinary importance to the subsistence economy of Inuit) in the *ICC Principles*, discussions of self-government and security are largely separated—even though as Gordon Robertson argued, self-government is indeed an important component of Arctic sovereignty, helping to enhance the security of the Arctic, especially now that the East-West, external orientation of the Cold War has largely receded into the past. Interestingly, at the start of the post–Cold War era, the 1992 ICC General Assembly in Inuvik hosted lively, and at times tempestuous, discussions about self-government and the environment, but little talk of peace and security. Without the Cold War to divide the Arctic, the Inuit were able to nimbly redefine their own "national" (or more accurately, tribal, substate, or trans-state) security agenda on a dime, and the essential ingredients of Arctic security for the post–Cold War world concerned internal dynamics. Therefore, the self-government aspirations of Inuit and the contemporary political structures through which they have sought to fulfill these aspirations deserve closer study—as do Inuit concerns regarding their environment.

The 1992 *ICC Principles* contain fifteen subsections addressing Inuit self-government, beginning with the Inuit right to self-government: "As Aboriginal peoples, Inuit have the right to exercise sufficient control over matters affecting their traditional territories, communities, and interests. An integral part of this right of self-determination within states is the right to self-government."[92] The ICC contextualized this right, refraining from declaring it as a sovereign right. Instead, they turn to sovereign states and their moral and international obligations to protect Inuit rights—accepting status as a protected people, not a formally sovereign, let alone a self-defending, nation: "States, which have signed and ratified these international covenants, are obliged to protect and promote the rights of Aboriginal peoples in a manner consistent with the rights guaranteed in such covenants."[93] The ICC based its legal argument for the right to self-government on international law and its commitment to the "fundamental collective right of peoples to self-determination."[94] It does not consider the realpolitik behind international law—that self-determination is asserted where it can defend itself, or where it can be promoted through external intervention. Seldom do states encourage the full self-determination of the indigenous minorities inside their borders, particularly when they predominate in a region that might seek secession or increased autonomy, as has been seen around the world, in ethnoculturally complex states as varied as Mexico, Guatemala, Bolivia, Burma, Thailand, China, Vietnam, Laos, Indonesia, and India. Even democracies such as the United States have been deeply conflicted, leaning more often than not throughout its history toward the suppression of indigenous rights rather than their affirmation. Canada is somewhat unique in its moral and constitutional outlook, having absorbed in its domestic polity the impulses of the old British Empire to integrate its full cultural complexity under the ultimate sovereignty of the Crown and to engage in the diplomatic process of treaty making as a continuation of conquest by other means, subsuming the indigenous nations along its periphery to the state's sovereignty as it expanded its sovereign footprint across continents. Rhetoric aside, most states, even democratic ones, are generally not persuaded by moral arguments—though from time to time, democratic states are forced to support such aspirations because of political pressures from their electorate, which occasionally swings toward idealist impulses. Something like this has pushed Aboriginal rights issues to very the top of the Canadian political agenda at several junctures, as seen during the Mackenzie Valley Pipeline Inquiry, and later during the Charlottetown Accord negotiations, and again at the birth of Nunavut—driven partly by Ottawa's sense of guilt, embarrassment, and moral confusion over its past policies, and reinforced during the armed uprising at Oka in 1990, when the specter of indigenous armed conflict paralyzed the nation, and hinted at the dangers that would ensue should the path of militancy and armed resistance, and an armed response by the state, be chosen.

The *ICC Principles* observed the impact of the lack of self-government on the Inuit homeland: "Presently, the lack of self-government fosters harmful dependency which is leading to serious deterioration of Inuit culture and society."[95] And yet at the same time, the ICC did not admit the dependence of Inuit political organizations, such as the ICC, on non-Inuit policy advisors who developed the platforms endorsed by the Inuit leadership, nor its exclusion of dissident Inuit representing the traditional, subsistence culture from positions of power. The Inuit Tapirisat of Canada, the Tungavik Federation of Nunavut (renamed Nunavut Tunngavik) and the ICC have depended upon numerous non-Inuit policy analysts for their research capabilities, conceptual vocabularies, and communications skills. Intellectually, the ideas and language of Inuit policy are inevitably influenced by non-Inuit. Indeed, the 1992 Inuit Circumpolar Conference experienced a vociferous internal debate between Inuit grassroots activists and advocates of democracy with roots in the early years of the land claims movement, acting independently and without non-Inuit advisors at their ear; and the more conservative, power-savvy elite of Inuit corporate and political leaders, with the former feeling marginalized by the more political sagacious power elite armed with their legal, economic, and political policy consultants and advisors. The *ICC Principles* blamed colonialism for many problems and challenges facing the Inuit homeland—but did little to acknowledge complaints by some Inuit of ICC's own exclusion of grassroots people, and the marginalization of community activists with a different point of view from the corporate and political elites. We must therefore be careful to not too readily accept at face value the speeches of northern leaders that are often written by and/or inspired by the conceptual taxonomy of non-native and, more often than not, non-northern consultants and advisors serving northern elites. These are the sorts of speeches presented to the media and that northern leaders make at international conferences, presented as the collective wisdom of Arctic peoples when in fact the ideas are often incubated far to the south, sometimes even bypassing the peoples of the Arctic themselves. Policy statements about northern issues are thus not necessarily the reflection of the will of the people from the outlying villages that dot the Arctic rim, even when presented as such. Indeed, the insularity and isolation of some northern leaders, who in pursuit of their objectives must spend large amounts of time outside the North, has become a periodic source of political controversy, resulting at times in the sudden loss of power of northern, Native leaders perceived to have grown apart from their home communities, and their replacement by more community-oriented hometown heroes who still reside in their community.

Many policy ideas about northern Canada have come from academic advisors and consultants in Ottawa and other decision-making centers. Of course, one can say the same of statecraft in general—ideas about foreign policy are generally those of a small elite far removed from mainstream society, who speak on behalf of their society's national interests while not necessarily truly representative of them. But on the whole, we accept the principles of foreign policy enunciated by experts who are part of an exclusive elite within a society. Needless to say, we should consider ideas about Arctic security as expressed by both the leaders and the led. Esoteric concepts derived from Western policy ideas seem to link Inuit leaders more to the southern intelligentsia than their own people. That educational systems based upon southern concepts, and such organizations as the northern service of the Canadian Broadcasting Corp. (CBC), have been the breeding ground of numerous northern leaders just as, in other colonial settings, new independent leadership was often borne of exposure to ideas at the colonial center, seems to be a reflection of colonial history in general. Bearing this in mind, we should not entirely discount ideas that seem borne of southern values when articulated by northern Native leaders. Furthermore, such statements still have value since they represent the official views of the organizations representing the people of the Arctic, and mirror to some degree the aspirations of their leaders—and as such, we cannot entirely discount them, even if they diverge from the aspirations of the grassroots Inuit. Nor should we.

But we must be careful not to presume that Inuit politicians always speak for their grassroots people, or that they will respect their aspirations when their power increases. Inuit politicians are not unlike politicians elsewhere in the world, gifted orators, shrewd backroom dealmakers, as susceptible to corruption as our own politicians in the non-Inuit world are, but as capable of greatness and inspiration as well. Inuit politicians seem to intuitively grasp the basics of Machiavelli's realism, knowing it is best to be both feared and loved but in a crunch, that it is safer to be feared than loved. The harshness of the Arctic landscape, its paucity of resources, the human toll of isolation, cold, and darkness reinforce the realist tenets of Machiavelli's thought, and have helped to nurture the emergence of a shrewd and powerful political elite that has helped the Inuit make huge political gains, particularly in comparison to the much larger Indian population to their south, who in many respects have suffered more, and yet have won far fewer concessions from the state. Indeed, in Canada there are some 30,000 Inuit, and yet they enjoyed the first truly comprehensive land claims settlement (the Inuvialuit Final Agreement), the first Inuit-controlled territorial government (Nunavut), three of the Aboriginal and northern seats at the constitutional negotiating table in Charlottetown in the early 1990s, at which an entirely new framework that promised a new Aboriginal order of government was negotiated (but later rejected by popular referendum), and a $10 million compensation package for the relocation and subsequent neglect of several Inuit families in the High Arctic communities of Resolute and Grise Fjord in the early 1950s. These political successes have positioned the Inuit to have the resources, and powers, to preserve their culture, identity, and heritage, while many other Aboriginal groups have continued to slide toward linguistic and cultural extinction. So while some advocates of Inuit rights argue that Canada must do more, go further, to atone for the sins of the past, a more objective analysis cannot overlook the tremendous gains made by Inuit, in part because of the tolerance and encouragement and support of the Canadian government, providing Inuit with greater autonomy, greater wealth, greater political power, and greater environmental control than any comparable indigenous minority group worldwide.

Indeed, the 1992 constitutional discussions at Charlottetown were a fascinating moment in Canadian history, reflecting to some degree a high point for indigenous rights and for the realization of Aboriginal self-government since Columbus and his followers brought the modernizing, economically globalizing, and militarily expanding states of Europe to the New World half a millennium ago. At the table were the now-famous "Mothers of Confederation," all strong, powerful women in positions of leadership, and all Inuit: ICC president Mary Simon, NWT premier Nellie Cournoyea, and ITC president Rosemary Kuptana, representing the 30,000 Inuit of Canada; with the chiefs of the Assembly of First Nations (AFN), the Native Council of Canada, and the Métis National Council (MNC) representing the other million Canadian Natives. The impressive Inuit role at these important constitutional discussions, and their predominant influence over the Aboriginal rights conversation taking place in Canada at that time, when so many of Canada's First Nations lived in a very different world, one that had been overrun, conquered by war or constitutionally subsumed by treaty, economically marginalized by the growing power of the federal, provincial, and territorial governments and their preference for industry or agriculture over subsistence, was a remarkable achievement. The "Mothers of Confederation" were indeed powerful, politically adept, and remarkably successful promoting the interests of their people, though the eventual rejection of the Charlottetown Accord by the Canadian electorate suggests that they may have miscalculated by over-reaching, and insisting on a level of autonomy that the rest of the country was not prepared for.

When the "Mothers of Confederation" spoke of the rights of their people, just as when the *ICC Principles* made similar assertions, they were speaking largely of an abstraction, while at the same time resisting genuine democratic movements led by less power-savvy leaders who spoke for the grassroots Inuit back home in the villages, as happened at the 1992 ICC general assembly. Inuit from Canada, Greenland, Alaska, and from the newly post-Soviet Russia had gathered in Inuvik and Tuktoyaktuk for the sixth general assembly in July, "to discuss issues critical to their future," read an ICC press release. Of all issues facing the Inuit future, none seemed to be more critical or to evoke more passion among delegates than the process of democratization spreading around the world as yearnings for independence, long ignored, were suddenly heard. Democracy was on everybody's minds in 1992, even in the Inuit homeland—and yet at the conference, the anti-democratic machinations of the political elite led to the acclamation of a new ICC president from Alaska without the opportunity for all aspiring candidates to be considered by the most basic of democratic tools: a vote. Indeed, much to the frustration of Inuit democracy advocates, the aspirations of some Canadian and Greenlandic Inuit were ignored by delegates from Alaska, who acclaimed as the next ICC president their own representative in the Alaska state House of Representative, Eileen MacLean, a bright and dynamic leader in both the Inuit community and at the state level who was a lifelong educator committed to the preservation of her culture and language.[96] Though an able and competent leader, and truly deserving of the post, the Alaska delegation acclaimed her as their candidate in spite of the efforts by three other hopefuls from Alaska, including the dedicated community activist Dalee Sambo, an outspoken advocate of subsistence rights, to be considered for the ICC leadership. Thus it was the process that came under fire, not the selection itself, which resulted in strong, capable leadership.

Many delegates at the ICC general assembly responded with disappointment at the process, including the sitting MP from Nunatsiaq, the legislative district that included the future territory of Nunavut, Jack Anawak, who told the general assembly they wanted a chance to nominate and vote for the presidential candidate of their choice.[97] Sambo observed with disappointment that her right to run for president of the United States was better protected than her right to run for president of the ICC.[98] Aqqaluk Lynge of Greenland, then an ICC vice president and currently the ICC vice chairman and the Greenland ICC's president, delivered a moving speech about democracy and how his elders had fought for basic rights denied to Inuit in Greenland a generation ago. He observed that the ICC had fought to become part of the democratic process: "We who were born in a colony, who want more autonomy, we have to defend democracy anytime there is anything to abuse it. One person who knows that, wants to be nominated for the president," said Lynge, who allowed Sambo to address the ICC.[99] "It is a sad statement that I was not allowed to be nominated," noted Sambo, "that there was a foreclosure by my own people."[100] She reminded the delegates that "these are not partisan politics," that the ICC stands for Inuit unity. "It is really important to go back to Inuit values," Sambo said. In spite of her popularity among delegates from Canada and Greenland, the politics of the day prevented Sambo from being nominated. But her words—and Lynge's—remain a powerful reminder of the passion for democracy, and a sobering critique of the process used by the Alaskan delegates to appoint a president without a vote.[101]

In the *ICC Principles*, the ICC asserts its commitment to accountability, proclaiming that for "purposes of self-government, Inuit have the right to determine their own institutions, according to the circumstances and needs in their respective regions. Such institutions must remain fully accountable to the people they serve and be capable of promoting all aspects of Inuit development."[102] Yet in reality, Inuit self-governing organizations like the Inuvialuit Regional Corporation, during their early post-settlement years, have generally resisted accountability. In the case of the Inuvialuit, their regional corporation appointed corporate directors within the Western Arctic region that were as dependent upon southern expertise as colonial administrators from an earlier time in history, a style of management that was later rejected by the Inuvialuit shareholders, who reclaimed control over their land claim after a scandal involving improper bonus payments made by board directors to themselves without merit, and without shareholder knowledge, was revealed.[103] And the still young territorial government of Nunavut continues to struggle with a host of governance issues, oscillating from representing the very best of hope for the future, to a deep sense of disappointment in the way business is conducted behind closed doors, with limited accountability to the Inuit people. As *Nunatsiaq News* editor Jim Bell observed in an article profiling his journalism titled "The Conscience of Nunavut" in the Summer 2005 edition of the *Ryerson Review of Journalism*, "so far, Nunavut has not lived up to its promise" a viewpoint shared by many Inuit that "likely includes the vast majority of Nunavummiut."[104]

In a *Nunatsiaq News* editorial written by Bell on March 14, 2008, "Leona makes a good point," he delved more deeply into the concerns of Inuit on the style of Inuit governance that so often generated grassroots frustration, "Leona Aglukkaq provoked a mini-squall of controversy late last month when she suggested in the legislative assembly that Nunavut's Inuit organizations must do more to make themselves transparent and accountable to beneficiaries. . . . Nunavut Tunngavik reacted in a predictable manner. They fired off a defensive press release saying Aglukkaq is 'simply misinformed' and that NTI staff and elected officials are as pure as the driven snow."[105] Bell believes otherwise, writing that "Aglukkaq's remarks constitute fair comment on a legitimate public issue and they deserve thoughtful attention."[106] That's because:

> In them, she calls attention to a problem that has frustrated many beneficiaries for many years. It's also a problem that may be impossible to fix, since it's rooted in the way that various Inuit groups organized themselves after the settlement of comprehensive land claim agreements with the federal government. In northern Québec, the western Arctic and Nunavut, each Inuit group opted for a corporatist model. In each one, the interests of a legally-defined Inuit collectivity is represented by one or more private corporations. For us, they're all household names: Makivik Corp., Nunavut Tunngavik Inc., the Inuvialuit Regional Corp., and so on. We're so used to their prominent public roles, we often forget what they really are: private corporations.[107]

Thus, Bell concludes, "in complaining about a lack of transparency within Inuit organizations, Aglukkaq expresses a type of frustration felt by numerous Nunavut and Nunavik beneficiaries. It's also worth noting that many of these beneficiaries, rightly or wrongly, feel they have no legitimate way to express that frustration."[108] Bell does credit the Inuit corporations for delivering many important benefits to their beneficiaries, and he acknowledges many important improvements in their management and accountability. But because of the dual nature of these corporate entities, as private corporations serving a public function, Bell believes these kinds of problems will "echo throughout the Arctic for many years to come."[109]

The *ICC Principles* noted the need to "provide for an adequate economic base for the full realization of Inuit self-government," as well as to develop "appropriate management, development and training programs" to help foster greater "Inuit self-reliance," and which can help to mitigate or prevent the sorts of problems experienced so far in all of the land claims settlement areas, where accountability issues have come to light. In addition, the *ICC Principles* argued that Inuit "must exercise sufficient control over the policies, programs and budgets directly affecting their respective regions," though without specifying that it's not just having control, but exercising responsible control, that can make or break the success of self-government, a challenge that has been faced from Alaska to Greenland as Inuit gained increased powers to manage their resources and govern themselves.[110] The problems have become particularly acute in Nunavut, which enjoyed the establishment of the most sophisticated and powerful model for Inuit self-government yet experienced in the Inuit homeland, combining the economic and environmental co-management structures of a comprehensive land claims accord with the governing structures of a territorial government. But instead of transforming Nunavut into a self-governing paradise, Nunavut has experienced several years of crisis, marked by disappointment and at times heartbreak, showing that Aboriginal self-government in practice was going to be a lot harder than Aboriginal self-government in theory.[111] But that doesn't diminish the achievement represented by Nunavut's existence; it simply grounds expectations in reality, and outlines the challenges that must next be overcome. Indeed, as Shelagh Grant has explained: "Considering that less than a half-century ago the Inuit were still denied the basic right of citizenship—the right to vote—their progress in regaining control of their lives, culture, lands and resources has been no less than phenomenal."[112]

During Nunavut's first five years, initial high hopes quickly turned to disappointment across the new territory. With the creation of the new territory of Nunavut in 1999, and its unique convergence of land claims and self-government, there was great hope for the future. But during the first half-decade of the new territory's existence, there have been many disappointments. According to Dafna Izenberg, "there are many hurts. Nunavut has fallen far short of the many hopes pinned on its creation, with 27 percent of all its deaths between 1999 and 2003 attributable to suicide; a higher rate of violent crime than anywhere else in Canada; and more students dropping out of high school than graduating."[113] And, when it came to the creation of jobs for Inuit, achieving satisfactory levels of Inuit employment in the new government of Nunavut, and developing an educational model to serve the unique cultural and linguistic needs of the predominantly Inuktitut-speaking population, things proved so disappointing that former B.C. Supreme Court Justice Thomas Berger, who rose to international prominence for his role in the Mackenzie Valley Pipeline Inquiry in the 1970s, and for his subsequent "Village Journey" through post-ANCSA Alaska, was called back to the North, appointed as Conciliator by Canada's Department of Indian Affairs and Northern Development on June 1, 2005, and asked to explore "new approaches to the implementation of the Nunavut Land Claims Agreement."[114]

As Berger observed in his final report: "It is now six years on since the creation of Nunavut. Nunavut today faces a moment of change, a moment of crisis."[115] And as described by Paul Mayer, a Montreal lawyer and the Senior Ministerial Representative for Nunavut Devolution to the Department of Indian and Northern Affairs, in his June 2007 Report on Nunavut Devolution, the Inuit are standing at a crossroads of hope and despair:

> Nunavut is at a crossroads today. On the one hand, it is a land of incredible op-
> portunity. It has vast mineral and natural resources wealth. At the briefings
> given by senior GN [Government of Nunavut] and Inuit association leaders in
> Nunavut, I heard many predict a bright and optimistic future for Nunavut. They
> outlined a vision of a self-reliant territory that would become less dependent on
> federal government transfers in which Nunavummiut would enjoy a standard of
> living comparable to that of southern Canadians. On the other hand, despite this
> optimism, the territory continues to face extremely difficult challenges. But the
> reality would best be described as a blend of optimism and despair.[116]

The *ICC Principles* accepted the principles of co-management and the continued necessity of jointly governing the Arctic, and consequently acknowledged the formal sovereignty of the modern state—and its territorial, provincial, state, and federal levels of government—that govern portions of their homeland, retaining final decision-making authority in most cases. And where there is self-governance, as in Nunavut or in the Labrador Inuit Settlement Area to its south, the federal government continues to control the capital flow into Inuit territory by means of implementation funds, resulting in a tug-of-war between Inuit territorial leaders and their federal funders and concerns of a potential financial strangulation of their young territory. The language of the 1992 *ICC Principles* suggests a pragmatic acceptance of the colonial powers that have extended their rule into the Inuit homeland over the past two centuries, and a respect for the constitutional order externally imposed onto the Inuit homeland: "Where competing federal, provincial, or state interests exist in regard to certain subject matters, mechanisms for joint management or control must be worked out. Such mechanisms must be consistent whenever possible with principles of self-government."[117] The *ICC Principles* go on to describe Inuit institutions of self-government. II:11 states that they "shall exercise their powers in a manner consistent with the fundamental collective and individual rights of Inuit and other peoples, who are subject to the jurisdiction of these institutions"; II:12 states that they "shall be subject to fair and independent procedures, through which decisions that are felt to be unjust or improper may be appealed"; II:13 states that "Inuit fundamental rights and freedoms must not be alterable by institutions of self-government without the free and informed consent of the people affected, obtained through formal and recognized procedures"; and II:14 states that "existing structures of self-government within the circumpolar regions, as well as Inuit aspirations towards significantly expanded forms of self-government, must be taken into account, where possible, in formulating and implementing an Arctic policy."

The *ICC Principles* are thus an enunciation of rights, and a declaration of Inuit aspirations. Yet it is power that brings change, and in other parts of the world, the inexorable movement toward self-government has been rooted in incrementally increasing power, not just declaring what is right. Indeed, many Inuit are as comfortable discussing the realpolitik of power as they are the ideals embodied in their Aboriginal rights. But the *ICC Principles*, by virtue of being principles, are at heart an idealistic articulation of Inuit aspirations rather than a discussion of realpolitik, and consequently overlooks the substantial military experiences and knowledge gained by many Inuit, especially in Alaska, where the territorial guard contributed to the security of Alaska during World War II and the Cold War, and also in northern and coastal Canada where the Canadian Rangers have helped to assert Canadian sovereignty during the same period. These experiences, and insights derived from them, could serve as a valuable incubator for an Arctic militia modeled on the EZLN, or independent Inuit defense force to protect a re-emergent Inuit nation much like the respected Israeli Defense Forces (IDF), helping the Inuit to assert greater sovereignty, and even if not ever a truly sovereign nation, at least to become more autonomous, self-governing, and self-defending. Indeed, even the experience of the Jewish Defense League, or JDL, which has helped to combat anti-semitism and to protect Jewish minorities, presents an intriguing subnational analogue that the Inuit could emulate should they seek to harness their potential military capacity.

Local militias have redefined sovereign boundaries before, from America's revolutionary Minutemen who asserted a uniquely American sovereignty, initiating a two-centuries long breakup of the British Empire; to the locally organized militia units of the old Yugoslavian army that became sovereign defense forces during and after the breakup of that state, to the Zapatistas' EZLN, which briefly engaged the Mexican army before agreeing to a ceasefire to enable its leadership to pursue political reforms for Mexico's ten million indigenous people. Inside post-Saddam Iraq, it was new, sectarian militias that defined the new political contours of that fractious state, and which enhanced the power of newly elected officials from each largely self-defending constituency. Afghanistan is much the same, where traditional warlords have long governed in a sovereign manner over tribally distinct regions, and where they again define the internal boundaries of that state. In most of the Inuit homeland, the Inuit are still the predominant demographic force; it would not be beyond the imagination for this locally demographic majority to arm itself (its hunters are already well armed) and assert a more formal role in the defense and security of their homeland.

Inuit Sovereignty, One Step at a Time

With their aspiration to re-assert their indigenous rights and traditions, the Inuit have proceeded to gain greater powers in numerous governmental and constitutional jurisdictions. Ever since the Alaska Native Claims Settlement Act was enacted in 1971, step by step the Inuit have sought to increase their powers in order to protect their traditional values and their indigenous rights. The environment and its security has been of vital importance to Inuit survival and thus central to Inuit culture; and the means to protect it, according to the ICC, the regional Inuit political organizations, and the many grassroots communities and their residents, is to create self-governing structures in the various Inuit regions, each adapting to its wider political environment. As Grant explains:

> To protect their environment from exploitation by others and at the same time preserve their culture, it was crucial to take back control of their lives. The process began in 1972; 20 years later, they stood at the brink of their overall objective. The Inuit of northern Québec had a land claims settlement. . . . In the western Arctic, the COPE settlement provided the Inuvialuit with an equal voice on land use and resource management boards. Then in 1992, a land claims agreement was signed in conjunction with approval of a separate Nunavut Territory, in essence granting Inuit of the central mainland and Arctic islands "self-government" within a non-ethnic government.[118]

The *ICC Principles* reflect the ideas and ideals of the Inuit, but because the ICC is itself an international organization, it does not represent the perspective of any single government—apart from the circumpolar equivalent of a government in exile, or perhaps more aptly, or underground in the face of continued colonial occupation by four militarily and economically superior states. Instead, their voices spread out across a vast and diverse region, cross-cut with numerous international, territorial, provincial, state, municipal, and other administrative boundaries. This complex political geography presents the Inuit with various governmental structures through which to articulate their ideals, some where they remain a predominant political force such as the relatively young territory of Nunavut, others where they are fast becoming a marginalized minority in their own land, as evident in rapidly growing administrative centers like Barrow, Alaska, and Inuvik, NWT.

So as sweeping as the *ICC Principles* are, they are not, at least not yet, the policies of any single government, and they thus lack the power of enforcement. However, in the many political entities created to govern various portions of the Inuit homeland, the Inuit have worked hard to gain not just a seat at the table, but when possible to take over the administration and governance of entire regions, as seen with the birth of Nunavut in Canada, and the emergence of some relatively powerful borough governments in Arctic Alaska where municipal power becomes a practical alternative to Aboriginal self-government, and since 2005 in the first truly indigenous Inuit governing structure in Labrador. So while the *ICC Principles* present a sweeping vision of environmental security, heavy on ideals, back home the Inuit understand the necessity for political realism to achieve their vision, and have learned that real power has resided in the regions, and that over time this power has substantially increased. Where the land claims become settled, new governing structures emerge to provide Inuit with real governing experience, whether through the partnership of co-management or with the real, albeit limited, powers of municipal and territorial administration. All of these structures are within the sovereign constitutional structures imposed upon the Inuit by the Arctic rim states, an inherently colonial arrangement even if not definitionally imperial. But in spite of this, or perhaps because of it and the unique political culture of North America, where indigenous rights have gained tremendous ground with the passage of time, the Inuit have in just three decades witnessed the completion of land claims across their entire North American homeland, from the Bering Sea to Baffin Bay.

With great political dexterity, and remarkable endurance, Inuit leaders have chipped away, a little bit at a time, over many decades, carving out zones of greater autonomy from their central governments far to the south that assert formal sovereignty over the Arctic, while depending on Inuit use and occupancy of Arctic lands to legitimize these claims. The ICC is thus akin to an international regime, representing the collective interests of the Inuit while not technically being a governing body, and thus without any practical levers for governing or administering their homeland. Lacking the power to implement the many ideals and objectives identified in the *ICC Principles*, the ICC members have had to look to the incremental gains back home to realize their vision, and to secure their most sacred values. In the process of increasing their autonomy, and broadening their political powers, the Inuit of Nunavut successfully negotiated the formation of their very own territorial government, which seceded from the Northwest Territories in 1999. As discussed in Jens Dahl, Jack Hicks, and Peter Jull in their edited volume, *Nunavut: Inuit Regain Control of Their Lands and Their Lives*, Nunavut reflects a unique synthesis of modern and ancient, North and South, public and indigenous: "The relationship between North and South, isolated hunter-gatherer village and networked industrial city, and Inuit and European . . . has been strengthened by the long years of negotiation, the many disputes, angry words and slammed doors, and eventual renewed discussion and final agreement which created Nunavut."[119] As further described by Jack Hicks and Graham White, "Nunavut is an attempt by the large Inuit majority to regain control over their lives and to ensure their survival and development as a people."[120] As Hicks and White explain, "the Nunavut 'package'—the provisions of the Nunavut Land Claims Agreement, and the resulting division of the Northwest Territories and the creation of the Nunavut territory and the Government of Nunavut—was designed to both accommodate Inuit self-government aspirations yet fit comfortably within established traditions of mainstream Canadian governance. It is not a radical departure."[121] But there are nonetheless "enormous challenges," including "a young work force with high levels of unemployment and dependence on social assistance, low (but rising) educational levels, high costs for goods and public services, inadequate public housing, poor health conditions, and escalating rates of substance abuse, violence and incarceration," and these challenges are so great that "a study commissioned by the federal government in 1988 predicted that Nunavut communities may become Arctic ghettos plagued by increasing rates of crime—with more in common with urban slums than with the independent, resourceful society that survived for thousands of years."[122]

Critics of the land claim model, and of the Nunavut experience specifically, have observed the risks associated with the Nunavut experiment, some coming under fire, such as Albert Howard and Frances Widdowson, who co-authored an article titled "The Disaster of Nunavut,"[123] and more recently the controversial and widely discussed 2008 book, *Disrobing the Aboriginal Industry: The Deception Behind Indigenous Cultural Preservation*. In "The Disaster of Nunavut," they argued the new territory was "fundamentally unviable," and would "not enable the Inuit to assert more control over their lives and thereby improve social conditions in their communities," and that the "racially defined territory's existence will depend almost entirely on federal transfers, and attempting to artificially retain Inuit culture will isolate Inuit people further from the modern world."[124] Hicks and White believe otherwise, and explain that the Nunavut experiment has in fact been fueled by a vision of hope, and a belief in its capacity to succeed: "The visionaries who gave birth to the Nunavut project and then negotiated it into existence did so in the belief that it would facilitate meaningful self-government, sustainable economic development and healthy communities. The challenge of overcoming Nunavut's economic and social problems, however, may well dwarf the considerable challenges of negotiating and implementing . . . the Nunavut project. And while the creation of Nunavut is undeniably a significant innovation within Canadian federalism, there is no guarantee that it will result in, for example, the kinds of community-based interventions needed to curb social pathologies such as suicides by young Inuit males."[125] They cite John Amagoalik, the well known "Father of Nunavut," who explained that Nunavut "won't solve all our problems overnight," and though "people will have a government they can relate to—a government that speaks and understands their language and understands their culture and priorities," he cautioned that "we cannot expect miracles. Sitting over a hole in the ice for hours, not moving, waiting for a seal, takes patience. It took a lot of patience to get self-government. Now it will take more patience to solve our many problems. Ultimately, however, the test of Nunavut's 'success' will be the degree to which its many benefits and opportunities are shared by *all* its residents—and the rate at which its social pathologies decrease over time."[126]

So how has Nunavut fared? Were the pessimists right in their pessimistic prognostications? Or were the optimists vindicated for their persistence of hope? While approaching the end of the first decade of Nunavut's existence as a territory, and having passed the fifteen year mark celebrating the signing of the Nunavut land claim, we can no longer exonerate the Nunavut Project for its youth or inexperience. But we can hedge our bets by recognizing that we are still standing at a crossroads, where success or failure still hang in the balance, both still possible, neither yet foreclosed. Supporters argue that conditions in Nunavut would have surely been no worse had Nunavut never been; all that would be absent would be its hope and promise. Opponents argue that there is a tragic inevitability in its failure, blaming this on the ultimate irreconcilability of Inuit traditions and modernity, and on the inherent contradictions of the land claim model that tries to balance a modern, corporate structure with the ancient traditions of subsistence and survival in the frozen land. More radical opponents among indigenous rights activists, of course, see a solution: the restoration of full, formal sovereignty, and the complete independence of the Inuit as a nation. Greenland is now on its way down this path, and with its close connection to Europe, where sovereignty takes many forms, the notion of a sovereign and independent Greenland is not so far-fetched. In Alaska, aspirations for formal independence have been largely ignored by the more pragmatic corporate modernists that have sought to come to terms with the state, but percolating on the sidelines, hidden within the sovereignty movement that looked to Washington for salvation from an oppressive or at least neglectful state government, lies a kernel that could one day sprout into a formal independence movement. Nunavut seems less likely to head down this road, but perhaps if the Nunavut project continues to stagnate and the young continue to take their own lives in such overwhelming numbers, an awareness will emerge as it has in Greenland, and to a lesser degree in Alaska, that the problem all along has been the colonial, semicolonial, and neocolonial dynamic, rooted in dependency on a more powerful neighbor to assert sovereignty and to bring security. If this awareness does emerge, then Nunavut has a compelling case to make, one that will be hard to rebut, particularly after Kosovo, the small province within a sovereign Serbia that was granted independence after its long neo-trusteeship under UN protection. On its own it could not assert or defend its own sovereignty, nor secure its independence, but with the blessing of the West, the military support of NATO, and enough stakeholders in the international arena to offset the preponderance of Serbian power, a formally independent Kosovo is now a reality. So why not the same for Nunavut?

Of course, should Nunavut articulate a desire to become independent, it could partner up with Greenland, and perhaps its circumpolar neighbors in Alaska and the Western Arctic region of Canada, and thereby strengthen its case by increasing its demographic base and broadening its territory, so much so that it would become a substantial member of the international community, with tremendous natural resource wealth and territorial waters that are poised to be emergent sea lanes linking the world's largest markets. The long-term economic potential is intriguing, but the awareness is not yet generally there, nor is the aspiration, with the exception of a few forward-looking sovereigntists. But one day this could change, as it has in Greenland.

How might this emergent Inuit nation approach issues relating to Arctic sovereignty and security? Before the Nunavut secession, the Government of the Northwest Territories (GNWT) administered a vast territory stretching from the Yukon-Alaska boundary in the west to Baffin Bay in the east. The NWT was still united during the final days of the Cold War and during the immediate post–Cold War period, and as such it was the GNWT that articulated what we can describe as the "territorial interest" on Arctic sovereignty and security. Only after the territorial division in 1999 would the new territorial Government of Nunavut (GN) and the Inuit of Nunavut share a singular perspective. We will turn next to the territorial perspective, in order to understand the differences between the Inuit conception of Arctic security as articulated in the detailed blueprint put forth by the ICC in 1992, and that of the broader GNWT prior to the territorial division, since at that time the territorial government reflected a distinct level of analysis, one that might shed some light on how a future Inuit nation might conceptualize and articulate a vision of Arctic sovereignty and security. Now, with Nunavut representing both the territorial and the Inuit voice, there is a less clear separation between the Inuit interest and that of the territorial government in the eastern and central Arctic, though in the post-Nunavut NWT, the territorial government is still very much a distinct level of analysis as compared to its many regional Aboriginal groups, such as the Inuvialuit and the many Dene tribes. Because of the diversity of viewpoints at the local and regional level, the GNWT had to find a balance, and assert a unified perspective from its diverse composition. A sovereign Inuit nation would have a similar challenge, and might articulate a balanced synthesis as the GNWT tried to do, at once recognizing the wide spectrum of viewpoints within its boundaries, and at the same time having to fulfill all the responsibilities and obligations that come along with governing a vast domain.

The Territorial Perspective

In November 1990, at the very end of the Cold War period and prior to the final dissolution of the Soviet Union, the GNWT issued a discussion paper on *Military Activity in the North and the Establishment of a Circumpolar Zone of Peace and Security*. The Northwest Territories, then and now, is not like many other places—apart from parts of Alaska, the Yukon, Nunavut, and Greenland. Its government runs, officially, by consensus—meaning there are no political parties and no official opposition. In actuality, the system has certain cleavages that are quite normal in regional politics: the Cabinet, which is elected by the legislative assembly, has a great deal of power, and the regular MLAs become a sort of sitting opposition to the Cabinet they establish. In spite of its flaws, the GNWT was until the Nunavut secession represented largely by Aboriginal people—and was as close to an operational Aboriginal self-government as Canada had at that time. Since Nunavut's formation, the new government in Iqaluit has become an even more powerful manifestation of Aboriginal self-government than the old Yellowknife government, but it has been hobbled by growing pains, including the relative inexperience of its leadership, its far less connective infrastructure, and its still evolving and notably strained financial relationship with Ottawa.

In its 1990 discussion paper, the GNWT sought to respond to the diversity of voices within the territory, and to articulate a policy that reflected a consensus among these diverse constituencies, and was a "response to the significant number of territorial residents, Aboriginal groups, non-government organizations and Members of the Legislative Assembly who have expressed their opposition to some aspects of northern military activity on moral grounds and encouraged the federal government to work with the superpowers and our other circumpolar neighbors toward demilitarization of Canada's north and circumpolar regions around the world."[127] It asserts that "Northerners have also been closely following the easing of tensions between the superpowers over the past three years and more recently, the dramatic events in Eastern Europe which, according to some world leaders, have brought about the collapse of the Warsaw Pact countries and an end to the Cold War."[128] It thus explained: "Given these encouraging developments, northerners are asking why governments continue to make massive expenditures on defense programs when there are so many other challenges—environmental, social, educational—facing the north, Canada and other nations."[129]

The position paper was also a response to several contentious issues relating to military activity in the NWT that "have prompted numerous motions and debates in the Legislative Assembly" including cruise missile testing, low-level training flights, and related military initiatives, such as Forward Operating Locations, on their potential impacts on "the lifestyle of northern residents, the protection of our environment and the interests of Native northerners as established through Aboriginal claims settlements."[130] As the report noted, "While the extent of opposition to, or concern about, these measures in the Northwest Territories varies from region to region, it is clear that northerners are seeking to have more influence over Canada's defense policy as it relates to certain military activities in the north.[131] At the same time, the GNWT recognized "that even if, or when, a circumpolar zone of peace and security is ever established, the Department of National Defence will continue to maintain a presence in northern Canada for national security and sovereignty reasons. Most northerners would agree with this assessment."[132] It added, "Overall, while the Canadian military's presence in the Northwest Territories is desirable and necessary from a national security and sovereignty perspective, it also represents a government institution which has contributed to development of the north and assisted other federal and territorial agencies in delivering a variety of programs and services to northern residences."[133]

The GNWT's introduction is an interesting articulation of the territorial perspective. Its realism concerning the need for, and the mission of, the military in the North stands in contrast to some of the more idealistic and pacifistic concerns of some of its residents—but it concluded that most residents of the NWT accept the continued need, and benefits of, a military presence in the region in spite of the profound changes in international affairs that quickly unfolded at the Cold War's end. It is interesting to note the GNWT's awareness and understanding of the new international environment of the post–Cold War era—and its regional perspective on the multifaceted role of the military in the North even in the face of these changes. While the GNWT did express concern for local values, an interest in Aboriginal land claims, and recognition of the need for impact assessments on local traditions, economies, and the environment, it seems to be very prudent in making a commitment to a continued military presence. Its reluctance to see a military withdrawal from the region has less to do with international security concerns, and more to do with a desire for continued developmental assistance for transportation, weather observation, and radar infrastructure; regional employment; and intergovernmental assistance during emergencies.

From the perspective of the GNWT, Arctic security is defined largely in regional terms. Although a regional perspective is, of course, to be anticipated, it is nonetheless interesting to observe the contrast between GNWT's outlook and the ICC's. Where the ICC developed a policy that asserts an interest in redefining the very limits of international relations in the Arctic, and moderating behavior at the global level to be more conducive to their regional interest, the GNWT's outlook seems to be a more pragmatic articulation of the regional perspective, with less of an ambition to influence the evolution of systemic-level events. Reading the GNWT position paper on military activity in the North one senses a regional appropriateness to its language and concepts. The paper is neither pretentious, nor does it not radiate with the nuance and idiom suggestive of an external influence or even an outside consultant hired for their policy expertise, as often is the case with policy development within the indigenous community. As the GNWT stated: "During the past decade, many residents of the Northwest Territories began to question this new presence of the military for a variety of moral, environmental, social and financial reasons."[134] The GNWT acknowledged the work of the ICC and numerous scholars promoting the demilitarization of the Arctic.[135] It commented on how "the international climate began to change in the late 1980s, producing more questions from northerners who felt that an easing of Cold War tensions between the superpowers should produce a corresponding decrease in military activity, thereby further contributing to prospects for reducing tensions and increasing the climate for world peace."[136]

The GNWT identified four issue-areas regarding northern security: The establishment of a circumpolar zone of peace and security; Canadian contribution to circumpolar and global peace; the ongoing role in the north for DND; and northerners' views about Canadian defense policy. The report summarizes military activity in the North, notes the Cold War military buildup in the USSR, and examines military activity in the Canadian North since World War II. The latter includes the military construction projects of World War II—the Alaska Highway and the Canol pipeline, the airfields for the Northwest Staging and Crimson routes—and after World War II, the construction of the DEW Line and permanent bases at Alert and Inuvik, and the Northern Command headquarters in Yellowknife. It noted that, "with the exception of these permanent facilities, and exercises involving cold weather training and testing of personnel, weapons, and aircraft, the military's presence in the Canadian North during the period 1960-1980 did not increase appreciably."[137] It was in the 1980s when "the climate began to change," and in 1983 the federal government entered into an agreement with the United States letting the U.S. military test their equipment in Canada—a five year agreement renewed again in 1988, and once more in early 1993—without any northern consultation, creating some tension in Parliament. With this agreement began the testing of cruise missiles over the Mackenzie River valley and northern Alberta.

The GNWT discussed the North American Air Defence Modernization (NAADM) project, whose origins date back to a 1985 agreement to replace the the aging DEW Line with more up-to-date radar systems—both short and long range—and the establishment of Forward Operating Locations (FOLs) through the upgrading of airstrips in the Inuvik, Yellowknife, Rankin Inlet and Iqaluit. A FOL planned for Kuujjuaq was stalled by an environmental review, and was subsequently cancelled by DND. The FOLs required runway extensions and/or upgrading, maintenance facilities for jet aircraft, and accommodation.[138] 1985 was also the year that the Polar Sea icebreaker traveled through the Northwest Passage without Canadian authorization, sparking another "sovereignty crisis"— and leading Ottawa to commence planning for a new Class 8 icebreaker, and to increase sovereignty patrols to assert Canada's territorial control over its Arctic waters, though it later scrapped the icebreaker plan—mainly for reasons of high cost. In 1987, the new Defence White Paper was released, which included a proposal for the purchase of several nuclear submarines to patrol the Arctic—but this plan, too, was never adopted.

The GNWT observed that, according to DND policy, Canada's defense obligations "must be carried out fairly and prudently in each and every region of Canada," including the North.[139] It also described the fundamental threats to Canadian security, "threats which stem from foreign military powers; threats which arise from foreign powers or individuals which violate Canadian laws or jurisdiction; and, finally threats from within Canada."[140] In regard to the first of these, the GNWT noted "the Canadian military is clearly anticipating a military attack on our borders or from across oceans which border Canada," and that "the Arctic is the shortest attack route between the two superpowers and while the threat of an attack over the Pole is currently quite remote, National Defence feels that the consequences are still too severe to ignore."[141] However, since 1990, this particular threat had become even less likely, for with the demise of the USSR came an end to hostilities between North America and Russia.[142] The second category regards "foreign governments, businesses or individuals breaking Canadian laws or violating its jurisdiction," including "poaching, smuggling, polluting the waters of the Arctic," and so forth.[143] These problems still exist, particularly in the fisheries of the Atlantic and Pacific, but increasingly in the Arctic, where shipping and oil and gas development present a risk, particularly with regard to pollution. But of most importance to the 1990s was the third category, which "covers threats to Canadian security which arise from within Canada," and includes natural disasters, human error–induced disasters, and "disruptions resulting from civil disobedience, riots and sabotage," a possibility that became ever more real after the Oka crisis of 1990. The GNWT examined the problem of internal security, noting: "With respects to threats to Canadian security which arise from within Canada, the Department of National Defence gets its authority to respond under the Emergencies Act, which replaced the old War Measures Act, and the National Defence Act, which was recently used when

Armed Forces were sent to Oka and Kanesatake. In both cases, a request for assistance from the Canadian military must come from responsible authorities in a provincial or territorial government."[144] In the NWT, a "request for military assistance to civilian authorities under the Emergencies Act must normally be made by the Minister of Municipal and Community Affairs through Northern Region Headquarters to the Department of National Defence."[145]

The GNWT summarized the main views that northerners have on the military in the North, and these views range from those who oppose military power altogether to those who want an expanded military presence in the North. In addition, there are those in the North whose main concern with the military is its need "to ensure that thorough and meaningful consultation takes place with local residents, their organizations and governments," and the GNWT concluded that "in the Northwest Territories, northerners appear to be unanimous on this issue—they want to know the military's plans for their communities and regions."[146] One of the GNWT's primary "thrusts" was its proposal for the establishment of a circumpolar zone of peace and security. Because of the profound changes in international relations in the late 1980s and early 1990s, which forced the western countries to "reconsider the principles or assumptions upon which their Cold War defence policies were based and develop new approaches which reflect the international climate of the 1990s," and because of the added "burdens" of "debt and pressing domestic problems," the GNWT observed that "the timing and circumstances are favorable for Canadians to play a more active role in terms of influencing Canada's defence policy."[147] As a consequence, the GNWT lent its support to the idea for a circumpolar zone of peace and security—an idea supported by the ICC among others: "Zones of peace and security can help to build confidence among nations that little or no military activity is taking place in a designated region or area," and "can help to establish trust among nations and generate a spirit of confidence in their neighbors."[148] They "may also encourage cooperation among nations," and as such the GNWT came to believe that "in this new post cold-war era, it is not unreasonable to reconsider proposals to negotiate and establish non-nuclear and demilitarized zones starting with a modest initiative in the circumpolar North."[149]

The GNWT made some recommendations, such as its proposal not to renew the U.S.-Canada agreement on the testing of cruise missiles—a recommendation later ignored by Ottawa, whose perspective on security was from the national level of analysis, requiring a less parochial view than the GNWT. Similarly, the GNWT opposed low-level flight training missions on the grounds of their potential environmental and social impact. In addition, it recommended that DND activity refrain from creating contaminated sites, that cold-weather testing of tanks and large-scale artillery be conducted in southern Canada, and that any future Arctic training center be considered in light of the GNWT's concerns over "the creation of contaminated sites, heavy weapons testing, and environmental damage."[150]

Yellowknife shared a deep concern for the Arctic's environmental security with the Inuit, illustrating how environmental security had already permeated upward from the local to the regional level, and from the tribal to the territorial, by 1990. However, it also shared a pragmatic assessment of the continued need for Arctic surveillance to monitor the northern frontier. The GNWT thus came out in support of DND's continued surveillance role in the Arctic, noting "there would appear to be general agreement that the Canadian Armed Forces must continue its surveillance and monitoring activities in the Northwest Territories," as "northerners are still concerned about foreign military incursions into northern airspace and waters."[151] It added that "particular reference has been made to the presence of foreign submarines in the Arctic Ocean."[152] Consequently, the GNWT recommended that "steps be taken to upgrade air and waterborne reconnaissance for foreign submarines in particular" and that DND "is encouraged to continue its close cooperation with federal and territorial agencies when assistance is required to more effectively enforce drug, poaching and environmental pollution laws."[153]

Naturally, the GNWT also concluded that the Canadian military "has an ongoing role to play in contributing to improving both transportation and community infrastructure in the Northwest Territories" and recommended "that it continue to work closely with federal, territorial and municipal authorities in responding to both the military's and northerners' requirements."[154] The GNWT recommended that DND work to improve its record on consultation with northerners and that the federal government ensures that military projects are "subject to thorough environmental, social and economic assessments."[155] It also recommended that DND personnel stationed in the North undergo cross-cultural orientation in an effort to more smoothly operate in the Arctic. GNWT supported the employment and training opportunities brought to the North by such programs as the Northern Region Rangers Program and the Northern Region Cadet program, recommending that DND "take steps to improve upon the Rangers Program by further upgrading training and increasing wages provided under the Program," and also expanding the role of the Rangers, such as through "maintaining and monitoring unmanned North Warning System sites."[156]

The GNWT recognized that the "Rangers Program has significant support in the Northwest Territories, particularly among the Inuit who view it as an opportunity to earn income, expand skills through training, spend more time on the land and contribute to the sovereignty and security of northern Canada."[157] This recognition of Inuit support for the Rangers program at the grassroots level by the GNWT stands in contrast to the views articulated by the ICC in the *ICC Principles*, which seemed more ideologically opposed to military activity in the Arctic, and out of touch with the strong community support for the Rangers found across the region. The GNWT also noted the economic benefits that have come to the North through military projects, and the millions of dollars contributed to the NWT's economy by the NAADM project, and stated its support of "the initiatives taken by DND and other federal agencies to insure that both short and long term benefits are realized from northern military projects," a view later accepted by the Inuit land claims corporations.[158] The GNWT similarly endorsed the support DND has provided to search and rescue, noting that the Canadian Rangers mission had been expanded to include SAR support. It recommended that DND contribute even further through additional training of search and rescue, as well as emergency preparedness responses. Lastly, the GNWT proposed to host workshops and seminars to allow northerners to participate in the dialogue concerning northern security "on an ongoing basis and in response to national and international events which determine the direction of Canada's defence policy."[159]

The GNWT sought to identify a place for its own voice, and the voice of its residents, in the policy-making process. It identified a northern perspective on defense matters, and with its proposal of a Circumpolar Zone of Peace and Security, it joined a litany of organizations including the ICC in seeking to redefine Arctic security in the 1990s. Its outlook was still sensitive to the need to respond to international conditions, but in a manner that was sensitive to regional issues. While it referred to social and environmental issues, its realistic appreciation of the economic and infrastructure contributions to the North by DND activities suggests that the GNWT was a stabilizing force in Northern politics, well aware of the region's strategic importance to Canada and its allies, and interested in working with Canada as a partner in building a stronger, more secure, and wealthier North. Its emphasis was not on issues of local or tribal sovereignty and empowerment; for these very issues not only threatened but in the end resulted in the division of the NWT—and with the subsequent risk of further fragmentation down the road if the ethnoculturally distinct subregions chose to follow in the footsteps of the architects of Nunavut, and aspired to form their own microterritorial governments and thus bypass, and potentially secede from, the government in Yellowknife. As such, the subregional, or tribal, political forces that once united to form the Dene Nation still threatened the very existence of the NWT as a singular and whole territory. It is thus natural that the GNWT looked to DND as an ally to help it more tightly bind its future to the rest of Canada, and help to keep both Canada and the NWT whole.

However, though the GNWT viewed northern security in this way, some Aboriginal residents of the NWT looked upon the non-Native bureaucracy in Yellowknife as something of a colonial presence and saw the GNWT as part of the problem and not the solution to their aspirations for self-government. The Inuit of the eastern and central Arctic had rejected the legitimacy of the GNWT for two decades, and negotiated a political accord that established their own territory by the end of the millennium, replacing the distant GNWT with their very own Nunavut. In other subregions, there has been a similar distrust of the GNWT bureaucracy, and a desire to fulfill their own tribal aspirations for greater self-governance, resulting in a movement for greater autonomy through the devolution of powers, or the formation of new regional, Aboriginal, or hybrid regional-Aboriginal governments. Should these local and subregional forces succeed in creating new micro-governments with powers comparable to the

GNWT, that territorial government could well wither away—and if that happened, the strong link that has bound the North to Canada through the GNWT, and its enduring respect for the federal government, and its mandate to assert the nation's sovereignty and defend its northern frontier, could become imperiled.

Chapter Two

Southern Perspectives on Arctic Sovereignty and Security

We will next examine concepts of Arctic sovereignty and security from the southern or state perspective, including the perspective of the national government in Ottawa. This perspective is traditionally described as the national level of analysis or, in Waltzian terms, the second image, but because of Canada's extreme variation between North and South—with profound differences in population density, urban development, industrialization, modernization of infrastructure, economic achievement levels, and a host of social metrics illustrating a north-south gap—describing this perspective as the "southern perspective" as distinct from the northern or tribal perspective is most useful analytically. In her innovative and above-mentioned discussion of the "levels of security" at the end of the Cold War, Canadian political scientist Erika Simpson observed that security, at the level of the nation, had been traditionally defined by "the realist paradigm," especially before the conclusion of the Cold War when alternative theories and definitions of security were widely adopted, from human security to soft power. Simpson cited Walter Lipmann, who wrote: "A nation is secure to the extent to which it is not in danger of having to sacrifice core values, if it wishes to avoid war, and is able, if challenged, to maintain them by victory in such a war. This definition implies that security rises and falls with the ability of a nation to deter an attack, or to defeat it."[1]

Simpson illustrated this realist tendency with an examination of President Reagan's Cold War foreign policy, which considered the Soviet military threat a real threat to America's core values. However, Simpson is not convinced that the realist paradigm was fully adequate, and criticized the "excessive" militarism inherent in realist rhetoric. Looking to psychology for an explanation, she explored attribution theory and the idea of "mirror imaging," cognitive dissonance, and the human tendency to fear the worst.[2] In contrast to realism and its dependence upon military strength for national security, Simpson considers the ideas of the "disarmers" and the nuclear "abolitionists," the Cold War's idealists when it came to issues of international security, with whom the Inuit leadership were aligned.[3] Citing Herz and Butterfield's "security dilemma," Simpson concludes that there is indeed logic to this alternative national security paradigm—and argued that "strategies based on disarmament seem to hold the promise of higher levels of security overall," a conclusion similar to that reached by the framers of the *ICC Principles*.[4] Historians of the interwar years in Europe might disagree with Simpson's assessment—as might a realist analysis of the collapse of Soviet communism, which appears to have succumbed to the high costs and internal contradictions that resulted from the superpower competition, fatally overwhelming the economically weaker of the two opponents, despite their military parity. But ethereal dynamics were in play and when the Soviet Union collapsed, it was in part because Soviet citizens no longer believed their system was superior and not long shared the values of Soviet Communism. The collapse was precipitated at least in part by an ideological revolution, as the ideals of East Europeans began to mirror those of their western counterparts. The people of the Soviet world came to agree that dismantling their security alliance, and joining the West, was a more secure path, validating Simpson's prescient views at the dawn of the post–Cold War era.

Simpson also examined "alternative security" concepts including neutralism, non-alignment, nuclear weapons free zones, civilian based defense, and non-provocative defense, many of which were embraced by the Inuit, and some of which were accepted by the territorial government as well—noting that their purpose "seems to be to gradually wean nations and leaders away from their dependence on force for security," and that such proposals are "principally intended to enhance the security of small states."[5] Or, one might add, substate, trans-state, and tribal entities like the Inuit. For many theorists, the Arctic has been an ideal laboratory between the superpowers and their allies where alternative paths to security could be developed, as observed in the work of Ron Purver, Oran Young, and Franklyn Griffiths—and adopted by such groups as the ICC, and as proposed by the reformist Soviet premier Gorbachev. Nuclear free zones, confidence-building measures, and other methods of reducing the probability of an East-West clash of arms were promoted by many academics, NGOs, and policy analysts during the Cold War as methods of utilizing the Arctic not as a theater of war but a theater of peace, and inspired Arctic and Aboriginal organizations like the Dene Nation and the ICC. Simpson credits the alternative security school with helping to "broaden [the] focus from thinking only about military threats and defences."[6] Of direct relevance to the Arctic in the post–Cold War world, where the military threat was greatly reduced, Simpson observed that "strategies to enhance or maintain the national security must also emphasize economic, social, environmental and political threats."[7]

Interestingly, Canada's Department of National Defence started to do just this—as articulated in its *1992 Defence Policy Statement*, its first coherent doctrinal re-assessment for the post Cold War period. In it, several alternative concepts of security became national policy, almost as if these alternative values and concepts for redefining security had migrated from the tribal and territorial agenda in the Arctic prior to the Cold War's end to the national agenda upon its conclusion. The Arctic thus became a laboratory for rethinking the very essence of security well ahead of the curve, long before the world of states was ready to implement these new, alternative ideas that were imagined, and developed, by northerners before the end of the Cold War. At Cold War's end, with the external military threat greatly reduced, and the bipolar system transitioning to something different—the world was ready to redefine security, and adopt some of the principles articulated by northern organizations for many years, and those local and regional values started to work their way from the periphery to the center, from the local, tribal, and regional level to the national and international level.

While the new concept of human security would soon take center stage, guiding the humanitarian interventions of the immediate post–Cold War period, one of the most notable and enduring contributions to the re-conceptualization of security after the Cold War was the introduction of environmental security as a core pillar of the national security calculus. And it is no coincidence that environmental security was a central ingredient, perhaps the key ingredient, to the *ICC Principles* as well as a cornerstone of Aboriginal land claims policy. In the Arctic, indigenous peoples had for years worked to preserve their environment and to protect the ecosystems that supported their traditional culture, engaging in long and fruitful negotiations with government officials, and upon enactment, these principles became embedded in the Canadian Constitution. As B. H. Liddell Hart might describe it, a route of indirect attack was selected, enabling a smaller but determined group of indigenous people to achieve a strategic victory over much more powerful opponents, and the impact of their victory has been so far reaching that their core values, and their understanding of the concept of security, have forever changed the way that the Government of Canada defines security. What was an Inuit value at odds with the industrializing, modernizing, expanding nation-state had become at last a truly national value, and increasingly a global value that would literally change the world, and whose advocates—whether Inuit leaders or the Nobel Peace Prize–winning former Vice President Al Gore—would aspire to unify the world, or at least the way the world is perceived, and security is defined, by those in charge.

Gordon Robertson, a former president of the Institute for Research on Public Policy, delivered a presentation to *The Arctic: Choices for Peace and Security—A Public Inquiry* in 1989 titled "The Human Foundation for Peace and Security in the Arctic," following on the heels of Inuit leader Mary Simon and leading Aboriginal rights advocate Thomas Berger, two well known proponents of the Aboriginal interest whose ideas have contributed greatly to the way Arctic security is now defined at all levels of decision-making and analysis. Robertson brings to this discussion of northern security some distance, and puts forth a thesis reminiscent of Shelagh Grant's analysis of the historical undulations between sovereignty and security as the attention of policy-makers shifted from internal and external concerns.

In a portion of his presentation published in the conference proceedings, but which he omitted from his oral presentation due to time constraints, Robertson observed that there "has been a tendency in our national attention, or inattention, to the North to oscillate between apathy and excitement; too little and too much in interest and enthusiasm, in hopes and disappointments."[8] He cites former Prime Minister St. Laurent, who said in 1954 that Canada had, up to that time, administered the North "in a state of absence of mind: few had cared about it and little had been done. Prime Minister Diefenbaker, four years later, lit up Canadian politics and aroused national fervor with 'The Vision'—a resource rich North on which our future greatness would depend. The picture was too glowing and disillusionment followed."[9] Robertson believes that "the risk is still with us," and proceeds to criticize those who have exaggerated the importance of the North. "It would be superficially attractive to suggest an 'ocean basin' focus in world history: the Mediterranean in the ancient world; the Atlantic Ocean and its bordering countries during the last four hundred years; the Pacific Rim today and in the coming century. One could move on to envision a future focus on the Arctic Ocean for the twenty-first century. That would be provocative and stimulating. It would also be a mistake. The Arctic is not going to be that central or that important."[10]

However, Robertson did acknowledge that the Arctic "is going to have much more importance in the future than it has had in the past," and since "a large part of the Arctic is ours," that "it is the area above all others where Canada can and should play a significant role."[11] Robertson cites the report by a group of northern specialists that he chaired in 1988, The North and Canada's International Relations, recommending that Canada seek "the achievement and maintenance of a secure and peaceful world in the Arctic," that would allow Aboriginal people to "preserve the essentials of their cultures while living in association with Canadians of other origins."[12] As such, "all of this question about self-government for the Inuit—and for the Dene and Métis in the western Arctic—is important if we are serious about Canada playing the role it ought to play in policies and international relations in the Arctic."[13] Says Robertson, with "virtually every question that will arise in our relations with other Arctic countries we will find our position stronger and more credible if we have a thriving, self-governing Inuit people in the Arctic."[14] One question is the issue of sovereignty: "Our argument for sovereignty is clearly needed to protect the environment and the economic base of a Native population that uses the resources of the land. That land includes the waters of the Archipelago even more than dry land of the islands that make it up. Our sovereignty is important if it is for a real purpose: for the welfare of real people who inhabit the Arctic. It will become largely empty symbolism if there is no self-reliant Arctic population there to benefit from our sovereignty."[15]

Thus argues Robertson, at the very heart of the concept of Arctic security must be the security of the indigenous people of the Arctic, and as a consequence, indigenous concepts of security must be reconciled with those at the national level. Not only does Canadian sovereignty depend upon the well-being of the Inuit, but it can be defined as much by its ability to enable Inuit security as by any traditional strategic calculus. The internal component—the essential trinity between people, government and the military examined by Clausewitz in his theory of military power presented in *On War*—demands that northern people become part of how we define Arctic security. In Robertson's words: "Peace and security in the Arctic are important for all Canadians and for the world generally. For whom are they more important than for the Native people who live north of the Arctic Circle? They are the ones our government should have most in mind"—and so Arctic security must ultimately be "in the interests of a proud, confident and self-governing people in the Canadian Arctic.[16] And to understand the interests of the Inuit requires comprehending the impacts on their society of the many changes that have buffeted the North in recent years. As noted by Graham Rowley in "An Arctic Affair," the North has changed profoundly in just a few decades since World War II, when:

one year was very like the year before, with living and travel conditions almost the same as they had been throughout the previous century. Since the war, air travel, radio, television, telephones, schools, health services, and so on have been introduced; houses have replaced igloos, in winter skidoos have replaced dog teams, and summer four-wheel Hondas have replaced feet. It is a different world from the North I first knew. (There is another north, as well—a North that a writer may describe but which never existed except in imagination.) The real North has changed so much and so fast that even the young Inuit today have little concept of how their parents and grandparents used to live.[17]

In 1935, he recalled, most Inuit still "hunted and trapped from small camps scattered along the coasts," and the "economy was based on white fox, which the Inuit trapped and traded, mainly for tea and tobacco, guns and ammunition, and blanket cloth. Virtually the only link between North and South was a ship that called at each post once a year to bring in supplies and take out the fur."[18] But all that would quickly change. As Shelagh Grant described:

The Second World War and the Cold War brought air fields, weather stations, the DEW Line and a wide assortment of other military activities to the Arctic, leaving in their wake pockets of PCBs and other contaminants. The United States Air Force patrolled the skies and their ships the Arctic waters, while under the frozen seas their submarines chased elusive Russians. Canadian Inuit, meanwhile, were catapulted into the twentieth century. Family allowances and day schools encouraged them to congregate around the trading posts. Tents and igloos were soon replaced by wooden homes, dog teams by snowmobiles and all-terrain vehicles, the Hudson's Bay Company by Co-ops. Community life brought television, rock concerts, new diseases, junk foods, alcohol and drugs. Social problems multiplied. School programmes taught in English created language barriers between children and parents, between youth and elders. Traditional values were under siege. Not until the mid 1980s would the tide begin to turn.[19]

These changes were precipitated to a large degree by the increasing strategic role of Canada's Arctic territories for national defense and international security, especially during World War II and later the Cold War. As described by Andrea Charron, a scholar in the War Studies program at the Royal Military College of Canada: "In the 1940s, Canada's attention was brusquely turned to the Arctic Archipelago. The nuclear age focused attention on the Arctic: Canada's undefended north and its proximity to the Soviet Union meant that the Canadian government had to abandon its laissez-faire attitude of the 1930's and pursue a policy of active monitoring and intervention."[20] She noted how because of its lack of financial and human resources, "Canada had little choice but to turn to the United States for military presence and weapons. These 'collaborative' defence efforts to guard against a common nuclear threat, while maximizing Canada's security, also maximized Canada's potential loss of sovereignty."[21]

When considering the national level of analysis, and the perspective of the Canadian government on Arctic sovereignty and security, it is important to recall how, as Ottawa looked north to defend its territory from external challenges, and to assert its national sovereignty over its new northern lands, it collided with the Inuit, and their ancient homeland, which was co-existent with its northern frontier. This resulted in a unique dialectical interaction which has in recent years moved toward a synthesis of tribe and state, as these two distinct levels of analysis came to know and understand one another, fusing a hybrid conception of Arctic sovereignty and security that balances the national and subnational perspectives. The Arctic has long been central to Canada's identity as a nation, and central to its security. As described by Joseph T. Jockel in his 1991 book, *Security to the North*, "Canada, like the United States, pushed back a frontier in its national development. Images of the north evoke for Canadians their great national achievement of building a second transcontinental country on the continent's less hospitable half."[22] He added that the Arctic "still represents for many Canadians their country's future."[23] Jockel cites Robert Page, who explained that Canadians "have had difficulty viewing the North with detachment because their future hopes have always involved the exploitation of its resource riches. Yesterday it was the yellow gold of Bonanza Creek; today it is the black gold of the Beaufort Sea."[24] As Jockel puts it, "The Arctic contributes to a northern mythology whereby Canadians can mark themselves as a tough, vigorous nation, the people, in the words of the Canadian national anthem, of the 'True North Strong and Free,'" and "Ownership of Arctic territories unquestionably does establish Canadians as custodians of one of the most starkly beautiful and environmentally fragile regions in the world. It is a responsibility many Canadians take very seriously, especially faced with the possibility the Arctic may eventually become an important source of oil and gas."[25] That's why, "as long as Canadians believe—and many fervently do believe—that their culture and national identity are in large part derived from their Arctic territories, they will be incensed at external challenges," and that means "no Canadian government can afford to be seen as failing to protect the Arctic."[26] This has contributed to "a kind of 'push resistant nationalism' which emerges in reaction to a concrete step taken by the United States that would affect Canada" in the course of its evolving defense partnership with Canada, there have been many "challenges to Canadian sovereignty on land that have been entirely inadvertent."[27] But it was the challenges at sea that had been "markedly different,"[28] as Washington has sought to define the waters of the High Arctic archipelago as high seas, in contrast to Ottawa which claims them as internal waters, a position Washington re-asserted in its January 2009 Arctic policy directive, and recommitted to early in the new administration in April 2009.

A detailed examination of Canada's evolving effort throughout the twentieth century to assert its sovereignty over the Arctic was presented by Nathaniel French Caldwell, Jr., in his 1990 book, *Arctic Leverage: Canadian Sovereignty and Security*.[29] He noted that "Canada shares a continent with a superpower and the United States' presence is overwhelming," and that in becoming an independent nation, "Canada did not gradually dissociate from Britain just to be absorbed by the United States."[30] Ottawa has thus sought "to stay an independent and sovereign nation on the North American continent," and as a consequence, "sovereignty protection has become a major goal of Canadian foreign and defense policies."[31] Caldwell recounts how "Canada acquired the islands of the Arctic archipelago in two transfers from the British government,"[32] and that:

> The first in 1870 transferred the British Northwest Territories and Rupert's Land, which was acquired from the Hudson's Bay Company. . . . The second transfer in 1880 included all remaining British holdings in North America with the exception of Newfoundland and Labrador. In 1895, the Canadian government indicated that the transfers included the Arctic archipelago, an area claimed but not occupied by Britain. The boundaries of the District of Franklin included all the Arctic islands north of the Canadian mainland plus the Boothian and Melville peninsulas on the continent. Canada's nineteenth-century claim to the Arctic archipelago has had profound consequences for Canadian sovereignty and security in the latter half of the twentieth century. Since World War II, technology has made military access to the Arctic feasible, and Canada has found itself in the role of buffer between the United States and the Soviet Union.[33]

According to Caldwell: "Senator Pascal Poirier first publicly raised the issue of Arctic sovereignty in the Canadian Senate on 20 February 1907," when he "proposed the sector principle" claiming Canada "has a right to all the lands that are to be found in the waters between a line extending from its eastern extremity north, and another line extending from the western extremity north."[34] The sector theory was rejected by Norwegian legal expert Gustav Smedal, who "asserted that a state's authority and sovereignty was limited to the area over which it exercised control, and specifically that the control of one island in an archipelago did not imply control of the whole group of islands."[35] While the sector theory "has never been generally accepted under international law," it was nonetheless "followed in the Arctic" where "disputed territories have gone to the country within whose sector they fall."[36] Nonetheless, Caldwell noted "it was disputable whether Canada had possession of the Arctic territory that Senator Poirier claimed," as there were still "no settlements or outposts, and Canada certainly did not have effective possession of the islands of the Arctic archipelago"—though a series of Arctic patrols were led by Captain Joseph Bernier in the next few years, "exercising jurisdiction over the waters in the Canadian Arctic" by enforcing whaling regulations, issuing fishing licenses, and even including the erection of a monument on Melville Island claiming the whole of the archipelago up to the North Pole as Canada's sovereign domain.[37] Ottawa's "inability to exercise effective authority in the Arctic archipelago became the subject of an investigation by the Canadian Reindeer and Musk-ox Commission of 1919," which "recommended that the government establish its authority in the archipelago," and to resist "competing claims from the United States, Norway, and especially Denmark to portions of Ellesmere Island."[38]

Canada thus "developed a plan by which it took possession of the Arctic archipelago in the 1920s," and "to meet the accepted criteria for 'effective possession' of the archipelago," including the establishment of "permanently manned Royal Canadian Mounted Police (RCMP) posts in the Arctic archipelago in 1922," starting with Baffin and Ellesmere islands, with posts later added to Devon and Victoria islands.[39] This helped Ottawa to overcome competing claims from Norway and Denmark, and to ensure that Knud Rasmussen's claim of Ellesmere Island on behalf of Denmark in 1921 was not accepted by Denmark. By 1930, Norway recognized Canadian sovereignty over the Sverdrup Islands.[40] As recounted by Ken Coates, Whitney Lackenbauer, William Morrison, and Greg Poelzer in their 2008 book *Arctic Front: Defending Canada in the Far North*, policing the Arctic became a symbolic and cost-effective means of asserting Arctic sovereignty, though at times its effectiveness could be questioned:

> Only the lonely vigil mounted by the Royal North West Mounted Police (RNWMP) in its isolated posts represented effective occupation in the Arctic. Of the three posts established in the summer of 1903, the one on Herschel Island was the most important, because that was where the threat to Canada's interests was felt to be most acute. A police post, of course, is a concrete example of sovereignty, but this is true only if it exercises its powers effectively. This was not the case with the Mounted Police detachment on Herschel Island during the whaling era. The detachment was staffed by two members of the force: Sergeant F.J. Fitzgerald and Constable F.D. Sutherland. When a steamer rented from the Hudson's Bay Company was wrecked, they were forced to go to the island from Fort McPherson that summer in an open boat, with very little in the way of supplies or equipment; nor did they have anywhere to live. As a result,

they were compelled to buy food and rent living quarters from one of the whaling companies. More significantly, because they had no proper boat, they were unable to make patrols at sea, so that the only way they could figure out the amount of tax to charge on trade goods was to accept the sums the captains reported to them.[41]

The authors note that "this approach was not very effective, but it was highly symbolic," and that as with the case of other efforts to assert Canadian sovereignty across its vast but sparsely inhabited northland, "once again success was achieved through lack of opposition," and "Canada's assertion of sovereignty on the cheap succeeded largely because it was unopposed."[42]

After the Canadian Arctic Expedition to the western Arctic from 1913–1918, Vilhjalmur Stefansson "campaigned for more Arctic exploration," invoking the natural resource potential of the region while also arguing "the Arctic was strategically significant as the shortest route for airplanes and submarines going between Europe, Asia, and North America," making him among "the first to envision the strategic significance of the Arctic," and whose "strategic vision led him to urge the Canadian government to grab as much unoccupied territory as possible while other nations still considered it worthless."[43] Ottawa even briefly claimed Wrangel Island after Stefansson led an expedition there, a hundred miles north of the Siberian mainland, but Moscow re-asserted its control over that island when it seized the island militarily in 1924, giving it "the dubious distinction of being the first country to enforce its Arctic claims by using naval force."[44] As Coates et al. recounted in *Arctic Front*, the Wrangel expedition both "concerned sovereignty and embarrassed the Canadian government," and:

> More dangerously, Stefansson's enthusiasm so infected the Mackenzie King government that it made approving gestures towards asserting sovereignty over the island, though it soon backed off. Given the uncertain sovereignty over its own Arctic islands, the thought that the Canadian government would assert its sovereignty over someone else's island seems foolhardy if not insane, and probably the government realized it. The episode was embarrassing, and made Stefansson persona non grata in Ottawa for the rest of his long life.[45]

By 1920, Coates et al. recount, "Canada had had title to the Arctic islands for forty years, and yet had no permanent presence on them," and when in the summer of 1919, Ottawa had asked Denmark "to restrain the Inuit of the Thule region from killing Canadian muskoxen"—and "Denmark, which did not officially proclaim its sovereignty over Greenland until 1921, asked the advice of Knud Rasmussen," who replied, "As everyone knows, the land of the Polar Eskimos falls under what is called 'No Man's Land,' and there is, therefore, no authority in this country except that which I myself am able to exert through the Trading Station.'"[46] Denmark agreed, and while "Canada hastened to reply that Ellesmere Island was not no man's land, but was part of Canada," many officials in Ottawa "were privately worried," and an "internal department memo suggested that Canada's sovereignty over this huge island (nearly four times the size of Nova Scotia), and in the rest of the High Arctic as well, was very tenuous."[47] As their memo explained: "The situation in the northern islands, therefore, appears to be that Britain has had an inchoate title which now probably through the lapse of time may be considered to have terminated; that the Low and Bernier expeditions may have established a 'fictitious' title which also has probably lapsed; and therefore, that Denmark or any other country is in a position to acquire sovereignty by establishing effective occupation and administration."[48] Coates et al. view this to have been a "startling admission."[49] Expanding Canada's police presence across the archipelago became an important method to reduce the Arctic sovereignty challenge. As Coates et al. recall: "By 1927, six RCMP posts had been opened in the Arctic islands"—including Craig Harbour and Pond Inlet in 1922, Pangnirtung in 1923, Dundas Harbour in 1924, Bache Peninsula in 1926, and Lake Harbour in 1927—and in 1925, "the Northern Advisory Board was set up to deal with sovereignty and other matters concerning the Arctic," composed of numerous senior government officials.[50] Coates et al. explain that the "impetus for the board's formation was another shock to Canada's assertion of Arctic sovereignty," when Ottawa learned "an American explorer named Donald B. MacMillan, a man with considerable Arctic experience, was planning a new expedition based at northern Greenland, with stations on Ellesmere and Axel Heiberg Island, to carry out aerial exploration of the polar region under the command of Admiral Richard Byrd."[51]

This challenged Canadian Arctic sovereignty, Caldwell observed, because "the Canadian Parliament passed a bill requiring expeditions in the Northwest Territories to have a government permit," the purpose of which was "to assert our sovereignty . . . right up to the North Pole."[52] Washington resisted Ottawa's assertions, and expedition leader MacMillan's memoirs "indicate his scorn for Canadian Arctic sovereignty," though his subsequent expeditions in 1926, 1927, and 1928 "all followed Canadian regulations."[53] Coates et al. observe that since Washington "had no interest in making claims to Ellesmere Island, nothing untoward came of this episode, but it did lead directly to the establishment of the most unusual Mounted Police post in the history of the force" on Ellesmere Island's Bache Peninsula, as "there was no one there to police, because no one lived there," making the post the "quintessential example of symbolic sovereignty," complete with a post office.[54] In contrast, the authors point out, "At the other detachments where there were people living—Pond Inlet, for example—the police carried out most of the functions of government, since there were still no other government officers anywhere in the Arctic."[55]

By 1933, Caldwell observes, "historian V. Kenneth Johnston concluded that Canada had validated its claim to the Arctic archipelago"[56] with its efforts to "establish effective occupation and, therefore, sovereignty in the Arctic," but Caldwell points out "that presence was meager," and that the "RCMP outposts were not followed by any wave of Arctic emigration nor by any significant growth of commercial activity."[57]

While "in the 1920s and 1930s Canada faced no more external challenges to its claims of sovereignty over the islands of the Arctic archipelago," Caldwell notes "by the end of World War II Stefansson's prophesy of the Arctic's strategic value was beginning to unfold."[58] But Ottawa's ability to defend the North has not always matched the region's strategic importance. In World War II, Canada quickly came of age as a naval power. Prior to the war, as Caldwell recounts, it "could count on the British navy for its maritime defense. Then suddenly, with Britain under siege, maritime protection was gone and Canada had to build a navy."[59] By the end of the war it possessed the world's third largest, with 400 ships, and it "had proven its effectiveness in anti-submarine warfare (ASW)."[60] But by 1947, this once formidable fleet had declined to just ten ships in commission, including one aircraft carrier, the Magnificent, that became the first warship to enter Hudson Bay—since "even with a drastically reduced navy, Canada had the rudiments of a maritime strategy that considered the Arctic's geostrategic location."[61]

By 1960, the Canadian navy was back up to 45 warships.[62] But Moscow began to nuclearize its submarine fleet, with the 1955 test firing of a SLBM from a Zulu diesel-electric submarine, five of which "were being converted to carry nuclear cruise missiles" capable of hitting major North American cities from Hudson Bay. By 1959, Moscow had deployed Hotel class ballistic nuclear subs and Echo class cruise-missile subs, creating the need for a "strategic defense dimension" to Canada's ASW capabilities. Early efforts at Canadian-U.S. cooperation on nuclear sub technology were limited, and in due course, the United States sought to restrict the transfer of its submarine technology "beyond Great Britain."[63] America's first ballistic nuclear sub was commissioned in 1961, but Canada's naval capabilities declined again, to 28 warships by 1968 and "no Canadian strategy to counter the increased maritime threat," though Caldwell notes Ottawa's "inability to control waters she claimed did not become visible until the voyage of the experimental tanker, Manhattan, through the Northwest Passage," precipitating that well known sovereignty crisis in 1969.[64]

Ironically, the Manhattan experiment was a multilateral endeavor, with the Canadian icebreaker, the John A. MacDonald, accompanying the Manhattan, albeit without an official request from the United States for escort support. The ice guides were provided by Canada, and a Soviet icebreaker had been invited to participate but could not due to bad weather.[65] Later, the newest Canadian icebreaker, the Louie St. Laurent, joined the transit of the Manhattan along with numerous U.S. vessels, though the smaller Northwind fell behind. Aerial surveillance by Canadian aircraft provided ice reports to aid navigation, and as Caldwell recounts the events, the John A. MacDonald "was the workhorse of the party, several times breaking the tanker free from ice."[66] As Caldwell points out, "Canada had as much to gain from the voyage as did the United States and, with the support of the John A. MacDonald, and aerial reconnaissance, did more than the United States to ensure the success of the experiment."[67]

The problem came about when Prime Minister Trudeau asked President Nixon to make "a formal request of permission for the Manhattan's transit," and

Washington refused, since that "might have given tacit acknowledgement of Ottawa's sovereignty over Arctic straits," and "the voyage was viewed as a private venture," and not an official government activity, though U.S. icebreaker support "tended to give the voyage official Washington sanction and contributed to public outrage in Canada."[68] This outrage was magnified by "the potential for an oil spill from the mammoth tanker," contributing to the "Canadian public's perception that Canadian sovereignty was being violated."[69] So while the Manhattan experiment was an "outstanding success" and showed "a tanker could be designed that would not need to be escorted by 'comparatively puny' icebreakers," Caldwell observes that "the political fallout from the voyage was significant," and "spurred the Canadians to pass the Arctic Waters Pollution Protection Act" in June 1970.[70] This enabled Ottawa to "claim some legal jurisdiction over all vessels operating in the Arctic archipelago, and it particularly discouraged tanker transits," though the "real intent was to prevent any future Manhattan incidents."[71] Ironically, only the Soviet Union recognized Ottawa's "jurisdiction over pollution control in the Arctic archipelago," as it "had long maintained effective control over the Northeast Passage," and thus would benefit from having such exclusive sovereign control over waters otherwise perceived to be international. While Soviet recognition of Canadian sovereignty over the waters of the Arctic archipelago "enhanced similar Soviet claims along the Northern Sea Route," [72] Caldwell notes "the United States and some of the Western European countries openly disputed Canadian jurisdiction over Arctic waters."[73]

Ottawa's 1971 White Paper on Defence, Defence in the 70s, reflected Ottawa's "desire to exert 'effective' control in the waters of the Arctic archipelago," and suggested Ottawa "planned to defend the waters of the Arctic archipelago as inland waters."[74] The Canadian armed forces would thus be assigned to "defend the 'sovereignty and independence' of Canada from 'external challenges'" such as infringements of Canadian law and territorial infringements including acts with "the potential of oil spills and challenges to Canadian control of resources on the seabed of the continental shelf."[75] The White Paper even ranked "the protection of [Canadian] sovereignty" as higher a priority than "the defence of North America in cooperation with U.S. forces."[76] It also "reduced Canada's NATO contribution," an "indication that Canadians perceived a reduced threat" from Moscow.[77] It appeared that the salient threat to Canada was perceived to be, post-Manhattan, from the United States.[78] And yet, Caldwell recalled how, "in 1970 right after a mid-life refit," Canada's sole aircraft carrier was "sold for scrap," and how "despite the precedence of Arctic sovereignty protection stressed in the 1971 White Paper, the Trudeau government supported no new maritime initiatives."[79] By the time Brian Mulroney became Prime Minister in 1984, Canada's navy had just three subs and 20 destroyers and frigates, with Canada's Maritime Command "in the worst shape of all the Canadian forces and . . . would be left in the mid-1990s with only ten serviceable warships."[80]

In 1985, another Arctic sovereignty crisis erupted with a new transit by a U.S. vessel through the Northwest Passage, the first since the Manhattan. This time, it was the USCGC Polar Sea, a Coast Guard vessel and not a private vessel as in the case of the Manhattan. As Caldwell observes, "All Canada could do was what it had done with the Manhattan—monitor the passage. In the Manhattan crisis, as well as in the Byrd-MacMillan affair sixty years earlier, Canada could only ask the United States to request permission," a situation that remained unchanged in 1985, but the "United States held that the waters of the Northwest Passage were an international strait, and therefore, neither permission nor notification was required."[81] Caldwell notes the irony, since it was Trudeau's government that had "promised to maintain 'effective control' of the Northwest Passage," while "the only defense strategy in the 1971 White Paper relating to 'effective control' was a proposal to increase aerial surveillance of Arctic waters," prompting him to ask: "What use was surveillance in sovereignty protection, when the intruder being watched tells you when and where he is going to violate your sovereignty, and when there are Canadian observers onboard the intruder to carefully note and assist the violation? Such was the case with the transit of the USCGC Polar Sea in 1985."[82] As T. C. Pullen recalled in *Northern Perspectives:*

> In August 1985, Canada's aging but redoubtable Coast Guard ice-breaker *John A. Macdonald* rendezvoused with the new American ice-breaker *Polar Sea* where Lancaster Sound joins Baffin Bay—gateway to the Northwest Passage. Together, the two ships sailed westward until reaching Viscount Melville Sound some days later. With the ice becoming progressively more difficult, they parted company—the Canadian to retreat, the American to press on in her determination to complete the Passage. . . . This incident, albeit not particularly significant, seems somehow to symbolize our inability—some might say reluctance—"to exercise Canada's full sovereignty in and over the waters of the Arctic archipelago." Surely, it would have been preferable had the accompanying Canadian ice-breaker led the *Polar Sea* westward through the heavy pack-ice, which we claim as our own, and into open water before turning back.[83]

Ultimately, the recurrence of this particular pattern of challenge to Canada's Arctic sovereignty—by the United States; with an icebreaker; and again transiting the Northwest Passage—was no coincidence, but reflects the underlying persistence of geopolitics, the asymmetry of power, and the contradictions inherent in the U.S.-Canada relationship. As Franklyn Griffiths explained in *Politics of the Northwest Passage*: "It is an irony that the challenge to Canada's control over its Arctic waters comes from the government and the people with whom Canadians have the most in common. The dilemma is compounded by the fact that whereas the United States is only secondarily an Arctic country and approaches the region from the standpoint of a maritime power with global interests, the Arctic figures prominently in Canadians' conceptions of themselves as a people and is viewed primarily from the perspective of a coastal and regional state."[84] Griffiths adds that in light of the "gross disparity of national power and Canada's economic dependence on the United States," it "becomes clear that Canada is engaged in a potentially very damaging dispute that will be difficult to resolve with success."[85] Canada's passionate and enflamed reaction was noted in the speech delivered by then–Secretary of State for External Affairs Joe Clark: "Sovereignty can be a very emotional issue in this country, and that is quite understandable, since sovereignty involves the identity and the very character of a people. We Canadians want to be ourselves. We want to manage our own affairs and control our own destiny, but we also want to go beyond this to play a constructive role in a world that is become increasingly interdependent. We have something to offer and at the same time we have something to gain."[86] As Clark explained: "The voyage of the Polar Sea demonstrated that Canada, in the past, had not developed the means to ensure our sovereignty over time. During that voyage, Canada's legal position was fully protected, but when we looked for ways to exercise our sovereignty we found that the Canadian cupboard was nearly bare."[87] As he noted:

> As the western country with by far the greatest frontage on the Arctic, we must come up to speed in a range of marine operations that bear on our capacity to exercise effective control over the Northwest Passage and our other Arctic waters. . . . Canada is an Arctic nation. The international community has long recognized that the Arctic mainland and islands are a part of Canada like any other, but the Arctic is not only a part of Canada, it is a part of Canadian greatness. The policy of the Government is to preserve that Canadian greatness undiminished.[88]

Clark's fusion of Canadian greatness with its vast Arctic possessions harkens back to the Victorian concept of the "Arctic Sublime," with Canadian identity inextricably linked to its status as an Arctic nation. The Arctic sea ice is thus viewed as something like connective tissue, like ligaments holding Canada's musculature to its inner skeletal structure. As Clark put it, "Canada's sovereignty in the Arctic is indivisible. It embraces land, sea, and ice. It extends without interruption to the seaward-facing coasts of the Arctic islands. These islands are joined, and not divided, by the waters between them. They are bridged for most of the year by ice."[89] And as many observers have argued, Canada's Arctic sovereignty is strengthened by the long habitation of its Inuit population, whose ice-based culture, which integrates land, sea, and ice, provides not just metaphor, but historical justification, for Ottawa's sovereign claim. Hence, as Clark observed, "From time immemorial Canada's Inuit people have used and occupied the ice as they have used and occupied the land."[90]

Indeed, according to "A Northern Dimension for Canada's Foreign Policy," the tenth chapter of the June 1986 report, Independence and Internationalism, issued by the Special Joint Committee of the Senate and of the House of Commons on Canada's International Relations, the Inuit play an especially important role in Canada's assertion of Arctic sovereignty. The report noted the unique role of the Inuit, and their contribution to Canada's Arctic sovereignty: "The

Inuit are Canada's most important support in the Arctic, and government policy should reflect this perception. Canada should give priority to achieving an acceptable land settlement in the North and encourage efforts to find governmental structures that would support Inuit cultural autonomy within the Canadian federation."[91] The report adds that "support should be given to the development of renewable resources, particularly fishing. Abroad, Canada should make strenuous efforts to reinforce the efforts of Indigenous Survival International, whose Canadian chapter addressed us in Yellowknife, to resist campaigns, especially in Europe, to ban the import of fur products, the trapping of which represents a major source of income for Inuit and Indian peoples in Canada."[92] In the September–October 1986 edition of the *Northern Perspectives* journal published by the Ottawa-based Canadian Arctic Resources Committee that addressed the sovereignty challenge post–Polar Sea, Jeff Richstone, a legal advisor to the Inuit Committee on National Issues, observed that the government's response to the Polar Sea's transit of the Passage was contrary to Inuit policy preferences, and its muscularity was dissonant with Inuit aspirations for a demilitarized Arctic: "The government also informed the House that it would increase military surveillance of the Arctic through aircraft overflights and naval manoeuvres, and would undertake construction of a Arctic Class 8 icebreaker. This announcement has caused concern to Inuit, since they fear that the government will be too easily lured into basing its northern policy on perceived threats to Arctic security."[93] As he explained, "In briefs before the Special Joint Committee on Canada's International Relations, national and regional Inuit associations stressed that Canada's claim to the Arctic is more securely founded upon continuing Inuit use and occupation of the area than upon the construction of ice-breakers, the promotion of increased tanker traffic, and investment in military hardware," as stability would be better achieved "by negotiating self-government and comprehensive claims agreements with Inuit. This would allow for the co-operative management and regulation of northern lands and the offshore, and would be a functional exercise of Canada's jurisdiction that could prove persuasive in international law."[94]

In addition to highlighting the role the Inuit play in Canada's claim of Arctic sovereignty, the Independence and Internationalism report examined the sovereignty challenges presented by the Manhattan and Polar Sea: "The deficiencies in backing up Canada's claim to sovereignty were highlighted by last summer's voyage through the Northwest Passage by the Polar Sea," and while "Canada's claim to sovereignty over the islands of the archipelago is beyond all doubt, the status of the Northwest Passage, which has both symbolic and defensive importance for Canada, is questioned by the United States." The report observes that the "spontaneous popular reactions to the voyages of the Manhattan and the Polar Sea show that Canadians feel strongly about their claims to these waters."[95] Indeed, as Caldwell observed, "Canadian public reaction to this transit was acrimonious," so Ottawa responded vigorously to the crisis, seeking and obtaining "Parliament's approval for actions to assert Canadian sovereignty in the Arctic archipelago," including a formal claim of the waters of the Arctic archipelago as internal waters, and the drawing of straight baselines to define Canada's Arctic maritime border, in seeming violation of UNCLOS, which does not allow coastal states to draw baselines that deviate from the contours of its coastline.[96] As noted by Andrea Mandel-Campbell in *The Walrus*, Ottawa "also pledged to build new icebreakers as well as spend up to $12 billion on a fleet of nuclear-powered submarines. Both plans were eventually scrapped."[97]

At around the same time, the Canadian government was in negotiations with Washington over the modernization of the DEW Line in the face of a renewed threat posed by Soviet bombers, this time armed with air-launched cruise missiles, making bombers "once again a first-strike threat," necessitating the modernization of North America's air defense capabilities with the North Warning System (NWS).[98] When the agreement was announced by U.S. President Ronald Reagan and Canadian Prime Minister Brian Mulroney in 1985, it "included guarantees of Canadian sovereignty, thus continuing the framework of defense cooperation conceived for the first early warning systems," and "would be Canadian-operated from the start."[99] Ottawa prepared a new White Paper, released in 1987, and it included plans for a nuclear submarine force with some ten to twelve attack subs envisioned for a total cost of around $8 billion to enable Ottawa to implement a "three ocean" concept of maritime defense, but this plan encountered both domestic opposition for its high cost, as well as resistance from the United States and other NATO allies, who preferred Ottawa to invest those defense expenditures in its ASW capabilities and on its forces in Europe.[100] While the "three ocean" concept would be well served by a nuclear sub force, in the end the high cost led Ottawa to pursue "other means" including "five new fighter airstrips in the High Arctic to accommodate recently acquired CF-18 interceptors," as well as "unmanned submarine listening posts" and the construction of a High Arctic military base at Nanisivik, announced in 1988 and later dusted off in 2007 when Ottawa felt its Arctic sovereignty again was being challenged, this time by renewed commercial interest in the increasingly accessible Arctic offshore resources.[101]

Ottawa and Washington reached a resolution to their dispute over access to the Northwest Passage by agreeing to "cooperative procedures," whereby the United States would seek permission prior to a transit "without recognizing any Canadian claim to jurisdiction over the waters of the Arctic archipelago," and for the first time, on October 10, 1988, the United States asked for permission to send the Polar Sea back through the passage, to which Ottawa agreed the very same day.[102] As Mandel-Campbell described, "In 1988, Prime Minister Brian Mulroney and US President Ronald Reagan signed the Arctic Co-operation Agreement, just three years after they sang together on stage at the Shamrock Summit in Quebec City. The agreement allows the US Coast Guard to use the passage after notifying Ottawa, but Canada in turn cannot deny the Americans access. The president also refused to include the US Navy in any agreement regulating Arctic waters."[103]

Caldwell described the evolution of Canada's Arctic security policy as reflected Ottawa's *1987 White Paper*, noting it "concentrated defense resources in the Arctic while maintaining international, NATO, and bilateral commitments. The 'three ocean' concept was designed to give Canada a near-continuous presence in the Arctic while still providing a force that could be used in NATO and Pacific theaters," and that from "the perspective of the West's policy of containment, the Arctic is the only area of the world where the Soviet presence has not been proportionately countered."[104] Even the Soviet Union took notice of the potential of the "three ocean" concept to foster "an increased Western presence in the Arctic," and in April 1989, "Soviet First Consul Alexey Makarov reiterated Soviet concerns over militarization of the Canadian Arctic."[105] A variety of issues scuttled Ottawa's planned nuclear submarine program, including a decline in popular support; vocal opposition from Minister of External Affairs Joe Clark; rising estimates for the nuclear submarine program's price tag, which the Department of External Affairs thought could rise as high as $20 billion; and a cabinet shuffle that removed Perrin Beatty, a proponent of the White Paper, as Minister of Defence.[106] In addition to the sub cancellation, Caldwell noted, "other forces that could play a role in Canada's sovereignty and security in the Arctic were affected"—including plans to purchase eight more Hercules aircraft that could resupply the CF-18 Arctic airstrips, which could in turn "affect the ability of the CF-18s to deter Soviet jets' incursions in the Arctic;" and "even construction of the Polar 8 icebreaker, the most symbolic and immediate response to the perceived violation of Canadian sovereignty by the USCGC Polar Sea in 1985, was slowed down."[107] Caldwell points out that "without a means to patrol Arctic waters the 'three ocean' concept is hollow,"[108] and Canada would thus "have to rely on its allies to patrol the Arctic."[109]

Caldwell noted "commercial activity in the Arctic continues to increase," and recalled how it was "commercial activity in the early part of the century" that had "prompted the government to send expeditions to exercise jurisdiction in the Canadian Arctic."[110] He believes that if Canada desires to exercise "effective control" in its Arctic waters, "it cannot depend on allies indefinitely."[111] Added Caldwell, prophetically: "As commercial development of the Arctic proceeds, the Canadian presence in the Arctic will grow and, consequently, so will the need to monitor the activity on and under claimed Arctic waters."[112] But by the final years of the Cold War, the Arctic remained largely undefended. As Joseph T. Jockel observed in 1991: "In the absence of much of a direct military threat to the Canadian Arctic region itself, the Canadian military presence has been scant. No ship or submarine of the Canadian navy is capable of operating in ice-covered or even moderately ice-infested waters, barring them from operations in high Canadian Arctic waters."[113] Jockel added that only "sixteen or seventeen northern patrol flights for visual observation . . . are conducted each year" and the Northern Region Headquarters of the Canadian Armed Forces in Yellowknife "is responsible for the largest military district in the world. Yet it has a staff of only seventy-seven and no military units under its direct command, except for a detachment of two Twin Otter search and rescue aircraft and the

Canadian Rangers, a paramilitary reserve force of about 700, largely Inuit hunt-ers."[114] Jockel points out that "beyond that, there are the minimally and un-manned stations of the North Warning System," and the Forward Operating Lo-cations (FOLs) which largely entail "relatively small scale upgrading of existing civilian airfields."[115] He cites Canadian defense analyst Harriet Critchley, who described Canadian defense capabilities in the Arctic as "quite modest," but given defense cutbacks in the preceding decades, "the provision of even such a modest capability places a noticeable strain on the overall defense capabilities" of Canada.[116] In 2005, Mandel-Campbell described a situation largely un-changed, even though fifteen years had passed since Jockel's writing: "Canada's token presence in the North consists of Canadian Forces Northern Area Head-quarters in Yellowknife, with a staff of 150, and two smaller detachments in Whitehorse and Iqaluit respectively to cover a four-million-square-kilometre territory. The navy has no ships with ice-breaking capability, and air patrols occur only a few times a year. Surveillance of the region is left to five Coast Guard icebreakers, scattered RCMP detachments, and 1,400 Inuit Aboriginal Rangers, still equipped with vintage Second World War rifles."[117] She added this "lack of military capability in the Arctic will not help Canada's historical claim to the passage if challenged in the International Court of Justice," and cited the view of international lawyer Donat Pharand, as presented in his book, *Canada's Arctic Waters in International Law*: "It's highly doubtful that Canada could suc-ceed in proving that the waters of the Canadian Arctic Archipelago are historical internal waters over which it has complete sovereignty."[118]

Arctic Security after the Cold War

The world quickly and profoundly transformed with the collapse of communism in Eastern Europe and the later break-up of the Soviet Union as a singular sover-eign state. These changes affected the whole world, including the territories above the Arctic Circle. Canada was quick to recognize these changes and to adapt its defense policy to meet the transforming security challenges of the im-mediate post–Cold War world. Consequently, the Department of National De-fence issued its 1992 Defence Policy Statement—recognizing that the world was profoundly different, and articulating a new doctrine for Canada's military in this new, and still emerging, post–Cold War world.

Three elements of change were reflected in the new doctrine: an articulation of environmental values as components of the national security, and a general "greening" of national defense; the dramatic collapse of Soviet power and with it the primary external threat to North America; and the increasing importance of Canada's vast and resource-rich northern frontier within the calculus of Cana-dian defense policy. In its section on "The International Environment," the *1992 Defence Policy Statement* stated: "The international environment in which Can-ada seeks its security and prosperity has changed dramatically in the recent past. For Canadian defense policy, the most significant of all recent international developments are undoubtedly the changes that have occurred in Central and Eastern Europe and the collapse of the Soviet Union. . . . The disintegration of the Soviet empire is only one of many events that have accelerated the transformation of the world. New as well as long-submerged forces are today stirring bright hopes and dark fears. Some are benign; others could be destabilizing."[119] Though not explicitly examined in the *1992 Defence Policy Statement*, many of the observations concerning changes in the international environment were also true of the Arctic environment, so one can readily deduce an emergent framework for redefining Arctic security. Though the *1992 Defence Policy Statement* only briefly discussed the Arctic, a chronic symptom consistent with Ottawa's tendency to neglect its northern frontier, the ideas and observations about changes in the post–Cold War world are every bit as relevant in the Arctic as they are to the world at large.

Nationalism and Tribalism

For instance, consider the following comments on the rise of nationalism in the vacuum created by the collapse of communism: "Nationalism is in the ascendant. It can be a powerful constructive force. Yet, as ancient nations reappear, ethnic hatreds also rekindle the violent confrontations of earlier eras . . . even as nationalism reshapes the borders of Central and Eastern Europe, the nations of the continent's western half are foregoing sovereign prerogatives in the interest of greater economic efficiency and political stability."[120]

Canada, as a multinational state, remains home to numerous ancient, indigenous First Nations—from the Inuit of the Arctic rim to the Mi'kmaqs of the Maritimes. However, the historical decimation of the southern Indian populations has left only tribal remnants of these ancient nations, though the Inuit population remains at historic demographic levels. Through inter-tribal and inter-regional alliances in national Aboriginal organizations like the Inuit Tapirisat of Canada and the Assembly of First Nations and through international organizations as the United Nations, or groups like the Unrepresented Nations and Peoples Organization, these tribal remnants have gained a louder voice, making it more likely that new political structures built to correspond with their traditional boundaries will appear, following in the path blazed by Nunavut.

Land claims are a big step in this direction. A new, third order of government for First Nations as negotiated at Charlottetown in 1992 would have been one more step—not necessarily toward the revival of the formal sovereignty of these ancient nations, but toward the creation of new governing structures, somewhere between a municipality and a territory, that correspond with the traditional tribal boundaries, an important step forward in their movement for greater autonomy and decreased dependence. As the armed standoff and military intervention at Oka clearly demonstrated in 1990—and as recurrent blockades of logging roads and Canadian rail lines in British Columbia and Ontario up to the present time further demonstrate, ancient hatreds still exist in many Aboriginal communities toward the "white man" and his governments. Canada has made some progress toward resolving some of the outstanding claims and conflicts, but many remain unresolved, estimated at more than 900 specific Native land claims in southern Canada, resulting in the June 12, 2007, announcement by Prime Minister Stephen Harper and Indian Affairs Minister Jim Prentice of the establishment of a quasi-judicial tribunal to resolve the growing backlog of claims.[121] According to a press release issued by the Prime Minister's Office, Prime Minister Harper "announced plans for a decisive new approach that will fundamentally change the way specific claims are handled in Canada," known as the Specific Claims Action Plan, designed to "address the huge backlog of unresolved treaty claims that has been the source of division and conflict in communities across the country."[122] As Harper explained, "Instead of letting disputes over land and compensation drag on forever, fuelling frustration and uncertainty, they will be solved once and for all by impartial judges on a new Specific Claims Tribunal."[123] Canada's Specific Claims Action Plan proposes four key initiatives that would create a new tribunal staffed with impartial judges who would make final decisions on claims when negotiations fail; make arrangements for financial compensation more transparent through dedicated funding for settlements in the amount of $250 million a year for 10 years; speed up processing of small claims and improve flexibility in the handling of large claims; and refocus the existing Indian Specific Claims Commission to concentrate on dispute resolution.[124]

What must be understood is that these sorts of conflicts do exist in Canada, just as they exist around the world: Though the populations of Canada's first nations are relatively small, combined, they pose a serious threat to the internal security and political stability of Canada. And in the North, where non-Native populations are also quite small, Aboriginal peoples and their communities still dominate the demographics, and in many parts of the North (outside the more populous and recently settled portions of Alaska, Yukon, and Labrador) the political machinery as well. The NWT, even after the secession of Nunavut, still has a large Native plurality, some 46 percent of its population of 42,000. Nunavut, which was created in 1999, and is approaching the end of its first decade of self-governance, is even more unified ethnically with its predominantly Inuit populace and its increasingly Inuit civil service. In Northern Québec, the situation is similar—though because Nunavik is part of a predominantly non-Native province (Québec), its relative political strength at the regional level is watered down considerably within the provincial context.

However, the high strategic and economic value of Northern Québec's rivers to Québec's and its neighbors' energy needs augments the power of its small, northern, indigenous population—as they ultimately possess the power to disrupt Québec's energy development program. All in all, the Native peoples of Canada's North are a force to be reckoned with—and to continue to ignore their needs, or to suppress their desire for greater autonomy through a continued colonial mindset, would only increase the frequency of local and regional conflicts, and invite more Okas. In the event of armed confrontations, not only could bridges be closed down as we saw with the Mohawk barricade of the Mercier Bridge linking Montreal to the southern townships in the summer of 1990; critical energy infrastructure, as well, could be vulnerable. By considering Canada's First Nations as real nations, albeit small micro-nations and tribal entities, and applying the logic of Canada's post–Cold War defense policy and its recognition of the potential threat of nationalism and tribalism to the country's hinterland, much grief could be prevented.

Environmental Security

A point of interest in DND's 1992 policy statement has to do with its enunciation of the environment as a bona fide component of the national security, albeit a secondary and not yet a primary security interest: "The adoption of a broader approach to national and global security, brought about by international concern over such issues as the environment, population growth, and the availability of critical resources, is a clear factor of stability. The inability of any one state on its own to solve these problems encourages greater cooperation and joint problem-solving across frontiers. Yet the same issues can also be divisive. Cross-border pollution and overfishing are major international irritants."[125] Environmental security is viewed not only as a global issue, but a domestic imperative: "The Department of National Defence is committed to ensuring that its policies and activities are consistent with safeguarding the environment."[126]

Concern about the environment was not entirely new to DND. Over the previous decade, the Department had demonstrated its environmental concerns in a number of ways. It had significantly reduced the amount of energy used in its facilities. Working with Forestry Canada and industry, DND conducted inventories and developed plans for the sustainable development of forests on departmental property. The Department devoted particular attention to responsible management of property used for operational training, and developed procedures to ensure that sites are returned to an environmentally sound state when no longer needed. In March 1992, an agreement was reached with Environment Canada to set aside 420-square kilometers on the eastern boundary of Canadian Forces Base Suffield, Alberta, as a national wildlife refuge.[127]

Of course, many Native communities that DND had displaced from their traditional lands over the years have found DND's commitment to the environment and its traditional use by Native people to be suspect. Similarly, Innu in Labrador wondered why their traditional lands were subjected to low-level supersonic bomber flights, which they found disrupted the migration of the caribou they depended upon to survive. Nonetheless, at least DND committed rhetorically to the preservation of the environment, and this marked an important beginning of a new, bona fide national security value—taking a long-term perspective on the matter that one might otherwise expect bureaucratic organizations, surviving from budget to budget, to overlook.

The U.N. Framework Convention on Climate Change, signed in Rio in 1992, which brought nations together from all over the world to deal with environmental risks that threaten global security, showed the potential of this universal value of environmental protection to rise to the top of the political agenda for the world community, but the on-again, off-again lack of sustained consensus, created in part by the unwillingness of the United States to place its own near-term interests after the longer-term interests of humanity, diluting the conference's outcome—and later by the U.S. withdrawal from the Kyoto regime entirely and continued U.S. resistance in Bali—shows that there is a long way to go before this new, green value takes root in the security calculus of American power. Though the willingness of the United States to commit to formal treaty negotiations in Bali in December 2007 did indicate that change was underway, albeit incrementally and at a slower pace than scientists believe is necessary to prevent an environmental and security catastrophe.

In recent years, high pollution levels found in the supposedly pristine Arctic—as illustrated by Arctic haze, dangerously high concentrations of DDT in Inuit breast-milk, and revelations of widespread nuclear pollution of the Arctic by the old USSR—has contributed to the increasing realization that we are one, small world, a fragile blue-green orb of life floating in the emptiness of space, vulnerable if not protected. For a long time, the environment has been a vital element of regional security. But now, it is finally a component of global security. The Clinton Administration, with the well known environmental advocate, theorist, and author of *World in the Balance* (and now the Academy Award winning documentary film producer of *An Inconvenient Truth*, and Nobel Peace Prize winner) Al Gore serving as Vice President, worked hard to facilitate an even greater commitment to the preservation of the environment as an element of both national and international security. In the years since, the Bush Administration has returned to an earlier concept of the environment being a repository of exploitable, extractable wealth, and has—for the moment—stepped back from this emerging concept of green security to some degree, though the White House continues to invest in the emerging hydrogen economy powered by fuel cells, and to promote energy independence for America as it announced in President Bush's 2003 State of the Union Address: "Tonight I'm proposing $1.2 billion in research funding so that America can lead the world in developing clean, hydrogen-powered automobiles," and "with a new national commitment, our scientists and engineers will overcome obstacles to taking these cars from laboratory to showroom, so that the first car driven by a child born today could be powered by hydrogen, and pollution-free."[128]

As Harriet Critchley told a conference sponsored by the Canadian Institute of Strategic Studies, Divided We Fall: The National Security Implications of Canadian Constitutional Issues, in 1992: "Even before the decline in traditional security threats began to occur, some Canadians were paying increased attention to non-traditional threats to security. The Palme Commission report, *Common Security*, was very influential in this emerging trend, but not the only stimulus.

In the early 1970s, for example, Prime Minister Trudeau identified marine-source pollution in the Canadian Arctic as a threat to Canada's security. At the time, such a notion of a threat to security seemed quite unusual to say the least, but by the 1990s the idea is quite acceptable."[129] She presented a broad taxonomy of "non-traditional" security threats, including global and regional environmental threats, air- and sea-borne pollutants, economic conflict, international terrorism, ozone depletion, and deforestation. Critchley noted the concept of security was already changing in Europe and the Persian Gulf at the Cold War's end, and believes that unless "the notion of security is broadened to incorporate both traditional and non-traditional types of threats," then Canadians "now, and even more so in the future, do not, and will not, feel safe. Rather, they will feel increasingly insecure. Therefore, it should come as no surprise when the public begins to expect the government to provide a defense, or defences, against such non-traditional threats to Canada's security and sovereignty."[130]

And as Canadian environmental activist and journalist Dr. David Suzuki told the Citizens Inquiry into Peace and Security in 1992, "I believe we still need a strong Department of National Defence, but now the 'mother of all battles' is environmental, not military. . . . We are in a real struggle to protect the life-support systems of the planet and their degradation is every bit as life-threatening as a bomb or bullet."[131] Consistent with this vision, the Commission presented three recommendations regarding environmental security: Canada "must take a leadership role in building the global institutions and agreements to monitor, study, regulate, protect and restore the global environment, and back that leadership with significant financial support"; "should make environmental protection a national priority, and put into place the legal, institutional and pro-grammatic tools to protect and restore the Canadian environment and to build an environmentally sustainable Canadian and global economy"; and "should stop further nuclear reactor sales, phase out uranium mining and uranium exports, and shift its nuclear development funding to the development of conservation and alternative energy technologies."[132] The Commission concluded that the "global environmental system faces a wide range of threats from human activity, including greenhouse gas build-up, ozone destruction, deforestation, desertification, loss of species/habitat destruction, toxic chemical contamination of water systems, and a wide variety of other forms of air, water and land pollution" and that "it is vitally important that work begin now in the areas where threats to the global environment have already been identified, such as global warming."[133]

As articulated by Canada's *1992 Defence Policy Statement*, the Department of Defense pledged to "contribute to the achievement of the overall environmental goals set by the Government. The Canadian Forces will continue to take environmental concerns into account when planning and executing training missions and operations. An environmentally sensitive approach to departmental decision-making will be pursued so that 'green' considerations are given equal weight along with operational, logistic, financial and human concerns."[134] The preservation of the environment is widely accepted nowadays as a national security goal, so much so that former Vice President Al Gore won a Nobel Peace

Prize for his efforts on behalf of the environment in October 2007, evidence that the greening of national security policy had fully matured, and what was once a local or regional value as articulated in the *ICC Principles* was now a recognized national security value around the world. But in 1992, this was still something quite new at the national level. The combined impacts on the human psyche of the Exxon Valdez disaster, the use of Agent Orange in the Vietnam War, the radioactive shadow cast by Chernobyl, the inherent risks to the environment of nuclear warfare—from fears of a global "nuclear winter" to higher levels of cancer in down wind from battlefields, and images of those ominous, oilfield infernos and the intentional oil spills in the Persian Gulf during the first Gulf War, have contributed to the emerging global realization that the environment is fundamentally tied to individual, national, and global security.

The Arctic is as relevant to these perceptions as any other part of the international environment, particularly the problems associated with the environmental pollutants. A major reason for the political mobilization of northern Natives has been their deep concern for the health of the environment—and one of the very key reasons for land claims was to establish a mechanism by which local people who live off the land can regulate, and minimize the external assault on, their physical environment. As we distance ourselves from the Cold War, the problem of Arctic pollution, particularly the environmental degradation caused by extraordinarily shortsighted nuclear waste management programs in Siberia, has become an international Arctic issue—bringing together experts and policy-makers from the entire Arctic basin, and paving the way forward for a global approach to Arctic environmental security that has carried into the current era, as climate change again threatens to transform the Arctic environment. The enormity of the environmental threats to the physical environment of the Arctic has caused the old Cold War divisions to quickly transform into a post–Cold War consensus.

The Inuit Circumpolar Conference has been concerned with Arctic nuclear and industrial pollution for many years, generating much interest in the academic and environmentalist communities. But not until the systemic Cold War division of the polar region ended could both sides sit down and work things out. Before the Cold War ended, it was virtually impossible to get the Russians to cooperate; but after Chernobyl, once Soviet industrial power was widely questioned inside the USSR and the risks and dangers more widely accepted, the diplomatic environment began to shift. Just as the Exxon Valdez spill affected policy-making in the Inuvialuit Settlement Region, Chernobyl affected the way the Russians dealt with their industrial and environmental policies. Glasnost allowed such problems to be discussed in public on the other side of the Arctic, in Siberia and northern Russia. When the Cold War finally ended, all sides finally agreed that there was quite a mess—and this mess was causing much risk to the local inhabitants of the Arctic littoral, especially the Aboriginal marine mammal hunters of the North. By the 1990s, the state of Alaska and the U.S. Federal Government were involved in assessing the damage caused by industrial and nuclear waste in what used to be the USSR. And Canada was implementing its Green Plan and its Arctic Environmental Strategy, beginning clean-up of the toxic wastes left over from the DEW Line, including PCB contaminated transformers that some researchers feared would pollute the fragile Arctic food-chain. As the problem of military security became less salient in the Arctic, environmental security—long a concern of the Native peoples of the Arctic—finally became an objective of both national and international security. Land claims, on a regional scale, reflected movement in this direction well before the Cold War ended—but it took systemic change to allow a new security paradigm to emerge internationally.

Fundamentalism

The threat of religious fundamentalism had been simmering throughout the Cold War and marked a new axis of conflict that challenged both East and West, with Soviet power dealt a mortal blow by the success of the Jihadist resistance in Afghanistan, and western power dealt a strategic setback with the loss in Iran to revolutionary Islamist forces. After the Cold War, religious fundamentalism gained strength and eventually inspired the events of September 11, 2001. As of the writing of the *1992 Defence Policy Statement*, fundamentalism was an emergent threat, one that DND recognized in its infancy: "Religion is once again becoming a source of tension and vision in various parts of the world. Fundamentalist solutions of one sort or another are seen as tempting alternatives to a failed past and a bleak future, particularly where experimentation with democracy and free-market economics have failed to achieve anticipated gains."[135]

In the domestic context, fundamentalism proved more latent, in contrast to the role, in America's heartland, of Christian fundamentalism. Though within the Aboriginal context, the movement for Native rights reflected an undercurrent of traditional Native spiritualism that could evolve into a domestic fundamentalist threat. During the Oka uprising in 1992, traditional Mohawk spiritualism played an indirect role in motivating the Warriors. Though Native spiritual traditions across Canada have been increasingly popular, the most notable movement toward religious fundamentalism in the Arctic has not been toward indigenous value systems but instead toward a rapid spread of revivalist Christianity not unlike that seen in America's bible belt. As Jimi Onalik explained to Dafna Izenberg in "The Conscience of Nunavut," rising disillusionment with the Nunavut experience has been "contributing to the growing popularity of the evangelical Christian movement in the North. James Arreak, a pastor with the Iqaluit Christian Fellowship, estimates that more than 1,000 people attended the 20th Arctic Bible Conference in Iqaluit in April 2004."[136]

Some observers find an active Dene mysticism and traditional spiritualism within the Dene Nation of the NWT, but so far, in the Inuit communities, traditional spiritualism, in particular the tradition of shamanism, is still only rarely discussed, after its long suppression by missionaries in the Arctic, either a sign of its disappearance or its continued underground status—and it is unclear whether shamanism or other elements of indigenous spiritualism will re-emerge as a social force in the Inuit homeland, or evolve into a new fault line of conflict. Traditional shamans are thought to still exist—but their suppression by the Catholic and Anglican missionaries forced them largely underground, and marginalized their social influence. However, it is plausible that, as we have observed in many Alaska communities, a tribal sovereignty movement will emerge in the Inuit homeland—and that this could be accompanied by a movement to restore traditional spiritualism. But whether this would or could result in the emergence of an indigenous, Inuit fundamentalism, is difficult to assess. But a grassroots rejection of the assimilationist policies of the past, and their more recent manifestations through such things as land claims corporations and other tools of westernization, is entirely likely, especially if disappointments with the land claims experience turns into a more bitter disillusionment. Such a traditionalist movement associated with tribal sovereignty would likely contain a spiritual element—but whether this would reflect traditional shamanism is impossible to predict. At the very least, just as fundamentalism has emerged throughout the world, particularly in areas that had unpleasant colonial and imperial experiences, we can speculate that it may also emerge in the North, though ironically, amidst Nunavut's social crisis since the territory was established in 1999, instead of such an indigenous fundamentalist backlash, there has been instead a robust evangelical movement.

The militancy of the Mohawk Warriors at Oka, and their sheer courage and moral strength, suggest that should Native fundamentalism emerge in the Canadian hinterland, there will be a serious security problem—one where insurgency in rural areas, terrorism, and sabotage of industrial and communication centers might become commonplace, paralyzing that geographically expansive nation. That fundamentalism has emerged among peoples the world over traditionally characterized as friendly, peaceful, and gentle, in regions where there is strong religious commitment to values like compassion, love, and justice, further suggests that it can happen in "Indian country." Isolated instances of sabotage in Northern Québec and Alaska, and the living memory of Oka, where Native warriors engaged in a gunfight with provincial police and then stared down the Canadian Army, suggest that the idea of Native fundamentalism in the North is not altogether unlikely, certainly not impossible. Ovide Mercredi's suggestion in 1992 after the failure of the Charlottetown Accord that there would be a wave of protest, blockades, and militancy in Native communities across Canada certainly struck a chord, one repeated over a decade later during a new round of Native militancy in Ontario and Manitoba. Indeed, despite efforts to evolve toward a more cooperative relationship between Native and non-Native, a generation after the land claims movement swept across the Arctic, the Native community in southern Canada has appeared to be edging again toward confrontation, frustrated by the relative lack of progress toward settling their land claims in the

South, with a series of blockades, culminating in the closure of Canada's busiest transportation corridor, on the National Day of Action on June 29, 2007.

The despair felt in Nunavut, where the Inuit won their own territorial government and the nation's most geographically expansive and financially remunerative land claim accord, mirrors the widespread sense of powerlessness and hopelessness in the southern part of Canada, where mechanisms of Aboriginal self-government are not nearly as powerful, and where land claims remain still just a distant promise, not a delivered fact as in the North. This time around, Canadian Forces, fresh from their counterinsurgency campaigns in Afghanistan, have not forgotten the dangers of the Oka crisis, and while Ottawa has worked hard in the years since to address the underlying causes of Native discontent that led to violence at Oka, the military internalized the lessons that it learned at Oka, culminating in the inclusion of Native radicalism as one of the potential threats to be met by Canada's new counterinsurgency doctrine. Renewed fears of Native radicalism are not without context; in 2006, a protracted land dispute in Caledonia, Ontario, led to violence between members of the Six Nations First Nation and non-Natives, with blockades, economic disruption, and occasional acts of violence, arson, and sabotage. A thirty-hour blockade of a major rail artery connecting Toronto to Montreal by Mohawks from the Bay of Quinte in Deseronto, Ontario, took place on April 20, 2007. Soon after with land claims negotiations under way, a blockade was erected by the Six Nations at nearby Hagersville, Ontario, on May 23, 2007, to protest a development project that had not properly consulted them: this led to a halt in negotiations as provincial negotiators cried foul, but both sides agreed to return to the table at the end of May 2007.

More blockades followed on the National Day of Action on June 29, 2007, which had been called by the Assembly of First Nations to bring attention to continued poverty in Indian Country. Though the AFN had urged its members to pursue peaceful means of protest, a more radical chief of the Roseau River First Nation in Manitoba urged Natives to make it a day of national rail blockades. *CBC News* reported that Manitoba Chief Terry Nelson had said that "blocking trains would send a stronger message about the poverty that Aboriginal communities face and the numerous land claims that are still being disputed. 'It's very clear that unless there's significant action—standing between the white man and his money—nobody cares, and that's the reality.'"[137] *CBC News* also quoted Nelson as saying, "There are two ways to deal with the white man. You either pick up a gun or you stand between him and his money."[138] A video showing how to blockade a rail line even showed up on *YouTube*, titled "When Justice Fails, Stop the Rails," calling "on Natives to take action by creating rail blockades similar to those recently staged near Tyendinaga, Ontario."[139] The video was produced by a group calling itself the Railway Ties Collective, which noted there remain over 800 outstanding land claims in Canada, and calculated that "the time it will take to resolve these things is expected to be more than 200 years."[140] Assembly of First Nations Chief Phil Fontaine told *CTV News* this "serves as evidence of mounting frustration among Canada's Native youth" and "suggested it's a sign of a frustrated and desperate segment of the First Nations population."[141]

Though Chief Nelson later called off his plans for a blockade, after Ottawa had agreed to increase his band's allotment of land by thirty hectares, several blockades were erected across Indian Country on the National Day of Action. The *Canadian Press* reported that Mohawks from Deseronto, Ontario "shut down Canada's busiest transportation corridor," with their first blockade going up three hours early, at nine p.m. on June 28th, closing down Highway 2; followed by a blockade of the CN Rail line, their second blockade of this rail corridor since April; and then, for the very first time, shutting down Highway 401, one of Canada's busiest roadways. Negotiations between the Mohawks and the Ontario Provincial Police led to the reopening of the 401 after eleven hours, but the other two blockades were kept up until the National Day of Action was over. *CBC News* reported that "Canada's busiest highway could be the target of future blockades," citing Mohawk activist Shawn Brant, who organized the blockades: "This is the first time ever we've shut down the 401, and I don't believe it's going to be the last. It was certainly a good test run for us."[142] CN Rail issued a press release calling attention to their frustration with the authorities for allowing the blockade to continue, despite a court order banning such activity: "CN today halted freight operations and embargoed all traffic on its Toronto-Montreal main line after reportedly armed native protesters erected an illegal blockade on the company's tracks near the eastern Ontario town of Marysville, located approximately 10 miles east of Belleville, Ont."[143] It had "obtained an injunction barring illegal occupation of the rail corridor when First Nations protesters blocked the line in April of this year. The Ontario Provincial Police (OPP) refused to enforce the order issued by Justice Campbell of the Ontario Superior Court at that time. First Nations protesters are again blocking CN's rail corridor and the OPP continues to refuse to intervene."[144] The company decided that "in the interest of ensuring the safety of its employees and operations, will indefinitely halt all rail operations on its Montreal-Toronto main line, including VIA Rail passenger trains, until the company has received assurances that the OPP will remove protesters and guarantee such safety."[145]

When pondering the specter of Native militancy and fundamentalism, the question to ask is this: How assimilated are the Aboriginal people of the North, and how resilient are the advocates of traditional culture? It is clear that Inuit leaders have become less distinguishable from their non-Inuit colleagues as they assume positions of power. But if the people they represent, and their values, remain largely traditional, there is potential for a backlash against them. When coupled with the poverty of the Arctic coastal communities, the alienation felt in post–land claims settlement areas—which widens the gulf between rich and poor in the North by creating corporate elites subsidized by public funds surrounded by a sea of poverty and despair—and the social dislocation experienced by youth caught between the world of their elders and the world of the white man, the concept of Inuit fundamentalism is not so farfetched after all. But by and large it hasn't yet emerged, but one may speculate that it eventually will, after the current wave of suicide and other self-destructive behaviors run their course, and after contemporary tools of social organization work their way North, much as we've seen in other parts of the world where new communications technologies have helped to redirect social alienation and anger outward, away from the self, and toward the symbols of their oppression and persecution.

Rich and Poor: The North-South Gap

Just as the gap between Third World nations in the world's South and industrialized nations in the world's North has grown, so has the gap between North and South in Canada, and between Native and non-Native: "Another concern is the widening of the gulf between the developed and developing worlds. The clash of ideas, cultures and economies, while no longer predicated on superpower rivalry, is continuing in a more varied and unpredictable form. The challenge is to overcome differences without resorting to force, through existing and possibly new instruments of multilateralism and cooperation."[146] As observed, to the shock of southern Canada over a decade ago in Davis Inlet when a wave of youth suicide swept that community, and more recently in Nunavut where Justice Berger again was called north to investigate why things were so slow to improve after more than five years of a land claim enhanced by the creation of a new, predominantly Inuit territory, the North continues to present many similarities to the developing world—and this is as true in Alaska and Siberia. In Alaska, the term "Fourth World" is often used to describe the similarity, which is further compounded by the climate and isolation of the Native villages across the state. With both a settled land claim accord and their own territorial government, the Inuit of Nunavut have at their disposal more tools, and greater powers, to shape their own destiny than any other Natives in the Americas. But thus far, their task has not been easy, as great challenges confront the Inuit of Nunavut as they seek to balance new and old, and re-learn to govern themselves.

As described by Paul Mayer, a Montreal lawyer and the Senior Ministerial Representative for Nunavut Devolution to the Department of Indian and Northern Affairs, in his June 2007 *Mayer Report on Nunavut Devolution*, the Inuit are standing at a crossroads of hope and despair: "Nunavut is at a crossroads today. On the one hand, it is a land of incredible opportunity. It has vast mineral and natural resources wealth. At the briefings given by senior GN and Inuit association leaders in Nunavut, I heard many predict a bright and optimistic future for Nunavut. They outlined a vision of a self-reliant territory that would become less dependent on federal government transfers in which Nunavummiut would enjoy a standard of living comparable to that of southern Canadians. On the other hand, despite this optimism, the territory continues to face extremely difficult challenges. But the reality would best be described as a blend of optimism and despair."[147]

Mayer examined Nunavut's challenges in detail, noting "Nunavut faces significant operational, financial and social challenges that raise serious concerns over the GN's ability to assume additional responsibilities," including the "immense challenges" posed by its geography and climate, the "enormous social challenges which, in the words of the GN, have reached crisis proportions'" such as prevalent alcohol and substance abuse problems, high crime, family violence and suicide rates that are "all well above the national average," an "acute housing shortage" and overcrowding that "contributes to health problems and learning disabilities," as well as a "major gap in the health status of Nunavummiut," who face "a lower life expectancy, higher infant mortality rate, and higher death rates from lung cancer" than elsewhere in Canada. And lastly, he pointed out, as Berger did, that "the low education levels and corresponding lack of employable skills in the Inuit population of Nunavut is one of the territory's most pressing issues."[148] On the suicide problem, he observed: "The suicide rate in Nunavut is shockingly high. Twenty-nine people in the territory took their lives in 2006, the second-worst year on record. Young men between 15 and 24 years of age in Nunavut are about 40 times more likely to commit suicide than the average Canadian in that same age group."[149] Berger believes the high suicide levels are a "a symptom of the current social malaise in Nunavut society caused by, among other things, rapid social change, high drop-out rates, poverty, unemployment and dysfunctional families."[150]

Despite the resolution of land claims from Alaska to Labrador, northern villages remain, by and large, isolated, with limited economic opportunity, inadequate housing, underfunded—and sometimes still culturally insensitive—education systems. Even in land claim settlement areas, wealth is often unevenly distributed, and many of the social and economic ills of the underdeveloped North remain common. The result is increased self-destruction and community violence, and increases in substance abuse, suicide, spousal assault, and elder abuse. With so much violence aimed inward, one may wonder if these self-destructive forces might eventually be redirected outward, under the influence of a more radicalized leadership, as we've seen in other parts of the world. If social conditions persist, or worsen, and if the current, pragmatic leadership is rejected by the community, it seems to be conceivable that these currently self-destructive forces could be redirected away from the self toward the non-Native power centers. Naturally, it is in Canada's interest to prevent this, and through land claims, it has started the process of bridging its internal North/South gap. But the reality of land claims implementation, and its rapid introduction of a corporate model into communities that have hitherto experienced only limited economic development, results in new divisions within the post-settlement environment, with corporate elites more closely aligned with the values of southern centers of economic and political power. The effort is thus ongoing to bridge the social and economic divides, narrowing the gap between haves and have-nots, and thereby reduce the risk of civil strife.

Though Canada's *1992 Defence Policy Statement* presented some new and innovative approaches to Canada's international security policies, it did not make an explicit connection to Canada's internal situation nor envision the risk of state failure in Canada's outlying territories. But as the Canadian Security and Intelligence Service (CSIS) revealed during the 1990s with its interrogation of Labrador Innu protesters who blockaded runways at Goose Bay to protest NATO low-level flight training, there was some emergent knowledge in Ottawa that Aboriginal protest could have the potential to threaten Canada's internal security—demanding a just and lasting solution to ensure the social peace, and a closing of both the North/South gap and the Aboriginal/non-Aboriginal gap. Even the largely industrialized province of Ontario, home of both Canada's political capital city, Ottawa, and its economic hub, Toronto, has been the flashpoint between Native and non-Native for more than a decade, ever since an Ontario Provincial Police sniper shot and killed Dudley George, an unarmed Native land rights activist at Ipperwash Provincial Park in September 1995. In the Report of the Ipperwash Inquiry, Commissioner Sidney B. Linden concluded: "Research in the course of the inquiry showed that the flashpoints for Aboriginal protests and occupations are very likely as intense today as they were at the time of Ipperwash. No one can predict where protests and occupations will occur, but the fundamental conditions and catalysts sparking such protests continue to exist in Ontario, more than a decade after Ipperwash." As Linden explained, "The immediate cost of conducting relations with Aboriginal people through confrontations and over the barricades is very high. All Ontarians risk even more if we leave long-simmering disputes unsettled until they boil over. Without effective and respectful means of resolving these disputes, an atmosphere of insecurity and uncertainty with respect to the lands at issue will persist.[151]

And in April 2007, the Canadian media reported that radical Native organizations such as the Mohawk Warriors Society had been listed in a draft DND counterinsurgency training manual as potential insurgents, alongside better known terrorist organizations like al-Qaeda, Hamas, and Hezbollah. AFN National Chief Phil Fontaine called "upon Prime Minister Stephen Harper to immediately and without reservation, reject and remove any references to First Nations from all versions of the training manual."[152] He stated that "any reference to First Nations people as possible insurgents or terrorists is a direct attack on us—it demonizes us, it threatens our safety and security and attempts to criminalize our legitimate right to live our lives like all other Canadians do. Just being referenced in such a document compromises our freedom to travel across borders, have unimpeded telephone and internet communications, raise money, and protest against injustices to our people."[153] Fontaine added, "It is shocking and outrageous to learn that the Canadian military would consider First Nations people as insurgents or equate us to Hezbollah or Hamas. Not only is there not a shred of evidence to make this link, First Nations have always served Canada well by their contributions to the Canadian services. Such absurd allegations only serve to undermine respect for the military and lead us to believe we will not be able to rely on their protection the way other Canadians do."[154] But the very fact that Canada's armed forces have contemplated applying its new counterinsurgency doctrine to the home front in Canada reflects the sober assessment by defense planners of what could happen, should that other path—of confrontation and not compromise—be followed by Canada's Natives.

Mary Simon, now president of Inuit Tapiriit Kanatami (ITK), and former ICC President as well as Canada's very first Arctic Ambassador, has described the persistence of the North/South gap, and the challenges that Inuit face as they struggle to close it, at the tenth general assembly of the Inuit Circumpolar Conference in Barrow, Alaska, on July 10, 2006: "The social economic gap between Inuit and other Canadians has not been closed, indeed for so many, particularly our young people, it has even widened. It is the children and youth whose culture and languages are under the most severe threat, who feel the pain most and are sadly, are the most at risk. . . . Above all, we need to maintain our determination that our rights are respected, our languages and culture protected and social economic equity is achieved, we should never accept no as an answer."[155]

Defending the North

An interesting, if only briefly presented, component of Canadian defense policy at the Cold War's end was the four-paragraph recognition in the *1992 Defence Policy Statement* of the need to defend the North. That the discussion of the North is only four paragraphs implies that DND, as of 1992, still did not feel that its northern security was particularly at risk, and later policy statements including the *1994 White Paper on Defence* and even the *2005 Defence Policy Statement*, the first such statement issued in over a decade, also paid only limited attention to northern security. But the seeds were planted as far back as 1992 in identifying the fundamental issues and challenges of northern security in the post–Cold War period, with its blend of external security issues relating largely to continental and maritime security, and internal security issues relating to the continuing struggle to pacify the northern frontier, preempt Native militancy through the promotion of greater political inclusion, as part of a broader model of sharing in the responsibilities of northern governance, uniting government and Aboriginal by their shared, and mutually reinforcing, sovereignty. While the *2005 Defence Policy Statement* lays a blueprint for securing the North, it would take the dramatic events of the summer of 2007 when Russia reasserted its claim to a vast stretch of undersea resources stretching from its northern shores to the North Pole, for Ottawa to be catalyzed to action. A year earlier, Canada's Arctic sovereignty and security had become a key campaign issue for the incoming Conservative Party of Canada, and soon thereafter with an intensification of Arctic diplomatic, military, and economic activities, the unique challenges of northern security have taken center stage.

Interestingly, the general principles that have blossomed in recent months as central policies pursued by Ottawa were articulated at the very dawn of the post–Cold War period. As noted in the *1992 Defence Policy Statement*: "The objectives of National Defence, with respect to the North, are to uphold Canadian sovereignty by exercising surveillance, demonstrating presence, helping civilian agencies cope with non-military contingencies and advising government on measures to deal with new challenges."[156] The latter phrase, "advising government on measures to deal with new challenges," is promising—for the North is sure to bring new challenges, as many are now noticing as a consequence of climate change and the increased commercial activities in the region. DND proposed to pursue these objectives "in various ways" in 1992, such as by expanding the Rangers, retaining an airborne battalion for reacting on short notice to emergencies in remote areas, and conducting R&D on new systems "of particular applicability to the North."[157]

Further, DND pledged to "coordinate its activities and plans with other departments and governments, assisting civil authorities in public welfare emergencies, including search and rescue operations," and to "continue to carry out surveillance of the North and its air and sea approaches." DND noted it would pursue a "number of specific initiatives are improving the ability of the Canadian Forces to contribute to sovereignty and security in the North," and that:

> The acquisition of three Arctic and Maritime Surveillance aircraft will make possible an increase in northern air surveillance patrols. The completion of the North Warning System will significantly enhance the capability of the Canadian Forces to monitor the use of Canadian airspace. The upgrading of northern airfields and the acquisition of Hercules aircraft with an air-refueling capability will enable the air force, for the first time in Canadian history, to deploy fighters anywhere across the Canadian North. The installation of a sub-surface acoustic detection system to monitor movements at a number of strategic choke-points in the Canadian Archipelago, and to monitor activity in the Arctic basin, will give Canada an unprecedented detection and surveillance capability in the North.[158]

These were ambitious plans—and if implemented, DND would be better prepared to meet some of the challenges of Canadian Arctic security. However, as the 1990s progressed, Canada's military engagement in its northern territories proved underwhelming, as noted in the work of University of Calgary political scientist Rob Huebert. As he explained in "Renaissance in Canadian Arctic Security?" in the Winter 2005–2006 edition of the *Canadian Military Journal*: "The security of the Canadian north has been a perpetual problem for Canadian policy-makers and for the Canadian military. The challenges of operating over the vast distances of the north, combined with the complex nature of security threats in the face of the extreme weather conditions, have created a security requirement that often appears insurmountable. As such, it frequently seems that Canadian political leaders and defence planners have preferred to ignore these challenges in the hope that nothing will happen."[159] And when Ottawa has decided to act, Huebert observes, it's "generally proven unwilling to commit the resources required to meet the needs of those decisions," and "when examining Canada's actions in defending its northern security without American assistance, it becomes apparent that the Canadian government has historically preferred to minimize its presence."[160] He described the Canadian military presence in the North, noting that the "largest force maintained in this region is the Rangers," the "volunteer militia force, whose purpose is to protect Canadian Arctic sovereignty through its presence, and also to provide a means of surveillance," and whose largely Native members possess "outstanding skills in navigating and surviving in the north" but who "are not heavily armed."[161] Additionally, he noted, the "permanent deployment of members of the Regular Forces in the North has been historically small, and, from the 1970s onward, normally has not exceeded 500 personnel stationed there at any given time," and whose field exercises have "declined in importance and size towards the end of the 1980s with the end of the Cold War."[162] Indeed, Huebert observed that "with the end of the Cold War, almost all activities that the Canadian Department of National Defence (DND) conducted in the north were either stopped or substantially reduced," adding that: "It is clear that the Arctic simply ceased being an area of significant concern for Canadian security during the 1990s. Indeed, when the Government did give any consideration to the role of the Canadian North in the emerging new international system, it was in the context of new multi-lateral institutions, the most important of which was the Arctic Council."[163] And as Huebert explained, even though the Arctic Council did "important work in the determination of environmental and social threats facing the Arctic, its founding document specifically forbids it from addressing security related issues," largely because the United States "still considered their Arctic security to be of a high priority, and did not want an international organization limiting their freedom of action in the region."[164]

Interestingly, the 1990s witnessed a profound transformation of Canada's domestic political structures in the North, most notably with the secession of the Nunavut Territory from the Northwest Territories, creating a new, territorial structure of governance that was largely contiguous with the Nunavut land claim agreement's settlement area, a bold experiment in Aboriginal self-government and a substantial augmentation of powers for the Inuit of the Eastern and Central Arctic regions. So while Ottawa may have neglected the external security challenges of its Arctic frontier, it had redoubled its efforts to enhance its internal security through political inclusion, devolution of governing powers, and tangible structural evolution in Aboriginal self-government in the Arctic. These domestic policy efforts were not necessarily perceived by decision-making elites to be part and parcel of its northern security calculus, but their practical impact no doubt will extend into the security sphere, owing to the impact of new self-governing and co-management structures on military activities in the North, and more broadly from the impact of increased participation by Inuit, and their more meaningful participation, in domestic politics. Thus the 1990s, with the Oka uprising marking the start of the decade, and the emergence of the Nunavut Territory in 1999 marking its end, witnessed a profound change, at least in northern Canada. In the South, with more complex political and ethnic topology, and greater resistance to Aboriginal self-government by non-Native stakeholders in the political process, progress was much less far-reaching.

One could thus describe the 1990s as a period of renewed internal focus for northern security in Canada, a time of institutional development as the Inuit quickly transitioned from managing their newly negotiated land claim in 1993 to the birth of their own territory in 1999. In hindsight, one can see the obvious benefits to northern security of this institutional development, but at the time the discussion of such changes was presented as part of the domestic policy framework for northern development, and a vast, northern Petrie dish for experimentation in Aboriginal self-government, as well as a highly touted public relations success story in a part of Canada where there were few non-Native interests to collide with Inuit aspirations. As the decade ended and the realities of self-government set in over the first five years of the next decade, this success story would shift to a tragic tale of missed opportunities, dashed expectations, and lost hope. But at the time of Nunavut's birth, the remapping of Canada and the emergence of a new territory governed of, by, and for the Inuit was widely celebrated.

Yet nowhere, other than perhaps in Ottawa's indirect comments on the northern security landscape—such as by "helping civilian agencies cope with non-military contingencies and advising government on measures to deal with new challenges" in the "Defence in the North" section of its *1992 Defence Policy Statement*—did DND suggest the possibility that its security challenges might in fact be domestic in their origin, or that, as demonstrated at Oka in 1990, there might be a place for military force, perhaps in the capacity of peacekeeping operations as performed by Canadian Forces during the Oka crisis—thus preventing greater escalation of violence between French and Mohawk residents in the summer of 1990.

The Challenge of State Collapse and Anarchy—at Home and Abroad

DND's *1992 Defence Policy Statement* presented Ottawa's first effort at new thinking on defense policy in response to the sudden transformation in international relations caused by the Cold War's end, and on the shift from Canada's Cold War defense policy to the less menacing but in many ways more complex post–Cold War era. Many of its principles were rearticulated two years later in Canada's *1994 White Paper on Defence* which reiterated the finality that "the Cold War is over" and noting that "the breakup of the Soviet Union significantly reduced the threat of annihilation that faced Canada and its allies for more than 40 years, and the dissolution of the Warsaw Pact and German unification marked an end to the division of Europe into hostile blocs."[165]

The *1994 White Paper* pointed out that Canada still faced "an unpredictable and fragmented world, one in which conflict, repression and upheaval exist

alongside peace, democracy and relative prosperity." Among the new and puz-
zling threats of the post–Cold War period were those presented by failed states,
which were like malignant time-bombs in the body politic, small but if untreated
potentially lethal. Canada, as a peacekeeping nation, was familiar with the dangers of state failure, having deployed its forces to hotspots throughout the Cold
War, and its unique approach to multiculturalism, and its rejection of assimilation as national policy in contrast with the United States, has made Canada a
natural and competent peacekeeping power. It's this peacekeeping tradition that
was called upon during the domestic uprising at Oka in 1990, and in many ways
is reflected by the interface connecting Canadian Forces with the indigenous
peoples of the North through the ongoing relationship of the Canadian Rangers
program.

Chapter 1 of the *1994 White Paper* examined the international environment,
and among the international considerations facing Canadian defense planners, it
noted that "the world's population is growing rapidly, putting pressure on global
political, financial and natural resources, as well as on the environment," that
"diminishing resources make it more difficult for advanced industrial states to
cope with global security challenges," and that "among the most difficult and
immediate challenges to international security are civil wars fuelled by ethnic,
religious and political extremism."[166] The *White Paper* further elaborated that
failed states would be a particular challenge of the new era.[167] In addition, the
rising tide of ethnic conflict and the "resurgence of old hatreds" was noted, an
issue of particular importance to Canada as a peacekeeping nation whose military was amongst the most active policing ceasefires and separating sides amidst
the intensity of civil conflict throughout the Cold War period.[168] Yet despite the
ferocity of these conflicts fueled by old hatreds, the situation was, at the grand
strategic and international level, more encouraging than during the Cold War,
owing to the less adversarial relations of world powers, in contrast to the Cold
War period.[169]

Chapter 2 of the *1994 White Paper* examined the domestic considerations
affecting Canadian defense policy; the primary issue addressed by the authors of
the *1994 White Paper* was economic, noting that "our prosperity—and with it
our quality of life—is threatened by the steady growth of public sector debt,"
and that "this situation limits governmental freedom of action in responding to
the needs of Canadians."[170] The *1994 White Paper* thus kept in mind the need
"to design a defence program that delivers capable armed forces within the limits of our resources."[171] In chapter 3, on Combat-Capable Forces, the authors of
the *1994 White Paper* wrote that Canada "must maintain a prudent level of military force" to be able to "deal with challenges to our sovereignty in peacetime,"
and "if and when required, in the defence of North America" in addition to challenges overseas.[172] In chapter 4 on the protection of Canada, the *1994 White
Paper* noted how, "taken together, the size of our country and our small population pose unique challenges for defence planners," and that despite the "dramatic
changes abroad," the authors argue that it "would be a mistake to dismantle their

capacity to defend our country. Canada should never find itself in a position where the defence of its national territory has become the responsibility of others."[173] Indeed, Canadian Forces must be capable of mounting effective responses to emerging situations at home, and thus:

> demonstrate, on a regular basis, the capability to monitor and control activity within Canada's territory, airspace, and maritime areas of jurisdiction; assist, on a routine basis, other government departments in achieving various other national goals in such areas as fisheries protection, drug interdiction, and environmental protection; be prepared to contribute humanitarian assistance and disaster relief within 24 hours, and to sustain this effort for as long as necessary; maintain a national search and rescue capability; maintain a capability to assist in mounting, at all times, an immediate and effective response to terrorist incidents; and, respond to requests for Aid of the Civil Power and sustain this response for as long as necessary.[174]

Providing "Aid of the Civil Power" had been required on dozens of occasions throughout Canada's history, when civil insurrection boiled to the surface of Canada's complex ethnic topology. And, as described in chapter 4 of the *1994 White Paper*: "The Canadian Forces may be called upon to assist civil authorities in situations other than Aid of the Civil Power. The Forces might, for example, be called on to counter acts of terrorism that exceed the capabilities of police forces. In addition to other military resources, the Canadian Forces maintain a special task force that provides an enhanced capability to respond to any such act immediately and effectively."[175] It further notes, "In recent times, the use of the Canadian Forces in this role has been comparatively infrequent. Nevertheless, the crisis at Oka in 1990 served to remind us that such situations can arise. The Forces played a crucial role in defusing the crisis. They demonstrated that the ability to call upon disciplined, well-trained, and well-commanded military personnel is invaluable in providing government with an effective means to deal with potentially explosive situations."[176]

The *1994 White Paper*, like the *1992 Defence Policy Statement* that preceded it, addressed the unique challenges of defending Canadian sovereignty over such a vast realm, noting that "taken together, the size of our country and our small population pose unique challenges for defence planners," as its "territory spans nearly 10 million square kilometres—fully 7% of the world's landmass," and is "bordered by three oceans which touch upon over 240,000 kilometres of coastline. We are charged with the control of our airspace as well as the aerial approaches to Canadian territory. Beyond our coasts, Canada seeks to maintain political sovereignty and economic jurisdiction over 10 million square kilometres of ocean in the Pacific, Atlantic, and Arctic."[177] It added that Canada's expansive geography "is not merely vast; it is also diverse and extremely demanding. It imposes significant burdens on our military personnel, their training, and their equipment. Canada's territory encompasses mountainous terrain, fjords, vast plains, rainforests, desert conditions, and the unique ecology of the Arctic. Our climate is harsh. Indeed, the economic livelihood of many Canadians is found in remote, difficult environments including three oceans, the North, and distant mines and forests."[178] But despite its harshness, and perhaps partly because of this, Canadians have a deep love for their country, and this love translates into a strong desire to defend its sovereignty across such a vast and resource-rich realm.

As the *1994 White Paper* described: "Canadians treasure their country, which is rich in both natural beauty and natural resources. They have made it clear to successive governments that they are firmly committed to the protection of both. They are concerned about environmental well-being in general, as well as the management of specific resources, such as the forests and fisheries, which have become urgent issues over the past several years and which will require renewed vigilance and enhanced management."[179] On Canada's sovereignty challenge in the post–Cold War period, the *1994 White Paper* explained:

> Sovereignty is a vital attribute of a nation-state. For Canada, sovereignty means ensuring that, within our area of jurisdiction, Canadian law is respected and enforced. The Government is determined to see that this is so. Some have argued that the recent dramatic changes abroad have eroded the traditional rationale for the role that the Canadian Forces play in the defence of Canada. It would be a grave mistake, however, to dismantle the capacity to defend our country. Canada should never find itself in a position where, as a consequence of past decisions, the defence of our national territory has become the responsibility of others.[180]

And while more than a decade would pass before concerns about global warming put the polar sea into play both diplomatically and strategically, Canada's defense planners foresaw the need to keep up their guard and not surrender its capacity to defend its sovereign territory, no matter how remote, thinly populated, or climatically extreme, right from the start of the post–Cold War period.

But with budgetary pressures, and a lag in perception as to the potential impact on the polar regions caused by climate change, Canada's defensive capabilities did begin to contract under the weight of shrinking budgets and reductions in forces, a situation that did not reverse course until after 9/11. The need to redouble its efforts to defend its sovereignty and ensure that its security remain protected was a theme that echoed throughout Ottawa's *2005 Defence Policy Statement*, its first formal, full articulation of Canadian defense policy since 1992. And while part and parcel of the ruling Liberal Party's policy platform on defense, when the Liberals lost power to the Conservatives in 2006, the new government brought along its own determination to redress what it portrayed during the campaign as a long neglect of Canada's northern security, and to redouble its efforts to defend its Arctic sovereignty. And yet the *1994 White Paper on Defence* had noted the importance of defending Canadian sovereignty across the land, including the ongoing conduct of peacetime surveillance and control:

> The provision of surveillance and control is an integral part of the Forces' activities in Canada. Even at a time when there is no direct military threat to Can-

ada, the Forces must maintain and exercise the basic navy, army, and air force skills to ensure effective control over our territory, airspace, and maritime approaches. In and of itself, maintaining the capability to field a presence anywhere where Canada maintains sovereign jurisdiction sends a clear signal that Canadians will not have their sovereignty compromised.

Responsibility for many of the Government's activities in the surveillance and control of Canadian territory, airspace, and maritime areas of jurisdiction lies with civilian agencies such as the Department of Transport. The Canadian Forces, however, make a valuable contribution to this demanding task, which often requires capabilities of greater readiness and reach than those available to civilian agencies. The capability to deploy highly trained Canadian Forces personnel and their specialized equipment anywhere in Canada at short notice also contributes to the attainment of national objectives in such areas as environmental protection, search and rescue, disaster relief, drug interdiction, and fisheries protection.[181]

Additionally, the *1994 White Paper* noted Canada's need to protect its fisheries, central to both its economy and its nutritional capacity.[182] Indeed, Canada asserted its naval power soon after issuing its *1994 White Paper*, seizing a Spanish fishing trawler in international waters in an effort to protect an ailing fishery that straddled the maritime boundary between Canada's territorial and international waters, thus putting in jeopardy a resource considered essential to Canada's economic and nutritional security. The result was an exercise in gunboat diplomacy described as the "Turbot War" of 1995, but which lingered on until 1997. As described on the Canadian Navy's Operations and Exercises web page, "Operation Ocean Vigilance" took place from 1995 to 1997 off the Grand Banks of Newfoundland: "Also known as the turbot dispute, this operation responded to the over-fishing of Grand Banks waters. Navy vessels were sent to observe Spanish fishing activity suspected of contravening fishing regulations. As a result, the Navy retrieved an illegal fishing net from seabed for the Department of Fisheries and Oceans, in a continued effort to protect Canada's shorelines."[183] According to an article in the *New York Times* published on March, 12, 1995: "Canada, acting unilaterally to protect depleted fishing stocks, has seized a Spanish trawler just outside Canadian territorial waters, in a confrontation with the European Union over North Atlantic fishing rights. 'You have chosen a government in Ottawa that will stand for Canadians,' Prime Minister Jean Chrétien told a cheering meeting of his Liberal Party in Winnipeg on Friday, a day after the trawler was seized off Newfoundland."[184] And as reported in the *New York Times* a month later: "Canada said on March 3 that it had the right to repel Spanish and Portuguese vessels even beyond its 200-mile territorial waters. On March 9, Canadian gunboats fired across the bow of a Spanish trawler fishing in international waters off Newfoundland, seized the vessel and diverted it to port."[185] And "Since that incident, Canada has cut the nets from one other Spanish trawler and tried to board a third. Tension along the Grand Banks has risen, with Canada threatening more such actions and with Spain sending a third patrol vessel on Thursday to protect its fishing fleet."[186]

Spanish Ambassador to Canada, José Luis Pardos, sarcastically wrote the following on the surreal high-seas showdown with Canadian naval might: "What a pity, indeed, that, contrary to some little turbot of our acquaintance, they did not have finger tips to cling to the sea bottom, waiting for a hero to save them at the 11th hour."[187] This was an interesting, albeit occasionally lampooned, display of Canadian sea power, and a seemingly uncharacteristically aggressive show of force for a nation perceived widely around the world to be a peacekeeping nation, particularly against a NATO ally. But when its national security was threatened as it was by foreign over-fishing, Ottawa remained fully committed to protecting its sovereignty, just as it would again be a decade later when its Arctic waters and undersea resources faced an emerging threat from foreign powers—in this case, Russia and Denmark. While Spain's Ambassador to Canada was surprised by Fisheries Minister Brian Tobin's aggressive response to the fishing dispute, had he more closely read Canada's *1994 White Paper on Defence*, he might not have been:

> Canadians have made clear their wish to protect Canada's fisheries from illegal and highly damaging exploitation. With the dwindling of major fish stocks, the issue has become more urgent. The Canadian Forces have made an important contribution to fisheries patrols for more than 40 years. The Department of National Defence and the Department of Transport now participate in a comprehensive federal effort, led by the Department of Fisheries and Oceans. The Canadian Forces will devote a significant number of flying hours and ship days to fishery patrols. This arrangement is a good example of interdepartmental cooperation yielding an efficient use of government resources. One of the most pressing issues in the current East Coast fishery crisis is that of predatory foreign fishing on Canada's continental shelf outside of our 200-mile exclusive fishing zone. Such fishing imperils the future of the fishery and contradicts the spirit of internationally agreed conservation measures. The Government has begun to take action against such activities.[188]

Protecting its fish stocks from predatory foreign fishing was but one objective amongst Ottawa's many defense priorities, which included environmental surveillance and protection as well, consistent with the general "greening" of its defense activities described in its *1992 Defence Policy Statement*. As explained in the *1994 White Paper*: "The Government has identified environmental protection as a major priority. It has emphasized the prevention of pollution and the promotion of 'green' practices in its day-to-day operations. The Department of National Defence and the Canadian Forces have been at the forefront of efforts to meet these goals. Indeed, all planning and operations (and this includes allied activity in Canada) are now designed with environmental stewardship firmly in mind."[189]

Chapter 5 of the *1994 White Paper* addressed Canada-U.S. Defence Cooperation, and recognized the importance and uniqueness of Canada's relationship with the United States, observing that "the United States is Canada's most important ally and the two countries maintain a relationship that is as close, complex, and extensive as any in the world."[190] It recognized that "potential challenges to continental defence remain," noting that "Russia retains strategic nuclear forces able to reach North America and a number of states have acquired, or are seeking to acquire, weapons of mass destruction and their means of delivery."[191] While the *1994 White Paper* did not anticipate Russia's renewed interest in Arctic resources and its potential to challenge Canadian Arctic sovereignty over a decade later, and does not explore the direct sovereignty challenges to Canada's Arctic waters presented by the United States in the past, it does consider the overall impact of its relationship with the United States on its security, finding that the defense cooperation relationship with the United States "continues to serve this country's fundamental interests extremely well."[192] The *1994 White Paper* observed that Canada will "maintain the ability to operate effectively at sea, on land, and in the air with the military forces of the United States in defending the northern half of the Western hemisphere," but noting the current climate of fiscal restraint, adds that "Canada will contribute to aerospace surveillance, missile warning, and air defence capabilities at a significantly reduced level."[193]

Chapter 7 of the *1994 White Paper*, on "Implementing Defence Policy," noted Canada's "new defence policy heralds a fundamental transformation of the way in which the Canadian Forces and the Department of National Defence will conduct their operations and do business in the coming years," adding that "most areas of defence will be cut. The relative weight of the naval, land and air establishments will be altered to allow for the transfer of more resources to where they are most needed—mainly to operational land forces. Everything is being made leaner. Everything is undergoing the closest scrutiny."[194] This fiscal reality, of budgetary restraint and a general downsizing of Canada's defense expenditures, was consistent with the worldwide "peace dividend" that followed the successful conclusion of the Cold War. With the Soviet threat gone, a fractured post–Cold War world presented less menacing threats, and while the world was no more peaceful, and in some places less so, the absence of an existential threat as posed by the Soviet Union during the Cold War led most western defense departments to reduce their budgets considerably, and it was within this budgetary context that Canada's contributed fewer financial resources to its northern defense operations in the immediate post–Cold War era.

The New Age of Mass Terror

It would not be until over a decade later that Ottawa updated its defense policy, with its Defence Policy Statement of 2005, "A Role of Pride and Influence in the World," part of Ottawa's effort to formally align Canadian defense policy with the complexities of the post-9/11 security landscape. As Minister of Defence Bill Graham noted in his introduction to the updated policy statement,

"This document represents significant change. It is the first review of Canada's defence policy in more than 10 years and it defines a new policy that is firmly grounded in the realities of the post–Cold War, post-September 11th world," and provides "the intellectual framework required to guide and shape the Canadian Forces to face the defence and security challenges of the 21st century."[195] He further explained that:

> The tragedy of September 11, 2001 proved to Canadians that we are vulnerable to the threat of terrorism and the spillover effects from failed and failing states. This policy, therefore, establishes the defence of Canada as our first priority. The Canadian Forces will be reorganized and retooled to tighten their focus on this primary mandate. The effective defence of Canada and North America has always required working collaboratively with the United States. We will build on the successful bilateral defence arrangements currently in place, such as NORAD. And we will seek to develop new, innovative approaches to defence cooperation with the United States, to better meet the threats to both countries.[196]

A summary of the *2005 Defence Policy Statement* presented on the DND website observed that "Canada's defence policy is at a defining moment," and that the "world has changed since the last defence white paper was released in 1994. The past decade has been characterized by failed and failing states, the emergence of global terrorism and the proliferation of weapons of mass destruction."[197] It further noted "an increasingly interdependent world has tightened the links between international and domestic security, as developments abroad can affect Canadians in unprecedented ways. Indeed, one failed state, Afghanistan, served as the breeding ground for the tragic events of September 11, 2001— events that brought home to Canadians the new reality of international terrorism striking in North America."[198] In order to be better prepared to respond to the world's new and pressing dangers, Ottawa pledged to "continue to maintain modern, combat-capable maritime, land, air and special operations forces," and that its military "will also need to become more effective, relevant and responsive. To that end, the Canadian Forces will concentrate on better integrating maritime, land, air and special operations forces to provide more 'focused effects' in operations—that is, the ability to deploy the right mix of forces to the right place, at the right time, producing the right result."[199] Further, Canadian Forces "will adapt their capabilities and force structure to deal with the new threats at home and abroad, including those that arise from the kind of instability that we have seen in failed and failing states. And they will enhance their ability to act quickly in the event of crises both in Canada and around the world."[200]

Mirroring efforts in the United States to modernize American forces through the process known as transformation, Canada similarly enunciated its own vision of "the transformation process on which the Canadian Forces are now embarked," including "adopting a fully integrated and unified approach to operations."[201] With the reality of the 9/11 attacks still fresh on their minds, the defense planners reiterated the continued commitment of Canadian Forces to performing traditional roles such as "protecting Canada and Canadians, defending North America in co-operation with the United States, and contributing to international peace and security."[202] Yet "within each of these roles," the policy statement explains that "significant change will take place," since given "the current security environment, the Government believes that a greater emphasis must be placed on the defence of Canada and North America. This will be our military's first priority. It will require the Canadian Forces to re-examine their approach to domestic operations. Most significantly, the Forces will now view Canada as a single operational area where the best available resources from our maritime, land, air and special operations forces can be brought to bear on a contingency, wherever it occurs."[203] Further, in "practical terms," the new policy explains,

> Canadian Forces will improve how they gather, analyze, integrate and use information gained from a combination of maritime, land, air and space surveillance systems, including satellites and unmanned aerial vehicles. They will also expand their presence—Regular, Reserve and Ranger—to respond more effectively to events across Canada, including the Arctic. . . . With demands of sovereignty and security in the North expected to increase in the next 10 to 15 years, the Canadian Forces will enhance specific capabilities for use in the region, including new aircraft and improved equipment for the Rangers. We will also consider the utility of basing search-and-rescue aircraft in the region. [204]

As has been the case since the *1992 Defence Policy Statement*, the Arctic is only briefly mentioned, though it is important to note that its presence in Canadian defense policy has been consistent, though it would take the more muscular approach to northern security of the Harper government in 2006 to really reprioritize the North within Canada's defense calculus. The *2005 Defence Policy Statement*, following in the tradition of past statements and white papers, briefly discusses the challenges of northern sovereignty and security: "The Canadian Forces have played an important role in asserting Canadian sovereignty in the North. Today, their activities include the work of Northern Area Headquarters in Yellowknife, the operation of the signals facility at Alert, overflights by our long-range patrol and Twin Otter aircraft, and periodic exercises. The Canadian Rangers, part-time Reservists who provide a military presence in remote, isolated and coastal communities in the North, report unusual activities or sightings, and conduct surveillance or sovereignty patrols as required."[205]

At the time of its writing, the *2005 Defence Policy Statement*, the primary strategic preoccupation was with state failure and the dangerous potential of leaving such threats unattended, as 9/11 demonstrated. Indeed, the introduction to the *2005 Defence Policy Statement* noted some of the challenges of the current period, and the dangers of the post–Cold War, and more particularly the post-9/11, era:

At the dawn of the 21st century, Canada faces a complex array of security challenges. The world remains an unpredictable and perilous place, where threats to
our well-being, our interests and our values persist. Failed and failing states dot
the international landscape, creating despair and regional instability and providing a haven for those who would attack us directly. Global terrorism has become a deadly adversary, and Canadians are now, in some ways, more indi-
vidually threatened than at any time during the Cold War. The proliferation of
weapons of mass destruction, whether to state or non-state actors, raises the
horrible prospect of massive civilian and military casualties. And intra- and in-
ter-state conflict continues throughout the world. These developments affect
Canadians as never before.[206]

The *2005 Defence Policy Statement* noted that in addition to protecting Canadians at home, the "Government also recognizes the importance of meeting threats
to our security as far away from our borders as possible, wherever they may
arise. Security in Canada ultimately begins with stability abroad."[207] It further
noted "while we need to be selective and strategic when deploying military personnel overseas, focusing on where our interests are at stake and where we can
make a meaningful contribution, the Canadian Forces must retain a spectrum of
capabilities to operate with our allies on international missions."[208] The particular risks and challenges presented by failed states are emphasized: "This is especially the case in failed and failing states. Canadians are proud of the role their
military has played in protecting people who cannot protect themselves, in delivering humanitarian assistance to those in desperate need, and in rebuilding
shattered communities and societies. The Canadian Forces will focus their expe-
ditionary capabilities on operations in these states, including in a leadership role
when it is in Canada's interest and ability to do so."[209] Both failed and failing
states "pose a dual challenge for Canada. In the first instance, the suffering that
these situations create is an affront to Canadian values. Beyond this, they also
plant the seeds of threats to regional and global security. They generate refugee
flows that threaten the stability of their neighbours, and create new political
problems for their regions. More ominously, the impotence of their governing
structures makes them potential breeding grounds or safe havens for terrorism
and organized crime."[210] Interestingly, if you look at Ottawa's formal articulations of defense policy throughout the post–Cold War era, you'll find a continuous, albeit somewhat taciturn, inclusion of Arctic sovereignty and security challenges. And at the same time, you see a continued focus on peacekeeping and
security-building operations and the lingering threat posed by failed states
abroad.

One continuous program designed to enhance northern security that has
maintained Ottawa's interest throughout is the budget-friendly Canadian Rangers program, which allows Ottawa to show the flag across its sparsely populated
Arctic frontier region while further developing its relationship with the Aboriginal people of the North, strengthening their partnership while at the same time
transferring greater powers of self-governance to the people of the North
through various processes including comprehensive land claims settlement and

implementation, Aboriginal self-government policy, and the unique programs and policies associated with the creation and implementation of the Nunavut territorial government. When viewed together, it becomes clear that Ottawa has not neglected its northern security challenges, though it did shift priorities away from external security concerns at the end of the Cold War, and toward domestic political development. But this nonetheless strengthened the body politic of the Canadian confederation, empowering the Inuit to play a greater role in the economic and political development of the North, the management of the region's resources, and thus strengthen Ottawa's sovereign claim to the Arctic region.

As discussed by Matthew Carnaghan and Allison Goody in their 2006 report to the Parliamentary Information and Research Service, *Canadian Arctic Sovereignty*, the "Canadian Forces Northern Area (CFNA) is headquartered in Yellowknife" and "comprises 65 Regular Force, Reserve, and civilian personnel." Its annual operations "include two 'Sovereignty Operations' (Army), two 'Northern Patrols' (flights of Aurora patrol aircraft, 10-30 'Sovereignty Patrols' (CFNA), and one 'Enhanced Sovereignty Patrol.'"[211] And as part of NORAD, Canada "maintains the chain of unmanned radar sites, the North Warning System (NWS)," and has launched Project Polar Epsilon to "provide all-weather, day/night (surface) observation of Canada's Arctic region" by satellite.[212] They add that as "part of Canadian Forces Transformation, CFNA will assume a greater command and control function," becoming "the 'Northern' regional headquarters of the new Canada Command in 2006," and that "within the CFNA, the Canadian Ranger Patrol Group provides a military presence in northern and remote areas by conducting patrols, monitoring Canada's northern territory, and collecting information. These part-time reservists comprise a significant element of Canada's northern presence."[213]

Ottawa's continued commitment to the Canadian Rangers program, from its reaffirmation in 1992 to its continued support for the program in later policy declarations in 1994 and again in 2005, demonstrated a willingness, indeed a creativity, in asserting its northern sovereignty, and providing an interface between Canadian Forces and the indigenous people of the Arctic, recognizing the importance of better integrating northern Aboriginal peoples into the social fabric of confederation and as an active contributor to the frontline defense of Canada's Arctic frontier. This has been discussed by P. Whitney Lackenbauer, an Assistant Professor of History at St. Jerome's University, University of Waterloo, and a widely renowned expert on the Canadian Rangers program: "Canada's vast northern expanse and extensive coastlines have represented a significant security and sovereignty dilemma since the Second World War. With one of the lowest population densities in the world, and one of the most difficult climatic and physical environments to conduct operations, a traditional military presence is prohibitively costly. As a result, the Canadian Rangers, a little-known component of the Reserves, have played an important but unorthodox role in domestic defence over the last sixty years."[214] He noted this reserve program, "managed on a community level, draws on the indigenous knowledge of its members, rather than 'militarizing' and conditioning them through typical military training regimes and structures. Embodied in its communities and peoples in isolated areas, the Canadian Forces continue to benefit from the quiet existence of the Rangers."[215]

Lackenbauer noted the Rangers are not a distinctly Arctic force, but that their "official role since 1947 has been 'to provide a military presence in those sparsely settled northern, coastal and isolated areas of Canada which cannot conveniently or economically be provided by other components of the Canadian Forces.' They are often described as the military's 'eyes and ears' in remote regions. The Rangers also represent an important success story for the Canadian Forces as a flexible, inexpensive, and culturally inclusive means of 'showing the flag' and asserting Canadian sovereignty while fulfilling vital operational requirements."[216] He cites Colonel Kevin McLeod, the former Commander of the Canadian Forces, Northern Area (CFNA), who explained that the "Centre of Gravity for CFNA is our positive relationship with the aboriginal peoples of the North, all levels of government in the three territories, and all other government agencies and non-governmental organizations operating North of 60. Without the support, confidence, and strong working relationships with these peoples and agencies, CFNA would be unable to carry out many of its assigned tasks." [217] As Lackenbauer himself explained, the Rangers "often represent the only CF presence in some of the least populated parts of the country, and serve as a bridge between cultures and between the civilian and military realms. The Rangers represent an example of the military successfully integrating national security and sovereignty agendas with community-based activities and local management. This force represents a practical partnership, rooted in community-based monitoring using traditional knowledge and skills, which promotes cooperation, communal and individual empowerment, and improved cross-cultural understanding." [218] He noted that "When Inuit members of the Rangers in Nunavut set out on exercises, they are members of their local and regional communities as well as representatives of the Canadian Forces. Their self-administering, autonomous patrols, rich in traditional knowledge and culture, allow them to represent both their peoples and Canada simultaneously."[219]

Lackenbauer understands the intimate connection and interplay between the Inuit and Canadian sovereignty aspirations and assertions in the Arctic, and views the Rangers as one of the threads connecting the two, a fragile thread sometimes overlooked in the South but one that in today's era of renewed Arctic sovereignty focus has been increasingly recognized: "First and foremost, Canada's sovereignty claims in the North rely partially on the idea of Inuit historic and contemporary use of the land and sea. "Canada is an Arctic nation," former Secretary of State for External Affairs Joe Clark explained in 1985, and "Canada's sovereignty in the Arctic is indivisible. It embraces land, sea and ice. . . . From time immemorial Canada's Inuit people have used and occupied the ice as they have used and occupied the land. . . . Full sovereignty is vital to Canada's security. It is vital to the Inuit people. And it is vital to Canada's national identity."[220] Lackenbauer believes that the Canadian Rangers "embody a partnership between peoples and ensure that Northern residents are represented on the front lines of Northern military operations," and cites a 2002 speech by former ICC president Sheila Watt-Cloutier that emphasizes the civic loyalty of the Inuit within the Canadian confederation: "Inuit are proud Canadian citizens and our commitment to the country is enduring; and Inuit will hold up the Canadian flag."[221] As Lackenbauer commented: "She used the Rangers as the prime example of how instrumental her people had been in exerting sovereignty in the Arctic. The Inuit would not tolerate being seen or treated, and would certainly not act, 'as powerless victims of external forces over which we have no control.' They were engaged, from the local to the international. The Rangers fittingly represent that the CF in the Arctic also has an indigenous face, and that security and sovereignty are priorities for all Canadians."[222]

Indeed, as the post–Cold War security environment evolved, and attention shifted from the strategic bipolarity of the Cold War era to the asymmetrical and complex strategic topography of the post–Cold War era, the first response after the collapse of communism and with it the military threat presented by the Soviet Union and its allies was to issue a peace dividend, and to scale back on military budgetary commitments until the abrupt wake-up call on 9/11 led governments to dig deeper into their pockets to fund their defense and security needs. The Rangers Program was inexpensive, requiring few big-ticket items, virtually no infrastructure, and only a modest budget; and it helped to consolidate Ottawa's claim to Arctic sovereignty by extending its commitment to a shared approach to managing and governing the region with its Aboriginal peoples. In short, it was the perfect solution for the immediate post–Cold War period when the economic strains of the prior years pushed many economies into recession, and new budget-balancing fiscal hawks entered into positions of power in the West, resulting in a widespread and deep-rooted aversion to expensive defense programs and in the initiation of a modernization effort guided by the principles of military transformation, enabling technology to lighten the military footprint in terms of manpower and expense while introducing laser-like precision and network-centric capabilities, thus preserving the West's military supremacy as demonstrated in both the first and, more than a decade later, the second Gulf War. Amidst such a climate, inspired by the metaphor of transformation, Ottawa's efforts to defend the North shifted toward a greater reliance on its largely indigenous militia force, the Rangers, just as northern governance itself transformed amidst the Nunavut land claims settlement and implementation on the one hand, and the birth of the Nunavut territorial government on the other.

Secession and State Failure in Canada

A curious parallel can be found in Ottawa's domestic Arctic policies, and its international policies with regard to the challenges of state failure. On the international front, Ottawa recognizes the dangers inherent in leaving state failure unaddressed and uncorrected, and thus works to combine "humanitarian assistance, stabilization operations, combat—all at the same time" and often within a few blocks of each other, in the complex, post-9/11 environment of the "three-block war."[223] As described in the *2005 Defence Policy Statement*: "Military experts have compared today's complex and chaotic operational environment to a 'three-block-war.' This term refers to the increasing overlap in the missions our personnel are asked to carry out at any one time and the resulting need for integrated operations. Our land forces could be engaged in combat operations against a well-armed militia in one city block, stabilization operations in the next block, and humanitarian relief and reconstruction two blocks over. Transition from one type of operation to another often happens in the blink of an eye, with little time to react."[224]

Along its northern frontier, Ottawa's approach is really quite similar. It remains committed to the domestic equivalent of humanitarian and stabilization assistance, through its ongoing effort at promoting the political and social development of Nunavut and the successful implementation of the Nunavut land claims agreement. And while at the moment the Arctic remains free of combat operations, the continuation of Ranger patrols, their contribution to coastal surveillance, the assertion of Canadian sovereignty, and to the strengthening of the relationship between the Aboriginal people of the North and representatives of the Crown and the Canadian Forces, fills a comparable role, as if Ottawa were applying the "three-block-war" metaphor to its northern front.

While the risks of international state failure, and the prospect of state failure in the Canadian Arctic, are not generally acknowledged nor linked together theoretically or doctrinally, the parallel has not gone unnoticed. Indeed, there are two dimensions where the domestic implications of state failure in Canada are relevant to the Arctic. First, there is the recurring issue of Québec's sovereign aspirations, as that restive province periodically maneuvers toward secession from Canada, and were secession to take place, it would dynamically transform the strategic environment of the Canadian Arctic. Second, there is the issue of localized state failure in the Arctic, where social conditions are reminiscent of many parts of the underdeveloped world where state collapse is a concern. This second dimension is contemplated in the work of Captain Alec Scott, who presented a paper on this topic, "A Failing State? The Canadian Forces' Role of Pride and Influence in Canada's North," to the Canadian Defence Academy conference on Aboriginals and the Canadian Military: Past, Present, Future, in Kingston, Ontario on June 21–22, 2006.

We will first examine the first of these issues, the evolving role of the Arctic in the event Canada itself fractures along the most likely fault line, that which separates Canada's original "two solitudes," Anglo-Canada and French Canada. While the focus of Prime Minister Harper's government has been on Canada's external security and the renewed strategic competition in the rapidly thawing Arctic where American, Russian, and Danish strategic interests collide with Ottawa's, in years past Ottawa's attention has been more focused on the unity of Canada and the potential secession of Québec, and on the reconciliation of Native and non-Native. But the role of the predominantly Native North in the event of Québec's secession from confederation is intriguing to consider, uniting in many ways these two strategic issues that have concerned policymakers for so many years, and which were both rooted in Canada's sovereign evolution, military and diplomatic history, and unique cultural origins. As many observers of Canadian politics have observed, the fragile relationship between largely Francophone Québec and Anglo-Canada has at times pushed the nation to the brink of breakup, with secessionists in Québec repeatedly pushing for independence, as they sought to do by referendum in 1995, missing their goal of 50 percent plus one by fewer than 30,000 votes. Out of more than 4.7 million votes cast, 50.58 percent voted "No" and 49.42 percent voted "Yes," with 1.82 percent of votes rejected, many without any obvious reason other than their being "No" votes in jurisdictions under the watchful eye of "Yes" supporters, resulting in an investigation by the Directeur général des élections du Québec who found some evidence of fraud, but only in isolated cases and not in sufficient numbers to have tipped the results to the "Yes" side. The defeat for the Parti Québécois (PQ) was a bitter loss, as reflected in the concession speech by then-Premier Jacques Parizeau, who said, infamously:

> My friends. It's lost, but not by much. But it's a success, it's a success in a way. If you could, let's stop talking about the Francophones of Québec. Let's talk about us. We'll talk about 60% of us. We voted for. We fought well, and we . . . we even showed clearly what we wanted. And we missed by a small margin, by several ten thousand votes. Well, in a case like this, what do we do? We spit in our hands and start all over again. I really wanted this to go through. I wanted it so badly, like all of you, that it would get through. We were so close to a country. Well, it's been delayed a little . . . not for long, not for long ... we won't wait 15 years this time . . . no, no . . . It's true, it's true that we have been defeated, but basically by what? By money and some ethnic votes, essentially. So all it means is that, in the next round, instead of being 60 or 61 per cent to vote YES, we will be 63 or 64 per cent and it will suffice. That's all.

While the issue has again receded, and the reconciliation between Québec and the rest of Canada appears back on track, the PQ continues to aspire for independence, and its party platform, adopted during the 2005 Parti Québécois National Council, includes holding a new referendum if it returns to power. But for the moment, that seems quite unlikely. But if Québec one day does secede, the area around the Hudson Bay and the Hudson Strait could take on a new military significance in relation to Québec's own ability to project power beyond its borders, and to defend its energy installations in Northern Québec. Furthermore, if Québec does secede, it may not bring its predominantly northern territories with it: Northern Québec and the adjacent Nunavut Territory could become an important theater for the containment of Québécois power by Anglo-Canada. Indeed, in anticipation of a victory by the "Yes" side in 1995, Aboriginal leaders in Québec began to assert their own right to self-determination, and to position themselves for either seceding from a newly independent Québec, or remaining in Canadian confederation at the time of Québec independence.

According to Jill Wherrett, author of the 1996 Parliament of Canada report, *Aboriginal Peoples and the 1995 Québec Referendum: A Survey of the Issues*, "In the debate surrounding the October 1995 Québec referendum and in subsequent discussions on the future of the province, Aboriginal issues have had a significant profile," and "most prominent among these has been the conflict over northern Québec, the traditional territory of the Crees and Inuit."[225] She observed that: "The Grand Council of the Crees (of Québec), under leadership of Grand Chief Matthew Coon Come, have been the most outspoken Aboriginal group. The Crees have asserted for many years that they are a people, with a right to self-determination recognized under international law. They argue that no annexation of them or their territory to an independent Québec should take place without their consent, and that if Québec has the right to leave Canada then the Cree people have the right to choose to keep their territory in Canada."[226] Indeed, the Crees "see themselves as a people bound to Canada by treaty (the JBNQA), and as citizens of Canada. The Crees have stated that a unilateral declaration of independence by Québec would be a violation of fundamental principles of human rights, democracy and consent. If secession were to proceed, the Crees argue they would seek protection through the Canadian courts as well as asserting Cree jurisdiction over its people and lands."[227]

> In the period leading up to the referendum, the Crees were active at both the domestic and international levels. A Cree Commission held 14 hearings in 10 different communities during August and September 1995.
>
> Its report, "The Voice of a Nation on Self-Determination," affirmed Cree opposition to secession without their consent, and restated their commitment to maintain a relationship with the federal government. In October 1995, the Crees released a study, *Sovereign Injustice*, which . . . emphasizes that Aboriginal peoples have a right to self-determination, including a right to stay in Canada. It argues that the forcible inclusion of the Crees in any future Québec state would lack validity and legitimacy from the viewpoint of international, Canadian, and Aboriginal law and practice. Such an action, the Crees assert, would also seriously detract from Québec's claims that it is resorting to fair or democratic process to achieve its goals. The study also argues that there is no rule under Canadian or international law that would ensure the present boundaries of Québec would become those of a sovereign Québec state.[228]

Indeed, Wherrett observed that "Québec's boundaries have been altered several times since Confederation in 1867," noting that:

> In 1870, Canada purchased Rupert's Land, which was inhabited by Inuit, Cree, Montagnais, Naskapi, Atikamekw and Algonquin, from the Hudson's Bay Company. Over the next few decades, Canada transferred portions of this territory to Québec. In 1898, Québec's northern boundary was set along the eastern shore of James Bay to the mouth of the Eastmain River, north along the river,

then due east to the Hamilton River and down the river to the western boundary of Labrador. In 1912, the vast territory bounded by the Eastmain River, the Labrador coast, and Hudson and Ungava Bays was transferred to Québec, extending the northern boundary to its present location. Cree, Montagnais, Naskapi and Inuit inhabited these lands. The Québec Boundaries Extension Act of 1912 included several provisions relating to the Aboriginal peoples of the territory: that the province would recognize the rights of Indians to the same extent as the government of Canada had recognized such rights and that the province should obtain surrenders to the territory in the same matter as the federal government had done elsewhere. The Act also stipulated that the trusteeship of Indians in the territory and management of lands reserved for their use would remain with the Government of Canada.[229]

Wherrett points out that the Cree study, *Sovereign Injustice*, "notes that portions of Québec annexed to the province in 1898 and 1912 constitute in large part the traditional territories of the James Bay Cree and other Aboriginal peoples, which were added to the province without their consent," and "concludes that the James Bay and Northern Québec Agreement provides for permanent federal obligations that could not be unilaterally undertaken by Québec."[230] Further, "to highlight their opposition to Québec secession, the Crees held a separate referendum on 24 October 1995. Cree voters were asked: 'Do you consent, as a people, that the Government of Québec separate the James Bay Crees and Cree traditional territory from Canada in the event of a Yes vote in the Québec referendum?' The Crees voted 96.3 percent to stay with Canada. Of 6,380 eligible voters, 77 percent participated in the Cree referendum."[231] She added that "Cree concerns over secession continue in the post-referendum period."[232]

Wherrett observes that the Inuit of Northern Québec have "also raised significant concerns over the future of their territory," and that "like the Crees, they assert the right to self-determination, and the choice to remain in the Canadian federation."[233] As well, like the Crees, "the Inuit held a separate referendum, on 29 October 1995," when Inuit voters were asked, "Do you agree that Québec should become sovereign?" And, "With about 75 percent of eligible voters casting ballots, 96 percent voted against Québec's becoming sovereign. This result was similar to the outcome of the vote carried out by the Inuit parallel to the 1980 Québec referendum, in which 94 percent had voted 'no.'"[234] Like the Crees, the Inuit of Northern Québec "continue to argue that they have rights to remain Canadian citizens and keep northern Québec within Canada, which are supported by section 35 of the Constitution Act, 1982 and the JBNQA. For reasons similar to the Crees', the Inuit opposed Bill C-110. They recommended that *the proposal be reconsidered, and if not, supported the adoption of an amendment identical to that put forward by the Crees.*"[235] Wherrett notes the "leaders of other Aboriginal peoples in Québec have also expressed their opposition to taking Aboriginal land out of Canada," noting that "in early October 1995, First Nations Chiefs, in a statement entitled 'Reaffirmation of Aboriginal Peoples of Québec and Labrador's Right to Co-Exist in Peace and Friendship,' articulated their resistance to the forcible inclusion of Aboriginal people in a new, independent state, arguing that it would be contrary to international law."[236] And "contrary to usual practice, many Aboriginal peoples exercised their right to vote, the exception being Mohawks of Kahnasetake, Kahnawake, and Akwesasne" who participated in an armed uprising in 1990. But "elsewhere, Indians registered a strong federalist voice," and "published referendum results show that more than 95 percent of Aboriginal peoples who participated in the referendum voted 'no.'"[237]

Québec officials, understandably, viewed things differently, and the "Parti Québécois position, as expressed in its sovereignty bill, is that Québec would retain its current boundaries in the event of secession."[238] Consequently, "in September 1995, Québec MNA David Cliche, then spokesperson on native affairs, argued before the Cree Commission on sovereignty that the province's borders could not be altered. He told the Commission that Québec does not require Cree consent to separate from Canada, and that Cree consent would be necessary only if changes were made to the James Bay Agreement. Otherwise, a separate Québec would simply assume Canada's responsibilities in the agreement."[239] Similarly, "during the referendum debate, Lucien Bouchard and Jacques Parizeau rejected claims that Aboriginal peoples have the same right to self-determination as Québeckers," and "asserted that under international law Québec has the right to maintain its current borders after secession. Once Québec was recognized as an independent state, Aboriginal peoples would simply be transferred to its jurisdiction."[240] Wherrett notes that "since the referendum, the Québec government has maintained its position that, in the event of secession, the province's territory could not be partitioned."[241]

Ottawa, however, has stood largely on the side of the Aboriginal community, and Wherrett observes that while "during the referendum debate, the federal government made few comments on Aboriginal issues," in May 1994, "Minister of Indian Affairs Ron Irwin stated his view that Aboriginal peoples have the right to stay in Canada with their territories if the province of Québec were to secede" and "in October 1995, Irwin told a meeting of First Nations chiefs in Ottawa that the federal government would protect Québec Aboriginal peoples and their territories if the province voted to separate, and repeated his position that Québec Aboriginal peoples have the right to stay with Canada."[242] She added that "the federal government entered more forcefully into the debate in early 1996. Commenting on a federal strategy in the event of a Québec vote to separate, both Intergovernmental Affairs Minister Stéphane Dion and the Prime Minister suggested that regions of Québec may be entitled to remain with Canada. Minister Irwin has also questioned Québec's right to the territory covered by the James Bay Agreement."[243]

With Aboriginal opposition to Québec's secession, federal support of the Aboriginal position, and Québec's determination to maintain its present borders, it is conceivable that in the event Québec does secede from Canada, civil war could break out in the North. With few roads connecting the northern communities to the southern commercial centers, and vast stretches of forested wilderness serving as a buffer between French Québec and the Aboriginal North, a newly independent government in Québec City might find it exceedingly difficult to wrest control of the Cree and Inuit communities from Canada's sovereign grip, especially as the strategic and commercial value of northern waterways offshore northern Québec increases due to climate change. The loyalty of the Aboriginal people of Québec would most assuredly remain with Ottawa, and this provides Ottawa with a strategic advantage in the event of Québec's separation. Already, there has been an increase in commercial shipping in the waters of Hudson Bay. The Port of Churchill in Northern Manitoba, which sits along the west coast of Hudson Bay, provides direct rail access to the sea from Canada's prairie provinces, the bread basket of the nation; and it has recently initiated trans-polar shipping to and from Russia through the Arctic Bridge project, and could become far more important strategically in the event of Québec's secession. According to the website of OmniTRAX, the company that owns and operates the Port of Churchill: "The Port of Churchill is Canada's only Arctic seaport, and is strategically located on the west coast of the Hudson Bay. The Port brings the world of ocean trade to the front doorstep of Western Canada. Churchill's unique location provides opportunities for the export of grain, manufactured, mining and forest products, as well as the import of ores, minerals, steel, building materials, fertilizer and petroleum products for distribution in Central and Western Canada."[244] The port features four deep-water berths, and is interconnected to the Hudson Bay Railway. As the Port of Churchill noted in a press announcement:

> Using the Port of Churchill eliminates time-consuming navigation, additional handling and high-cost transportation through the Great Lakes and St. Lawrence Seaway. The 2007 shipping season, which normally runs from July to early November, was the biggest in over 30 years. And, in mid-September, the Hudson Bay Port Company celebrated a first at the Port of Churchill when an empty Artic Supply ship which had just offloaded cargo to the Hudson Bay, was loaded with 12,500 tons of HBR-transported prairie wheat to be delivered domestically. On October 18, 2007 the port received its first inbound shipment in seven years and the first ever from Russia, a shipment of fertilizer imported by Farmers of North America. This shipment from Russia is said to be the beginning of an Arctic Bridge between the two countries.[245]

Shipping directly from Churchill, through Hudson Bay and Hudson Strait, could become a vital trade route to Europe in the event Québec secedes, which would in effect sever Canada in two, separating its agricultural heartland from its maritime provinces and their ports along the sea lanes to Europe. Its northern sea route from Churchill would enable Canada to remain economically independent, and to neither depend upon the goodwill of the United States, nor upon the newly independent Québec, to keep its current trade links to Europe. That would in turn put the Hudson Bay and Hudson Strait into play strategically, increasing the likelihood that Ottawa will endeavor to retain sovereignty over Northern

Québec, lest its shipping lanes become vulnerable to closure by Québec naval power.

Thus, partitioning Québec becomes a likely strategic outcome in the event of Québec's separation from Canada; indeed, the proposal made by Lionel Albert and William Shaw in *Partition: The Price of Québec's Independence* in 1980 was fairly well received. Scott Reid, in his *Canada Remapped*, observed that the Albert-Shaw proposal for partition is "the most influential partition plan." Summarizing the plan, he writes: "Albert and Shaw argue that if Québec attempts to gain independence, it should be deprived of about 80 percent of its territory. Québec's legal claim to most of this land, they believe, is founded solely upon the province's continued participation in Confederation. If Québec were to secede, it would forfeit its right to control the northern two-thirds of its landmass, as well as all land south of the Saint Lawrence River."[246] He notes that the authors "call for Canada to assume control of certain other areas of the province—the Outaouais, all of Montreal west of St. Denis Street, the north coast of the Gulf of Saint Lawrence—on the grounds that these areas contain sizable non-Francophone minorities and considerable numbers of pro-Federalist Francophones."[247] Reid observed that Albert and Shaw hoped their plan would dissuade Québec from seceding: "They would rather have a large province than a small country. That is why separation will not happen."[248] But Reid is not so sure of that, and he writes that Lionel Albert has revised his partition plan in response to the increased likelihood of Québec gaining independence. Reid examines three other similar partition plans that exclude the portion of Québec that used to be part of Rupert's Land. One is Kenneth McDonald's proposal, which, like the Albert-Shaw proposal, is "particularly harsh" in order to deter Québec's secession. Reid cites McDonald:

> Without Rupert's Land, without land access to the United States save through Canadian territory, Québec would be little more than an island state: Montreal, plus a quadrilateral roughly 650 miles by 250. . . . Such a sovereign Québec might still be economically viable—as Singapore is, as Taiwan is—but it's unlikely to appeal to many Québeckers when the alternative is to retain all of its present territory, and much of its present quasi-sovereignty, within the Canadian framework.[249]

Reid also examines the partition proposal of David Jay Bercuson and Barry Cooper in their book, *Deconfederation: Canada Without Québec*. This plan is similar to the Albert-Shaw plan, though slightly more generous to Québec. Unlike Albert and Shaw, their plan is not meant to be a deterrent to secession, and while Shaw and Albert suggest the French of Québec might "prefer a large province to a small country," Reid believes "the rest of us would be better off if Québec were a small country and not a large province."[250]

But Reid is most impressed by a partition plan proposed by David Varty, in *Who Gets Ungava?* which "examines the wording of the Act Respecting the North-Western, Northern and North-Eastern Boundaries of the Province of Québec of 1898, and the Québec Boundary Extension Act of 1912, as well as the meaning in law of the concept of sovereignty. His conclusion is that Québec would have no legal claim to the two sizable pieces of territory that were transferred to it in 1898 and 1912."[251] As Reid explained: "Varty's proposal is a refreshing change from the others; it tries to be reasonable. He suggests acting on partition within a legal framework, while most others seem to propose illegal seizures of territory."[252] This notwithstanding, can we expect Québec to willingly give up its northern territories, with their vast potential for hydro-power and mineral wealth? More realistically, we can expect Québec's separation—with or without Ungava—to cause a steep rise in tensions between Anglo, French, and Aboriginal cultures in the North.

One other partition plan that Reid looks at briefly is that of Ian Ross Robertson. Reid observes that Robertson's "real interest" is in "the establishment of a corridor of Canadian territory between Ontario and New Brunswick." Because there are so many Anglophones along the South Shore of the Saint Lawrence River, he calls for a narrow corridor, with "a width of thirty to fifty kilometers" along the U.S. border.[253] The problem with this corridor is that Québec would be in an ideal position to close the corridor, harass its English-speaking residents, and otherwise provoke problems between Ontario and the Maritime Provinces in an effort to drive the Anglophones out and create a more stable Francophone country. The vulnerability of the corridor to Québec intervention would make it even more likely that the Port of Churchill will become increasingly important—as will the defense of the Hudson Strait. Whether Ungava remains part of Québec or not, Québec's separation would force Canada to look to Ungava and Nunavut as regions where power must be balanced, borders secured, and Québec's influence contained. Especially if an independent Québec develops the capacity to project military power beyond its borders.

In *Security to the North*, Joseph T. Jockel contemplates this potentiality among three distinct scenarios of secession. The first independence scenario is for "Québec becoming 'sovereign' and negotiating an association with Canada which includes leaving defense in the hands of the Canadian government."[254] The second is "Québec becoming sovereign, with or without an economic association with Canada, and opting for the establishment of Québec armed forces," which "would protect the sovereignty of Québec's territory, airspace and possibly waters, and could undergird Québec diplomacy through the provision of token forces, while a Québec defense budget could be used as a form of economic subsidy, especially to the aerospace industry located in the Montreal area."[255] Jockel noted that the Parti Québécois calls for the formation of a "moderate armed forces (une armée de taille modérée), equipped with conventional, non-nuclear forces, which would have tasks of territorial protection and assisting the population in a natural disaster," which would be offered "for participation in United Nations peacekeeping operations" and to "maintain its commitments to NATO and NORAD, defensive alliances permitting the maintenance of a climate of stability and security which enhances disarmament initiatives."[256] The third scenario is "the breakup of the country into more than two sovereign states," with the English-speaking provinces going separate ways to pursue their own regional interests, a scenario Jockel considers "highly unlikely."[257]

However, this third and least likely scenario, which would see a true Balkanization of Canada, might be the scenario that would be most conducive for the formal restoration of Inuit sovereignty: if the western provinces pursue regional independence, and the maritime provinces become separate sovereign entities, the relative poverty of an independent Atlantic Canada and its need to protect the security of its new borders with an independent Québec might create an opening for Nunavut to break away as well, since the emergent mini-states of the former Canada will have their hands full securing their new frontiers and the territorial breadth of the Arctic might be beyond their capacity to defend. Thus this least likely scenario of a post-Québec Canada might be the most likely path for Nunavut to become formally independent. In the event of this scenario unfolding, Jockel believes the "United States would have to undertake itself all operations essential to the security of North America, including those located in Canada," as it is "hard to imagine that several Canadas would be able to manage, pay for, or coordinate coherent armed forces."[258] A singular Anglo-Canada would be much easier to manage than a multi-state fragmentation, though there would be "thorny command and control issues," and the need to make some big decisions with regard to air defense of eastern Canada, which is "conducted by aircraft based at Bagotville, Québec, with several aircraft from Bagotville on alert in Goose Bay, Labrador," that are all "controlled by Canadian NORAD region headquarters at North Bay, Ontario," and a "Forward Operating Location (FOL) for northern air defense operations . . . also located in Québec, at Kuu-jjuaq."[259] But since the North American Air Defense Modernization program, "there are no air defense radars located in Québec."[260] Air defense problems would thus "emerge readily," as the new sovereign nations figured out such things as "whose aircraft would be responsible for air defense operations in Atlantic Canada," and "would Québec build its own area defense control center" or instead "propose that North Bay become a joint Canada-Québec control center?"[261] And "inevitably there would be the NORAD issue," since it is likely Québec "would be eager for close relations with both the United States and Canada."[262] But it may be "very difficult for the United States to accept the tri-nationalization of NORAD," and Jockel believes "the interests of North American defense would be served" by Québec leaving air defense "in the hands of the United States and Canada" and by Québec "restrict[ing] itself to an army."[263] Because "North American air defense would be complicated by an active Québec role" after its independence, Jockel thinks Washington "should encourage it to leave North American air defense in the hands of the United States and Canada" but to also support Québec's "candidacy to be a signatory to the North Atlantic Treaty" and to "seek with both the Canadian and Québec governments ways to incorporate Québec in discussions of North American security."[264]

In the years since the nail-biter of a referendum on Québec separation held in 1995, Québec and Anglo-Canada have worked hard to patch up their differences, and on November 22, 2006, Prime Minister Stephen Harper preempted a renewed effort by Québec separatists to assert their enduring nationhood in a referendum that would unravel the Canadian confederation, and "surprised the House of Commons . . . by announcing his party wants to recognize Québec as nation within a united Canada. Harper said the party is putting forward a motion to recognize Québec's nationhood within Canada in order to supersede a Bloc Québécois motion that he says would virtually be a vote for separation from the rest of Canada."[265] For the moment, the issue of Québec's distinctiveness, and its yearning for independence, seemed to have been alleviated, but the perennial nature of this issue suggests it will resurface again, and when it does, the role of the Arctic as a potential strategic counter-balance to an independent Québec will have to be assessed. Within this context of Anglo-French relations and the recent move toward reconciliation, the strategic value of the Arctic as a potential counterweight to an independent Québec's military power has become somewhat diminished—but this does not mean these balance of power considerations should now be overlooked entirely.

Indeed, just as systemic changes allowed for a reduction of tension between East and West along their shared northern frontier during the 1990s just as it did along the old "Iron Curtain" along the East-West divide, a lasting rapprochement between Québec and Anglo-Canada would likewise pacify the potential maritime frontier along the Hudson Strait between Ungava and Nunavut, in terms of post-secession security concerns for both an independent Québec and the remaining Anglo-Canada, whether united or itself divided into smaller sovereign units. But in anticipation of a future secessionist threat from Québec, a tighter integration of the Inuit homeland with the rest of Anglo-Canada would enhance the loyalty to Canada of the people of the Arctic—and this can be achieved by a closer collaboration between Ottawa and Nunavut in their land claims implementation and co-management efforts, and through continued recruitment, training, and deployment of Canadian Rangers that patrol the Arctic coast, engage in surveillance, and assist in search and rescue in partnership with the crown.

But just as the aspiration of Québec to become independent will likely never entirely be extinguished, it is possible that a greater desire by the Inuit for independence might emerge. In Greenland, which is one of the world's largest islands, and which within the context of long-term global warming shows many potential attributes of sovereign independence; with its own language, a distinct culture, vast offshore and potential onshore resources, the case for independence, and the end to its colonial dependence on Denmark, is indeed compelling. For the Inuit of North America, who inhabit the coastal strip along the continent's northern shore as well as the islands further north, the issue is more complicated—owing to their habitation of the North American mainland where the United States and Canada have asserted formal sovereignty, and to the resolved nature of their land claims, through which the Inuit and the national governments mutually recognized one another, and agreed to subordinate tribal sovereignty to that of the state with whom they have partnered through a lengthy series of negotiations and the formal implementation of their final accords, which included "cede and surrender" clauses legally extinguishing Aboriginal title to their homelands. But just because the Inuit have entered into these binding, constitutional arrangements does not mean that they will always accept their legitimacy, particularly in light of the passionate reaction against the extinguishment clause, and what has been perceived by many Inuit to be a less than candid, or at least less than clear, explanation by their leadership of the full extent and implications of their surrender of Aboriginal rights and title. In the effort to sell the land claims as negotiated to the beneficiaries who must ratify the accords, Aboriginal leaders tend to understate the risks inherent in the surrender and to emphasize the benefits. As time passes, and in particular as the climate warms and the Arctic basin opens up to all manner of new external influences, challenges, and opportunities, the yearnings for more formal Inuit independence could begin to be felt. Especially if the bold and ambitious Nunavut experiment continues to disappoint the Inuit, and if the Inuit continue to perceive indifference, and at times bad faith, from Ottawa when it comes to implementation of their land claim accord.

As recalled by Andrea Mandel-Campbell in her January 2005 *Walrus* magazine article, "Who Controls Canada's Arctic?" if the Inuit "were indeed being used strategically during the Cold War, then Iqaluit, the capital of Nunavut, is perhaps the most enduring legacy of that American presence. The windswept town of six thousand is the site of a former US military base, which operated on-and-off between 1942 and 1963. Remnants of the base, including old hangars, are still used, and the former barracks now serves as a residence for Nunavut Arctic College."[266] She recounts how during this period, "Ottawa largely neglected the region's sparse aboriginal population, which suffered from rampant tuberculosis, lack of housing, and even starvation. The dire situation facing the Inuit forced St. Laurent to admit at the time that Ottawa had 'administered these vast territories of the north in an almost continuing state of absence of mind.'"[267] After Prime Minister John Diefenbaker launched "what became known as a golden age in Arctic science and research during the 1960s and 1970s," a general decline set in and since the 1980s, "Canada's underfunded programs in Arctic research have lagged behind most other northern nations," and "just as international interest in the Arctic is growing as a result of climate change, Canada's aging scientific infrastructure is crumbling, and a number of research stations have been mothballed."[268] Part of the problem, Mandel-Campbell writes, is that while Canada is an Arctic state, "most Canadians do live within one hundred miles of the border, and are more obsessed with U.S. trade and culture than a dwindling scientific and military presence in the North," and as a consequence, "the Arctic remains an imagined place far from their daily realities."[269]

The continuing perception of neglect, when combined with the historical grievance from broken promises, mistreatment, and cultural insensitivity during the 1950s relocation of the "High Arctic Exile" families, when further compounded by the despair experienced in the communities where shockingly high youth suicide rates remain a deep social wound, could become politically potent, and boil over to rage—and that rage, if no longer directed inward but instead becomes directed outward, toward the government and its neglect, could result in a bona fide independence movement. The seeds are already planted, as reflected in the Circumpolar Inuit Declaration on Arctic Sovereignty, which stopped well short of declaring independence but established a compelling legal, historical, and political context for one to later emerge—should the modern state fail to assert Arctic sovereignty in a manner that is respectful of Inuit values and inclusive of Inuit participation. When communism collapsed in Europe, many sovereign political entities that did not adequately or justly address the aspirations of their underlying nations, tribes, or sects—which had until then been content with increased autonomy within the modern state—quickly broke apart, fracturing into their constituent parts as they found sovereign expression in a smaller form. Many long-standing, internationally recognized constitutional frameworks and formal sovereign structures of governance evaporated—as if works of fiction.

Should Nunavut fail, and other Inuit regions—whether governed by municipal, territorial, or tribal systems of governance—continue to stagnate and to endure the persistence of despair, their failure could turn Canada's bold experiment in Aboriginal self-governance into a catalyst of a secession struggle, much as the original structures of the Alaska Native Claims Settlement Act—in particular the twenty-year window when exclusive Native title to lands and shareholder equity was at risk, and newborns were excluded from the claim—left many Alaska Natives with the perception that their land claim was designed either to fail, or worse, to eradicate Native culture, as chronicled by Thomas Berger in *Village Journey*. This fueled a Native sovereignty movement that swept like a prairie fire across village Alaska during the 1980s, culminating in an Inupiat secession threat in 1992, Alaska's very own Balkanization crisis.

So far, however, Inuit aspirations for independence have been largely episodic, ebbing and flowing without a sustained build-up of momentum, enabling decisive government action to preempt a formal independence movement—thus far at least. With the exception of Greenland, there is currently no active movement to form an independent Inuit nation, at least none that commands a significant political following. But that does not mean this always will be the case. In Canada, as in Alaska, the movements for secession have been thus far contained within the broader sovereign and constitutional framework of their countries. In Alaska, the Inupiat called for a fifty-first state, not their own country. And in Canada, during the formation of Nunavut, the Inuit seceded from the Northwest Territories to create their very own territory, while remaining a part of Canada—indeed helping Canada to more credibly assert sovereignty in the Arctic in the process. And with the formation of the North Slope Borough in Alaska, the Inupiat remained part of both the United States, and part of Alaska, with their own municipal authority but without their own state-level government.

Until now, the Greenlandic Inuit have remained part of Denmark, albeit with their own autonomous Home Rule government, with substantial authority on domestic issues and an increasing role in diplomatic and strategic affairs—with an eye to eventually gaining formal independence once they achieve economic self-sufficiency due to the effects of global warming, as evident in their decisive "Yes" vote in the November 26, 2008, non-binding referendum on Greelandic independence. But it remains to be seen if the Inuit aspiration for sovereignty and that of the modern state can remain integrated in a mutually reinforcing and balanced fashion, especially if the Arctic demographic balance begins to shift as greatly and as rapidly as seen in the Yukon during the Klondike Gold Rush, or like Alaska experienced during World War II and in the years preceding statehood, when a non-Native influx forever altered the political balance in favor of non-Native interests—or even more recently, as seen in Yellowknife during the Diamond Rush of the 1990s, with its indigenous Native majority becoming a minority in less than a single generation, making an indigenous assertion of sovereignty that much harder to implement. Even along the Arctic coast, where the Inuit maintain their demographic predominance, the larger administrative centers such as Barrow, Inuvik, Iqaluit, and Nuuk have seen a dramatic influx of non-Inuit, helping to fulfill the need for skilled workers to staff the positions in the new governments—as what some scholars have recently described as the "Aboriginal Industry" sets up shop purportedly to help Natives achieve self-government, but then becomes a permanent drain on the Arctic economy, siphoning off resources meant for the Inuit and desperately needed in the villages into the coffers of consultancies that ultimately contribute to a continued economic stagnation that persists at the village level, where jobs remain scarce, and marketable skills continue to elude local residents who long to participate as equals in the new, northern economy.

Even a decade after Nunavut was formed, a crisis persists, with hope in retreat and despair on the rise—requiring the attention of the highest levels of the Government of Canada, and the return of the famed retired B.C. Supreme Court Justice, Thomas Berger, to facilitate a solution. At a constitutional conference in Yellowknife in 1995, one Gwich'in leader noted in his remarks to the delegates that behind every chief, behind every tribal leader, stood a non-Native consultant. Fifteen years later, that situation remains unchanged—though a much-needed public discussion has at last begun, as awareness of the depths of this problem leapt into Canada's national consciousness in 2009.[270] Ironically, the movement for greater Inuit self-governance has unwittingly contributed to the declining demographic prominence of the Inuit in their homeland, as a new class of government administrators migrate north to fill the many positions left vacant owing to the continued lack of fully credentialed locals with the proper degrees and accreditations. Rather than adapt the new job descriptions to reflect the educational realities of the Arctic, and commit to on-the-job training to enable the creation of a truly Inuit government, Nunavut has become as dependent upon non-indigenous experts as the old territorial government the Inuit worked so hard to separate from. Berger has proposed a recommitment to the preservation of Inuit language and culture as the backbone of the new government, but his program requires a substantial commitment of new educational funds to be viable. In the meantime, Nunavut continues to be pulled in two directions, as the dueling assertions of state and tribal sovereignty continue to collide. Berger delivered the seventeenth annual John Holmes Memorial Lecture at the Glendon Campus of York University in Toronto on March 31, 2009, on the topic of "From the Mackenzie Valley to Nunavut: Northern Challenges," in which he noted "30,000 people live in Nunavut on a land the size of India," and "while 85 percent of its population is Inuit, only about 50 percent of government employees come from that background, doing mostly lesser-paying jobs. The problem lies in education, because there are not enough qualified Inuit to fill the jobs requiring higher skills."[271] Berger reaffirmed his belief that "Canada has an obligation to help the Inuit improve their situation and take their place in running their own affairs," adding that "societies find strength in diversity," and concluding that "we have an obligation to keep our promise to help them succeed."[272]

But add to this the new uncertainties and challenges of climate change, which could usher forth a new wave of migration of non-Inuit into the Arctic, and the situation promises to become even more complex—and finding a balance that reconciles the interests and sovereign aspirations of the Inuit and the modern state will become even harder to strike. Mandel-Campbell considers a solution proffered by Canadian Arctic sovereignty expert, and author of *Politics of the Northwest Passage*, Franklyn Griffiths, to overcome what he calls Canada's "two-faced approach to sovereignty."[273] As she describes it, Griffiths "advocates the establishment of a consultative committee for the archipelago similar in design to the Arctic Council, a Canadian-inspired international body, which brings together the world's eight circumpolar countries and aboriginal groups. The committee would serve as a forum for government departments to consult with the Inuit on such issues as shipping and seabed mapping. 'We should be taking the lead from the Inuit,' says Griffiths."[274] Such an approach is precisely what the Inuit have called for in their Circumpolar Inuit Declaration on Arctic Sovereignty at Tromsø, Norway, on April 28, 2009—where they reaffirmed their desire to achieve a synthesis of these two competing perspectives on sovereignty, and thereby find a balance in the sovereign aspirations of the Inuit and the modern state throughout the Arctic. Section 4.3 of the declaration observes, "Issues of sovereignty and sovereign rights in the Arctic have become inextricably linked to issues of self-determination in the Arctic. Inuit and Arctic states must, therefore, work together closely and constructively to chart the future of the Arctic."[275] As ICC chair Patricia Cochran explained, "We have lived here for thousands and thousands of years and by making this declaration, we are saying to those who want to use Inuit Nunaat for their own purposes, you must talk to us and respect our rights."[276] ICC vice-chair Duane Smith added that the declaration's provisions "make it clear that it is in the interests of states, industry, and others to include us partners in the new Arctic, and to respect our land claims and self-government agreements."[277]

Chapter Three

Toward a Synthesis of Tribe and State: Foundation of a Stable Arctic

The Canadian military's relationship with the people of the Arctic, and Canada's other remote littoral regions from Newfoundland to Vancouver Island, has developed through its long history of recruiting, training, and conducting field exercises with the Canadian Rangers to patrol its coastal frontiers, and to assist with search and rescue operations in these isolated regions. The Rangers Program has thus been an important point of contact between Canada and its Native peoples, instilling loyalty to Canada while enhancing local capabilities for territorial defense. This loyalty might, in times of crisis, play an instrumental role in securing the Arctic, whether against an external threat, or potentially an internal one should social conditions deteriorate to the point of armed rebellion. In the Inuvialuit Settlement Region, the Canadian Rangers have developed a network of committed Ranger militia members whose loyalties to their own regional leadership do not necessarily exceed their loyalties to crown and country, as seen during a dispute between DND and the Inuvialuit leadership over Ranger exercises planned to be held, but not approved, in the Inuvialuit Settlement Region in 1991. Dividing loyalties can, when properly balanced, effectively enhance the national interest, as the Romans well knew, preventing local tyrannies from becoming a threat. Alexander the Great realized this, keeping the threat of Spartan hegemony alive in order to help unite the weaker Greek states under the banner of Macedonian rule early in his reign. As Muktuk Marston realized in Alaska during World War II, northern Native people can play a very important role in the defense of the North from enemy attack—and an important sociopolitical role in breaking down old barriers between Native and non-Native.

Through the Canadian Rangers program, DND has been able to provide opportunities for Inuit who prefer to live on the land, something local leaders have been less than successful in developing through the corporate orientation of post–land claims decision-making structures. In Arctic Canada, the Canadian Rangers thus help strengthen the bond between the Inuit and the Crown—further solidifying the place of the Arctic in confederation, and further democratizing the Arctic, as we saw take place in Alaska, by fostering the emergence of an alternative power center to the private corporations that dominate the post-land claims environment, and which cast a tremendous influence over local politics. And, by jointly promoting the security of the Arctic, and reinforcing the sovereignty of the Arctic, while at the same time helping to preserve the traditional culture of the Inuit, the Canadian Rangers can help to redefine Arctic sovereignty in a manner that is at once compatible with Inuit traditions and with the objectives of the modern state. Such a cross-pollination can help to integrate Inuit concepts of human security with Ottawa's concepts of national security, and help to prevent the domestic equivalent to state failure in Canada's North.

One prescient military theorist, with an intimate knowledge of the Arctic and its many social and economic challenges, and of the Canadian Rangers program and its historical contributions to Canadian sovereignty and security, has called for just such a role for the Canadian Rangers. As noted above, Captain Alec Scott has explicitly made the connection between Ottawa's international policy with regard to state failure, and Canada's own internal challenges with regard to the human security of its indigenous peoples, who continue to live in poverty and in conditions that he perceives as comparable to those in parts of the world experiencing state failure.[1] He thus believes Canada's true Arctic imperative is to prevent state failure in Canada's North, and he believes the Canadian Rangers could prove essential in achieving this goal.

As Scott has written, "Canada's International Policy Statement on Defence asserts that the primary adversary in the new security environment is global terrorism supported and bred by failed and failing states," and "establishes an 'integrated strategy of using diplomatic, defence and development assets to help rebuild states.'"[2] He adds that the "Policy Statement goes further to assert that failed and failing states contribute to cycles of poverty, misery and violence, and that these conditions are 'an affront to Canadian values,'" and notes that "it condemns failed and failing states as having governments that are unable to maintain political authority, to provide security and other basic services, and to protect essential human rights."[3] And yèt, he points out that "in some ways, descriptions of these foreign failing states are hauntingly and disturbingly similar to the terms many use in dialogue about Canada's Aboriginal Peoples and their communities in Canada's Arctic and near North," where "poverty, truncated education, loss of language, unemployment, lack of adequate housing, suicide, marginalization, and loss of access or connection to the land are some of the biggies."[4] He further cites the Policy Statement on Defence, noting it "continues: 'the Government is committed to enhancing Canada's ability to . . . restore stability in failed and failing states," and "this will require a whole of government approach" by "bringing together military and civilian resources in a focused and coherent fashion.'"[5] He thus proposes "that we simply commit to do at home what we propose to carry out across the world."[6] As he clarifies:

> Now, I'm not proposing rolling a battle group into Resolute Bay, I am suggesting that the concept of defence and development working together can be just as effective at home as abroad. Why not? It says right there on page 11 that, "Our military will become more effective, relevant and responsive, and its profile and ability to provide leadership at home and abroad will be increased." I think this is especially true in the context of security, sovereignty and stability. And I must add that, to me, security, sovereignty and stability are inextricably joined, and each contributes to the other.

> Stability is perhaps the key concept here. In Afghanistan, stability is the cornerstone to creating a safe environment for rebuilding. The CF contributes to stability there by supporting local authority and demonstrating commitment to an end result. Domestically, the CF is already contributing through assistance to other government departments, most notably in anti-criminal and natural disaster response deployments. These high profile and conditional domestic operations have deservedly brought praise and attention to the CF at home, but perhaps only scratch the surface of the real day-to-day threats to Canadian safety and security.[7]

Scott cites a 2006 Conference Board of Canada report, *Facing the Risks: Global Security Trends and Canada*, which "forecasted that in the next 15 years, 'Health and social issues could be the most important human security challenges for Canada. These challenges will pivot around marginalized groups and individuals. The gap between the living conditions of Aboriginal People and the rest of Canada will still exist and in many areas it will widen. . . . The consequences of their vulnerabilities will generate wider social ills that will affect all Canadians.'"[8] He also cites Berger's March 2006 *Conciliator's Report on the Implementation of the Nunavut Land Claims Agreement*, in which Berger noted: "Nunavut today faces a moment of change, a moment of crisis. It is a crisis in Inuit education and employment, a crisis magnified by the advent of global warming in the Arctic and the challenge of Arctic sovereignty. . . . Inuit leaders are deeply concerned that the housing, education, health and suicide situation have reached crisis proportions..."[9] And he refers to "themes in the Royal Commission on Aboriginal Peoples that talk about severe disruption to Aboriginal culture, community and economics, marginalization, and denial of land and natural resource bases."[10] Scott observes that "most poignantly for those of us working with youth are the overwhelming statistics on suicide in Aboriginal and especially Northern Aboriginal communities," and to this he adds, "Through my little window this is a distant early warning that our state government is failing to provide basic services."[11]

Scott suggests Canadian Forces may play a "constructive role in restoring stability in this potentially failing state" by "walking the walk," and cites the 2004 National Security Policy: "There can be no greater role, no more important obligation for a government, than the protection and safety of its citizens."[12] Looking to some of the new measures to defend Canada's Arctic sovereignty, he explains that "satellite monitoring of the northern land and waterscapes is like the new roof," while "surface and subsurface radars on the Northwest Passage are like new doors and locks. All very nice and shiny, but remember those waves rolling in day after day? The foundation to security and sovereignty in the North and near North are the people who live there. And the waves keep pounding against these people without pause and in some cases with increasing harshness and effect."[13] Scott believes that Canadian Forces must thus "be diligent not to simply project 'security' as a net over the North using aerospace and southern-based military assets," but "must develop a long-term collaborative and inclusive strategy that is influenced by Aboriginal principles of security and participation in defence. It needs to stand by a firm commitment to enhance and sustain the role of Aboriginal Canadians in the defence and sovereignty of the North. To quote John Merritt from Inuit Tapiriit Kanatami: 'Building sovereignty means building hope.'"[14] As Scott elaborates: "Following the Defence policy intent of using current assets in new and innovative ways, this stability strategy involves the CF members who are already living in Canada's North and near North—our Canadian Rangers. Rangers are already well celebrated across Canada and the CF for their historical and current contributions to the efforts of the CF in 165 communities from Newfoundland and Labrador, to Ellesmere Island, to Vancouver Island."[15] He added that much of the effort of Canadian Forces to demonstrate "control and use of the unpopulated areas of the Arctic archipelago" has been through "Ranger long-range patrols. Many community emergencies, from lost hunters, to mass evacuations or natural disasters, have seen Rangers respond as CF representatives or community members."[16]

As a consequence, Scott finds that "investments in the Canadian Rangers have always been dollars well spent," as "the organization has a low overhead, flexibility of construct, and a proven track record in engaging people from coastal, remote and isolated communities," and also "has the highest participation rate by Aboriginal people of any component of the CF, so much so that the Aboriginal members easily outnumber the non."[17] Accordingly, he explains:

> The list is long of those who sing their praises for the Rangers' knowledge of the land and water. Let's return for a moment to our patch of sea ice I talked about earlier. Rangers have lifetimes of experience passed down to them about this ice—when it is safe to cross, when it breaks up, etc.—they would usually be the ones to show us our path across. But lets not forget that things are changing around us on this ice. Cracks are forming, ice is melting, gaps between the floes are getting larger, and our snowmobiles have a lot more miles on them if you know what I mean.[18]

Scott notes that the Rangers' mission was "structured after Cold War conventional threats, and retain tasks very much relevant to that era of strategy and operations," and argues that their "reason for being as the watchers, ever vigilant on the shore or on the tundra, is slowly melting with the ice cap. A transformation is required here to align with the rest of the CF in operational orientation and relevance to Canada and Canadians."[19] As well, what the Rangers are "also facing now are growing gaps in technology, and other tools, between them and the rest of the CF," as well as "limits of 6-10 days of employment a year, with the chance that staff shortages, weather delays, or regular employment obligations may mean missing a year's training."[20] Scott believes that it's "nearly impossible to derive a collective identity without regular and cumulative training and education opportunities," and "while Rangers have always prided themselves on not needing training, as they arrive at the Patrol with the prerequisite on the land skills, a significant risk has been created that lack of a common understanding and inability to act in integrated environments suggests that Rangers will continue to be denied access to positions of control or influence in their own component. The Canadian Rangers currently is the only component of the CF where a member cannot be employed in their own chain of command at a headquarters."[21]

Further challenges include the impact of "compulsory education over the last 25 years—this means, for example, the youth can use computers, but have not spent their childhood on the land in significant terms," bringing a "growing risk that the traditional skills that have brought honour and employability to the Rangers for the last 60 years could be fading."[22] Captain Scott recommends that Canada "reinvest in these traditional skills" as "both a strategy to sustain the profession of being a Ranger, and more importantly . . . to return a condition of value to the skill sets." He describes this as a "conscious and focused effort to promote and support stability in a mixed wage economy. It is getting more people active on the land, where their language was created and thrives. It is reinforcing the people who are already voluntary members of the CF."[23] He believes that the "Rangers should continue to carry out their primary tasks as they now exist—essentially the Neighborhood Watch for the North and coastal regions. Added to this should be direct support for on the land training and experience, and a significant improvement in access to technology. Professional development and job aids must be provided to enhance and sustain Rangers' leadership role for the Junior Canadian Rangers Programme."[24] That's because "an active and valued Ranger Patrol in a community also contributes heavily to community stability," and "in many communities in the North and near North, the hunters are the ones who can afford the time and resources required to get out on the land or water—many cannot afford it. A Ranger strategy that acts in a similar fashion to Hunter Support Programs in Northern Québec may increase the duration of on the land activity as well as increase the amount of country food returning. Also, through direct support, Rangers will be able to undertake more activities under their own leadership and initiative, leading to more consistent and authentic results."[25]

Scott probes further, and finds that "digging down to the next level, it means reviewing the philosophical basis of Duty with Honour to ensure that the 'Canadian Values' that direct the military ethos reflect the values of Aboriginal Peoples, and that 'Western thinking on the nature of the profession of arms' is moderated by Aboriginal thinking on the hunter-sentinel-warrior—an element of a culture that has not evolved in the same social/political construct. It means honestly examining a structure of a component of the CF that has separated geographically and by component the officer and NCM corps—a structure that shares perhaps too much with a colonial past."[26] Captain Scott adds that "concurrently, reaching out across government and even private sector—General Hillier calls this the Team Canada approach—to coordinate and focus efforts and effects is crucial. Increased Ranger stability can act as a force multiplier in many other social, cultural, and economic initiatives. Rangers are also community and business leaders, elders, and/or active citizens in their own right."[27]

Scott concludes that "when we do traverse this formidable new environment of transformation, and have adopted an innovative 'walk the talk' strategy for domestic operations, there is also a side effect—we have created a valuable working model for the CF to engage other Aboriginal People in voluntary service in the CF. By creating meaningful participation in a valid and relevant component of the CF, close to home, and in an environment that embraces and values traditional skills, knowledge and military heritage, we will have a formula for success in applications like basing Primary Reserve units on First Nation Reserves. From active participation in the Reserves, the jump is very small to the Regular Force."[28] Adds Scott: "You cannot escape the conclusion that 4500 more active and engaged Canadian Rangers in 165 communities across Canada will have a tremendous impact, especially in areas of highest socioeconomic risk. In fact, it will have much the same impact and long-term value as CF missions and efforts in Afghanistan. This defence and development approach will create and sustain the Canadian Forces' Role of Pride and Influence in Canada's North."[29]

A Renaissance in Tribal Sovereignty

There is indeed a harmony of sorts between the skills required for national defense and those required for survival and subsistence through hunting in the Arctic environment—good tracking skills, excellent marksmanship, strong survival skills on the land, keen eyesight, and the ability to operate with stealth. Alaska's legendary frontier military strategist, "Muktuk" Marston, the state's equivalent to Lawrence of Arabia who created a "Tundra Army" to defend Alaska from an anticipated Japanese attack of the mainland during World War II, nurtured these common bonds, creating the Alaska Territorial Guard, and providing Alaska Natives with an organization through which they could develop new skills, self-confidence, and leadership. As noted in "Native Americans in the Military," in World War II, "the Alaska Territorial Guard—commonly known as Eskimo

Scouts—faithfully patrolled 5,000 miles of Aleutian coastline and 200,000 miles of tundra, rescuing downed U.S. airmen." The ATG was organized by army major Marvin 'Muktuk' Marston, who "organized the Eskimo Scouts, Alaska's tundra army, at Nome and other areas, to defend Alaska against attack," and "since 1949, the Army National Guard has retained scout battalions in rural Alaska. These units, largely comprised of Alaskan Natives that were residents of their respective rural areas, have been referred to as the 'eyes and ears of the North.'"[30] Further, the Scouts were the only members of the National Guard who had "a continuous active duty mission," and:

> Scouts currently patrol ice flows in the Bering Straits, monitor movements on the tundra, and perform Arctic search and rescue efforts as required. With the dissolution of the Soviet Union in the early 90s, the necessity for scout battalions was significantly reduced. The National Guard, when forced by the end of the Cold War to re-examine the mission of the guard in rural Alaska, decided to convert the scout units to more conventional support battalions.[31]

As former Adjutant General of the Alaska National Guard and past chairman of the Alaska Federation of Natives, John Schaeffer has observed, these skills helped shape the prior generation of Alaska's Native leaders who spearheaded the Alaska Native Claims movement. Schaeffer credited the Territorial Guard as the birthplace of the movement for Alaska land claims and Native political independence in Alaska can be traced in part to the local armory of the Territorial Guard: the discipline, respect for the land, and increasingly color-blind meritocracy of the armed forces proved a good match for Alaska's Inuit. Many Alaska Native leaders from the 1960s, who pushed for the first comprehensive land settlement in the North, look back with fondness and pride on the spirit of independence that their military experiences nurtured.

General Schaeffer saw the Alaska Territorial Guard as an important incubator for Alaska Native leadership, and as powerful tool to help cement the relationship of the Native community to the federal government, and to provide important leverage to counterbalance the continued efforts by the state of Alaska to assimilate, marginalize, or otherwise disempower Alaska Natives. Schaeffer was serving as the chairman of the Alaska Federation of Natives and a delegate to the 1992 Inuit Circumpolar Conference general assembly in Inuvik, where the Inuit leadership endorsed a motion from the Alaska delegation on their desire to further study the idea of secession from the state of Alaska, and to form their own fifty-first state in the Union—much like the Inuit of the Northwest Territories would later do in forming Nunavut.

Schaeffer attributed the intensity of the sovereignty movement to the policies and attitudes of the state government in Juneau. "I'm not the only Native in Alaska that's getting disillusioned with the quality of government," said Schaeffer, "We don't see anything but continued repression. Especially by the state."[32] The problem, he said, was that the state was primarily concerned with the rights of individuals—which is "easy to do when most individuals in Alaska are non-Native." He explained that "states exist primarily to support individualism," but "as tribal groups, we're not primarily interested in individual rights: We're always coming into conflict with laws that protect individual rights." That's why, he explained, the North Slope Borough commissioned a "special study about a fifty-first state . . . to ensure self-government for our people. Things are not getting better: We're facing even more pressure from other interests in the world."

Schaeffer categorized the sovereignty movement that swept across tribal Alaska into distinct components that he believed were, in essence, "different movements." The first movement sought "tribal government under the Indian Reorganization Act," which was passed by the U.S. Government as a way for the "federal government to control Native people." However, he noted that since ANCSA was passed in 1971, there had been "only a few IRA governments" in Alaska, though "there were lots before '71." The second movement sought to "use existing structures like borough governments," as allowed under the Alaska constitution. "They are expensive—and need a tax base," added Schaeffer. The borough model worked "okay in North Slope Borough with oil," and "the Northwest Arctic is another" where that structure has proved compatible with Native aspirations and available resources. But most of Alaska's other rural regions are poor, and thus could not support a borough government financially, lacking their own tax base. Schaeffer said the third movement sought a distinct "state structure, if not more," as proposed by the Inupiat in 1992, and at earlier times in their struggle to regain land rights and to re-assert their sovereignty over the North Slope, which meant to secede from the state of Alaska and form a separate state for Alaska Natives much like the Inuit of Nunavut did when they seceded from the Northwest Territories. "The idea surfaced out of frustration with the state and its handling of subsistence," Schaeffer observed, but "there exists skepticism among non-Natives" about the idea's viability. Nonetheless, the state of Alaska took the "sovereignty challenge seriously," and within the Native community, at a recent "leadership retreat there was lots of support, even in Southeast."

Schaeffer found that the areas where the support was strongest for establishing a fifty-first state were the "three areas that have youth" included as new shareholders—the Nana, Doyan, and Arctic Slope regional corporations. The involvement of youth in the corporate structure had infused into these regions the ideals of independence, making them "the biggest supporters of a new state." Schaeffer noted that the Governor and state officials, including the Attorney General, were "talking about it," and that the state's Attorney General recently visited the North Slope to hold a hearing on Alaska's sovereignty challenge. "We've exhausted the 'Autonomous region within the state' concept, but we're beyond that." Schaeffer believes that Alaska Natives were "open to debate" about what their future state would look like—and whether it would resemble a separate state of the union, a self-governing territory, or a commonwealth. "What you have here is a concept that's being embraced by a good part of the

Alaska Native leadership." Schaeffer described the Native leadership as "political realists" that have sought to "do what's possible within the confines of existing structures," like the borough and municipal government structures allowed under the state constitution, and the corporate structures established by ANCSA. But many Alaska Natives desire something more sovereign: "This is the first time," Schaeffer pointed out, that Alaska Natives have been "able to voice this kind of desire," which he recalls "wasn't an acceptable concept in the 1960s and 1970s" when Alaska Natives were "just grappling with independence." But the ideas of utilizing existing structures, as favored by the political realists, "isn't enough" according to many Alaska Natives who aspire to greater sovereignty, and doesn't "take care of what we need." One of the problems with existing structures, like the corporate model established by ANCSA, is that they favor continued assimilation of Alaska Natives: "Alaska and the U.S.—they want integration. It doesn't matter what they tell you. In the United States, it's not okay to be different."

Schaeffer recounted how Alaska's Native leadership was shaped to a large degree by the military's presence in the state—which established a kernel of leadership that survived the cultural pressures of the missionaries. Schaeffer described a "positive part" of the Native experience with the U.S. Military as "the re-establishment of Native leadership," as "Non-Natives, missionaries, took away Native leadership." But the Alaska National Guard, and its predecessor, the Alaska Territorial Guard, created by "Muktuk" Marston during World War II, "established armories—places for the Native leadership to meet," and "out of that came leadership. Political, land claims leadership" emerged from the independence-minded Native leaders trained by the Guard. Schaeffer recalled how he told Muktuk Marston that the impact of the Guard on today's Native leadership was significant, greater than Marston himself expected: The armories were "the only place to train leaders," and it was there that they were "given the opportunity to lead again." After WWII, "almost all leaders in western and northern Alaska came out of the Guard, a whole generation of leadership."

At various times, Schaeffer said, the idea of a separate state had come up in Alaska Native community, rooted in the chronic inability of Alaska Natives to "get along with the non-Native community." Alaska Natives were "courted by courts and the present administration," but there remained an "inability of the state structure to deal with us on an equitable basis," as "we believe in diversity," and "we choose to be Inuit instead of melting into the hodgepodge." Politically, Natives had been "frustrated by 'one man, one rule.' 500,000 whites move in and dictate to us how to do things. The frustration is just beginning." How far might this frustration one day lead? And, is it feasible that a secession movement could be waged to achieve formal Native sovereignty rather than merely synthesize Native and national concepts of security? In the early 1990s, Schaeffer did not think this was likely—but over the longer run, he believes the idea is plausible. Already, "the Native leadership has been given permission to use civil disobedience if it is necessary to get our point across—we never had that before," noted Schaeffer. In the past, civil disobedience was rarely used in the North—though on isolated occasions, such as during the famous "duck-in" that challenged federal restrictions on the subsistence harvesting of migratory fowl, it was successfully employed. Generally, however, Schaeffer has found that "it was not our style," despite the largely pacific outlook of the ICC. But during the sovereignty movement in the 1990s, "it just came out"—as if from thin air—and was "never considered before. We didn't riot, burn cars, not our style. Giving us permission to break the law is a radical move for our people. Of course, we haven't used it yet. But the people have given us that authority if we want it." At an intellectual level, Schaeffer said Alaska Natives were not historically well informed about nonviolent civil disobedience as a tactic for achieving freedom and independence: "Alaska Natives don't even know Gandhi and King. We used the legislature, courts—other backroom tactics" rather than street protests and other traditional methods of nonviolent resistance. One thing was becoming clear, however, according to Schaeffer: "An alternative is needed. One man one vote works against us," especially as the state of Alaska's non-Native population now dwarfed its Native population, with a five-to-one demographic majority. If it came down to a military show-down, Alaska Natives are well ahead of Native people elsewhere in the Americas, Schaeffer believes, as there are "hordes of the people that could be trained" by veterans of the Territorial Guard experienced in combat, with military training dating back to the Second World War, and more recently through the Alaska National Guard's scout battalions that have replaced the old Territorial Guard.

As noted on *GlobalSecurity.org*, the Alaska National Guard (AKNG) has two main units, the Air National Guard, with bases near Fairbanks and Anchorage and a largely urban and hence non-Native membership, and the Army National Guard, the latter with 116 armories, and a presence in 88 communities and bases in 76 of them, with most members in rural parts of the state and predominantly Native. Three of the units are known as scout units, and the scout battalions have detachments across village Alaska, and provide around half the state's manpower to Alaska's Army National Guard. As further described by *GlobalSecurity.org,* "The AKNG is charged with both a state and federal mission. It provides search and rescue operations and a host of other community support operations such as rural medevac, natural disaster preparation, civil disorder preparation, law enforcement support, Reserve Officer Training Course (ROTC), Junior ROTC, and ChalleNGe Youth Corps Program. To meet its federal mission of augmenting the active Army and active Air Force in time of war or national emergency, it must meet the same readiness criteria as the active Army in personnel, training, maintenance and worldwide deployability."[33]

Schaeffer described Alaska's scout battalions as "elite forces, with guerrilla warfare tactical training." Schaeffer explained that during World War II, the Alaska Territorial Guard, a militia, was formed by the Army with 3,000 plus Eskimos and Indians. It was disbanded in 1946. But he observed that in many Eskimo villages, "they kept meeting, kept weapons and uniforms." Then, at the dawn of the Cold War, in 1949–50, the Alaska National Guard formed, with the old Territorial Guard as its nucleus. By the 1990s, Schaeffer noted there were "three battalions of around 1,500 Natives," composed primarily of Yu'pik, Inupiat, and some Athabaskan companies. "In Alaska, they are part of the National Guard. Same pay structure and training," and "their missions are part of the forces assigned to the Pacific Command," with the Scouts playing an active role in search and rescue (SAR) "for everybody"—from the Air National Guard to the Coast Guard. Schaeffer added that the Scouts "have a battalion headquarters, their units are scattered, with a minimum of fifteen per village," and some "bigger units with fifty to sixty" that are "organized in a cellular organization like the Special Forces, with five-man teams." According to Schaeffer, "the headquarter teams can run any number of scout teams," and "they have airlift with Twin Otters, and two Black Hawks," as well as "ground vehicles, Swedish tracked vehicles—three per company, fifteen in each battalion. The Scouts are mobile, not on foot," and "each scout team has two snow machines." They are also "equipped with M-16 rifles, one grenade launcher," and "in every two-man team, there is one sniper in general. Each group has an M-60 machine gun." As Schaeffer described the Scouts, "they are heavily armed for a light patrol meant for surveillance," and "each scout team has a boat, to travel between communities and conduct SAR. There are communications, radios set up in each village armory, portable equipment, the latest available to the military." An outpost was even maintained on Little Diomede Island to "provide intelligence along the border" with the Soviet Union. The Scouts were "able to provide this very cheaply compared to regular troops."

In all, the Scouts seem to be very well armed and equipped when compared to the Canadian Rangers in Canada, who lack virtually all of the heavy equipment the Scouts have, and who are armed largely with Lee-Enfield, World War I–style rifles. Because Alaska is adjacent to Russia, and during the Cold War served as both a vital strategic buffer and a forward theater between the United States and Soviet Union, the Scouts were considered important to the national defense—and were accordingly integrated into the U.S. military, with top-of-the-line equipment and state-of-the-art training. But until the sovereignty show down in the 1980s and 1990s, such capabilities weren't of immediate tactical value, "because," as Schaeffer explained, "we're not that type of people. We haven't considered small demonstrations, let alone anything else." Indeed, before World War II brought the reality of armed violence into the Arctic theater of operations, Schaeffer said the idea of war had been foreign to most Inuit: "We were told they shoot at human beings: I hunt seals, but to shoot at human beings?" However, Schaeffer acknowledged that he himself had "threatened to use force when the state tried to ram roads down our throats" into the isolated Northwest of Alaska. "Even I threatened to blow up equipment if the state tried to build a road in our area." As for acquiring weaponry for the conduct of military operations, Schaeffer pointed out that Alaska is a virtual supply depot. "We know where the weapons are," noted Schaeffer. "They are easy to get in stores, through legal access." In addition, there are the military weapons caches deployed throughout the state for use by the National Guard. Schaeffer also believes the elite skills of the Scouts could prove useful: "The way we train in Scouts," he explained, to operate "with a minimum distance of 800 yards," would suit armed conflict on the tundra, through "long distance warfare. We train snipers."

In addition to the use of snipers to defend the Inuit homeland from a challenge to its security could be the application of targeted infrastructure attacks. One natural target would be the Alaska Pipeline. Schaeffer noted that military plans exist "to protect the pipeline" from hostile attack, but that there had been at least one unsuccessful attempt to blow up the pipeline, and in recent years, it has experienced at least one random act of sabotage when a drunken gunmen opened fire on the pipeline in October 2001. But Schaeffer recalled an earlier bomb attack that had failed: "There was one failed attempt to sabotage the pipeline, shortly after it was constructed. The explosives didn't do the job." And during the 1970s oil embargo, when the U.S. Government regarded Arab states as a potential threat, "exercises were conducted to secure the pipeline" from an external terror attack. Again in 1991, when Iraq posed a "possible threat" during the first Gulf War, precautions were taken. But Schaeffer said that the real problem was that the "pipeline is not really defendable. Anybody could disrupt its flow." Though he believes "the longest anybody could stop the flow would be for two days. It's not really worth it," since to repair the pipeline would require only two hours if no pipe needed to be fixed, and only two days if a pipe did need to be fixed. "The worst thing," he reflected, would be "to destroy a pumping station." But even in such a case, that "would be bypassed," and in the end would only "slow down the flow."

According to Schaeffer, the two areas of strategic vulnerability of the pipeline are the gathering stations at Prudhoe Bay, "where there is tight security" in place, and at Valdez, where the oil is stored and loaded onto tankers for its journey to southern markets, where there is "also tight security." Schaeffer noted that Prudhoe Bay's security has been provided by a Northwest Arctic Borough–owned company, but he added that this did not necessarily provide the Inuit with a tactical advantage in the event of an independence movement: "It's a business; you don't convert a business to nationalistic aims very easily." Schaeffer added that the pipeline security business was made up mostly of "cops, not soldiers," and that the Alaska state troopers' SWAT team "practice some on pipeline" to be ready to respond to a security problem. Because the pipeline is the primary method by which the state of Alaska extracts wealth from Native land, its continued functionality would be important if a new, Native state was established in order to continue to move North Slope oil to market, though likely under the terms of a more equitable royalty-sharing and taxation arrangement than currently exists. One can postulate that the pipeline would be mutually defined as neutral ground in the event of intra-state hostilities, owing to the mutual dependence on that singular natural resource deposit by both Natives and the state. But the use of force in other ways was conceivable—especially if a new or emergent

Native, fifty-first state faced a military threat from the remaining rump of non-Native Alaska, or from abroad.

The major reason for Alaska's post–World War II growth—the strategic threat that the Soviet Union posed—is now gone. But the state's vast potential as a source of natural resources has not yet been fully tapped. Whether the struggle over developing Alaska's untapped resources sparks an eventual division into two, separate states, one Native and the other non-Native states, or encourages the continued unity of the state, remains to be seen. So far, unity has been maintained, though in Native Alaska, social conditions remain as grim as they do in Arctic Canada, with epidemic levels of suicide, overwhelming social problems, persistent poverty, and new challenges ushered forth by climate change including permafrost degradation, which has impeded access to the land during hunting season. In the event of a Native secession, it is conceivable, down the road, that the Scouts could form the nucleus of an Inuit Defense Force, and instead of helping to unify the nation and integrate tribe and state, and to cement the sovereign bond that unites Native and non-Native, it could now defend the new boundary between the two.

The Scouts are well armed and are linked historically with the emergence of an independent-minded Native leadership that governs an increasingly frustrated and alienated people denied the full fruits of the resources extracted from their traditional homeland. Schaeffer responded to the idea advocated by state officials during the peak of the sovereignty movement that dealing with the state was far preferable to dealing with the far-away federal government, because, as former state cabinet member Edgar Blatchford explained, "if you can do it locally, you can effect change easier, and be a bigger fish in smaller pond." Schaeffer countered that the "Inuit communities are some of the poorest in the country—with Third World country problems in Alaska and Canada." Schaeffer held out hope that a "new state," even with "lower standards" of economic development would probably "share goods" more equitably along traditional Native lines. A new, fifty-first state need not be all that different from other states, he explained, as Alaska Natives had "been in America long enough. Whatever we do, we're likely to adopt American systems. Who knows, we may reinvent tribal government, maybe a hybrid of tribal governments." Secession from Alaska made sense, since he expected a better relationship with the federal government in Washington than with the state government in Juneau. But "when the facts are all in," Schaeffer added, "we may not want to be part of Alaska or even a state" in the Union at all, but instead pursue formal sovereignty. But then again, the very process of discussing so openly ideas about sovereignty and independence could help to change things. As General Schaeffer suggested, "Maybe the effort will be enough to change things so the state is more accommodating."

Some Inuit leaders have gone even further in their articulation of Inuit sovereignty, calling for a formal restoration of their sovereign independence. At the end of the Cold War period, as independence was regained by the many captive peoples of the Soviet Union, including the tiny Baltic states occupied by the Red

Army since the end of World War II and annexed by Moscow, one of Alaska's earliest land claims activists, Charles Edwardsen, Jr., advocated formal Inuit independence, a declaration which was made on August 1, 1991, at the Kasigluk Elders Conference for an Inuit republic. As Edwardsen explained in "Attributes of Original Sovereignty: A Memorandum from the Kasigluk Elders Conference," on September 19, 1991:

> Alaska Native Nations have never ceded or recognized the annexation of Alaska by the Russians or the United States. This military occupation of Alaska by the United States must come to terms with the Alaska Native Peoples' Declaration for the creation of the Republic of the Arctic. This occurred on August 1, 1991 by the Kasigluk Elders of Alaska. This Inuit declaration is more sacred than the one which was declared by the Americans on the Fourth of July, 1776. The Inuit claim to sovereignty is based upon the longest peaceful coexistence on the North American continent. . . . In our northern world, the Eskimos and the Indians of the circumpolar regions were never fought, never conquered, and never signed treaties relinquishing their rights to the land.[34]

And in a later article, "Science and the Indigenous Arctic," which Edwardsen submitted to the Center for World Indigenous Studies on June 15, 1993, he explained: "The Inuit, of the Circumpolar Region, qualify as a nation-state under international law" and that the "Inuit of Canada, Denmark, United States, and Russia have met the criteria of Article I of the Montevideo Convention on the Rights and Duties of States. Our inherent rights to sovereignty as defined by longest peaceful existence have never been extinguished by the claims of discovery by the Spanish, Russians, British, Portuguese, Danes, Americans, nor Canadians."[35] Indeed, Edwardsen argues that: "Unlike the origins of the United States, France, and Russia, the Inuit call to freedom maintains our tradition of the longest peaceful occupation, co-existence, territorial integrity and sovereignty of the Arctic since time immemorial. Based upon our self-determination and supported by International Law, we make this Declaration of Sovereignty which signifies Inuit Independence from all Anglo-European original or derivative states, and from any infringement of Inuit Sovereignty."[36] He questioned the legal and constitutional basis for American sovereignty over Alaska, noting there "was never a treaty nor consensual relationship between Czarist Russia and the indigenous tribes of Alaska. Secondly, the Treaty of Cessions of 1867 between Russia and the United States is not a transfer of sovereignty nor a secession of lands from the indigenous population. Therefore, the United States government is an occupational force within Alaska."[37] Edwardsen this sought to challenge America's occupation of Alaska under international law, and explained that neither the United States nor Russia could legitimately "manufacture, between themselves, sovereignty which they have not acquired nor can ever acquire either on March 30, 1867 nor through the ratification of the Maritime Boundary Treaty of September 16, 1991. For the last 250 years in Alaska, Russia and the United States have been outside of civilized international law and outside of their own constitutions. The United States and Russia have been the benefactors of this unconstitutional occupation and have enjoyed one trillion dollars of ill-gotten gains."[38] Edwardsen's historical analysis is largely accurate, though his aspiration for formal sovereignty and independence is not widely shared among the Inuit leadership, at least not currently. And though he notes that "the Arctic Slope Native Association (ASNA) voted 'No' to ANCSA" and that "they seem to have been the only representatives within the Alaska Federation of Natives with the ability to see into the future and to recognize a land robbery in the guise of a poor third world contract," the legitimacy of the land claims concept has nonetheless been widely accepted across the Arctic by Alaska Natives and non-Natives alike.

While ASNA voted against ANCSA, they were a minority voice within the Alaska Native community, the majority of which welcomed the protections and compensation of ANCSA as the best possible deal at that time, albeit with some misgivings about ANCSA's structural flaws. But land claims have evolved considerably since, with a more democratic ratification process adopted when land claims migrated to Canada, so now all individual Natives within the affected settlement area have a say in the process, and not just the leadership; and there are now far stronger protections of Aboriginal traditions. Land claims have thus become an important vehicle for the enhancement and formalization of state sovereignty over the Arctic territories, especially in Alaska and Canada, with the Home Rule Government in Greenland serving in a similar function, legitimating the aspiration of continued sovereign control by the colonial power through the devolution of powers to the regional level. Thus, in more recent years, the Native secessionist impulse has begun to ebb, as has the climate of more radical tribalism seen during the early 1990s when tribalism was resurgent the world over, as the Arctic states have endeavored to maintain unity, address the concerns of their indigenous populations, and increase their role in governing their homelands. More often, pragmatic considerations have led the leadership to pursue increased autonomy within the existing constitutional structures of the national governments that assert sovereignty over their homeland, pursuing land claim settlements and self-government accords rather than formal independence.

Even in Russia, efforts are being made to secure approvals from the Native community prior to the development of large-scale energy projects, a notable change from the Soviet era. As reported in the April 24, 2008, edition of the *Barents Observer*, Gazprom has even "got the necessary consent from regional indigenous peoples for the development of the huge Bovanenkovskoe field in the Yamal Peninsula," and the chief of the Gazprom Dobycha Nadym subsidiary had claimed "the intrusion of the oil industry in a zone managed by indigenous peoples is conducted in a highly careful and civilized manner" and that "all decisions regarding the laying of pipelines and infrastructure in the area are made only after consultations with representatives of the regional indigenous peoples."[39] While these sorts of consultations may fall well short of the powers gained by Natives in the North American Arctic, it does suggest some movement in this direction.

Land claims in the Arctic were thus the first concrete step in the process of decolonizing the North by devolving decision-making authority from what many northerners perceive to be far away, colonial centers of administration and decision-making to local communities: by letting go, central government authorities have in fact been strengthening their hand, gaining greater political legitimacy through their new spirit of collaboration, co-management, and devolutionary policies. After nearly four decades, the process begun by land claims that started in Alaska is still by no means complete. Indeed, throughout large portions of Canada, hundreds of specific and regional land claims agreements are either still in the process of being settled, or have yet to be started, having proceeded at a snail's pace for over three decades, precipitating a political crisis in June 2007 when renewed fears of Native militancy began to spread. Ottawa has since redoubled its commitment to a just and lasting reconciliation between Native and non-Native, promising to empower its Indian Claims Commission, created in 1991, by creating a new, independent tribunal to more speedily resolve Native claims.

Furthermore, nearly four decades after the U.S. Congress enacted ANCSA, many Native villages remain critical of the land claims model, and favor alternative approaches to Native empowerment, such as through the restoration of tribal governing structures as sought by members of the "sovereignty movement" in the 1980s and 1990s, such as through the creation of IRA Councils under the terms of the federal Indian Reorganization Act of 1934. However, most of the Arctic region has come to embrace the land claims model as an important step forward in their effort to restore Aboriginal rights, political control, and some elements of their tribal sovereignty. As a result, the many Inuit communities along the Arctic littoral have now settled their land claims, and have moved on to the challenges of restoring self-government to their homeland. Generally speaking, the tribal experience in the Arctic mirrors the tribal experience around the world. One major differentiator, of course, is that the United States was fundamentally transformed by its own civil rights movement, which solidified the ideals that were militarily victorious during the U.S. Civil War. It took a long time, but by the end of the 1960s, minority rights of all sorts, including Aboriginal rights, had worked their way into the psyche of decision-makers at all levels of government, providing a more supportive environment for land claims negotiations and other processes of Native empowerment than experienced elsewhere in the world. Even in Alaska, where strong state interests have been pitted against the Native community in a long battle over who controls the resource wealth extracted from the land, the situation between state and tribe is far more harmonious than in other parts of the world where ethnic violence and civil warfare have erupted in response to the same centrifugal forces.

In the Arctic, as in many parts of the world that were once colonized, colonial impulses long dictated the pace of the North's political development. What the North offered the South, in terms of economic opportunity as well as military security, drove the northward expansion of government, which in turn contributed to a growing indigenous, pan-Arctic movement for greater autonomy that ultimately redrew the map of northern Canada and Alaska, as these new institutions of local and regional self-governance proliferated, first gaining regulatory powers and later, governmental authority—most dramatically illustrated by the birth of the Nunavut territory in 1999, an Inuit-governed territory. The very roots of this drama thus date back to the expansion of commerce by Europe's great powers into the northernmost reaches of North America: Russia expanded its empire from Siberia to Russian America, extending juridical sovereignty over Alaska in the nineteenth century; Britain, through the Hudson's Bay Company, penetrated the interior northern territory known as Rupert's Land even earlier, transforming the political economy of the indigenous northland from pure subsistence to commercial hunting and trapping.

Across the Arctic, there has been a long legacy of government from afar, and generations of northerners have felt a deep and troubling concern with the ongoing neglect by distant government administrators. In time, however, the concept of Aboriginal rights evolved—and gradually transformed the political relationship between governments and the people of the Arctic, as colonialism gave way to democratic impulses and greater political participation by Native peoples in the governing of the Arctic. While the forces of modernism and traditionalism would continue to clash in the years ahead, these conflicts would be managed by the structures of co-management, corporate development, and self-government created by the region's comprehensive land claims settlements.

What Natives have achieved in northern Canada, through peaceful negotiation, with their negotiation partner many times more powerful by any military or economic measure, is remarkable. Especially when compared to the chaos and violence that have resulted from other tribal aspirations along the Cold War's other peripheral regions where other tribal and subnational movements emerged to challenge the old state boundaries. The age of land claims has transmuted this very same tribal force into something else altogether in the Arctic: a peaceful force to spawn the emergence of new structures of Aboriginal self-government. Caught between their tribal past and the demands of a modern future, Native leaders have crafted a synthesis between these two competing, dialectical forces. The outcome of this clash between tribe and state, a blending of contemporary economic, political, and constitutional institutions to preserve age-old traditions, defines the very essence of neotribalism—neither a surrender to the forces of assimilation, colonialism, or even imperial occupation; nor a rejection of the modern state outright. Instead, the Natives of the Arctic, walking in two worlds, have found ways to blend elements of both, forging a unique and one might hope enduring synthesis. As new strains work their way into the North, from increased fuel and food prices to the many impacts of climate change on the Arctic environment, social alienation from the Arctic rim states could again begin to rise, and if it does, a movement for Native secession, and for the restoration of formal sovereignty, could again emerge. Indeed, in recent years, there has been more and more discussion of, and aspiration to, formal, sovereign independence in Greenland, with the former Danish colony and current far-flung

Danish province re-asserting traditional Inuit place names, and introducing its own flag and quitting the European Community in 1985.[40] As the climate warms, both Denmark and Greenland's Home Rule government expect to see benefits from direct trans-polar trade, hydroelectric power development, onshore mineral exploration, and offshore oil and gas development—and an agreement updating the division of resource revenues between the two has recently been negotiated, which paves the way forward for eventual independence. Greenland is already starting to experience a continental greening as a result of its thawing ice sheet, with increasing agricultural output, and in time a continued thaw is expected to open up the island's vast interior to human habitation and development, contributing to the island's economic self-sufficiency, and making independence economically viable.

But while the Inuit of Alaska and Canada inhabit the coastal strip of the nations that assert formal sovereignty over their traditional homelands, the Inuit of Greenland inhabit their own giant island—at 840,004 square miles the world's largest, larger than all the independent, sovereign island countries in the world, such as Indonesia (735,358 square miles), Madagascar (226,917 square miles), Papua New Guinea (178,704 square miles), Japan (143,939 square miles), the Philippines (115,831 square miles), New Zealand (103,883 square miles), Great Britain (88,787 square miles), Cuba (42,804 square miles), and Iceland (39,769 sq miles)—and thus by virtue of its vast territorial scale, and its geophysical isolation from Denmark, the Greenlandic Inuit have a compelling justification to assert formal sovereignty over their homeland.[41] By the same argument, the Inuit of Baffin Island, whose island is 194,574 square miles in size, and the Inuit of Ellesmere Island, which is 71,029 square miles, could make a similar argument, as could the Inuit of Cornwallis Island. And combined, the Inuit of Nunavut's archipelago communities inhabit an island group that would become the world's third largest island country if it became formally independent. While the Inuit of Alaska and Canada cohabit the mainland with an overwhelmingly non-Inuit demographic majority, the situation in the High Arctic islands remains quite distinct, and the case for a formal secession with a natural and stable border is quite compelling, especially if Greenland becomes an independent country or if Québec one day secedes from Canada.

A sovereign, independent Greenland need not differ so much from Iceland, a sovereign island country with a relatively small population numbering some 310,000, or even the many micro-states of Europe and Oceania. If the tribal emirates of Arabia can maintain their sovereign status as the United Arab Emirates in today's world, or the city-states of Liechtenstein (population 34,000), Monaco (32,400), San Marino (28,900), or even tiny Vatican City (920), the four smallest sovereign states in Europe by population, or the Pacific island states of Tuvalu (11,600), Nauru (13,000) or Palau (20,300), then the case for the formal independence of Greenland is within the realm of the possible.[42] Greenland's population, estimated at 56,300 in 2007, is greater than the populations of these small, sovereign city-states, and around the same size as the Marshall Islands (59,000), Antigua and Barbuda (68,700), Dominica (69,000), and Andorra (70,600). Indeed, just as the tiny emirates of Arabia united under one flag, and thus avoided colonization or foreign conquest, one can imagine something like a United Inuit Republic much like that called for in 1993 by Alaska Native leader Charles Etok Edwardsen.

As the climate warms, aspirations for independence in Greenland have indeed grown, fueled in part by the emergent economic opportunities that have accompanied the warming trend, from inexpensive hydro-electric power to potentially vast reserves of underground minerals and offshore oil and gas. As reported by Colin Woodard in the *Christian Science Monitor*: "For 30 years, Greenland's 56,000 people have been pushing for greater control over their own affairs. Despite their best efforts, it was assumed that poor, remote Greenland would remain tied to Denmark indefinitely. But with the recent surge in global oil and mineral prices—and melting ice on land and sea improving access to potential reserves of both—the prospects for Greenland's independence have never looked better."[43] He cited Aleqa Hammond, Greenland's Minister of Finance and Foreign Affairs, who explained: "If Greenland becomes economically self-sufficient, then independence becomes a practical possibility. We know that we have gold and diamonds and oil and great masses of the cleanest water in the world. . . . It may be closer than we think."[44] And as Paul Brown reported in *The Guardian*, "The dash for minerals is fuelling another debate in Greenland: whether the country should go for independence from Denmark."[45] He also cited Aleqa Hammond, who said she "hopes that the oil and mineral companies moving in will create sufficient wealth for her country to break from colonial rule."[46] As she explained, "It is natural for a country to want to be independent. We do not feel ourselves part of Europe—we are an Arctic people—but our way of life is changing and we have to change with it."[47] Hammond's case for sovereign independence was further elucidated in an article by Brian Cathcart in the *New Statesman*, which also profiles Hammond. While climate change news coverage has been dominated by "thousands of stories" that present "depressing dispatches from the global-warming front lines," in Greenland "the story is different, because for the Greenlanders there is hope, albeit hope of a kind to make the rest of us uncomfortable. For Greenland is booming, and it is all down to climate change."[48] Roger Boyes, in an article titled "Global Warming Could Help Greenland to Independence" in *The Times*, writes that "a new national anthem may soon be needed. Greenland has taken its first tentative steps towards becoming an independent state. Anders Fogh Rasmussen, the Danish Prime Minister, traveled to Greenland—which has been part of Denmark since 1721—to present a report that sets out the road to full sovereignty," and which envisions "phasing out of subsidies from Copenhagen as the huge island makes increasing use of its rich mineral and oil resources under a thick layer of ice."[49] Boyes observes that when it comes to climate change, "Greenlanders cannot get enough of it. The melting of the icebergs may, as some climate scientists predict, ultimately end up by flooding American cities, but it has given political bargaining muscle to the 57,000 inhabitants of the world's largest island,"[50] as new fisheries and offshore oil reserves open up. Boyes cites Jesper Madsen of the DMU National Environmental Research Institute in Roskilde, Denmark, who noted that the U.S. Geological Survey "calculates that the greatest unused oil reserves on Earth are in the Greenland waters—and they are in the east, where the ice is melting fastest."[51]

According to Krista Mahr, reporting in *Time* magazine, "as the increasingly alarming news of its melting 1.8 million square kilometer (695,000 square mile) ice cap has trickled south and the race for polar resources has officially started, the international community is paying more attention to its largest island."[52] So much so, that Mahr notes that "by the end of this summer, some 3,400 scientists from 60 countries were working on the landmass. Both German Chancellor Angela Merkel and U.S. House Speaker Nancy Pelosi had dropped by to see the melting glaciers for themselves. And singer Björk dedicated a song to Greenland (and the Faroe Islands)—Declare Independence—on her latest album."[53] Asks Mahr, "Why? Because while people may be learning more about Greenland through global warming's effects on its fragile environment, what's less well known is that a grassroots movement for greater self-rule has been brewing in the Danish territory for the last 30 years."[54] She noted that "long before Russia planted a metal flag in the sea floor beneath the North Pole last month, Greenland had been eyeing its own potential reserves of oil and gas surrounding the island. Shrimp processing is the biggest contributor to the territory's GDP today, but big oil could offer a much shorter path to self-reliance."[55]

Indeed, as *Bloomberg* reporter Christian Wienberg reported, on June 13, 2008, "Denmark and Greenland agreed to divide future oil proceeds from the Arctic Island, which may hold reserves equivalent to those of the North Sea."[56] He noted that Danish Prime Minister Rasmussen and Greenland's Premier Hans Enoksen, had "signed an oil income agreement that also included steps toward increased independence for Greenland."[57] Wienberg's article cited Enoksen, who said "this agreement recognizes us as a people, it makes Greenlandic our official language and it gives us our right to our underground resources."[58] Under the new agreement, "Greenland will receive the first 75 million kroner ($15 million) generated from oil production, while the two governments will split additional proceeds until Denmark has received an equivalent of the 3.2 billion kroner it pays in annual subsidies to the Arctic Island. Greenland will receive all additional proceeds after that."[59] As Danish Prime Minister Rasmussen told Wienberg, "'It's only natural that we share the proceeds that may come. It's of utmost importance that Greenland improves the ability to generate income' before it can become more independent."[60]

But not everyone is confident Greenland's increasing resource wealth will lead the Arctic island to independence. So long as Greenland remained hidden by its ice cap, largely impenetrable to resource development, it was of little economic interest, and was largely integrated into world politics through its strategic military relationship with the United States, which had come to the island's defense during World War II much as it had Newfoundland's, further strengthening its military presence throughout the Cold War with continued interest in the post–Cold War era, with its geostrategic position of value to North America's air defense, maritime security and now ballistic missile defense. As noted by *Christian Science Monitor* reporter Woodard, Greenlandic geologist Minik Rosing of the University of Copenhagen "doesn't share the belief that finding oil will serve the cause of independence," and cites Rosing as stating, "It's inconceivable that a country as large as Greenland wouldn't be rich in natural resources. As everyone else gets more and more desperate for this commodity, you don't want to have it and be a very, very small, very, very independent country, very, very far from anything else. My personal view is if Greenland finds oil, that is the end of the idea of independence."[61] Woodard also cites longtime Greenlandic ICC representative Aqqaluk Lynge, who explained, "We are afraid that the United States will take over Greenland if the Danes get out. If Americans can take Iraq, then why not Greenland?"[62] Woodard notes that the U.S. military "has been active in Greenland since World War II, when it occupied the island to prevent it from falling under Nazi control and to provide mid-Atlantic refueling bases for ships and aircraft," and then in the Cold War, "radar stations were added to detect incoming missiles, and Thule Air Force Base in northernmost Greenland is expected to play a central role in plans for a national missile-defense system."[63]

Paul Brown of *The Guardian* also notes that "some argue that independence has dangers," as "Greenland is the land mass closest to the North Pole and has rapidly assumed greater strategic importance as its much more powerful and populous neighbors vie for a slice of the Arctic's supposed mineral wealth," and this accounts for why the United States is "strengthening its air base at Thule on the extreme north of the island and the Russians have already planted flags on the sea bed."[64] *Time*'s Mahr writes, "the thought of big nations finding yet another vested interest in their landscape isn't universally thrilling in Greenland, which has been a strategic military outpost for the U.S. and Denmark since the Cold War. Inuit hunters were displaced when the American military set up camp at the Thule Air Base on the island's northwest shore in the 1950s, and Inuit hunters were the first to be exposed when a B-52 carrying hydrogen bombs crashed near the base in 1968."[65] She cites the ICC's Greenlandic president, Aqqaluk Lynge, who remains concerned about the potential risks to the Inuit: "We are fragile, both in terms of the climate crisis and because of the military buildup in the Arctic," and as a consequence, "Every night I pray they don't find oil and gas in Greenland."[66]

It was Greenland's vulnerability to external aggression that brought American military power to the island, a year after Denmark was invaded and occupied by Nazi Germany on April 9, 1940. According to a statement from the U.S. Department of State issued on April 10, 1941, one day after the United States and Denmark entered into a defense agreement for Greenland, "during the summer of 1940 German activity on the eastern coast of Greenland became apparent" when "three ships proceeding from Norwegian territory under German occupation arrived off the coast of Greenland," and "in the late fall of 1940, air reconnaissance appeared over East Greenland under circumstances making it plain that there had been continued activity in that region." The next year, on March 21, 1941, "a German bomber flew over the eastern coast of Greenland and on the following day another German war plane likewise reconnoitered the same territory. Under these circumstances it appeared that further steps for the defense of Greenland were necessary to bring Greenland within the system of hemispheric defense envisaged by the Act of Habana."[67] So on April 9, 1941, an agreement "between the Secretary of State, acting on behalf of the Government of the United States of America, and the Danish Minister, Henrik de Kauffmann, acting on behalf of His Majesty the King of Denmark in his capacity as sovereign of Greenland" was agreed to, granting "to the United States the right to locate and construct airplane landing fields and facilities for the defense of Greenland and for the defense of the American Continent," but only "after explicitly recognizing the Danish sovereignty over Greenland."[68]

The agreement recognized that "as a result of the present European war there is danger that Greenland may be converted into a point of aggression against nations of the American Continent, and accept[ed] the responsibility on behalf of the United States of assisting Greenland in the maintenance of its present status."[69] The United States asserted it had "no thought in mind save that of assuring the safety of Greenland and the rest of the American Continent, and Greenland's continuance under Danish sovereignty."[70] The agreement further pledged, in Article IX, to respect the interests of the Inuit: "The Government of the United States of America will respect all legitimate interests in Greenland as well as all the laws, regulations and customs pertaining to the native population and the internal administration of Greenland. In exercising the rights derived from this Agreement the Government of the United States will give sympathetic consideration to all representations made by the Danish authorities in Greenland with respect to the welfare of the inhabitants of Greenland."[71] In an exchange of notes with the U.S. Secretary of State, Danish Minister Henrik de Kauffmann, whose formal title was described in the text of the 1941 treaty as "Envoy Extraordinary and Minister Plenipotentiary of His Majesty the King of Denmark at Washington," wrote that "the proposed agreement, arrived at after an open and friendly exchange of views, is, under the singularly unusual circumstances, the best measure to assure both Greenland's present safety and the future of the island under Danish Sovereignty. Furthermore, I am of the opinion that the terms of the agreement protect, as far as possible, the interests of the native population of Greenland whose welfare traditionally has been the paramount aim of Denmark's policy in Greenland."[72]

Early in the Cold War, the external threat to Greenland and to North America was no longer from Germany, which had been decisively defeated at the end of World War II, but from the Soviet Union. And so on April 27, 1951, the defense treaty with Greenland was updated with the signing of the "Defense of Greenland: Agreement between the United States and the Kingdom of Denmark."[73] Article I of the 1951 treaty affirmed that both countries, "in order to promote stability and well-being in the North Atlantic Treaty area by uniting their efforts for collective defense and for the preservation of peace and security and for the development of their collective capacity to resist armed attack, will each take such measures as are necessary or appropriate to carry out expeditiously their respective and joint responsibilities in Greenland, in accordance with NATO plans."[74] Article VI of the 1951 treaty affirmed that "due respect will be given by the Government of the United States of America and by United States nationals in Greenland to all the laws, regulations and customs pertaining to the local population and the internal administration of Greenland, and every effort will be made to avoid any contact between United States personnel and the local population which the Danish authorities do not consider desirable for the conduct of operations under this Agreement."[75]

On August 10, 2004, Denmark, Greenland, and the United States updated their 1951 defense agreement, when "after two years of negotiations, all three parties—the U.S. on one side, and Denmark/Greenland on the—reached consensus on the terms of the treaty. The United States was granted permission to upgrade Greenland's Thule Radar Station as part of the American Missile Defense (MS) program. The agreement itself implicitly recognized former Danish colony Greenland as an equal partner with influence over its own foreign affairs."[76] Among the most notable changes in the treaty's language was the emphasis on "partnership with Greenland," the inclusion of Greenland as a party to the treaty, and the evident spirit of equality among these three parties. According to Greenland's minister for foreign affairs, Josef Motzfeldt, "For us at home, this date marks the day that Greenland took a decisive step toward equality and responsibility on par with other countries of the world, and away from the indignity and indifference of the colonial era. By entering this agreement complex, Greenland has taken an active step toward increased foreign policy independence."[77] Colin Powell, then serving as the U.S. Secretary of State, echoed Motzfeldt's sentiment, adding that "it is important to demonstrate that Greenland is a full-fledged member of this partnership. And the best way of showing that is by being on hand today."[78]

Greenland took a step toward regaining formal independence in late 2008, when it voted overwhelmingly in favor of a referendum on increased autonomy from Denmark. As reported by Alan Cowell in the *New York Times*: "In a referendum on greater autonomy leading to eventual independence, the people of Greenland, the world's biggest island, voted overwhelmingly on Tuesday in favor of loosening their 300-year-old ties to Denmark," and "turnout was more than 70 percent and almost 76 percent of the voters were in favor."[79] According to Cowell, Denmark, "will maintain influence over matters including foreign policy and defense," but a "new law will allow Greenlanders the option of taking more responsibility in several areas. It will also permit them to be recognized as a separate people under international law and make the Eskimo-Inuit tongue known as Greenlandic the island's official language."[80] These new measures will "come into force next June following approval by both the Greenland and Danish parliaments," and "will allow Greenland to take control of revenues from potential oil, gas and mineral finds, but the full extent of those natural resources is not yet clear."[81] An article in *AFP* noted that Greenland's Prime Minister, Hans Enoksen, "predicted independence from Denmark by 2021," but cautioned that "while the new status, which takes effect on June 21, 2009, is widely seen as a first step towards independence, many doubts remain over the viability of sovereignty for the territory of just 57,000 inhabitants."[82]

The historic vote was celebrated across the Inuit homeland. An announcement was issued by Canada's national Inuit organization, Inuit Tapiriit Kanatami (ITK), whose president, long-time Inuit leader Mary Simon, "acknowledged the importance of this week's three-to-one vote by the people of Greenland in favour of greater self rule," and stated it "has been by any test a decisive vote," said Ms. Simon, "and no doubt reflects the confidence of Greenlanders in moving forward to the next stage of their political evolution."[83] Simon drew parallels to the gains made by Inuit in Canada, who "have also decided many important events in relation to their self determination by direct popular votes, including ratification of land claims agreements and the creation and boundaries of Nunavut," and who explained that "votes of this kind are testimony to the fundamental and abiding strength of democratic values among Inuit."[84]

Sovereign Struggles

Asserting sovereignty over the Arctic has never been an easy task for the Arctic rim states. From time to time, they try to demonstrate their capacity to defend their Arctic frontiers through sovereignty patrols, joint exercises between local militia forces and regular armed forces, and symbolic displays of national power in the otherwise vast expanses of the Arctic. In 2007, a 24-member patrol including Regular Forces, Canadian Rangers, and a member of the RCMP dubbed "Operation Nunalivut 2007" traveled some 8,000 km across the High Arctic over a three-week period to assert Canada's sovereignty. "Nunalivut" means the "land that is ours" in Inuktitut, raising, perhaps unintentionally, the interesting but politically charged question of whose land the Arctic really is—and perhaps challenging any incipient sovereign aspirations that could be simmering among the political leadership of Nunavut.

But how two dozen members of the armed forces and the police, traveling for three weeks across an otherwise sparsely settled frontier region, actually enhances Canada's sovereign claim begs to be asked. Indeed, the very need for such a mission seems to suggest there is still a deep and unresolved feeling of sovereignty insecurity in Ottawa. A June 2008 *Associated Press* news report, titled "Warfare Course Shows Canadian Military is Still Struggling in the Arctic," examines Ottawa's efforts to assert a more visible and active military presence in the Arctic, revealing many of the practical problems that hamper efforts at asserting Arctic sovereignty through such sovereignty patrols, undermining their very intent: "As Canada prepares to spend billions defending the Arctic with icebreakers and deep-water ports, the soldiers who will actually stand guard over that frigid frontier have a shopping list of their own. Warm boots would be nice. So would snowmobiles that run, food that doesn't freeze and shovels that dig. Internal assessments released to *The Canadian Press* of a Canadian Forces advanced winter warfare course last March in Resolute, Nunavut, depict a military still learning the basics of working in the North and vulnerable to challenges that extreme weather can bring."[85] Lieutenant Colonel Marco Rancourt, commander of the Canadian Forces Land Advance Warfare Centre was quoted as saying "A lot of things popped up," evidence that "Conducting operations in the Arctic is difficult," but that "compared to those other forces that actually have an active part in the North, we're probably equal to them—if not better."[86] Active operational experience in the Arctic has long been a challenge, as noted by John Honderich in his *Arctic Imperative*: "Studies have shown that when Canadian troops have trained in the high Arctic, approximately 80 percent of their energy is consumed in mere survival. That leaves little with which to do battle. Throw in all the equipment, weapons, provisions, and fuel needed for an invasion, and the task becomes that much more daunting."[87] Honderich added, "The islands of the Canadian archipelago are a desert of endless permafrost, an equally inhospitable terrain. More importantly, there is little of strategic importance to anyone other than a few radar stations farther south."[88]

Asserting Ottawa's sovereign claim to its Arctic territories has become a priority for Ottawa. And yet, while Prime Minister Harper has announced sweeping plans for a new generation of Arctic offshore patrol vessels, a High Arctic training base for regular armed forces as well as the Canadian Rangers, and the re-development of the Nanisivik port into a deepwater naval facility at the entrance to the Northwest Passage, he has largely overlooked one of Canada's most powerful claims to Arctic sovereignty: its increasingly supportive, collaborative, and interdependent relationship to the Inuit of the Arctic, their enduring stewardship over the Arctic lands, seas, and wildlife since time immemorial, and the mutual recognition of each other's sovereignty through the resolution brought forth by Native land claims. When Ottawa dusted off the old Mulroney-era proposal that called for a much less expensive repurposing of the old Nansivik deep water port facility instead of construction of a new deep water facility at Iqaluit, which would have required extensive dredging, the decision disappointed the territorial government. Ottawa's decision, and its exclusion of input by the Government of Nunavut, was discussed by University of British Columbia international law expert Michael Byers in an interview in Canada's progressive news site, *Rabble.ca*: "If we're going to address these challenges effectively, we need to engage the experience and insight of those who live in the North. It has to be a collaborative exercise. And yet Mr. Harper went to northern Baffin Island to announce a new port for Canada's navy without any consultation with the Government of Nunavut, and then flew right over Iqaluit on his way back to Ottawa without stopping to meet with Inuit leaders—an astonishing example of his dictatorial approach."[89]

Prime Minister Harper, when making his announcement at Nanisivik in August 2007, justified his pledge to defend Canada's Arctic sovereignty in terms reminiscent of the "Arctic Sublime," and not in the more pragmatic language of geopolitics and national security. As described by Fred Chartrand of *Canadian Press*: "This remains a place where the principal forces of nature still hold sway, a place where men and women are braced into vigour by the huge trackless landscapes and the often harsh elements," and a "place so stunningly beautiful that no Canadian can experience it without feeling an overwhelming sense of romantic patriotism for our country." Even those who have never experienced it personally understand this, as "It's embedded in our history, our literature, our art, our music and our Canadian soul."[90] But Arctic sovereignty is about more than "romantic patriotism," and requires the people of the North to be braced by more than vigor. Nunavut blogger and retired RCMP officer Clare Kines, in "Of Ships and Sovereignty," found Nanisivik to be a logical location for the Arctic port, but argues like Byers that Ottawa's approach to sovereignty needs to focus more on stewardship and not just the security of the Arctic: "The choice of Nanisivik as the port is the only logical one for the government to make. For one thing, it already exists. Nanisivik has been a deep water port, with fifty feet of water port side, since 1975. To construct a new port in Iqaluit or Resolute or elsewhere would be much more expensive and needless."[91] And secondly, it "also is situated on the Northwest Passage, the only existing port on the Northwest Passage." Kines predicted that "there will be people in Iqaluit jumping up and down saying a port should have been built there," but added, "give me a break, Iqaluit is about 600 nautical miles south of the Passage, and the costs of construction would be enormous."[92] Additionally, Kines notes "there is also additional infrastructure at Nanisivik that makes it a logical choice (although not as much as there used to be). Fuel tank facilities, proximity of a 6,400' runway, and a utilidor for fresh water all still exist in Nanisivik. No, Nanisivik is the smart choice if you're needing a base for Arctic Patrol vessels."[93] So from a logistical perspective, and a cost perspective, the decision was sound. But as Kines reflects, the Prime Minister has taken "the wrong approach to sovereignty," and while correct that "when defending sovereignty you must 'use it or lose it,'" he has overlooked something very basic:

> As far as the waterways of the Northwest Passage go, Canada already uses them, and has for years. A fleet of Canadian Coast Guard icebreakers spend all summer in the Arctic waters. And more importantly, Canadian Inuit make use of the frozen and unfrozen waters, to travel, and hunt, and live. The Inuit have been living lives up here for thousands of years, long before there was a Canada, and now they are Canadians and their lives, and those of other Nunavummiut, are the strongest possible argument for Canada's sovereignty in the Arctic that there is.[94]

Inuit leader and former ICC chair Sheila Watt-Cloutier has noted that the "Inuit remain closely connected with the land, sea, ice, snow, and wildlife," and that "the truth and wisdom of our elders is helping to reconnect the Arctic with the lives of people throughout the world."[95] Mary Simon has also written about the interconnection of the Inuit to Canadian sovereignty in the Arctic: "For generations, Canadians have professed to be a 'people of the North.' The reality, however, is that the Arctic has been on the margins of Canadian consciousness. This is about to change, not because there has been a radical shift in the Canadian collective consciousness, but rather because the Arctic has become a geopolitical hot potato. Climate change and sovereignty have parachuted the region into the media spotlight."[96] And yet, "At the same time, the current federal government has backed away from commitments to Inuit" and "is sending mixed signals about its commitments to the Arctic. The federal Conservatives have done away with our ambassador for circumpolar affairs, shelved the Northern Strategy initiative launched by the Martin Liberals, missed opportunities to build vital scientific research infrastructure, which could have been a legacy of the International Polar Year, downgraded Canada's attendance at last year's Arctic Council ministerial meeting in Salekhard, Russia, and backed away from election promises to build heavy icebreakers."[97]

Simon recalls how "for the past half-century, Arctic sovereignty crises have appeared every ten to fifteen years," and that "current iteration is the 'use it or lose it' tour by Prime Minister Harper, which accompanied announcements of a deepwater port at Nanisivik and an army training base at Resolute Bay."[98] Asks Simon: "What does Harper mean? Have Inuit not been using the region for millennia? Amid the latest round of promises, has Canada forgotten the northern governments and aboriginal institutions that have been negotiating and implementing arrangements for the better governance of the Arctic for the past thirty-five years?" She added, "Luckily for Canada, the Inuit are always here. Without the Inuit, could we really claim to be masters of the Arctic house? Probably not. Ultimately, the Arctic sovereignty issue will depend on people, not ports or training facilities or military exercises. If Canada is to secure a long-standing and unimpeachable claim to the Arctic, it must be grounded in the daily realities of the Inuit and other Canadians who make this region their home."[99]

> Canada's mistreatment of the Inuit in using them as human flagpoles to assert sovereignty was laid out with excruciating honesty during hearings convened by the Royal Commission on Aboriginal Peoples in the early 1990s. A settlement was finally achieved and a semi-apology delivered. How ironic now for Canada to brandish the fact that Canadian citizens—Inuit—live in the Arctic in order to add legitimacy to its sovereignty claims.[100]

Simon observed that "the time has come to listen to Arctic voices on the subject of integrating the region with mainstream Canada," and asks rhetorically: "Would not a better strategy be to make this bountiful and magnificent region a part of Canada's daily experience?"[101]

But according to Section VII of Thomas R. Berger's March 2006 Conciliator's Final Report on Climate Change, Sovereignty and the Future of the Inuit, rather than looking to successful and effective land claims implementation as a means of affirming its sovereign claim to the Arctic, Ottawa has largely abandoned any genuine effort to fulfill the promises articulated at the Nunavut land claim signing in 1993. As I observed at that time: The signing of the historic land-claim settlement with 17,500 Inuit in the Central and Eastern Arctic—an agreement that sets in motion the creation of Nunavut, Canada's third northern territory—was greeted with much hope for the future. Mr. Mulroney, Northern Affairs Minister Tom Siddon, and many Inuit leaders spoke of the children of Nunavut, for whom the agreement promises so much. But while moments like this make for ideal headlines and provide terrific photo and video opportunities for the political elite, there is good reason to resist the seduction of such a political love-in and to be prepared for a challenging future. As one young Inuk said, the moment was both exciting and frightening at the same time.[102] The Inuvialuit enjoyed such a day in 1984 when their land claim accord was signed, and the years that followed oscillated between hope and fear, with several early challenges arising that threatened to jeopardize the intended benefits of their land claim accord. But they persevered, learning from their early mistakes, and made their land claim work for their community. The Inuit of Nunavut are still at an early stage of their learning curve, still struggling to overcome a wide array of challenges that face them, still searching for solutions to their new challenges. Ottawa has not made things easy for the Inuit, putting on the brakes when it came to implementation of the historic Nunavut land claim accord. As Berger explained in his final report: "Implementation of comprehensive land claims agreements is commonly 'ghettoized' in the Department of Indian Affairs and Northern Development, far from the locus of national and international policy debate between central agencies. This is not surprising, perhaps, in light of the small scale and local nature of many comprehensive land claims agreements. This is not, however, the case with the 1993 Nunavut Land Claims Agreement which intersects with Canada's national and international interests and obligations, and foreign policy objectives."[103] That's because of "the sheer size of Nunavut and the length of its coastline," and the geographical fact that "nearly forty percent of Canada is above the 60th parallel."[104]

But now Arctic warming has greatly added to the importance of this Northern dimension. As Berger explains, "With Arctic warming, the landscape and seascape may be greatly altered," as "the Nunavut Settlement Area includes huge offshore waters such as the Northwest Passage and the other passages through the Arctic Islands."[105] And while the "experts disagree on whether the retreat of the ice in the Arctic archipelago represents an impending threat to sovereignty, as other countries and shipping firms challenge Canada's claim over Arctic waters, or a law enforcement problem," Berger concludes that "either way, though, all agree that the Inuit are key to demonstrating and maintaining Canada's control over the Arctic."[106] He cites renowned Arctic sovereignty expert, Franklyn Griffiths, who believes that Canada "should build a stronger capacity for collective choice in the Canadian Arctic," as the "Inuit know the area best. They are constant in their attachment to it in ways that southerners cannot equal. In partnership with the Federal government, they will insist on an exercise of control which is not remote but sensitive to local conditions, not agitated about a distant place but grounded in that place."[107]

Inuit and the State: Mutually Enhanced Sovereignty

The Inuit have shown themselves to be shrewd political pragmatists, and thus far have recognized that the benefits of being part of Canada outweigh the benefits of separation. That is why there has not yet been a movement for independence or for a formal restoration of sovereignty. Berger recalled that "the preamble to the Nunavut Land Claims Agreement recites the considerations that impelled the Parties to in 1993 enter into the Agreement," one of which recognizes "the contributions of Inuit to Canada's history, identity and sovereignty in the Arctic."[108] He added "this provision is unique in Canadian relations with Aboriginal peoples," as "no other comprehensive land claims agreement or historic treaty acknowledges the contribution of an Aboriginal people to Canada's sovereignty in this way."[109] As well, by signing their 1993 land claim accord, he noted how the Inuit "formally ceded to Canada their Aboriginal title to Nunavut," and how "only with this formal cession was Canada's claim to the Arctic and the Arctic Islands complete, unburdened by Aboriginal title. The signing of the Nunavut Land Claims Agreement was thus a vital step in strengthening Canada's claim of sovereignty."[110] As Canada continues to assert its claim to the Arctic amidst increased international competition by its neighbors, Berger explains that "the Inuit presence in the Arctic, their use of the sea and the sea ice, is the surest proof of Canada's claim. As the ice melts and shipping lanes open and resources become accessible, their longstanding occupation of the land and the waterways (every one of Nunavut's 27 communities is on tidewater) will work to Canada's advantage."[111]

On October 16, 2007, Prime Minister Harper, who ascended to Canada's highest office on a pledge to secure Canada's Arctic and defend its northern sovereignty, delivered his Throne Speech, in which he recognized that stewardship of the North was an essential component to asserting sovereignty over the North, indeed a key ingredient in Ottawa's effort to resolve its simmering security dilemma on its northern flank. Just as his Esquimalt, B.C., speech in the summer of 2007 used that historic naval port for its metaphorical symbolism of Canada's aspiration to secure its coasts from foreign foes, integrating its historical imagery to make his case to defend the Arctic through an augmentation of Canada's Arctic naval power, Harper's Throne Speech emanated a deep sense of a historical yearning for Canada to secure its place in the world, its way, according to its traditions. Titled "Strong Leadership, A Better Canada," it was at once a defense of his earlier policies to build up Canada's Arctic military capabilities and presence and a refinement of those policies by linking them to the plight of the Inuit, whose presence in the Arctic, and survival as a people, had now been recognized as the missing ingredient from his earlier policy articulations. In his discussion of "Strengthening Canada's Sovereignty and Place in the World," he observed that: "The Arctic is an essential part of Canada's history. One of our Fathers of Confederation, D'Arcy McGee, spoke of Canada as a northern nation, bounded by the blue rim of the ocean. Canadians see in our North an expression of our deepest aspirations: our sense of exploration, the beauty and the bounty of our land, and our limitless potential. But the North needs new attention. New opportunities are emerging across the Arctic, and new challenges from other shores."[112] He thus pledged to "bring forward an integrated northern strategy focused on strengthening Canada's sovereignty, protecting our environmental heritage, promoting economic and social development, and improving and devolving governance, so that northerners have greater control over their destinies. To take advantage of the North's vast opportunities, northerners must be able to meet their basic needs."[113]

Mary Simon had been calling upon Ottawa to reconnect its Arctic sovereignty policies with its policies toward the Inuit, and had cautioned that to pursue Arctic sovereignty was impossible while neglecting the people of the Arctic. And so the Prime Minister affirmed his commitment to Inuit, in particular their housing, a pledge made by his predecessor that he had until now distanced himself from. Simon responded to Harper's speech and its singular sentence on the Inuit approvingly, noting, "It opens doors and creates opportunities. That is welcome."[114] She added that Harper's Throne Speech "has some key strengths from the vantage point of Inuit, the majority and permanent population of the Arctic. First of all, it accepts the importance of the Arctic at both the international and national levels. Secondly, it recognizes that coherent domestic policies for the Arctic have large economic and social development components, and the federal government must be an active player in those vital areas. Thirdly it proposes the development of a long overdue integrated northern strategy."[115] Just a few days after Harper's Throne Speech, Simon participated in an online discussion of Arctic sovereignty with Canada's *Globe and Mail* newspaper, responding to over a dozen questions from the newspaper's readers. As she observed, "I am encouraged by the interest from Canadians on this topic, and further on the level of support for the Inuit in the Arctic on this issue," adding she was about to embark upon "a cross-Canada speaking tour on the issue of Arctic Sovereignty," and that she was "eager to meet Canadians from coast to coast, and engage in positive and progressive discussions about sovereignty, and a host of issues facing Inuit in the Arctic today."[116] When asked by one resident of British Columbia, "What do you want the Canadian to do to help your people and to protect your lands and Canada's sovereignty in the Arctic? What are your greatest concerns today about the Arctic region—both land and sea?" Simon replied, "Act in partnership with us, not in disregard for us and our rights. Implement our land claims agreements with honour. Help us tackle some distressing social and community development problems. Take global warming seriously. Communicate with your government representatives. Insist on action."[117]

Simon later commented that she was "encouraged by this debate among Canadians, and look[s] forward to generating more of it beginning tomorrow in Ottawa, and in the weeks and months to come across Canada."[118] Simon's cross-Canada speaking tour was titled "Inuit and the Canadian Arctic: Sovereignty Begins at Home," and she explained that "our concept of asserting Canadian sovereignty in the Arctic goes well beyond the much needed military and legal measures anticipated and recently announced by the Government of Canada," and that "the best way to assert Canadian sovereignty in the Arctic is through its residents who live in the region. The Inuit approach to asserting sovereignty is holistic in nature and calls for the development of healthy people and healthy communities alongside the military and legal measures."[119] Simon asked Canadians to write to their Members of Parliament (MP) in support of the Inuit approach to the issue, which ITK described as "positive, progressive, collaborative, and participatory."[120]

Canada is now engaging in a national dialogue on Arctic sovereignty, and in the process, the gap between the people of Arctic and their national governments far to the south is beginning to narrow. The issue is high atop the national agenda, so much so that there was a book on Arctic sovereignty that won the prestigious Donner Prize for "for the best book on Canadian Public Policy" on April 30, 2009: *Arctic Front: Defending Canada in the Far North.* The chair of the Donner Prize jury, Grant Reuber, described the winning book as a "very useful, topical and policy-relevant book," adding that "unquestionably, this book deals with a subject of major public importance and interest." Dean Del Maestro, Parliamentary Secretary to the Minister of Canadian Heritage, congratulated the winners, noting that Ottawa "has an Integrated Northern Strategy resting on four pillars—protecting our environmental heritage, promoting economic and social development, exercising our sovereignty, and improving and developing governance—so I'm pleased to see that these outstanding writers have made a contribution to public policy development in our True North."

This dialogue has been precipitated by the convergence of two trends. The first is the thawing of the Arctic ice due to global warming, which will over time have the effect of melting away its hitherto impassible frontier perimeter defense that's been in place since the last ice age, somewhat akin to the Great Wall of China turning to dust and scattering to the wind. And the second is the realization, in Canada, that the Nunavut experiment, blending an historic, comprehensive land claim settlement with the creation of a new, predominantly Inuit territorial government, could fail, despite its structural innovations and paradigm-shifting advances in self-government. Success will require closer, and more continuous attention, by Ottawa, and more time, experience, training, and education will be required by the Inuit. Many ideas have been presented, such as Berger's proposed recommitment to the "Nunavut Project" calling on Ottawa to pursue a bilingual education project to enable the Nunavut government to fulfill the cultural aspirations of the Inuit, and to offer government services in a culturally and linguistically appropriate manner, without surrendering to the assimilating forces that so often accompany modernization. With the melting of the Arctic ice, Ottawa has begun to awaken to its Arctic obligations, and in the process of asserting its sovereignty over the Arctic, it has begun to recognize the full extent of its responsibilities to the peoples of the Arctic, and to its citizenry North and South who will depend increasingly on efforts to secure the northland and the waters of the archipelago as the ice melt continues. Ottawa has had to confront some tough Arctic realities, including challenges posed by record high suicide and substance abuse rates, a persistent housing shortage, and the continued economic challenges of the young Nunavut territory. Its embrace of land claims, and increased devolution of political power to the Arctic communities, has contributed to its assertion of Arctic sovereignty, though clashes with the Inuit leadership over its pace of implementation, and its financial support for the new territory, do present a reality check on its progress to date and the need to try harder. Asserting sovereignty has never been easy in the vast, climatically harsh landscape of the Arctic, but its efforts do provide a normative model for the other Arctic rim states to follow despite the many challenges that remain.

Arctic Sovereignty and a Warmer Earth

Ever since Russia's symbolic flag-planting beneath the North Pole in August 2007, Ottawa and its Arctic neighbors have been put on notice that Moscow will be increasingly active in the Arctic, having already realized in recent years that its natural resource wealth was its ticket back to the center stage of world politics. Each of the Arctic rim states has felt a similar lure of the Arctic, with its untapped resource wealth beckoning as the ice melts accelerate. No longer is the region considered the very ends of the Earth; indeed, the possibility is now firmly planted, as firmly as the Russians' titanium flag beneath the pole, that to the world of tomorrow, it might well become its epicenter. With this realization, of course, come new responsibilities, as what was once perceived to be a distant frontier is now catapulted to center stage. Indeed, while Berger has observed that "experts disagree over the rapidity of climate change and the extent to which it can be attributed to human activity, there is no question that global climate change is a reality."[121] He explains that although "we are accustomed to news of climate change, of the challenge that global warming may represent; nevertheless, for most of us in the temperate zones it is a distant rumble. In the Arctic, however, climate change is not remote. It is already happening."[122] And while "we are now calling it climate change," he notes that "in the Arctic it is the *warming* that is apparent. It can be seen everywhere: Permafrost is melting, storm surges across extended open water are eroding the banks of coastal communities, the ice goes out earlier and forms again later than it did before, shifting patterns of ice and snowfall impede the migration of caribou as well as the seasonal movements of polar bears and seals."[123]

Berger cites the 1,800-page November 8, 2004 report of the Arctic Climate Impact Assessment (ACIA) sponsored by eight Arctic countries and conducted by some 300 scientists, which found that "the Arctic is warming much more rapidly than previously known at nearly twice the rate as the rest of the globe, and increasing greenhouse gases from human activities are calculated to make it warmer still."[124] Further, "Arctic summer sea ice is projected to decline by at least 50 per cent by the end of this century with some models showing near-complete disappearance of summer sea ice. This is very likely to have devastating consequences for some Arctic animal species, such as ice-living seals and for local people for whom these animals are a primary food source. At the same time, reduced sea ice extent is likely to increase marine access to some of the region's resources."[125] The report predicts that "warming over Greenland is projected to lead to substantial melting of the Greenland Ice Sheet, contributing to global level rise at increasing rates," with the potential to boost sea levels by more than twenty feet; Berger adds that "global warming may be accelerating" and notes "NASA's study of the Arctic ice, released on September 28, 2005 shows that Arctic ice cover has shrunk by 10 per cent in the last four years."[126]

And the decline in Arctic sea ice continues to break records, with 2007 experiencing the biggest ice-melt since satellites began keeping an eye on the Arctic in 1979. According to an October 1, 2007, press release from the National Snow and Ice Data Center (NSIDC): "Arctic sea ice during the 2007 melt season plummeted to the lowest levels since satellite measurements began in 1979," and NSIDC senior scientist Mark Serreze commented that the "sea ice cover is in a downward spiral and may have passed the point of no return. As the years go by, we are losing more and more ice in summer, and growing back less and less ice in winter. We may well see an ice-free Arctic Ocean in summer within our lifetimes. . . . The implications for global climate, as well as Arctic animals and people, are disturbing."[127] As Berger explained, "Every year, it is said, the polar ice cap is smaller by an area the size of Lake Superior.," and the "springtime melting in the Arctic has begun much earlier; in 2005 it started 17 days sooner than expected. In Greenland, across Davis Strait, the past two years were the warmest ever recorded in some of the coastal communities."[128] Indeed, "ten years ago the people at Cape Dorset could travel in September or October over the ice of Telluk Inlet to Baffin Island. Last year they couldn't make the journey over the ice until mid-December. In Iqaluit, in December, Inuit were putting to sea in Frobisher Bay in small pleasurecraft; I was told that, even a few years past, they could far more easily have walked across the frozen Bay. Birds such as robins are appearing for the first time. The anecdotes were universal; no one who has more than a few years' experience in the Arctic doubts that change is upon us."[129] Berger cites a presentation by James Hansen, director of NASA's Goddard Institute for Space Studies, to the American Geophysical Union on December 6, 2005, in which he observed that "Earth's climate has neared, but has not passed a tipping point beyond which it will be impossible to avoid climate change with far-ranging undesirable consequences. This includes not only the loss of the Arctic as we know it, with all that implies for wildlife and indigenous peoples, but losses on a much vaster scale due to rising seas."[130]

Berger notes that "the increasing warming of the North has obvious ramifications for economic development," and that "the warming of the Arctic will make Nunavut's minerals, its oil and gas more accessible. The opening of the Northwest Passage and the other passages through the Arctic Islands will bring navigation and shipping."[131] To this he adds: "Arctic warming, however, may bring accelerated industrial activity. And it may mean the loss of animal species the Inuit have depended on for centuries. Polar bear, walrus, and other marine mammals and birds may over time be at risk of extinction. The hunting and food sharing culture of Inuit may be under significant threat. I know it is said that with global warming species will flourish in the new climate and replace the species that are gone. But no one can predict such things with any confidence."[132] Berger writes that "the melting of polar ice has brought the world's attention to the fact that the Northwest Passage and the other passages through the Arctic Islands may in the quite foreseeable future be navigable for substantial periods of each year," and as a consequence, the "ownership of the resources and authority over the sea routes—in short, sovereignty over the North—is a topic of increasing discussion."[133]

When it comes to Canada's assertion of sovereignty to the Arctic, Berger explains that "effective occupation is one of the keys to sovereignty under international law," and the "immemorial presence of the Inuit in Canada's Arctic, as much as British and Canadian voyages through the Arctic Islands, is fundamental to Canada's claim."[134] That's because, "For centuries, the Inuit were the sole occupants of the Arctic Islands and most of Canada's Arctic coastline. They lived on the land and on the ice; they harvested the resources of the land and the sea. . . . In Canada we now know, through Aboriginal mapping projects conducted in recent years, that before Europeans came the Arctic was already mapped by the Inuit—traced all over by their hunting patterns."[135]

Berger recalls how "Canada's desire to establish its sovereignty in the High Arctic also led, at least in part, to the 1953 decision of the federal government to resettle some Inuit families farther North," when "seven families from the Inukjuak (Port Harrison) area in northern Québec and three families from Pond Inlet in what is now Nunavut were resettled in communities at Resolute Bay on Cornwallis Island and at Grise Fiord on Ellesmere Island. Over the next three years, the number of resettled families rose to seventeen. These Inuit communities remain the most northerly Canadian."[136] As reported by Jim Bell in the October 15, 1999 edition of *Nunatsiaq News*, "The heart-rending story of the forced relocation of the High Arctic exiles from Inukjuak to Resolute Bay and Grise Fiord in the 1950s is well-known throughout the Arctic, and well-known even among many southern Canadians," and has been "the subject of documentary films, numerous newspaper and magazine articles, and a variety of reports produced by governments and independent researchers. Thanks to their own prodigious efforts, and a special set of televised hearings organized by the Royal

Commission on Aboriginal Peoples, the High Arctic exiles and their immediate families eventually received $10 million in compensation—but no apology—from the government of Canada."[137] Bell observes there were numerous other cases of Inuit exiles, in addition to the well known exile to Grise Fjord and Resolute, as Ottawa "sanctioned relocations of Inuit occurred again and again throughout the 1950s and 1960s from one end of the Arctic to the other," starting in 1936, "when the Hudson's Bay Company, with the encouragement of the federal government, relocated 53 people from Cape Dorset, Pangnirtung and Pond Inlet to Devon Island."[138] Bell recounts that in "Baffin, the people of Padloping Island were relocated to Broughton Island in 1968," and "as late as 1978, the people of Killiniq—or Port Burwell—were dispersed throughout northern Quebec after the government of the Northwest Territories closed their community," while in Labrador, "the Newfoundland government moved the people of Hebron and Nutak to three communities to the south in 1959."[139]

There has been much controversy over the particular plight of the "High Arctic exiles," with numerous accounts written describing their poor treatment and near-abandonment by Canadian authorities during the early years of their relocation, such as Wil Haygood's August 1992 feature on the *Boston Globe*, "The Lie at the Top of the World," and several books including Alan Rudolph Marcus' 1995 *Relocating Eden: The Image and Politics of Inuit Exile in the Canadian Arctic*, and Melanie McGrath's 2008 *The Long Exile: A Tale of Inuit Betrayal and Survival in the High Arctic*. Berger correctly points out that their relocation to the High Arctic was driven largely by Ottawa's desire to establish a permanent population, and thus bolster its otherwise tenuous sovereign claims to the region. Because of the painful history of their relocation, and the chronicled neglect and mistreatment by government officials, Ottawa agreed to a $10 million financial settlement with the survivors of the original relocation and their descendants. But because Ottawa asserts the relocation effort was mutual and not a forced internal exile, and that its intention was in part to alleviate the threat of famine near Port Harrison (Inukjuak), it did not proffer an apology.

University of British Columbia international law expert Michael Byers recently reiterated the case for a formal apology to the High Arctic exiles in an op-ed in *The Globe and Mail* titled "Mr. Harper, apologize to the 'High Arctic Exiles': Not only is this the right thing to do, but it would help cement Canada's northern claims."[140] In his op-ed, Byers recalls how "Prime Minister Stephen Harper has apologized for the behaviour of previous Canadian governments on three occasions now: the Chinese head tax, Maher Arar, and residential schools." Byers notes while "others are, or will, also be seeking apologies," he believes that "none is more compelling—both morally and politically—than a small group of Inuit who were arbitrarily relocated half a century ago."[141] Byers sees a link between the apology issue and Canada's recent efforts to strengthen its sovereignty in the Arctic, and believes Ottawa's decision in the 1950s to move the exiles to the Elizabeth Islands "was motivated by concerns about possible Danish or American claims," and that "the Inuit, identified by government officials by numbers rather than their names, were essentially treated as flagpoles."[142] Byers notes that "for the Inuit, it was like landing on the moon."[143] Byers adds "the survivors call themselves the 'High Arctic Exiles,' and they include some of the Inuit's most influential leaders. John Amagoalik, the 'Father of Nunavut,' was five years old when he was relocated. So too was Martha Flaherty, who later became the president of Pauktuutit, the Inuit Women's Association. Senator Willie Adams, then a teenager, had the foresight to jump ship at Churchill."[144] Byers recalls how Ottawa "refused to apologize" when negotiating the $10 million compensation package in the mid-1990s, and that this "refusal was described by Mr. Amagoalik as a 'real slap in the face for us.'"[145] Byers argues that "for a Prime Minister who cares about sovereignty, apologizing to the High Arctic Exiles would be an excellent next step."[146]

But while an apology would be dramatic, and would in all likelihood be cheered by Inuit, the situation of the exiles is complicated by the fact that their presence in the High Arctic has resulted in some substantial benefits to the Inuit. Among these benefits are the large tracts of High Arctic lands selected for the Nunavut land claim, which contribute substantially not only to the land and resource wealth of the Inuit, but also to the territorial breadth of the Nunavut territory. By many measures, including the size of the new territory, the amount of land owned outright by the Inuit, the extent of their subsurface rights as well, and the inclusion of the High Arctic communities of Grise Fjord and Resolute and their continued stream of operational funding and infrastructure investments in Nunavut, the relocation of the exile families to the High Arctic has proven to be a long-term collective gain for the Inuit overall. Further, as Byers noted, Inuit leaders like John Amagoalik—considered by many to be the "Father of Nunavut"—emerged from the relocation experience; so as difficult as the experience was for the families involved, it made the Inuit stronger and not weaker for their suffering, contributing to the emergence of a strong and dedicated leadership that ultimately triumphed by creating Nunavut.

Michael R. Marrus, in his 2006 University of Toronto report on historical apologies, observed that we are "awash in apologies, both trivial and highly consequential," and that "extending across cultures, apologies have become a familiar part of our relational landscape. In particular, apologies have emerged as an instrument for promoting justice for historic wrongs."[147] He describes a "Wave of Apologies," noting that "recent years have seen a wave of official apologies, or near apologies, for wrongs committed in the distant past—and sometimes the far distant past."[148] As he elaborates: "University of San Diego law professor Roy Brooks, in a 500-page book entitled *When Sorry Isn't Enough*, refers to our 'Age of Apology;' Janna Thompson, an Australian philosopher who has written an important work on historical justice identifies an 'epidemic of apology;' historian Elazar Barkan refers to an 'avalanche of apologies;' and ethicist Lee Taft, writing in the *Yale Law Journal* on apologies' role in civil litigation, speaks about an 'apology mania.'"[149] Among the many examples considered in his report, Marrus presents two Canadian Prime Ministers' contrasting approaches to historical apologies, both concerning the plight of Japanese Canadians during

World War II. First is Pierre Trudeau: "On his last day as prime minister, Trudeau refused, apparently heatedly, a request that he apologize to Japanese Canadians for wartime removals and internments. 'I cannot rewrite history,' he said. 'It is our purpose to be just in our time and that is what we have done in bringing in the Charter of Rights.'"[150] Marrus also considers Brian Mulroney, who agreed to issue just such an apology that Trudeau had rejected, and who "in his 1988 apology for Japanese Canadians, won respect when analogized with interpersonal apologies: 'We have all learned from personal experience that as inadequate as apologies are they are the only way we can cleanse the past so that we may, as best we can, in good conscience face the future.'"[151] Marrus believes that "societies may need to find unconventional solutions in a continuing quest for justice," and that "under the right circumstances and appropriately delivered, apologies may well be worth considering."[152]

But it has long been my view that an apology, given the many tangible benefits to the Inuit that have come from the relocation, would not properly reflect this bittersweet mix of consequences, some negative and some positive. I prefer a different solution: Rather than issue an apology to the Inuit, I believe Ottawa should instead present a very heartfelt, and very public, "thank you"—or as it is said in the Inuktitut language: "Qujannamik." An apology would only feed into the psyche of victimhood, perpetuating a self-perception among Inuit of victimization that has only undermined Inuit self-confidence; while in contrast, a very public, and very heartfelt "Qujannamik" campaign would be uplifting, contributing to Inuit self-esteem by recognizing the inherent sovereign duality of Canada, reaffirming the dual nature of Canadian Arctic sovereignty, where state and tribe co-exist, and mutually strengthen one another. A Qujannamik campaign would not be about winners and losers, only winners. There would be no victims, only partners. This seems to be a more appropriate response, one that recognizes the equal contributions of tribe and state to the affirmation of Canada's Arctic sovereignty. A Qujannamik campaign would show Ottawa's sincere appreciation to the Inuit for all their contributions; for sharing their land with Canada; for selflessly joining the Canadian Rangers during times of war and peace, becoming the "eyes and ears" on the frontlines of Canada's northern defense, and contributing to search and rescue as well as sovereignty assertion missions; for welcoming the U.S. Air Force during the early Cold War era for DEW Line construction, and later contributing to the operations and maintenance of the new North Warning System and to the cleanup effort of the old DEW Line sites; in short, for being there, and staying there, and helping to make Canada more secure in the process.

Mistakes were made, and early on there was according to several accounts a pronounced insensitivity to the unique cultural requirements of Canada's most northerly citizens; but the story of Canada's exiles is not just a story of tragedy and suffering, but also of resilience and of hope. A Qujannamik campaign would recognize this resilience and hope, and not undermine its positivity. It would recognize all that has been learned, on all sides, from Ottawa to Iqaluit and beyond—about how to co-manage and to share in the development of the North, and how to self-govern, and administer a vast territory. Yes, there is much room for improvement, and so much more to learn—about improving existing health care and education policies to achieve the same levels of health security and educational accomplishment as seen in the South, while at the same time embracing and preserving Inuit cultural and linguistic traditions; about investing resources for much-needed infrastructure improvements, so that adequate housing and roads and port facilities can be achieved. Together, both sides can do better; but they already have much to be proud of. They have come a long way from those days of first contact between North and South, and have gone far beyond those first symbolic sovereignty patrols to a more tangible, meaningful, and legitimate expression of Arctic sovereignty. The partnership that has been built between the Inuit and the modern state can help both Ottawa and the Inuit to find further strength in their unity. And for that a heartfelt Qujannamik, and not a questionably sincere apology, would go much further.

Arctic Spring

Over the centuries, interest in the Arctic and the commercial and strategic potential of its sea lanes and resources has been persistent, but climatic conditions prevented the region's full potential from being achieved before now—holding back its development, and limiting its contribution to the world economy, making it neither a rimland or a heartland but something that the geopolitical theorist Mackinder called "Lenaland," named for the isolated Lena river valley in Russia. This long isolation now looks to be changing—as a result of the rapid warming of the Earth's climate and accelerated ice melts, several decades earlier than most had imagined could be possible. This puts the region in play strategically, as the historic promise of unlocking its full potential renews interest in the region among numerous stakeholders.

During the Cold War, with the threat of nuclear apocalypse hanging over all our heads, some strategic theorists sought to "think about the unthinkable," and prepare for all potential scenarios that might unfold. Herman Kahn, a former RAND Corporation analyst and founder of the Hudson Institute, was amongst this era's most colorful and controversial thinkers, becoming the template for the character of "Dr. Strangelove" in the popular Kubrick dark comedy. One of Kahn's books was called *On Escalation: Metaphors and Scenarios*, and it sought to present various metaphorical potentialities in order to help his readers comprehend the full range of scenarios that might unfold. But Kahn is more famous for his *Thinking About the Unthinkable*, which was one of the first explicit attempts to resist political correctness in "defense of thinking," even about frightening things like nuclear war. His other magnum open, *On Thermonuclear War*, made him a celebrity, and was one of the sources of the more apocalyptic elements of *Dr. Strangelove*'s unique conceptual vocabulary, like doomsday machines and mine-shaft gaps. What, you might ask, does Herman Kahn and the literature of nuclear warfare have to do with Arctic sovereignty? Quite a lot:

from our need to think about some pretty unthinkable things like the collapse of the polar ice pack and the end of a frozen Arctic, to a dramatic increase in Arctic shipping, resource development, urbanization, industrialization, and even the long-term possibility of forestation; as well, with the destabilization of the permafrost and warming of the polar sea, there's the specter of methane dumps inducing rapid temperature increases with the potential of outpacing evolution's adaptive capability, which as Al Gore has noted in *An Inconvenient Truth*, could mean the end of life itself. This is all huge, and potentially historic, stuff, no different than the issues faced in the nuclear age in terms of the underlying risks. With the stakes of climate change so high, in the Arctic and around the world; and with the clash between the optimists and pessimists every bit as intense as that witnessed during the Cold War's doctrinal debates, a look at some metaphors and scenarios for our age makes as much sense as it did for Kahn and the other strategic thinkers of the Cold War.

During the Cold War there were two fundamental strategic concepts that emerged to handle nuclear weapons. One was Bernard Brodie's "deterrence" concept, which sought to maintain stability by balancing mutual fear, creating MAD, Mutual Assured Destruction, or what some called the Balance of Terror. Then there was Kahn's response which was to imagine nuclear warfighting at every level from localized nuclear wars to a general, total war that would result in tens or hundreds of millions killed. One was guardedly optimistic about the prognosis for peace, while the other was more optimistic about the potential outcome of a nuclear war, and our ability to both survive and win one. With the Arctic, we have a similar divergence in optimism and pessimism: some have postulated that what we think of as the Arctic is actually coming to an end, and that we now stand at what might very be the threshold of a "post-Arctic" world. The Arctic Ocean and its increasingly active basin will of course still be there— more obviously so as the ice retreats. But its currently dominant characteristics are changing rapidly—in particular the massive, permanent, continent-sized barrier of multi-year ice that sits atop the pole, which could in time disappear. As the ice pack retreats, the polar barrier that marked the very "ends of the Earth," or what was long ago called "Ultima Thule" has the potential to become a trans-polar crossroads, or what mapmakers long ago imagined to be the "Midnight Sea," and already shipping experts are considering potential routes across the top of the world between Asia and Europe.

What Rob Huebert and Brooks Yeager call a "New Sea" in their January 2008 World Wildlife Fund Report will soon emerge, and what was once the "ends of the Earth" now has the potential to become its center, a profound transformation from "terra incognita" to a true "medi-terranean." The concept of a post-Arctic world is not a new one. One of the first to articulate this concept was Canadian journalist Ed Struzik, who authored a 1992 *Equinox Magazine* article titled, appropriately, "The End of the Arctic?" More recently, of course, is Al Gore's "Inconvenient Truth" thesis which echoes Struzik's earlier argument that we are witnessing the end of a unique part of the Earth's heritage. Gore goes further, suggesting a potential global catastrophe that threatens to end most life on our planet. Even if such an apocalyptic end does not result from climate change, Arctic peoples and their governments will have to contend with the impacts of shifting wildlife migration patterns, coastal erosion and permafrost thaws that jeopardize much northern infrastructure. And even new opportunities such as increased trans-polar shipping will bring new risks and challenges, especially as multi-year ice breaks up and drifts south into the emergent sea lanes, requiring much investment and infrastructure development to ensure adequate safety, search and rescue, environmental cleanup, and marine service capabilities are in place.

There are also many optimists who see us standing at the start of a new era, much like Francis Fukuyama viewed the end of the Cold War as a Hegelian "End of History," and the dawn of a new era of hope. This more optimistic viewpoint believes we're now entering the dawn of the "Age of the Arctic," the title of the well known book and 1986 *Foreign Policy* article by Oran Young or as described by the phrase made famous in 1973 by former Alaska Governor Walter Hickel, that we're approaching the "Day of the Arctic." One can look even further back, all the way to William H. Seward's 1853 "Destiny of America" speech that predicted the expansion of America to include "new equal States, alike free, independent and united" whose borders "shall be extended so that it shall greet the sun when he touches the Tropic, and when he sends his glancing rays towards the Polar circle." Seward helped fulfill his prediction when he negotiated the purchase of Alaska from Russia in 1867—though at the time he was much criticized for "Seward's Ice Box," or "Seward's Folly." Whether we stand at a precipice before the tragic "End of the Arctic," or at the gateway to the promising "Age of the Arctic," depends ultimately on whether we approach the climate issue with hope or fear, and whether we anticipate great opportunity, or severe danger.

I think of the coming era as the onset of the Arctic Spring. It has the potential to transform the Arctic basin much like Prague Spring promised to open up and integrate Czechoslovakia with the West, but which in the end was crushed for another generation. However, the hope expressed in 1968 was finally fulfilled twenty years later, when the Velvet Revolution, a people-powered insurgency against the Communist state, succeeded in bringing down the Moscow-backed tyranny. As we think about this coming transformation, this looming Arctic Spring, we should remember that this is a new chapter of history—with the potential for new ideas and innovation. Soviet Premier Gorbachev had such a vision for the Arctic at the Cold War's end, expressed in October 1987 in his Murmansk Initiative, which called for the Arctic to become a "Zone of Peace," and to lead the way forward to an end of the Cold War. But events quickly sped beyond his control, with the fall of the Berlin Wall more speedily integrating East and West than his Arctic diplomatic efforts. But the idea was a good one, and perhaps worth revisiting. At Ilulissat in May 2008, a similar vision of an Arctic united and governed by international law was asserted; it remains to be seen if this vision ultimately triumphs. It is possible that the Arctic basin will become a new arena for cooperation between Russia and the West, much as Gorbachev foresaw at Murmansk. But much depends on the evolution of political attitudes in all of the Arctic states, and whether the political climate warms along with the geophysical climate. It is notable that at Ilulissat, only the top foreign affairs officials of the Arctic rim states were present, suggesting that even as they pledge to collaborate in their efforts to resolve future Arctic disputes, they have yet to fully integrate the input of the region's inhabitants, and in particular its indigenous peoples. This was noted by the Inuit leadership, who one year later issued their own declaration on Arctic sovereignty, calling for the rightful, and central, place in determining its future.

But on the other hand, the Ilulissat Summit did take place in Greenland, and not a southern capital like Copenhagen or Washington or Ottawa; and further, it pledged to walk the path of cooperation, not conflict. Both are important steps forward. The next step should be to broaden the circle of stakeholders, so that the dynamic and creative efforts of the indigenous peoples of the region, and their many interests and perspectives, can help to shape the world's response to the changes taking place at the top of the world. With the new regional governing structures across the Arctic now fully integrating the Inuit, and settled land claims empowering indigenous peoples with huge tracts of lands and substantial economic resources, their participation is not only enabled: it is essential, as the internal and external dimensions of Arctic security have come together at the top of our world.

Sea Change in America's Arctic Policy

Many of the policies of President Bush's administration were controversial, and some believe unnecessarily unilateral and divisive; but in the closing hours of his presidency, he issued the first new American Arctic policy since 1994, a fascinating document full of multilateralism, pledging the United States to work with international, regional, local, and even tribal organizations. It was so unexpected that the initial response was largely one of denial, with media attention focusing on the few unilateral components relating to national and homeland security but not on the dozens of other more collaborative dimensions. Those reflected a sophisticated awareness of the transformation of the Arctic, and showed an appreciation of the increasing role of its indigenous peoples— marking a collaborative and multilateral conclusion to his highly controversial presidency.

A tectonic shift—toward greater collaboration with, and participation of, the numerous tribal, national, and international actors on the circumpolar stage— was evident in the first comprehensive re-articulation of U.S. national policy on the Arctic region since 1994. Indeed, it is noteworthy that among the six policy objectives identified in Section III, part A of National Security Presidential Directive 66/Homeland Security Presidential Directive 25 (NSPD-66/HSPD-25)— issued on January 9, 2009, in the final days of the Bush administration—were to

"Strengthen institutions for cooperation among the eight Arctic nations" (objective number four) and to "Involve the Arctic's indigenous communities in decisions that affect them" (objective number five.) This is historically significant, and demonstrates both an increased awareness of, and respect for, the growing political and economic participation of the Arctic peoples in governing their own affairs, as well as a continued commitment to a collaborative, multilateral approach to solving the region's challenges.

Also of significance: while the very first policy objective listed in Section III, A, is to "Meet national security and homeland security needs relevant to the Arctic region," a point that has dominated news coverage and commentaries on the new Arctic policy, the second objective listed is to "Protect the Arctic environment and conserve its biological resources," while the third to "Ensure that natural resource management and economic development in the region are environmentally sustainable," which will directly benefit the foundational pillars upon which the indigenous Arctic cultures depend for their cultural, nutritional, and economic survival. That the sixth policy objective listed is to "Enhance scientific monitoring and research into local, regional, and global environmental issues," which further reinforces America's renewed commitment to multilateralism at the top of the world, and increasing environmental knowledge at all levels, from the local to the global, during this time of Arctic transformation.

These important dimensions to the new U.S. Arctic policy were largely overlooked by many observers, in particular by the op-ed pages of several newspapers north of the border that emphasized the national security and unilateral dimensions of America's new Arctic policy. For instance, as *The Chronicle Herald* opined in its January 15th editorial, "Arctic Sovereignty: No More Northern Lite":

> Just a week before the White House changes hands, it has released a new policy directive on the Arctic that calls for a more assertive American role. The bedrock of the policy is the same—that the U.S. considers the Northwest Passage international waters, not Canadian domestic waters. But the document also calls for a stronger U.S. presence in the Arctic for economic and security reasons and for a resolution of Arctic border disputes so the region's natural resources can be better exploited.

The Calgary Herald published an article on January 13th by *Canwest News Service* reporters Mike Blanchfield and Randy Boswell, titled "Bush Asserts Power Over Arctic," which was linked to, and cited by Andrew C. Revkin on January 13th, in his widely read *Dot Earth Blog* in *The New York Times*. And, in a national news story in *The Globe and Mail* newspaper on January 14th ("Northwest Passage: Harper plays down threat to Arctic sovereignty"), Katherine O'Neill reported that Northwest Territories (NWT) Premier Floyd Roland believes the "increased U.S. interest in the region is of deep concern and the federal government should respond with more than rhetoric," as "too much is at stake in the Far North."

O'Neill cited Premier Roland, who told her: "Let's not lose it for the sake of being nice. Canada can no longer afford to maintain a passive approach to our northern interests." O'Neill reported the new U.S. policy directive "reasserts the Americans' long-held claim that the fabled Northwest Passage is an international waterway, open to all. Canada argues that the route is an internal waterway." She added the new policy "also states that the United States should develop a greater presence in the Arctic for security reasons, as well as resolve outstanding border disputes, including one with Canada in the Beaufort Sea, so it can tap into the region's vast natural resources." She also cited from the directive the following passage: "The United States has broad and fundamental national security interests in the Arctic region and is prepared to operate either independently or in conjunction with other states to safeguard these interests." And she quoted Canada's well known Arctic security expert, Professor Rob Huebert from the University of Calgary, who "said Mr. Bush's directive has effectively 'thrown a grenade into Canada-U.S. relations' and that it will be interesting to see what the new president does with it. 'This is a very blunt statement . . . they didn't play any political niceties here.'"

Somehow, the unprecedented level of collaboration that the White House has embraced—with its top-level commitment to indigenous as well as global participation, and its refreshingly holistic approach to the region's environmental and ecological health as well as to continued scientific research in the interest of protecting this fragile domain—got overlooked in the first round of commentary, analysis, and opinion that greeted the release of the directive. Clarifying its policy, on January 13th the U.S. State Department provided a statement in response to a question at its daily press briefing in which it explained: "The new directive is the culmination of an extensive interagency review process undertaken in response to rapid changes taking place in the Arctic, the principal drivers of which are climate change, increasing human presence in the region, and the growing demand for Arctic energy deposits and other natural resources," and noted the "directive focuses on seven broad areas of Arctic policy," including:

1. National security and homeland security,
2. International governance,
3. Extended continental shelf and boundary issues,
4. Promotion of international scientific cooperation,
5. Maritime transportation,
6. Economic issues, including energy resources, and
7. Environmental protection and conservation of natural resources.

The State Department also reiterated its commitment to Arctic cooperation, noting that "States safeguard their national security interests in numerous ways, some on their own, and some in cooperation with others. The United States wants to cooperate with other governments in the Arctic. The best way to address both the challenges and opportunities of the Arctic is through cooperation. Any U.S. action would respect international law."

It is true that Sec. III, B, of the directive addresses U.S. national and homeland security issues, and observes that "human activity in the Arctic region is increasing and is projected to increase further in coming years," requiring the United States "to assert a more active and influential national presence to protect its Arctic interests and to project sea power throughout the region." And, consequently, the directive does describe America's Arctic national interests to "include such matters as missile defense and early warning; deployment of sea and air systems for strategic sealift, strategic deterrence, maritime presence, and maritime security operations; and ensuring freedom of navigation and overflight." And, to be fair, the directive does re-assert America's long-held view of the Northwest Passage as an international strait. But to take away from the directive only these policy issues, and not the many others that demonstrate a deep commitment to multilateralism and an historically unprecedented sensitivity to the needs, interests, and perspectives of the indigenous peoples of the Arctic, does something of a disservice, and suggests an incomplete reading of the directive. For instance, Sec. III, C, specifically addresses issues of international governance, noting U.S. participation in "a variety of fora, international organizations, and bilateral contacts that promote United States interests in the Arctic," including the Arctic Council, which "has produced positive results for the United States," and which also "provides a beneficial venue for interaction with indigenous groups." Further, the directive urges the U.S. Senate to "act favorably on U.S. accession to the U.N. Convention on the Law of the Sea promptly, to protect and advance U.S. interests, including with respect to the Arctic," and doing so "will give the United States a seat at the table when the rights that are vital to our interests are debated and interpreted."

The directive calls upon American officials to "continue to cooperate with other countries on Arctic issues through the United Nations (U.N.) and its specialized agencies, as well as through treaties such as the U.N. Framework Convention on Climate Change, the Convention on International Trade in Endangered Species of Wild Fauna and Flora, the Convention on Long Range Transboundary Air Pollution and its protocols, and the Montreal Protocol on Substances that Deplete the Ozone Layer," and to "consider, as appropriate, new or enhanced international arrangements for the Arctic to address issues likely to arise from expected increases in human activity in that region, including shipping, local development and subsistence, exploitation of living marine resources, development of energy and other resources, and tourism." Additionally, Sec. III, E, commits the United States to continued promotion of international scientific cooperation, including "the sharing of Arctic research platforms with other countries in support of collaborative research that advances fundamental understanding of the Arctic region in general and potential Arctic change in particular," and the "active involvement of all Arctic nations in these efforts in order to advance scientific understanding that could provide the basis for assessing future impacts and proposed response strategies." Even Sec. III, F, on maritime transportation in the Arctic, takes a collaborative approach, across not only the various levels of domestic governance but national boundaries, as "effective search and rescue in the Arctic will require local, State, Federal, tribal, commercial, volunteer, scientific, and multinational cooperation," as "safe, secure, and environmentally sound maritime commerce in the Arctic region depends on infrastructure to support shipping activity, search and rescue capabilities, short- and long-range aids to navigation, high-risk area vessel-traffic management, iceberg warnings and other sea ice information, effective shipping standards, and measures to protect the marine environment."

And Sec. III, G, on economic and energy issues, directs U.S. officials to "seek to increase efforts, including those in the Arctic Council, to study changing climate conditions, with a view to preserving and enhancing economic opportunity in the Arctic region," and that "such efforts shall include inventories and assessments of villages, indigenous communities, subsistence opportunities, public facilities, infrastructure, oil and gas development projects, alternative energy development opportunities, forestry, cultural and other sites, living marine resources, and other elements of the Arctic's socioeconomic composition." It also calls upon U.S. officials to "work with other Arctic nations to ensure that hydrocarbon and other development in the Arctic region is carried out in accordance with accepted best practices and internationally recognized standards," and to "consult with other Arctic nations to discuss issues related to exploration, production, environmental and socioeconomic impacts." Lastly, Sec. III, H, on environmental protection and the conservation of natural resources, notes with concern that "the Arctic environment is unique and changing," and that "increased human activity is expected to bring additional stressors to the Arctic environment, with potentially serious consequences for Arctic communities and ecosystems." As with the earlier sections of the directive, it calls for "cooperation with other nations," so as to "respond effectively to increased pollutants and other environmental challenges," and to "continue to identify ways to conserve, protect, and sustainably manage Arctic species and ensure adequate enforcement presence to safeguard living marine resources, taking account of the changing ranges or distribution of some species in the Arctic."

And for those species "whose range includes areas both within and beyond United States jurisdiction," it calls upon the United States to "continue to collaborate with other governments to ensure effective conservation and management." It also calls upon officials to "seek to develop ways to address changing and expanding commercial fisheries in the Arctic, including through consideration of international agreements or organizations to govern future Arctic fisheries; pursue marine ecosystem-based management in the Arctic; and intensify efforts to develop scientific information on the adverse effects of pollutants on human health and the environment and work with other nations to reduce the introduction of key pollutants into the Arctic." None of these issues suggest a go-it-alone attitude by the United States. Quite the contrary, it reflects an awakening to the increased participatory role of indigenous peoples, circumpolar neighbors, and international organizations in the management of the Arctic, and the continued need for a multilateral approach to managing the Arctic's unique challenges in the years ahead. While the new policy does not reflect a change of perspective on the legal status of the Northwest Passage, or a softening in America's commitment to freedom of the seas, it does suggest a sea change is underway in its perception of, and sensitivity to, the numerous challenges mounting at the top of the world as the ice continues its retreat, and the prospect of a post-Arctic world enters the realm of the possible. Most importantly, it shows a far greater sensitivity to the interests and perspectives of the indigenous peoples as well as America's Arctic neighbors, and a willingness to work together in a joint effort to resolve these challenges in the years ahead.

Circumpolar Inuit Declaration on Arctic Sovereignty

On April 28, 2009, a delegation of Inuit leaders from Greenland, Canada, Alaska, and Russia presented a Circumpolar Inuit Declaration on Arctic Sovereignty in Tromsø, Norway, where the Arctic Council was meeting. It represented the Inuit response to their exclusion at Ilulissat, and while it does not directly consider the many details presented in the new U.S. Arctic policy, it nonetheless illustrates that both the Inuit and the modern state are converging in their conceptualization of Arctic sovereignty, with both viewing it to be an increasingly collaborative and mutually reinforcing concept. The declaration emerges from the work of the first Inuit Leaders' Summit on November 6–7, 2008, in Kuujjuaq, Nunavik, in Northern Quebec, where they "gathered to address Arctic sovereignty" and "expressed unity in our concerns over Arctic sovereignty deliberations, examined the options for addressing these concerns, and strongly committed to developing a formal declaration on Arctic sovereignty."[153] There, the Inuit leaders "noted that the 2008 Ilulissat Declaration on Arctic sovereignty by ministers representing the five coastal Arctic states did not go far enough in affirming the rights Inuit have gained through international law, land claims and self-government processes."[154] In many ways, their declaration was their direct response to the foreign ministers of the Arctic states for their exclusion at Ilulissat, and it constructively redresses this exclusion, and persuasively argues for their central role in determining the fate of the Arctic. As the ICC observed at this start of their effort in November 2008, "Sovereignty is a complex issue. It has a variety of overlapping elements, anchored in international law. But fundamentally it begins with the history and reality of Inuit use and occupation of Arctic lands and waters; that use and occupation is at the heart of any informed discussion of sovereignty in the Arctic. Arctic nation states must respect the rights and roles of Inuit in all international discussions and commitments dealing with the Arctic."[155] ICC chair Patricia Cochran noted that "one clear message from the convening of our meeting is that for all sorts of reasons—law, politics, and the very practical reason that the world stands to learn the most about the Arctic from the people who know the Arctic best—Inuit have an essential role in international discussions about Arctic waters, marine transportation plans, environmental initiatives and mechanisms, and the future of international Arctic institutions and relations generally."[156]

The April 2009 declaration unveiled at Tromsø updates the Inuit policy on sovereignty in the Arctic, following in much detail their vision and blueprint as put forth by the ICC in 1992 just as the Cold War era came to an end. Their new declaration on sovereignty notes the Inuit "live in the vast, circumpolar region of land, sea and ice known as the Arctic" and "depend on the marine and terrestrial plants and animals supported by the coastal zones of the Arctic Ocean, the tundra and the sea ice. The Arctic is our home."[157] It asserts that Inuit "use and occupation of Arctic lands and waters pre-dates recorded history" and that their "unique knowledge, experience of the Arctic, and language are the foundation of our way of life and culture."[158] The declaration notes while the "Inuit live across a far-reaching circumpolar region," they remain "united as a single people," and that their "sense of unity is fostered and celebrated by the Inuit Circumpolar Council (ICC)."[159] It further notes that Inuit "enjoy the rights of all peoples," and that these "include the rights recognized in and by various international instruments and institutions" as well as "the rights and responsibilities of all indigenous peoples" as "recognized in and by international legal and political instruments and bodies."[160] In what may be viewed as a prelude to a later bid for independence, the declaration asserts that "central to our rights as a people is the right to self-determination," which "is our right to freely determine our political status, freely pursue our economic, social, cultural and linguistic development, and freely dispose of our natural wealth and resources. States are obligated to respect and promote the realization of our right to self-determination."[161]

The declaration notes that Inuit rights as indigenous peoples include those rights "recognized in the United Nations Declaration on the Rights of Indigenous Peoples (UNDRIP), all of which are relevant to sovereignty and sovereign rights in the Arctic."[162] The Inuit note that they are specifically "an indigenous people of the Arctic" whose "status, rights and responsibilities as a people among the peoples of the world, and as an indigenous people, are exercised within the unique geographic, environmental, cultural and political context of the Arctic," something that "has been acknowledged in the eight-nation Arctic Council, which provides a direct, participatory role for Inuit through the permanent participant status accorded the Inuit Circumpolar Council."[163] But the Inuit are also "citizens of Arctic states" and as such "have the rights and responsibilities afforded all citizens under the constitutions, laws, policies and public sector programs of these states."[164] Because the Inuit are "indigenous citizens of Arctic states," they "have the rights and responsibilities afforded all indigenous peoples under the constitutions, laws, policies and public sector programs of these states."[165] The Inuit are likewise "indigenous citizens of each of the major political subunits of Arctic states (states, provinces, territories and regions)" and thus "have the rights and responsibilities afforded all indigenous peoples under the constitutions, laws, policies and public sector programs of these subunits."[166] All of these rights and responsibilities, the Inuit contend, "do not diminish the rights and responsibilities of Inuit as a people under international law."[167]

Section two of the declaration concerns the "Evolving Nature of Sovereignty in the Arctic," and notes sovereignty "has often been used to refer to the absolute and independent authority of a community or nation both internally and externally" but that it remains a "contested concept, however, and does not have a fixed meaning."[168] Further, the declaration notes, "Old ideas of sovereignty are breaking down as different governance models, such as the European Union, evolve," where "sovereignties overlap and are frequently divided within federations in creative ways to recognize the right of peoples."[169] Therefore, for the Inuit, "issues of sovereignty and sovereign rights must be examined and assessed in the context of our long history of struggle to gain recognition and respect as an Arctic indigenous people having the right to exercise self-determination over our lives, territories, cultures and languages."[170] The Inuit further note that "recognition and respect for our right to self-determination is developing at varying paces and in various forms in the Arctic states in which we live," and that:

> Following a referendum in November 2008, the areas of self-government in Greenland will expand greatly and, among other things, Greenlandic (Kalaallisut) will become Greenland's sole official language. In Canada, four land claims agreements are some of the key building blocks of Inuit rights; while there are conflicts over the implementation of these agreements, they remain of vital relevance to matters of self-determination and of sovereignty and sovereign rights. In Alaska, much work is needed to clarify and implement the rights recognized in the Alaska Native Claims Settlement Act (ANCSA) and the Alaska National Interest Lands Conservation Act (ANILCA). In particular, subsistence hunting and self-government rights need to be fully respected and accommodated, and issues impeding their enjoyment and implementation need to be addressed and resolved. And in Chukotka, Russia, a very limited number of administrative processes have begun to secure recognition of Inuit rights. These developments will provide a foundation on which to construct future, creative governance arrangements tailored to diverse circumstances in states, regions and communities.[171]

The declaration observes that in "exercising our right to self-determination in the circumpolar Arctic, we continue to develop innovative and creative jurisdictional arrangements that will appropriately balance our rights and responsibilities as an indigenous people, the rights and responsibilities we share with other peoples who live among us, and the rights and responsibilities of states," and that in "seeking to exercise our rights in the Arctic, we continue to promote compromise and harmony with and among our neighbours."[172] It notes that "international and other instruments increasingly recognize the rights of indigenous peoples to self-determination and representation in intergovernmental matters, and are evolving beyond issues of internal governance to external relations,"[173] and that the Inuit are "permanent participants at the Arctic Council with a direct and meaningful seat at discussion and negotiating tables."[174] However, even though the Ilulissat Declaration pledged the Arctic rim states to "use international mechanisms and international law to resolve sovereignty disputes," thus far "in their discussions of Arctic sovereignty" they "have not referenced existing international instruments that promote and protect the rights of indigenous peoples. They have also neglected to include Inuit in Arctic sovereignty discussions in a manner comparable to Arctic Council deliberations."[175]

Section three of the declaration considers "Inuit, the Arctic and Sovereignty: Looking Forward," and asserts that the "actions of Arctic peoples and states, the interactions between them, and the conduct of international relations must be anchored in the rule of law,"[176] and that the "actions of Arctic peoples and states, the interactions between them, and the conduct of international relations must give primary respect to the need for global environmental security, the need for peaceful resolution of disputes, and the inextricable linkages between issues of sovereignty and sovereign rights in the Arctic and issues of self-determination."[177] It advocates the role of Inuit as "active partners" and notes that "inextricable linkages between issues of sovereignty and sovereign rights in the Arctic and Inuit self-determination and other rights require states to accept the presence and role of Inuit as partners in the conduct of international relations in the Arctic."[178] Furthermore, the declaration notes that a "variety of other factors, ranging from unique Inuit knowledge of Arctic ecosystems to the need for appropriate emphasis on sustainability in the weighing of resource development proposals, provide practical advantages to conducting international relations in the Arctic in partnership with Inuit."[179] Thus, it concludes, "Inuit consent, expertise and perspectives are critical to progress on international issues involving the Arctic, such as global environmental security, sustainable development, militarization, commercial fishing, shipping, human health, and economic and social development."[180] Thus, "as states increasingly focus on the Arctic and its resources, and as climate change continues to create easier access to the Arctic, Inuit inclusion as active partners is central to all national and international deliberations on Arctic sovereignty and related questions, such as who owns the Arctic, who has the right to traverse the Arctic, who has the right to develop the Arctic, and who will be responsible for the social and environmental impacts increasingly facing the Arctic."[181]

The declaration asserts that the "inclusion of Inuit as active partners in all future deliberations on Arctic sovereignty will benefit both the Inuit community and the international community,"[182] and that "extensive involvement of Inuit in global, trans-national and indigenous politics requires the building of new partnerships with states for the protection and promotion of indigenous economies, cultures and traditions."[183] These partnerships, the declaration contends, "must acknowledge that industrial development of the natural resource wealth of the Arctic can proceed only insofar as it enhances the economic and social well-being of Inuit and safeguards our environmental security."

The declaration calls for "enhanced international exchange and cooperation in relation to the Arctic, particularly in relation to the dynamics and impacts of climate change and sustainable economic and social development," as "regional institutions that draw together Arctic states, states from outside the Arctic, and representatives of Arctic indigenous peoples can provide useful mechanisms for international exchange and cooperation."[184] The Inuit contend that the "pursuit of global environmental security requires a coordinated global approach to the challenges of climate change, a rigorous plan to arrest the growth in human-generated carbon emissions, and a far-reaching program of adaptation to climate change in Arctic regions and communities,"[185] and note that the "magnitude of the climate change problem dictates that Arctic states and their peoples fully participate in international efforts aimed at arresting and reversing levels of greenhouse gas emissions and enter into international protocols and treaties."[186] Further, the declaration asserts that "these international efforts, protocols and treaties cannot be successful without the full participation and cooperation of indigenous peoples."[187] The "pursuit of economic opportunities in a warming Arctic" requires states to "act so as to: (1) put economic activity on a sustainable footing; (2) avoid harmful resource exploitation; (3) achieve standards of living for Inuit that meet national and international norms and minimums; and (4) deflect sudden and far-reaching demographic shifts that would overwhelm and marginalize indigenous peoples where we are rooted and have endured."[188] Ultimately, the very "foundation, projection and enjoyment of Arctic sovereignty and sovereign rights all require healthy and sustainable communities in the Arctic," as "sovereignty begins at home."[189] The Inuit pledge to build upon "today's mechanisms for the future," and to "exercise our rights of self-determination in the Arctic by building on institutions such as the Inuit Circumpolar Council and the Arctic Council," and "the Arctic-specific features of international instruments."[190]

Section four of the declaration contains the heart of the "Circumpolar Inuit Declaration on Sovereignty in the Arctic," asserting that the "conduct of international relations in the Arctic and the resolution of international disputes in the Arctic are not the sole preserve of Arctic states or other states" but "are also within the purview of the Arctic's indigenous peoples."[191] Accordingly, the "development of international institutions in the Arctic, such as multi-level governance systems and indigenous peoples' organizations, must transcend Arctic states' agendas on sovereignty and sovereign rights and the traditional monopoly claimed by states in the area of foreign affairs."[192] Because "issues of sovereignty and sovereign rights in the Arctic have become inextricably linked to issues of self-determination in the Arctic," the declaration asserts that the "Inuit and Arctic states must, therefore, work together closely and constructively to chart the future of the Arctic."[193] Thus, the Inuit affirm that they are "committed to this Declaration and to working with Arctic states and others to build partnerships in which the rights, roles and responsibilities of Inuit are fully recognized and accommodated."[194]

Toward a Post-Arctic World

In the years ahead, the Arctic promises to become much less isolated than in the past. As Heritage Foundation analysts Ariel Cohen, Lajos F. Szaszdi, and Jim Dolbow have observed: "The Arctic is quickly reemerging as a strategic area where vital U.S. interests are at stake. The geo-political and geo-economic importance of the Arctic region is rising rapidly, and its mineral wealth will likely transform the region into a booming economic frontier in the twenty-first century."[195] As they describe:

> The coasts and continental shelf of the Arctic Ocean are estimated to hold large deposits of oil, natural gas, and meth-ane hydrate (natural gas) clusters along with large quantities of valuable minerals. With the shrinking of the polar ice cap, extended navigation through the Northwest Passage along the northern coast of North America may soon become possible with the help of icebreakers. Similarly, Russia is seeking to make the Northern Sea Route along the northern coast of Eurasia navigable for considerably longer periods of the year. Opening these shorter routes will significantly cut the time and costs of shipping.[196]

With increased commercial and strategic activity in the Arctic basin, competition for the region's resources will surely grow. As this competition intensifies, it will become increasingly vital for the Inuit and the modern states that surround the Arctic basin to work collaboratively, to defend their shared interests and values, and to protect their shared homeland from new and emerging threats. As Cohen, Szaszdi, and Dolbow noted: "In recent years, Russia has been particularly active in the Arctic, aggressively advancing its interests and claims by using international law and by projecting military might into the region."[197] While post-Soviet Russia has been far less menacing to the security of North America than the old Soviet Union was, the region continues to be of strategic interest to all the Arctic rim and non-rim states as well as the industrial states further to the south in both Northeast Asia and Europe—particularly with the advent of global warming and its potentially profound impact on the Arctic region.

In the past few years, record ice melts have been experienced, with the long frozen Northwest and Northeast passages becoming simultaneously ice-free in the summer of 2008. In time, a seasonally ice-free Arctic may become the rule and not the exception, with some scientists predicting an ice-free Arctic could emerge as early as the summer of 2013, though others anticipate a later polar thaw in mid-century. Consequently, the "trickle" of Arctic commerce that was on the rise in the mid-1980s, as described by Nathaniel French Caldwell, is widely expected to become a veritable deluge, and this will create new challenges for both the Inuit and the Arctic states in their continuing efforts to assert a meaningful and enduring sovereignty over the Arctic.

Much of Ottawa's current Arctic defense build-up, announced in 2007 after Moscow laid claim to a vast stretch of the Arctic seabed—including plans for a new fleet of Arctic offshore patrol vessels and a new naval facility in the High Arctic—is in direct response to this rising tide of commercial interest in the region, and the increased attention to the undersea resources by the Arctic rim states, which each seek as large a slice of the pie as they can legitimately claim and effectively defend, and non-rim states eager for much of the Arctic to be recognized as High Seas. The new palette of issues faced by Ottawa's strategic planners remains much the same as in the Cold War, albeit driven by a different sort of threat—one that is more commercial in nature, at the moment, than military. As Caldwell observed, it was commercial interest in the Arctic that first drove Ottawa's attention to its northern territories, resulting in its continuing efforts to assert jurisdictional control over the region early in the twentieth century. And it is again commercial interests that have led Canada and its neighbors to redouble their focus on their Arctic territories and seas, and in the case of Ottawa, to dust off plans from 1988 to establish a more robust naval presence in the High Arctic.

As Oran Young wrote in 1992, just as the post–Cold War era began, "there are reasons to believe that the Far North will continue to be an arena of considerable strategic significance during the foreseeable future."[198] Young noted that "the rising tide of human activities in this environmentally sensitive region demands an increased effort to coordinate actions, not only to reap mutual benefits but also to avoid mutual losses. The result is a growing challenge requiring both innovative political thinking and effective leadership."[199] He recalled how during the Cold War, "international relations among the ice states seemed simple and unambiguous," since the strategic challenges inherent in the bipolar division of the world, and the Arctic, resulted in two military blocs facing off against one another across the Arctic Ocean.[200] "From this perspective, it was easy to treat the Arctic as a peripheral area presenting no distinctive issues in its own right."[201] But no more. As the Cold War came to an end, this perceived simplicity was no longer tenable. As Young explained: "By contrast, the situation now emerging as a result of the militarization and industrialization of the Arctic, the end of the Cold War, and the break-up of the Soviet Union is far less straightforward and unambiguous."[202]

Indeed, these emergent complexities will challenge the young institutional structures created by land claims and self-government negotiations across the Arctic, which have yielded novel and innovative governing structures from Alaska's North Slope Borough, formed in 1972 and governing over 89,000 square miles of Arctic coastal territory; to the vast 770,000 square mile Nunavut Territory created in 1999; to the traditional system of Inuit governance reestablished in the 28,000 square mile Labrador Inuit Settlement Area in 2005. Consider the recent tensions observed in the co-management process between Inuit and Ottawa that were exacerbated by the additional pressures of climate change, as reported by John Bird in *Nunatsiaq News*. Bird describes the observations of Doug Clark, the lead author of a study on polar bear management who "found a growing breakdown in the relationship between Inuit hunters and government managers who rely on science," and who explained the problem is that the management system was developed "in a simpler time, when climate change was not on the agenda and land claims were only a concept."[203]

> Now, he said there are four sets of stakeholders: the Inuit and Inuvialuit who live with the bears, and who clearly have the most at stake in terms of livelihood and cultural identity; the scientific management proponents; environmental groups using the polar bear to "mobilize the public and pressure governments to act on climate change;" and those who would deny climate change is an issue or that there is any reason to be concerned about polar bears. . . . As a result, polar bear management strategies have become "polarized and politicized."[204]

But Clark still believes "it's not too late to save the system," and that a "good starting point . . . is that scientific management advocates, who now wield most of the power, must make sure they fully understand the Inuit position," and "they can do that by becoming more involved with the Inuit on concrete, local concerns."[205] As Clark explained: "Trust and respect are the two kinds of glue that hold co-management together. And that glue is running thin. They need to be repaired."[206] Therein lays the ultimate challenge of Arctic sovereignty, from the Bering Sea to Baffin Bay and beyond—reaching as far away as Greenland, Lapland, and Siberia. It is up to all of us, North and South, to repair that glue, and restore the bond of trust that unites tribe and state in the Far North, and which reconciles our two distinct perspectives on Arctic sovereignty.

There has always been a fundamental ambiguity along this "Last Frontier," as the line that defines the boundary between North and South, internal and external, tribe and state, has traditionally been blurred—like the ubiquitous Arctic ice fog that so often induces a sense of vertigo, making it all but impossible to identify where the land ends and ice and sky begins. To Ottawa, the waters of the Northwest Passage and its High Arctic archipelago have long been perceived to be internal waterways, and for much of the year as frozen extensions of its sovereign territory. To Washington, these waters, frozen or not, have always been perceived to be international straits, high seas with the self-same navigational freedoms as all the world's oceans. And to the Inuit, who have always called the Arctic home, the land and waters fused together for much of the year, as water hardened into ice, and the ice, like the land, became covered by a pervasive blanket snow. All across the Arctic, the aspiration for a restoration of Inuit self-governance has not, generally speaking, meant a rejection of the overarching reach of state sovereignty into the region, but rather an acceptance of a continuing state of sovereign duality, with the Inuit becoming loyal citizens of the modern state, often coming to its defense in time of war, and like other minority peoples, aspiring to become more equal and meaningful participants in the modern political economy—while still maintaining, in the face of so many pressures of modernization and assimilation, their proud and ancient traditions.

The re-emergence of this sovereign duality, which was prevalent throughout the medieval period in European history, suggests there has been an inherent limit to the modern state's ability to assert sovereignty across so vast and sparsely settled a frontier region, a limit reinforced by the Arctic's climate and isolation. But with the prospect of an Arctic thaw, this isolation may soon end, and that could mean an end as well to its restraint upon state sovereignty. This could explain the recent movement in the Arctic for greater Inuit participation in national and international issues, as exemplified by the Circumpolar Inuit Declaration on Arctic Sovereignty in May 2009, and the previous year's referendum on Greenlandic independence, both catalyzed by the increased commercial, diplomatic and military activity in the Far North. For the state to effectively assert sovereignty across the Arctic region, it has increasingly turned to the Native peoples of the region, fostering a reciprocal recognition of each other's sovereign rights as codified by treaty, land claims agreements, constitutional reform, and new institutions of self-governance.

In Canada, the state has recognized an inherent and unsurrendered Aboriginal right to self-government, even though the Canadian populace remains less committed to notion of inherency—as revealed by its rejection of the 1992 Charlottetown Accord, in part because of its provisions to empower Canadian Natives with a third order of government. In return for the state's recognition of Native rights, the Inuit have recognized in turn the constitutional authority of the modern state, and through the exchange engineered by their land claims accords, they have freely surrendered their Aboriginal rights for the clarity of these new Constitutional rights, formally embracing superior state sovereignty. Such a surrender of Aboriginal rights remains controversial, but nonetheless undergirds all land claims accords, though the articulation of constitutionally protected Native rights has grown increasingly expansive, with the most recent articulation, the Labrador Inuit Constitution of 2002, filling 160 pages of text. The Arctic land claims movement defined a generation-long transitional stage in northern development, an evolutionary bridgehead from earlier policies of assimilation to a new era of self-government, a portal through which the tribal and national levels of analysis could interface, and which, through their ongoing dialectic, a new political reality could emerge across the Arctic, where Inuit leaders—with one foot in the modern and the other in the traditional worlds—now interact with equal ease in the boardroom, at the negotiating table with their federal and international counterparts, and out on the land and sea ice, hunting with their elders.

This new generation of Inuit leaders, at home in both worlds, embody within their hearts and souls a bit of both worlds, navigating a path from past to future with both in mind. The Inuit leaders thus reside in a localized universe defined by clan, tribe, or village, as well as in a national and international universe of growing political power, economic vitality, and strategic influence. In the Arctic, where state and tribe come together, where land and ice unite as one, the Inuit stand at this nexus. Land claims provided a powerful and evolving interface between these two worlds that meet at the top of the world, becoming the

engine of transformation for the entire region. While land claims formally transferred the vast majority of land title to the state, leaving only around one-tenth
of the land base under the direct ownership of the Inuit, they augmented Inuit
powers tremendously throughout their vast settlement regions, making them
powerful stakeholders in the emergent Arctic political economy, and precipitating a subsequent process of greater political devolution.

Together, state and tribe have thus far accommodated one another, giving
birth to something that is both medieval and modern, mutually dependent and
yet independent. It is a complex relationship, one that reflects complex realities.
It may not always be this way, and both the overwhelming victory of the yes-
vote in the November 2008 Greenlandic referendum on autonomy, and the more
recent articulation of Inuit sovereignty in the May 2009 Circumpolar Inuit Declaration on Arctic Sovereignty, indicate the Inuit are currently rethinking their
stance on sovereignty and independence, while hoping their long and in so many
ways successful partnership with the modern state becomes renewed, and their
exclusion from the negotiating table at Ilulissat becomes the exception and not
the rule.

Out along the very last of Earth's frontiers to be tamed by modernity, it has
been the endurance of tribal sovereignty, and its accommodation with modernity, that has provided the modern state with much of its sovereign legitimacy in
the Arctic. This will prove essential going forward, as climate change transforms
the region, increasing the risks of strategic competition in the Arctic, and the
potential clash of competing sovereign ambitions as states collide at the top of
the world. Now, as the Arctic takes center stage again, the challenge of Arctic
sovereignty is becoming ever more complex, reflecting the challenges of not just
the post–Cold War and post-9/11 worlds, but with the additional challenges presented by the rapid geophysical transformation induced by climate change. Now
with the Arctic warming, its veil of ice and snow is giving way to a rising tide of
liquid water, and these waters are reconnecting with the world ocean at the top
of the world. "Ultima Thule" is fast becoming the "Midnight Sea" of ancient
legend.

As observed by Matthew Carnaghan and Allison Goody in their 2006 report, *Canadian Arctic Sovereignty*, the Arctic "has featured prominently in debates about Canadian sovereignty," with a "renewed focus on the Arctic due to
the effects of climate change in the region, notably the melting of the polar ice
caps. At the same time, there are continuing strategic issues relating to potential
incursions into Canadian Arctic territory at various levels."[207] They believe it's
"important to note that the Arctic is a vast and remote territory that presents
many difficulties in terms of surveillance, regulation, and infrastructure development," and that the "definition of sovereignty is somewhat elusive, with varying emphasis given to the elements of control, authority, and perception"—while
"another important dimension of the assertion of Canadian sovereignty includes
stewardship, an issue that has been raised by Canada's northern Inuit and Aboriginal peoples," whose use and occupancy "is significant in terms of the valid-
ity of Canada's sovereign claims."[208] In recent years, stakeholders on all sides of

the Arctic, at the state and tribal level, have come to understand these fundamental dimensions, and their interconnections.

Indeed, this understanding undergirds the remarkable transformation of the Arctic's political economy, and the emergence of new governing structures that attempt to reconcile the interests of tribe and state that have proliferated at the top of the world. These institutions provide a foundation for resolving the challenges that lay ahead, so long as the "glue" described by Doug Clark continues to bind tribe and state together, as partners in managing the Arctic, and in defining what Arctic sovereignty means. Just a single generation after the Arctic's strategic environment rapidly transformed at the conclusion of the Cold War, up-ending the strategic calculations of the Arctic rim states as the primary external threat quickly disappeared, the Arctic's geophysical environment is now undergoing its own transformation—further impacting the strategic calculus of all the Arctic's stakeholders, from the solitary hunter on the sea ice to the diplomatic and strategic actors on the world stage.

For all of the Arctic's stakeholders—from the tribal to the global level—a new day is coming. Over thirty-five years ago, Alaska Governor Walter J. Hickel foretold of the "Day of the Arctic"—an era in which the top of the world would lead the way forward, helping to solve the world energy crisis, transform global maritime shipping and rail transportation, and even alleviate problems of drought—as the region's bountiful resources and strategic location fostered the emergence of a truly northern approach to sovereignty and security. That day now looks to be just around the corner. And as we approach it, bound together by the enduring partnership between North and South, the Inuit and the modern state, we're better prepared to embrace the limitless potential that Hickel so presciently imagined, and to overcome the many challenges as well—and to welcome the arrival of this new day together.

Afterword by Ed Struzik
The Next Chapter in Arctic History Must Be Co-Authored by Northern Peoples

Ed Struzik is an award-winning journalist and author of three books on the Arctic: Northwest Passage, The Quest for An Arctic Route to the East *(1991);* Ten Rivers: Adventure Stories from the Arctic *(2005); and* The Big Thaw: Travels in the Melting North *(2009). He has received over thirty awards and fellowships, including the Sir Sandford Fleming Medal for an outstanding contribution to the understanding of science; an Atkinson Fellowship in Public Policy; and the 2009 Michener-Deacon Fellowship.*

In August 2007, two Russian icebreakers converged at the North Pole on a mission that was supposed to be mainly scientific. The geopolitical purpose of the venture didn't become apparent until veteran Arctic explorer Artur Chilingarov, a member of Russia's lower house of parliament, descended 14,000 feet in a deep sea submersible and deposited a Russian flag, cast in rust-free titanium, on the sea floor.

Lest anyone failed to notice, the entire event was choreographed and filmed in a way that was clearly intended to announce to the world that the seabed under the Pole, the 1,200-mile-long Lomonosov Ridge, was an extension of Russia's continental shelf. Expedition members were treated like heroes when they came home. "We were there first and we can claim the entire Arctic, but if our neighbors want some part of it, then maybe we can negotiate with them," said Vladimir Zhirinovsky, the populist leader of Russia's ultra-nationalist Liberal Democratic Party.

Curious, as it seemed at the time, given the legal regime in place to resolve ocean boundary issues, Zhirinovsky's comments reflected in some measure what the Russians were thinking. A few days after the flag planting, the Russian military dispatched strategic bombers over the Arctic Ocean for the first time since the Cold War ended. "The division of the Arctic," *Rossiiskaya Gazeta,* the Russian daily newspaper declared some time later, "is the start of a new redistribution of the world."

Not to be outdone by any of this, Canada shot back in the spring of 2009 with survey flights that went beyond the North Pole into a region that Russia had already staked out and claimed. The flights were a clear sign that Canada was not going to back down in the face of Russia's aggressive behavior. "It shows that we're going to do the maximum of what we can scientifically claim," said Rob Huebert, the military and security expert who wrote the foreword to this timely and very important book. "It clearly indicates that Canada is making good on its pledge not to be intimidated in the High Arctic."

The redrawing of the map of the Arctic is just one of a number of challenges that Arctic nations face. In the western Arctic, the United States and Canada have yet to agree on a maritime boundary line extending from the Alaska/Yukon border. The boundary line between Alaska and Siberia was supposed to have been resolved in 1990 when the United States and the Soviet Union signed an agreement to divide the area. The Russian parliament, however, has refused to ratify it. Parliamentarians claim that the deal robbed them of 30,000 square miles of territory. In the meantime, Canada and Denmark are still at odds about who owns Hans Island, a tiny kidney-shaped chunk of rock that lies off the coast of Ellesmere Island. Last but not least, is the dispute over the Northwest Passage, which Canada claims as part of its territorial waters. That claim is disputed by both the United States and the European Union.

Mercifully, most countries have been content to settle border disputes amongst themselves peaceably or to leave it to the 21-member U.N. technical committee that oversees the Convention of the Law of the Sea to review and recommend which country owns what in the Arctic. In dealing with territory beyond the 200 nautical mile limit, the committee makes its recommendation on the merits of geological data submitted by each nation. The deadline for doing so depends on when a submitting country ratifies the Convention on the Law of the Sea. Ten years is currently the time a signing country has to make submission.

The planting of a Russian flag at the North Pole notwithstanding, and the recent revelation that Russia may be willing to go to war to protect its interests there, the UN Convention on the Law of the Sea remains one of best ways of resolving the boundary issues beyond the 200 nautical mile economic zone. The redrawing of that part of the Arctic map, however, will take some time. Russia has until the end of 2009 to complete its case; Canada and Denmark have until 2013 and 2014 respectively. No one knows when the U.S. claim is going to be resolved because the Americans have still not ratified the Convention on the Law of the Sea.

Whether the Russians are willing to wait to exploit what they think is rightfully theirs remains to be seen. What's missing at this juncture in the ongoing debate about the Arctic's future is a meaningful recognition that this vast polar region is a homeland for a distinct group of people. Nearly two million people live in Russia; 650,000 in Alaska; 130,000 in Canada; and a little over a million in Greenland, Iceland, the Scandinavian countries and the Faeroe Islands combined. The welfare of many of these people, the Inuit in particular, will be seriously affected by the military, economic, and climatic events that are now unfolding.

If there is one thing among the very many important things to be learned from Barry Zellen's book, it's that history has not served the interests of these people especially well. Whether it was the construction of DEW Line sites that littered the Arctic with PCBs, the relocation of Inuit from northern Quebec that made them exiles in the High Arctic, the energy and mining developments that flew southerners in and out rather than employing northerners, or the schools system that forced children and their families off the land, the culture and well-being of these people have been either ignored or violated much too often and far too long.

That is slowly changing. Land claims have given many of these people control over their own territory. Self-government, especially in Nunavut and Greenland, has aided many of them in their quest for self-determination. The institution of northern-hiring preferences and the establishment of aboriginal-owned companies have also helped. Still, Mary Simon's memorable plea when she was president of the Inuit Circumpolar Conference in 1989 is as valid today as it was back then. Arctic countries "must look beyond geographical and political borders and alliances." she said. "Like Inuit, they must begin to perceive and value the Arctic as an integral whole that not only sustains our Inuit way of life but also determines the Earth's future in many ways."

"We do not wish our traditional territories to be treated as a strategic military and combat zone between Eastern and Western alliances," she added. "For thousands of years, Inuit have used and continue to use the lands, waters and sea ice in circumpolar regions. As Aboriginal people, we are the Arctic's legitimate spokespersons."

The human history of the Arctic is a complicated one. It is rich in human drama that was fueled by both courage and recklessness in the pursuit of rewards rarely won. The last Great Ice Age, however, is now coming to an end, and the new warmer world that is replacing it is going to open the door to all that wealth that eluded so many explorers for more than five hundred years.

This end of the Arctic as we know it will likely enrich southern populations increasingly starved for energy resources. But it may also open the door to border conflicts, smugglers, illegal aliens, and terrorists. Unless something is done to curb the forces that are warming the Arctic world, it will also result in a series of ecological collapses. Inevitably, this will lead to extinctions, extirpations, and more species being added to the endangered list. These catastrophic changes will, in turn, rattle the foundations on which Inuit cultures are built.

As Barry Zellen poignantly reminds us in this book, the Arctic is no longer a no-man's land of interest only to missionaries, military strategists, and outdoor adventurers. In the not-too-distant future, the forces of climate change are going to transform this icy world into a new economic frontier. The end of the Arctic, as we once knew it, will be the beginning of a new chapter in history. That new chapter in history must be co-authored by the people who live there.

Notes

Preface

1. Ned Rozell, "Ice Fog a Product of Temperature, Topography, Dogs," *Alaska Science Forum*, Article 1319, January 8, 1997. Online at: http://www.gi.alaska.edu/ScienceForum/ASF13/1319.html.
2. Rozell, "Ice Fog a Product of Temperature, Topography, Dogs."
3. Carl von Clausewitz, *On War*, edited and translated by Michael Howard and Peter Paret (Princeton: Princeton University Press, 1976), 101, 140. As Clausewitz wrote, "war is the realm of uncertainty; three quarters of the factors on which action is based are wrapped in a fog of greater or lesser uncertainty" (101), and "all action takes place, so to speak, in a kind of twilight, which, like fog or moonlight, often tends to makes things seem grotesque and larger than they really are" (140).

Chapter One

1. Barry Zellen, "Cold Front Rising: As Climate Change Thins Polar Ice, a New Race for Arctic Resources Begins," *Strategic Insights* 7, No. 1 (February 2008), http://www.ccc.nps.navy.mil/si/2008/Feb/zellenFeb08.asp.
2. To gain a sense of the controversy surrounding the 1985 Polar Sea transit of the Northwest Passage, see the *CBC News* archives where the news report filed by *CBC News* reporter Whit Fraser can be played. "The Polar Sea Controversy," *CBC News*, July 29, 1985. Available online at: the CBC archives: http://archives.cbc.ca/IDC-1-73-2349-13655/politics_economy/northwest_passage/clip7
3. Zellen, "Cold Front Rising."
4. For instance, see Shelagh D. Grant, *Sovereignty or Security? Government Policy in the Canadian North, 1936-1950* (Vancouver: University of British Columbia Press 1988). As well, see: Richard Rohmer, *The Arctic Imperative; an Overview of the Energy Crisis* (Toronto: McClelland and Stewart, 1974); John Honderich, *Arctic Imperative: Is*

Canada Losing the North? (Toronto: University of Toronto Press, 1987); Nathaniel French Caldwell, Jr., *Arctic Leverage: Canadian Sovereignty and Security* (Westport: Praeger, 1990); and Joseph T. Jockel, *Security to the North: Canada-U.S. Defense Relations in the 1990s* (East Lansing: Michigan State University Press, 1991). Franklyn Griffiths, ed., *The Politics of the Northwest Passage* (Montreal: McGill-Queens, 1987), presents various perspectives on the Arctic, from the systemic to the local, with its contributors presenting a diverse mosaic of cause and effect in Arctic political history.

5. Oran Young, the pioneering theorist of regional subsystems in international relations theory and international regimes, published *Resource Management at the International Level* in 1977, which explores the unique regional subsystem of Beringia, followed by numerous other works on Arctic politics, Arctic international relations, and various topics relating to international relations, international security, and international relations theory. Among Young's many contributions to the literature are his *Resource Management at the International Level: The Case of the North Pacific* (London: Frances Pinter; New York: Nichols, 1977); *The Age of the Arctic: Hot Conflicts and Cold Realities*, co-authored with Gail Osherenko (Cambridge: Cambridge University Press, 1989); *Arctic Politics: Conflict and Cooperation in the Circumpolar North* (Hanover: Dartmouth University Press, 1992); *Polar Politics: Creating International Environmental Regimes* (Ithaca: Cornell University Press, 1993); and *Creating Regimes: Arctic Accords and International Governance* (Ithaca: Cornell University Press, 1998).

6. Oran Young, "Governing the Arctic: From Cold War Theater to Mosaic of Cooperation," *Global Governance: A Review of Multilateralism and International Organizations* 11 (2005): 9–15.

7. Young, "Governing the Arctic," 9–15.

8. Young, "Governing the Arctic," 9–15..

9. Young, "Governing the Arctic," 9–15.

10. Young, "Governing the Arctic," 9–15.

11. Kenneth Waltz, *Man, the State, and War* (New York: Columbia University Press, 1954), 238

12. Kenneth Waltz, "Political Structures," in Robert O. Keohane, ed., *Neorealism and Its Critics* (New York: Columbia University Press, 1986), 94.

13. Kenneth Waltz, *Theory of International Politics*, 99.

14. Kenneth Waltz, "Political Structures," 95.

15. Kenneth Waltz, "Political Structures," 96.

16. Kenneth Waltz, "Political Structures," 90.

17. Kenneth Waltz, "Political Structures," 90.

18. Kenneth Waltz, "Political Structures," 90.

19. Kenneth Waltz, "Political Structures," 90.

20. For more on human security as the concept evolved, see: "New Dimensions of Human Security," in the *United Nations Development Program, Human Development Report 1994* (Oxford: Oxford University Press, 1994), 22–40. Available online at: http://www.undp.org/hdro/hdrs/1994/english/94ch2.pdf. Also see: Roland Paris, "Human Security: Paradigm Shift or Hot Air?" in Michael Brown et al., eds., *New Global Dangers: Changing Dimensions of International Security* (Cambridge, Massachusetts: MIT Press, 2004), 249–64.

21. Erika Simpson, "Redefining Security," *The McNaughton Papers* 1 (Toronto: Canadian Institute for Strategic Studies), March 1991, 57–75.

22. Simpson, "Redefining Security," 57.

23. Simpson, "Redefining Security," 57.

24. Simpson, "Redefining Security," 57.

25. Simpson, "Redefining Security," 57.

26. Simpson, "Redefining Security," 59.

27. Simpson, "Redefining Security," 61.

28. Mary Simon, "Security, Peace and the Native Peoples of the Arctic," *The Arctic: Choices for Peace and Security—A Public Inquiry* (West Vancouver: Gordon Soules Book Publishers, 1989), 31–32.

29. Simon, "Security, Peace and the Native Peoples of the Arctic," 32.

30. Simon, "Security, Peace and the Native Peoples of the Arctic," 32–33.

31. Simon, "Security, Peace and the Native Peoples of the Arctic," 32–33.

32. Simon, "Security, Peace and the Native Peoples of the Arctic," 32–33.

33. Simon, "Security, Peace and the Native Peoples of the Arctic," 33.

34. Simon, "Security, Peace and the Native Peoples of the Arctic," 34.

35. Simon, "Security, Peace and the Native Peoples of the Arctic," 33.

36. Simon, "Security, Peace and the Native Peoples of the Arctic," 33.

37. Simon, "Security, Peace and the Native Peoples of the Arctic," 34.

38. Simon, "Security, Peace and the Native Peoples of the Arctic," 34.

39. Patrick E. Tyler, "Soviets' Secret Nuclear Dumping Causes Worry for Arctic Waters," *New York Times*, May 4, 1992.

40. Alex Kirby, "Russia's Growing Nuclear Dustbin," *BBC*, March 3, 1999.

41. Simon, "Security, Peace and the Native Peoples of the Arctic," 34.

42. Simon, "Security, Peace and the Native Peoples of the Arctic," 34.

43. Simon, "Security, Peace and the Native Peoples of the Arctic," 34.

44. Simon, "Security, Peace and the Native Peoples of the Arctic," 36.

45. Inuit Circumpolar Conference, *Principles and Elements for a Comprehensive Arctic Policy*, 1992, II.1.

46. ICC, *Principles and Elements*, II.2.

47. ICC, *Principles and Elements*, II.3.

48. ICC, *Principles and Elements*, II.4.

49. ICC, *Principles and Elements*, II.5.

50. ICC, *Principles and Elements*, II.7.

51. ICC, *Principles and Elements*, II.7.

52. Inuit Circumpolar Council Press Release, "Canadian Inuit Call for Direct Say on Arctic Sovereignty," June 2, 2008.

53. ICC Press Release, "Canadian Inuit Call for Direct Say on Arctic Sovereignty."

54. ICC Press Release, "Inuit Leader Reminds Foreign Ministers: Much of the Arctic Belongs to all Inuit; Pan-Inuit Sovereignty Summit to Convene in November," Ilulissat, Greenland, November 29, 2008.

55. ICC, *Principles and Elements*, II.9.

56. ICC, *Principles and Elements*, II.11

57. ICC, *Principles and Elements*, II.14.

58. ICC, *Principles and Elements*, II.16.

59. ICC, *Principles and Elements*, II.18.

60. ICC, *Principles and Elements*, II.19.

61. ICC, *Principles and Elements*, II.20.

62. ICC, *Principles and Elements*, II.21.

63. Dan O'Neill, *The Firecracker Boys* (New York: St. Martin's Press, 1994).

64. D. M. McRae, "The Negotiation of Article 234," chapter 5 in Franklyn Griffiths, ed., *Politics of the Northwest Passage* (Montreal: McGill-Queens, 1987), 101.

65. McRae, "The Negotiation of Article 234," 101.

66. John Kirton and Don Munton, "The Manhattan Voyages and Their Aftermath," chapter 4 in Franklyn Griffiths, ed. *Politics of the Northwest Passage* (Montreal: McGill-Queens, 1987), 67.

67. John Kirton and Don Munton, "The Manhattan Voyages and Their Aftermath." Chapter Four in Franklyn Griffiths, ed. *Politics of the Northwest Passage* (Montreal: McGill-Queens, 1987), 67.

68. Woods Hole Research Center, "The Kyoto Protocol," in the "Warming Earth" section of the Woods Hole Research Center website (WHRC.org): http://www.whrc.org/resources/online_publications/warming_earth/kyoto.htm; "2007 United Nations Climate Change Conference," *Wikipedia*, http://en.wikipedia.org/wiki/2007_United_Nations_Climate_Change_Conference.

69. Chad Bouchard, "Bali Roadmap Officially Kicks Off New Round of Climate Change Negotiations," *Voice of America News*, December 17, 2007.

70. Inuit Tapiriit Kanatami Press Release, "Strong Inuit Presence at UN Climate Change Conference UNFCCC COP-13 in Bali," November 30, 2007.

71. See Robert Penner, "Is Canada a Silent Nuclear Power?" *The True North Strong & Free?* (West Vancouver: Gordon Soules, 1987), 55. Penner described ways that Canada helped fuel the arms race through its close support of the U.S. nuclear weapons program, and that it allowed the United States to test cruise missiles and other weapons in Canadian territory, to plan to disperse its strategic bomber fleet to Canadian airfields in the event of war, to put nuclear-armed vessels into Canadian ports, to test deep-water torpedoes in Canadian waters, to fire mock neutron bomb artillery shells in Canada, to use Canadian territory to communicate with its strategic bomber force and to use Ellesmere Island in the High Arctic to test satellite communications designed to control weapons delivery during protracted nuclear war, and to participate in the North Warning System that replaced the aging DEW Line. He said this was just the beginning of a list and that some 140 sites in Canada participate in the business of nuclear war planning, and that as a result Canada was a silent nuclear power.

72. ICC, *Principles and Elements,* III:1.

73. ICC, *Principles and Elements,* III:2.

74. ICC, *Principles and Elements,* III:3.

75. ICC, *Principles and Elements,* III:3.

76. ICC, *Principles and Elements,* III:4.

77. ICC, *Principles and Elements,* III:5.

78. ICC, *Principles and Elements,* III:7.

79. Grant, "Arctic Wilderness—and Other Mythologies."

80. Grant, "Arctic Wilderness—and Other Mythologies."

81. Grant, "Arctic Wilderness—and Other Mythologies."

82. Grant, "Arctic Wilderness—and Other Mythologies."

83. Grant, "Arctic Wilderness—and Other Mythologies."

84. Grant, "Arctic Wilderness—and Other Mythologies."

85. Grant, "Arctic Wilderness—and Other Mythologies."

86. Grant, "Arctic Wilderness—and Other Mythologies."

87. Grant, "Arctic Wilderness—and Other Mythologies."

88. According to Parks Canada, Ivvavik, meaning "a place for giving birth, a nursery" in Inuvialuktun, is the first national park in Canada to be created as a result of an aboriginal land claim agreement. It protects a portion of the calving grounds of the Porcupine caribou herd and represents the Northern Yukon and Mackenzie Delta natural

regions. Aulavik, meaning "place where people travel" in Inuvialuktun, protects more than 12,000 square kilometres of Arctic lowlands on the north end of Banks Island. The park encompasses a variety of landscapes from fertile river valleys to polar deserts, buttes and badlands, rolling hills, and bold seacoasts. At the heart of Aulavik is the Thomsen River, which offers visitors a chance to paddle one of the continent's most northerly navigable waterways. This pristine Arctic environment is home to both the endangered Peary caribou and to the highest density of muskox in the world. The wildlife and land have supported Aboriginal peoples for more than 3,400 years, from Pre-Dorset cultures to contemporary Inuvialuit. And Tuktut Nogait, at 16,340 square kilometres, is Canada's fifth largest national park. Like the other two parks created inside the ISR, a park management board, with representatives from Canada, the Northwest Territories, and the Inuvialuit, will work with Parks Canada to plan and manage the park.

89. Grant, "Arctic Wilderness—and Other Mythologies."

90. Grant, "Arctic Wilderness—and Other Mythologies."

91. Alootook Ipellie, "Thirsty for Life: A Nomad Learns to Write and Draw," in John Moss, ed., *Echoing Silence: Essays on Arctic Narrative* (Ottawa: University of Ottawa Press, 1997), 94.

92. ICC, *Principles and Elements*, II.1.

93. ICC, *Principles and Elements*, II.2.

94. ICC, *Principles and Elements*, II.3.

95. ICC, *Principles and Elements*, II.4.

96. Barry Zellen, "One Arctic, One future?" *Arctic Circle Magazine*, September 1992.

97. Zellen, "One Arctic, One Future?"

98. Zellen, "One Arctic, One Future?"

99. Zellen, "One Arctic, One Future?" Lynge continues to be a passionate and outspoken advocate of Inuit rights. He told *AFP* on June 16, 2008, "The Inuit have been marginalised in the current debate on the Arctic by those who now control our land and waters. . . . We no longer want to accept the isolation and harsh treatment that has been inflicted upon us in the past. . . . We paid the price of the sovereignty of these governments who steal our land, our resources. Enough is enough, we don't want to be displaced by force, as was the case in Thule and we demand to be treated humanely." AFP, "Stop Stealing Our Land, Inuits Say, as Arctic Resources Race Heats Up," *AFP*, June 16, 2008.

100. Zellen, "One Arctic, One future?"

101. Zellen, "One Arctic, One future?"

102. ICC, *Principles and Elements*, II.4.

103. Glenn Taylor, "Former IRC Chair Under Investigation." *Inuvik Drum*, August 15, 1997; Frances Widdowson, "The Inherent Right of Unethical Governance," presented to the Annual Meeting of the Canadian Political Science Association at York University, Toronto, Ontario, on June 1–3, 2006; and Pedro Van Meurs, *"Ten Years IFA"— Successes and Failures, A Report Card*, December 1993.

104. Dafna Izenberg, "The Conscience of Nunavut: Nunatsiaq News Editor Jim Bell on a Mission," *Ryerson Review of Journalism*, Summer 2005.

105. Jim Bell, "Leona Makes a Good Point," *Nunatsiaq News*, March 14, 2008.

106. Jim Bell, "Leona Makes a Good Point," *Nunatsiaq News*, March 14, 2008.

107. Jim Bell, "Leona Makes a Good Point," *Nunatsiaq News*, March 14, 2008.

108. Jim Bell, "Leona Makes a Good Point," *Nunatsiaq News*, March 14, 2008.

109. Jim Bell, "Leona Makes a Good Point," *Nunatsiaq News*, March 14, 2008.

110. ICC, *Principles and Elements*, II,6.

111. ICC, *Principles and Elements*, II.8.

112. Grant, "Arctic Wilderness—and Other Mythologies."

113. Izenberg, "The Conscience of Nunavut."

114. Thomas R. Berger, "Letter to the Minister of Indian Affairs and Northern Development," *Nunavut Land Claims Agreement Implementation Planning Contract Negotiations for the Second Planning Period: Conciliator's Final Report, 'The Nunavut Project,'* Vancouver, BC, March 1, 2006, ii. Available online at: http://www.ainc-inac.gc.ca/pr/agr/nu/lca/index_e.html.

115. Berger, "Letter to the Minister," i.

116. Paul Mayer, Senior Ministerial Representative for Nunavut Devolution, *Mayer Report on Nunavut Devolution*, Department of Indian and Northern Affairs, Government of Canada, Ottawa, Ontario, June 2007, 8. Available online at: http://www.ainc-inac.gc.ca/nr/prs/m-a2007/2-2891-m_rprt-eng.pdf.

117. ICC, *Principles and Elements*, II.9.

118. Grant, "Arctic Wilderness—and Other Mythologies."

119. Jens Dahl, Jack Hicks, and Peter Jull, eds., *Nunavut: Inuit Regain Control of Their Lands and Their Lives* (Copenhagen: International Work Group for Indigenous Affairs, 2000), 13.

120. Jack Hicks and Graham White, "Nunavut: Inuit Self-Determination through a Land Claim and Public Government?" in Dahl, Hicks, and Jull, eds., *Nunavut: Inuit Regain Control*, 30.

121. Hicks and White, "Nunavut: Inuit Self-Determination," 31.

122. Hicks and White, "Nunavut: Inuit Self-Determination," 92.

123. Hicks and White, "Nunavut: Inuit Self-Determination," 81.

124. Hicks and White, "Nunavut: Inuit Self-Determination," 81.

125. Hicks and White, "Nunavut: Inuit Self-Determination," 93.

126. Hicks and White, "Nunavut: Inuit Self-Determination," 93.

127. Government of the Northwest Territories, *Military Activity in the North and the Establishment of a Circumpolar Zone of Peace and Security*, Yellowknife, NWT, November 1990, 1.

128. GNWT, *Military Activity in the North*, 1.

129. GNWT, *Military Activity in the North*, 1–3.

130. GNWT, *Military Activity in the North*, 1–3.

131. GNWT, *Military Activity in the North*, 1–3.

132. GNWT, *Military Activity in the North*, 1–3.

133. GNWT, *Military Activity in the North*, 1–3.

134. GNWT, *Military Activity in the North*, 8.

135. GNWT, *Military Activity in the North*, 8.

136. GNWT, *Military Activity in the North*, 9.

137. GNWT, *Military Activity in the North*, 6.

138. GNWT, *Military Activity in the North*, 7.

139. GNWT, *Military Activity in the North*, 9.

140. GNWT, *Military Activity in the North*, 9.

141. GNWT, *Military Activity in the North*, 9.

142. GNWT, *Military Activity in the North*, 9.

143. GNWT, *Military Activity in the North*, 9.

144. GNWT, *Military Activity in the North*, 9.

145. GNWT, *Military Activity in the North*, 9.

146. GNWT, *Military Activity in the North*, 14.

147. GNWT, *Military Activity in the North*, 17. The GNWT discussion paper draws heavily from the Panel on Arctic Arms Control at the Canadian Centre for Arms Control and Disarmament—renamed the Canadian Centre for Global Security in 1992, and which issued a detailed report on a circumpolar zone in 1989 proposing a regional security perspective; gradual demilitarization in the zone; non-military cooperative measures; a role for circumpolar citizens; and the establishment of an Ambassador for Circumpolar Affairs.

148. GNWT, *Military Activity in the North*, 18.

149. GNWT, *Military Activity in the North*, 18.

150. GNWT, *Military Activity in the North*, 31.

151. GNWT, *Military Activity in the North*, 31.

152. GNWT, *Military Activity in the North*, 32.

153. GNWT, *Military Activity in the North*, 32.

154. GNWT, *Military Activity in the North*, 33.

155. GNWT, *Military Activity in the North*, 34.

156. GNWT, *Military Activity in the North*, 35.

157. GNWT, *Military Activity in the North*, 35.

158. GNWT, *Military Activity in the North*, 38.

159. GNWT, *Military Activity in the North*, 39.

Chapter Two

1. Simpson, "Redefining Security," 62

2. Simpson, "Redefining Security," 62.

3. Simpson, "Redefining Security," 63.

4. Simpson, "Redefining Security," 63.

5. Simpson, "Redefining Security," 64.

6. Simpson, "Redefining Security," 65.

7. Simpson, "Redefining Security," 65.

8. Gordon Robertson, "The Human Foundation for Peace and Security in the Arctic," *The Arctic: Choices for Peace and Security—A Public Inquiry* (West Vancouver: Gordon Soules Book Publishers, 1989), 88. Also see Gordon Robertson, "Nunavut and the International Arctic," *Northern Perspectives* 15, No. 2 (Ottawa, Ontario: Canadian Arctic Resources Committee, May/June 1987).

9. Robertson, "The Human Foundation for Peace and Security in the Arctic," 88.

10. Robertson, "The Human Foundation for Peace and Security in the Arctic," 88.

11. Robertson, "The Human Foundation for Peace and Security in the Arctic," 88.

12. Robertson, "The Human Foundation for Peace and Security in the Arctic," 89.

13. Robertson, "The Human Foundation for Peace and Security in the Arctic," 91.

14. Robertson, "The Human Foundation for Peace and Security in the Arctic," 91.

15. Robertson, "The Human Foundation for Peace and Security in the Arctic," 91.

16. Robertson, "The Human Foundation for Peace and Security in the Arctic," 92.

17. Graham Rowley, "An Arctic Affair," in John Moss, ed., *Echoing Silence: Essays on Arctic Narrative* (Ottawa: University of Ottawa Press, 1997), 15–16.

18. Rowley, "An Arctic Affair," 15–16.

19. Grant, "Arctic Wilderness—and Other Mythologies."

20. Andrea Charron, "The Northwest Passage Shipping Channel: Is Canada's Sovereignty Really Floating Away?" presented to the CDAI-CDFAI 7th Annual Graduate Student Symposium, RMC, October 29–30 2004.

21. Charron, "The Northwest Passage Shipping Channel."

22. Joseph T. Jockel, *Security to the North: Canada-U.S. Defense Relations in the 1990s* (East Lansing: Michigan State University Press, 1991), 21.

23. Jockel, *Security to the North*, 21.

24. Jockel, *Security to the North*, 21.

25. Jockel, *Security to the North*, 21.

26. Jockel, *Security to the North*, 22.

27. Jockel, *Security to the North*, 22.

28. Jockel, *Security to the North*, 22.

29. Nathaniel French Caldwell, Jr., *Arctic Leverage: Canadian Sovereignty and Security* (Westport: Praeger, 1990). Also see Joel J. Sokolsky, *Defending Canada: U.S.-Canadian Defense Policies* (New York: Priority Press, 1989); David G. Haglund and Joel J. Sokolsky, eds., *The U.S.-Canada Security Relationship: The Politics, Strategy, and Technology of Defense* (Boulder: Westview Press, 1989); and Gerard S. Vano, *Canada: The Strategic and Military Pawn* (Westport: Praeger, 1988).

30. Caldwell, *Arctic Leverage*, 2.

31. Caldwell, *Arctic Leverage*, 2.

32. Caldwell, *Arctic Leverage*, 2.

33. Caldwell, *Arctic Leverage*, 2–4.

34. Caldwell, *Arctic Leverage*, 7.

35. Caldwell, *Arctic Leverage*, 8.

36. Caldwell, *Arctic Leverage*, 89.

37. Caldwell, *Arctic Leverage*, 7–8.

38. Caldwell, *Arctic Leverage*, 9.

39. Caldwell, *Arctic Leverage*, 9–10.

40. Caldwell, *Arctic Leverage*, 11.

41 Ken S. Coates, P. Whitney Lackenbauer, William R. Morrison and Greg Poelze, *Arctic Front: Defending Canada in the Far North* (Markham, Ontario: Thomas Allen Publishers, 2008.) As reprinted by *The Globe and Mail*, April 24, 2009, online at: http://www.theglobeandmail.com/servlet/story/RTGAM.20090424.wbkdonnerexcerpt_arctic/BNStory/globebooks.

42. Coates, et al., *Arctic Front.*

43. Caldwell, *Arctic Leverage*, 12–13.

44. Caldwell, *Arctic Leverage*, 14.

45. Coates, et al., *Arctic Front.*

46. Coates, et al., *Arctic Front.*

47. Coates, et al., *Arctic Front.*

48. Coates, et al., *Arctic Front.*

49. Coates, et al., *Arctic Front.*

50. Coates, et al., *Arctic Front.*

51. Coates, et al., *Arctic Front.*

52. Caldwell, *Arctic Leverage*, 15.

53. Caldwell, *Arctic Leverage*, 15–16.

54. Coates, et al., *Arctic Front.*

55. Coates, et al., *Arctic Front.*

56. Caldwell, *Arctic Leverage*, 16.

57. Caldwell, *Arctic Leverage*, 17.
58. Caldwell, *Arctic Leverage*, 17.
59. Caldwell, *Arctic Leverage*, 42.
60. Caldwell, *Arctic Leverage*, 41.
61. Caldwell, *Arctic Leverage*, 42.
62. Caldwell, *Arctic Leverage*, 42.
63. Caldwell, *Arctic Leverage*, 44.
64. Caldwell, *Arctic Leverage*, 45.
65. Caldwell, *Arctic Leverage*, 46.
66. Caldwell, *Arctic Leverage*, 46.
67. Caldwell, *Arctic Leverage*, 47.
68. Caldwell, *Arctic Leverage*, 46–47.
69. Caldwell, *Arctic Leverage*, 47.
70. Caldwell, *Arctic Leverage*, 49.
71. Caldwell, *Arctic Leverage*, 49.
72. Caldwell, *Arctic Leverage*, 94.
73. Caldwell, *Arctic Leverage*, 50.
74. Caldwell, *Arctic Leverage*, 50.
75. Caldwell, *Arctic Leverage*, 51.
76. Caldwell, *Arctic Leverage*, 51.
77. Caldwell, *Arctic Leverage*, 51.
78. Caldwell, *Arctic Leverage*, 51.
79. Caldwell, *Arctic Leverage*, 51.
80. Caldwell, *Arctic Leverage*, 51.
81. Caldwell, *Arctic Leverage*, 56.
82. Caldwell, *Arctic Leverage*, 56.
83. T. C. Pullen, "That Polar Icebreaker," *Northern Perspectives* 14, No. 4 (September/October 1986).
84. Franklyn Griffiths, "Beyond the Arctic Sublime," chapter 12 in Franklyn Griffiths, ed., *Politics of the Northwest Passage*. Montreal: McGill-Queens, 1987, 241.
85. Griffiths, "Beyond the Arctic Sublime," 241.
86. Joe Clark, "Statement on Sovereignty to the House of Commons," Ottawa, Ontario, Canada, September 10, 1985. As presented on page "Appendix: Statement on Sovereignty," in Franklyn Griffiths, ed., *Politics of the Northwest Passage* (Montreal: McGill-Queens, 1987), 269.
87. Clark, "Statement on Sovereignty to the House of Commons."
88. Clark, "Statement on Sovereignty to the House of Commons."
89. Clark, "Statement on Sovereignty to the House of Commons."
90. Clark, "Statement on Sovereignty to the House of Commons."
91. Government of Canada, Special Joint Committee of the Senate and of the House of Commons on Canada's International Relations, Ottawa, Ontario, *Independence and Internationalism*, 1986.
92. Government of Canada, *Independence and Internationalism*.
93. Jeff Richstone, "Arctic Sovereignty: The Search for Substance," *Northern Perspectives* 14, no. 4 (September/October 1986).
94. Richstone, "Arctic Sovereignty: The Search for Substance."
95. Government of Canada, *Independence and Internationalism*.
96. Caldwell, *Arctic Leverage*, 58.

97. Andrea Mandel-Campbell, "Spies, Submarines, and Foreign Ships May Signal That Our Claim to the North is Melting," *The Walrus*, January 2005, http://www.walrusmagazine.com/print/2005.01-national-affairs-Arctic-global-warming/.

98. Caldwell, *Arctic Leverage*, 61.

99. Caldwell, *Arctic Leverage*, 61.

100. Caldwell, *Arctic Leverage*, 64.

101. Caldwell, *Arctic Leverage*, 67.

102. Caldwell, *Arctic Leverage*, 67.

103. Mandel-Campbell, "Spies, Submarines, and Foreign Ships."

104. Caldwell, *Arctic Leverage*, 71.

105. Caldwell, *Arctic Leverage*, 82.

106. Caldwell, *Arctic Leverage*, 80–82.

107. Caldwell, *Arctic Leverage*, 83.

108. Caldwell, *Arctic Leverage*, 84.

109. Caldwell, *Arctic Leverage*, 85.

110. Caldwell, *Arctic Leverage*, 85.

111. Caldwell, *Arctic Leverage*, 85.

112. Caldwell, *Arctic Leverage*, 96.

113. Jockel, *Security to the North*, 20.

114. Jockel, *Security to the North*, 20.

115. Jockel, *Security to the North*, 20.

116. Jockel, *Security to the North*, 20.

117. Mandel-Campbell, "Spies, Submarines, and Foreign Ships."

118. Mandel-Campbell, "Spies, Submarines, and Foreign Ships."

119. *Canadian Defence Policy 1992* (Ottawa: Department of National Defense, April 1992), 2.

120. *Canadian Defence Policy 1992*, 2–3.

121. Prime Minister's Office Press Release, "Prime Minister Harper announces major reforms to address the backlog of Aboriginal treaty claims," June 12, 2007.

122. PMO Press Release, "Prime Minister Harper Announces Major Reforms."

123. PMO Press Release, "Prime Minister Harper Announces Major Reforms."

124. PMO Press Release, "Prime Minister Harper Announces Major Reforms."

125. *Canadian Defence Policy 1992*, 3.

126. *Canadian Defence Policy 1992*, 19.

127. *Canadian Defence Policy 1992*, 20.

128. George W. Bush, 2003 State of the Union Address, Washington, DC, The White House, January 28, 2003. Available online at: http://www.whitehouse.gov/news/releases/2003/01/20030128-19.html.

129. Harriet Critchley in Alex Morrison, ed., *Divided We Fall: The National Security Implications of Canadian Constitutional Issues* (Toronto: Canadian Institute of Strategic Studies, 1991), 44–45.

130. Critchley, *Divided We Fall*, 45.

131. Critchley, *Divided We Fall*, 20.

132. Critchley, *Divided We Fall*, 50–51.

133. Critchley, *Divided We Fall*, 49.

134. *Canadian Defence Policy 1992*, 20.

135. *Canadian Defence Policy 1992*, 3.

136. Dafna Izenberg, "The Conscience of Nunavut," *Ryerson Review of Journalism*, Summer 2005.

137. CBC News, "Manitoba Chief Calls for National Day of Rail Blockades," *CBC News*, May 23, 2007.

138. CBC News, "Manitoba Chief Calls off Blockade Plans," *CBC News*, June 21, 2007.

139. CTV News, "Young Natives Becoming Desperate: Fontaine," *CTV News*, May 16, 2007.

140. CTV News, "Young Natives."

141. CTV News, "Young Natives." As *CTV* cited Fontaine, "As for our young people, absolutely there are some very serious concerns, frustration, building and building, frustration turning to anger because our young people have no hope. They feel a deep sense of hopelessness because conditions in our communities are so desperate." *CTV* reported that "the video calls on Natives to take action in order to press the federal government to solve longstanding land claim disputes," stating: "Creating the political will for just and timely resolution will take your help. Real solidarity means shouldering some of the burden of struggle." But Fontaine told *CTV*, "I still believe diplomacy is the most effective way of bringing about change and that is how we will continue to press our case. But I also should point out I understand the deep frustration felt by many of our leaders and I share their concerns, I share their frustration, and I want to assure them we will continue to work with them, we will continue to work together to build the kind of future our people, especially our young people, deserve."

142. Sue Bailey, "Protest Leader Willing to Talk," *Canadian Press*, June 29, 2007; Toronto AM 640, "UPDATE: 401 Closed as Mohawk Protest Begins," *640Toronto.com*, June 28, 2007; CBC News, "Highway Blockade May Not be the Last, Mohawk Activist Warns," *CBC News*, June 29, 2007; Canadian Press, "Rogue Mohawk Protesters Warn of More Barricades; Busy Ontario Road Opens," *Canadian Press*, June 29, 2007.

143. CN Rail, "CN Halts Rail Operations, Embargoes All Traffic in Toronto-Montreal Corridor, Following Illegal Blockade of Rail Line," CN Rail Press Release, June 29, 2007. Available online at: http://www.marketwire.com/2.0/release.do?id=747305.

144. CN Rail, "CN Halts Rail Operations."

145. CN Rail, "CN Halts Rail Operations."

146. *Canadian Defence Policy 1992*, 3.

147. Paul Mayer, Senior Ministerial Representative for Nunavut Devolution, *Mayer Report on Nunavut Devolution*, Department of Indian and Northern Affairs, Government of Canada, Ottawa, Ontario, June 2007, 8. Available online at: http://www.ainc-inac.gc.ca/nr/prs/m-a2007/2-2891-m_rprt-eng.pdf.

148. Mayer, *Mayer Report*, 8–11.

149. Mayer, *Mayer Report*, 10.

150. Mayer, *Mayer Report*, 10.

151. The Honourable Sidney B. Linden, Commissioner, "Commissioner's Statement: Public Release of Report," *Report of the Ipperwash Inquiry*, Government of Ontario, May 31, 2007, pages 12 and 13. Available online at: http://www.ipperwashinquiry.ca /report/index.html.

152. "Assembly of First Nations National Chief Demands that Federal Government Immediately Repudiate and Remove Reference to First Nations from Military's Terror Manual List," Assembly of First Nations Press Release, Ottawa, Ontario, April 1, 2007.

153. "AFN Chief Demands," April 1, 2007.

154. "AFN Chief Demands," April 1, 2007.

155. "New ITK President Mary Simon Tells International Conference Canadian Inuit Need to Take Tougher Approach in Dealing with Governments," Inuit Tapiriit Kanatami Press Release, Barrow, Alaska, July 10, 2006; and "Mary Simon's First Speech as ITK President at the Inuit Circumpolar General Assembly in Barrow, Alaska," Inuit Tapiriit Kanatami Speech, Barrow Alaska, July 10, 2006.

156. *Canadian Defence Policy 1992*, 18.

157. *Canadian Defence Policy 1992*, 19.

158. *Canadian Defence Policy 1992*, 19.

159. Rob Huebert, "Renaissance in Canadian Arctic Security?" *Canadian Military Journal* (Winter 2005–2006): 17.

160. Huebert, "Renaissance in Canadian Arctic Security?" 18.

161. Huebert, "Renaissance in Canadian Arctic Security?" 18.

162. Huebert, "Renaissance in Canadian Arctic Security?" 19.

163. Huebert, "Renaissance in Canadian Arctic Security?" 20–21.

164. Huebert, "Renaissance in Canadian Arctic Security?" 22.

165. Department of National Defence, *1994 White Paper on Defence*. Government of Canada, Ottawa, Ontario, 2. Available online at: http://www.forces.gc.ca/admpol/newsite/downloads/1994%20White%20Paper%20on%20Defence.pdf.

166. DND, "Chapter 1: International Environment," *1994 White Paper on Defence*, 12.

167. DND, "Chapter 1: International Environment," *1994 White Paper on Defence*, 12. As noted in "Failed States" in chapter 1, "The breakdown of authority in certain states is another source of instability. It is characterized by chaos, violence and the inability of political leaders to provide the population with the most basic of services. In recent years, this problem has not been confined to any specific region of the world or even to countries with particularly low standards of living. Examples as diverse as Somalia, the former Yugoslavia, Rwanda and Afghanistan illustrate the extent of the problem. The international community remains heavily engaged in attempts to respond, but success in confronting challenges engendered by scarcity and war is not easily achieved." DND, "Chapter 1: International Environment," *1994 White Paper on Defence*, 12.

168. DND, "Chapter 1: International Environment," *1994 White Paper on Defence*, 12. As noted in "Resurgence of Old Hatreds" in chapter 1, "Among the most difficult and immediate challenges to international security are the civil wars fuelled by ethnic, religious and political extremism that broke out in the Balkans and areas of the former Soviet Union following the collapse of communism. In recent years, rival groups have clashed in a number of these states. Other regions of the world, most notably parts of Africa and Asia, have seen the strength of fundamentalist groups grow considerably, with civil wars and other violent manifestations showing no signs of abating. Many of these conflicts have proven relatively immune to regional or multilateral diplomacy and intervention. The task of maintaining ceasefires in the midst of civil wars is especially difficult, given the absence of coherent front lines, lack of discipline among the warring sides, civilian populations subject to horrible depredations and atrocities and, most important, a reluctance by combatants to respect such ceasefires." DND, "Chapter 1: International Environment," *1994 White Paper on Defence*, 12.

169. DND, "Chapter 1: International Environment," *1994 White Paper on Defence*, 12. As further noted in "Resurgence of Old Hatreds" in chapter 1, "However horrendous the impact for the local populations caught in the middle of civil wars, the absence today of adversarial relations among the world's great powers suggests that these conflicts are

more likely to be contained. At the same time, Canada cannot escape the consequences of regional conflict, whether in the form of refugee flows, obstacles to trade, or damage to important principles such as the rule of law, respect for human rights and the peaceful settlement of conflicts. Even where Canada's interests are not directly engaged, the values of Canadian society lead Canadians to expect their government to respond when modern communication technologies make us real-time witnesses to violence, suffering and even genocide in many parts of the world. Thus, Canada continues to have an important stake in a peaceful and stable international system." DND, "Chapter 1: International Environment," *1994 White Paper on Defence*, 12–13.

170. Department of National Defence, "Chapter 2: Domestic Considerations," *1994 White Paper on Defence*, 14.

171. Department of National Defence, "Chapter 3: Combat-Capable Forces," *1994 White Paper on Defence*, 16.

172. DND, "Chapter 3: Combat-Capable Forces," *1994 White Paper on Defence*, 15.

173. Department of National Defence, "Chapter 4: Protection of Canada," *1994 White Paper on Defence*, 17.

174. DND "Chapter 4: Protection of Canada," *1994 White Paper on Defence*, 19.

175. DND, "Chapter 4: Protection of Canada," *1994 White Paper on Defence*, 17.

176. DND, "Chapter 4: Protection of Canada," *1994 White Paper on Defence*, 17. As chapter 4 of the *1994 White Paper* states, "Throughout Canadian history, provinces have been able to call upon the armed forces to maintain or restore law and order where it is beyond the power of civil authorities to do so. Section 275 of the National Defence Act states that the Canadian Forces: are liable to be called out for service in aid of the civil power in any case in which a riot or disturbance of the peace, beyond the powers of the civil authorities to suppress . . . is, in the opinion of an attorney general, considered as likely to occur. The role of the Canadian Forces in this context is very precisely defined. When a riot or disturbance of the peace occurs or is likely to occur that is beyond the powers of the civil authorities to control, a provincial attorney general may require the Canadian Forces to be called out in Aid of the Civil Power. In this situation, the Chief of the Defence Staff determines the nature of the response. The Canadian Forces do not replace the civil power; they assist it in the maintenance of law and order. In recent times, the use of the Canadian Forces in this role has been comparatively infrequent. Nevertheless, the crisis at Oka in 1990 served to remind us that such situations can arise. The Forces played a crucial role in defusing the crisis. They demonstrated that the ability to call upon disciplined, well-trained, and well-commanded military personnel is invaluable in providing government with an effective means to deal with potentially explosive situations." DND, "Chapter 4: Protection of Canada," *1994 White Paper on Defence*, 17.

177. DND, "Chapter 4: Protection of Canada," *1994 White Paper on Defence*, 17.

178. DND, "Chapter 4: Protection of Canada," *1994 White Paper on Defence*, 17.

179. DND, "Chapter 4: Protection of Canada," *1994 White Paper on Defence*, 17.

180. DND, "Chapter 4: Protection of Canada," *1994 White Paper on Defence*, 17.

181. DND, "Chapter 4: Protection of Canada," *1994 White Paper on Defence*, 17–18. Additionally, the *1994 White Paper* noted the importance of securing Canada's border against illegal activities as one of its sovereign responsibilities: "Canadians face an increasing challenge from those who would exploit the vast size and resources of our country for illegalactivities. This applies to the illegal trade in narcotics and other contraband substances, as well as the smuggling of illegal immigrants into Canada. In supporting the activities of other government agencies, the Canadian Forces play a significant role in countering such activities. During the renewal of the North American Aerospace

Defence (NORAD) Agreement in 1991, Canada and the United States agreed to give NORAD a role in counter-narcotic monitoring and surveillance. This is an ancillary mission to which the capabilities of our maritime and land forces have also been applied, and illustrates how existing structures and capabilities can be adapted to address new problems." DND, "Chapter 4: Protection of Canada," *1994 White Paper on Defence*, 18.

182. DND, "Chapter 4: Protection of Canada," *1994 White Paper on Defence*, 18.

183. Canadian Navy Website, Operations and Exercises section, located online at: http://www.navy.dnd.ca/cms_operations/operations_e.asp?id=460.

184. Clyde H. Farnsworth, "Canada and Spain Face Off Over Fishing Zone," *New York Times*, March 12, 1995.

185. John Darnton, "Spanish Stirred by 'War' Over a Fish They Don't Eat," *New York Times*, April 15, 1995.

186. Darnton, "Spanish Stirred by 'War.'"

187. Paul Gessell, "Spanish Envoy Tackles Tobin, Canada on Internet," *Ottawa Citizen*, March 27, 1996.

188. DND, "Chapter 4: Protection of Canada," *1994 White Paper on Defence*, 18.The *1994 White Paper on Defence* further stated: "Interdepartmental cooperation has been markedly enhanced in response to the recommendations of the Osbaldeston Report and the 1990 report of the Standing Committee on National Defence on maritime sovereignty. Secure communications have been installed, standard operating procedures have been developed, and acquisition policies are addressing the potential benefits of having common and interoperable equipment." DND, "Chapter 4: Protection of Canada," *1994 White Paper on Defence*, 18.

189. DND, "Chapter 4: Protection of Canada," *1994 White Paper on Defence*, 18. The *1994 White Paper on Defence* further stated: "Beyond this, the Department of National Defence has concluded a memorandum of understanding with the Department of the Environment with respect to the use of the Canadian Forces in environmental surveillance and clean-up" which "sets out the role of the Department and the Forces in assisting the Department of the Environment in the event of a serious environmental incident. In addition, as the Forces carry out their routine surveillance missions, they will seek to identify and report potential and actual environmental problems." DND, "Chapter 4: Protection of Canada," *1994 White Paper on Defence*, 18. Also included among Canada's sovereignty-related defense activities was the protection of Canadians, in the form of disaster relief as well as search and rescue activities: "The Canadian Forces play a key role in responding to natural and man-made disasters. Not only is the Minister of National Defence also the Minister Responsible for Emergency Preparedness, but, as part of a broader initiative to reduce the size of government, the administration of emergency preparedness planning—once carried out by a separate agency—has been absorbed by the Department of National Defence. Memoranda of understanding between the Department and other government agencies govern the coordination of resources in response to emergencies, and the Department will make an immediate and effective contribution to disaster relief." DND, "Chapter 4: Protection of Canada," *1994 White Paper on Defence*, 18. And on search and rescue: "The Department of National Defence and the Canadian Forces make a vital contribution to the maintenance and operation of Canada's search and rescue capability," as "[s]earch and rescue represents a significant challenge for Canadian Forces personnel and their equipment. The distances involved can be enormous and the operating conditions very difficult. Nevertheless, for Canadians, safeguarding human life remains an absolute priority, and the Canadian Forces will continue to play a

major role in this vital area." DND, "Chapter 4: Protection of Canada," *1994 White Paper on Defence*, 19.

190. Department of National Defence, "Chapter 5: Canada–United States Defence Cooperation," *1994 White Paper on Defence*, 19.

191. DND, "Chapter 5: Canada–United States Defence Cooperation," *1994 White Paper on Defence*, 19.

192. DND, "Chapter 5: Canada–United States Defence Cooperation," *1994 White Paper on Defence*, 20.

193. DND, "Chapter 5: Canada–United States Defence Cooperation," *1994 White Paper on Defence*, 22.

194. Department of National Defence, "Chapter 7: Implementing Defence Policy," *1994 White Paper on Defence*, 31.

195. Bill Graham, Minister of Defense, "Message from the Minister," *Defence Policy Statement of 2005*, Department of National Defence, Government of Canada, Ottawa, Ontario, i.

196. Graham, "Message from the Minister," i.

197. Department of National Defence, "Summary," *Defence Policy Statement 2005*, Government of Canada, Ottawa, Ontario.   Formerly available online at: http://www.mdn.ca/site/reports/dps/summary_e.asp.

198. DND, "Summary," *Defence Policy Statement 2005*.

199. DND, "Summary," *Defence Policy Statement 2005*.

200. DND, "Summary," *Defence Policy Statement 2005*.

201. DND, "Summary," *Defence Policy Statement 2005*.

202. DND, "Summary," *Defence Policy Statement 2005*.

203. DND, "Summary," *Defence Policy Statement 2005*. Also, as noted in the "Summary" of *Defence Policy Statement 2005*, "The expanded JTF2 will be able to deal with emergencies in different parts of the country. The enhanced Joint Nuclear, Biological and Chemical Defence Company will increase its support to civilian authorities in responding to a major incident in Canada. As a result of this new policy direction, our maritime and air forces will place greater emphasis on protecting Canada when deploying their personnel and assets. The maritime forces, for example, will play a prominent role in implementing the National Security Policy's six-point plan to strengthen marine security. Canada's Reserves will also increase their efforts in protecting Canada and Canadians. Building on their nation-wide presence, the Reserves will support civilian authorities in responding to domestic emergencies, focusing on their expertise in chemical, biological, radiological and nuclear response, information operations and civil-military cooperation."

204. DND, "Summary," *Defence Policy Statement 2005*.

205. Department of National Defence, "A New Vision for the Canadian Forces," *Defence Policy Statement 2005: A Role of Pride and Influence in the World*, 10. While northern security is briefly considered, more attention is devoted to the contribution of Canadian Forces to the continental defense of North America, in partnership with the United States through NORAD: "It is clearly in our sovereign interest to continue doing our part in defending the continent with the United States. Our intent to do so was clearly reflected in the security and defence measures announced in recent budgets, the signing of the Smart Border Declaration in 2001, the establishment of the Bi-National Planning Group in 2002, the publication of the National Security Policy (which calls for closer cooperation with the United States in protecting and defending our coasts and territorial waters) and the 2004 Joint Statement on Common Security, Common Prosperity: A New

Partnership in North America. These initiatives, while significant, are not enough. As part of our new, more sophisticated approach to our relationship with the United States, we will renew our commitment to continental defence, including through enhancing our domestic capabilities and establishing a single national command structure. The Government will also pursue further practical ways of strengthening our continental defence architecture and bilateral consultative mechanisms." Department of National Defence, "The Canada–U.S. Defence Relationship in a Changing World," *Defence Policy Statement 2005: A Role of Pride and Influence in the World*, 22. Among the future tasks identified for Canadian Forces is the enhancement of their role in defending the North American continent, including such efforts as:

- strengthening their ability to counter threats in Canada, especially in terms of monitoring and controlling activity in the air and maritime approaches to our territory;
- continuing to contribute Canadian aircraft and other assets to the NORAD mission;
- ensuring that maritime forces, both regular and reserve, cooperate even more closely with the U.S. Navy and Coast Guard;
- improving their ability to operate alongside American forces, including through more frequent combined training and exercises;
- exploring with the United States ways to enhance our bi-national defence cooperation, especially in the areas of maritime security and military support to civilian authorities; and
- continuing to participate in international operations overseas to address threats at their source.

206. Department of National Defence, "Introduction," *Defence Policy Statement 2005: A Role of Pride and Influence in the World*, 1. The introduction continued: "In this dangerous environment, Canadians look to their government for reassurance and protection. The Government has responded. In the immediate wake of September 11, 2001, it announced nearly $8 billion in measures aimed at enhancing the security of Canadians. In April 2004, the Government released its first National Security Policy, which sets out a broad range of new initiatives in areas such as intelligence, emergency planning and management, public health crises, and transportation and border security, to counter the major threats to Canadians. In Budget 2005, the Government made the largest reinvestment in Canada's military in over 20 years, totaling approximately $13 billion. This sum includes new baseline funding and significant additional resources for capital programs. Now, the Government has released the International Policy Statement that establishes the priorities and principles governing Canada's relations abroad, and leaves no doubt that defence and security are an integral part of our international strategy."

207. DND, "Introduction," *Defence Policy Statement 2005: A Role of Pride and Influence in the World*, 2.

208. DND, "Introduction," *Defence Policy Statement 2005: A Role of Pride and Influence in the World*, 2.

209. DND, "Introduction," *Defence Policy Statement 2005: A Role of Pride and Influence in the World*, 2–3. In its section on "The International Security Environment at the Beginning of the 21st Century" of *Defence Policy Statement 2005*, DND observes: "Whether in Somalia, Afghanistan, Haiti or Sudan, the past 15 years have confronted us with the concept and consequences of failed and failing states. The inability of governments in these countries, and others like them, to maintain political authority, to provide security and other basic services, and to protect essential human rights has trapped mil-

lions of vulnerable civilians in a cycle of misery, poverty and violence," and "Canadian Forces will continue to participate across the spectrum of international operations, with a focus on the complex and dangerous task of restoring order to failed and failing states. . . . As the concept of the three-block war suggests, these operations have become more challenging. Our soldiers, sailors and air personnel must increasingly operate in environments where the lines between war and peace have blurred. These situations are volatile, and a humanitarian mission can swiftly turn into a combat operation, particularly when warlords, criminal gangs and other irregular combatants remain part of the equation. They call for a wide variety of tools, from negotiation, compromise and cultural sensitivity to precision weapons. The aim is always to produce focused effects that put a premium, even in conflict situations, on the sanctity of human life." DND, "The International Security Environment at the Beginning of the 21st Century," *Defence Policy Statement 2005: A Role of Pride and Influence in the World*, 5.

210. DND, "The International Security Environment at the Beginning of the 21st Century," *Defence Policy Statement 2005: A Role of Pride and Influence in the World*, 5.

211. Matthew Carnaghan and Allison Goody, *Canadian Arctic Sovereignty*, Political and Social Affairs Division, Parliamentary Information and Research Service, Library of Parliament, Ottawa, Ontario, January 26, 2006, 8.

212. Carnaghan and Goody, *Canadian Arctic Sovereignty*, 8.

213. Carnaghan and Goody, *Canadian Arctic Sovereignty*, 8.

214. P. Whitney Lackenbauer, "The Canadian Rangers: A 'Postmodern' Militia that Works," *Canadian Military Journal* 6, No. 4.

215. Lackenbauer, "The Canadian Rangers."

216. Lackenbauer, "The Canadian Rangers."

217. Lackenbauer, "The Canadian Rangers."

218. Lackenbauer, "The Canadian Rangers."

219. Lackenbauer, "The Canadian Rangers."

220. Lackenbauer, "The Canadian Rangers."

221. Lackenbauer, "The Canadian Rangers."

222. Lackenbauer, "The Canadian Rangers."

223. DND, "Introduction," *Defence Policy Statement 2005: A Role of Pride and Influence in the World*, 3.

224. Department of National Defence, "A New Vision for the Canadian Forces," *Defence Policy Statement 2005: A Role of Pride and Influence in the World*, 8.

225. Jill Wherrett, "Introduction," *Aboriginal Peoples and the 1995 Québec Referendum: A Survey of the Issues*. Parliament of Canada, Political and Social Affairs Division, February 1996. As cited by Barry Zellen, Arctic Security Project Report, Part 2: State Perspectives on Arctic Sovereignty, Center for Contemporary Conflict, Naval Postgraduate School, http://www.ccc.nps.navy.mil/events/recent/2009-OnThinIce-Part2.asp.

226. Jill Wherrett, "The Referendum and Post-Referendum Debates; A. Aboriginal Perspectives; 1. The Crees of Quebec," *Aboriginal Peoples and the 1995 Québec Referendum*.

227. Wherrett, "The Referendum and Post-Referendum Debates; A. Aboriginal Perspectives; 1. The Crees of Quebec."

228. Wherrett, "The Referendum and Post-Referendum Debates; A. Aboriginal Perspectives; 1. The Crees of Quebec."

229. Jill Wherrett, "Background; B. The Province of Quebec's Current Boundaries," *Aboriginal Peoples and the 1995 Québec Referendum*.

230. Wherrett, "The Referendum and Post-Referendum Debates; A. Aboriginal Perspectives; 1. The Crees of Quebec."

231. Wherrett, "The Referendum and Post-Referendum Debates; A. Aboriginal Perspectives; 1. The Crees of Quebec."

232. Wherrett. "The Referendum and Post-Referendum Debates; A. Aboriginal Perspectives; 2. The Inuit of Northern Quebec," *Aboriginal Peoples and the 1995 Québec Referendum*. As Wherrett observed: "In late January 1996, Coon-Come urged the prime minister to make a formal declaration in the House of Commons supporting the Cree decision to remain in Canada if Québec secedes. The Crees again asserted that the JBNQA is a treaty that binds the federal government to protect Cree interests in the event of a unilateral declaration of independence by Québec.(8) The Crees also appeared during Senate Committee hearings on Bill C-110 (An Act respecting constitutional amendments). They opposed the bill, arguing that reforms should not be made at the expense of the Crees and other Aboriginal peoples.(9) In their view, Bill C-110 could constrain the federal government from tabling constitutional initiatives to protect the rights of Aboriginal peoples in the context of Québec secession. The Crees proposed an amendment in the event that the Senate supported the bill, a non-derogation clause to ensure that the Act would not constrain the powers of Parliament to propose or to authorize an amendment to the constitution in order to: a) recognize, affirm or protect the Aboriginal peoples and their Aboriginal and treaty rights or other rights and freedoms, or b) preserve and protect the national unity and territorial integrity of Canada. The Crees also called for their inclusion in federal unity initiatives."

233. Wherrett, "The Referendum and Post-Referendum Debates; A. Aboriginal Perspectives; 2. The Inuit of Northern Quebec."

234. Wherrett, "The Referendum and Post-Referendum Debates; A. Aboriginal Perspectives; 2. The Inuit of Northern Quebec."

235. Wherrett, "The Referendum and Post-Referendum Debates; A. Aboriginal Perspectives; 2. The Inuit of Northern Quebec."

236. Jill Wherrett, "The Referendum and Post-Referendum Debates; A. Aboriginal Perspectives; 3. Other Aboriginal Groups," *Aboriginal Peoples and the 1995 Québec Referendum*.

237. Wherrett, "The Referendum and Post-Referendum Debates; A. Aboriginal Perspectives; 3. Other Aboriginal Groups."

238. Wherrett, "The Referendum and Post-Referendum Debates; B. Quebec Government."

239. Wherrett, "The Referendum and Post-Referendum Debates; B. Quebec Government."

240. Wherrett, "The Referendum and Post-Referendum Debates; B. Quebec Government."

241. Wherrett, "The Referendum and Post-Referendum Debates; B. Quebec Government."

242. Jill Wherrett, "The Referendum and Post-Referendum Debates; C. Federal Government," *Aboriginal Peoples and the 1995 Québec Referendum.*

243. Wherrett, "The Referendum and Post-Referendum Debates; C. Federal Government."

244. For the Omnitrax website, see: http://www.omnitrax.com/portservice.aspx.

245. Omnitrax website, http://www.omnitrax.com/portservice.aspx.

246. Scott Reid, *Canada Remapped: How the Partition of Québec Will Reshape the Nation* (Vancouver: Pulp Press, 1992), 39.

247. Reid, *Canada Remapped*, 39.
248. Reid, *Canada Remapped*, 41.
249. Reid, *Canada Remapped*, 41.
250. Reid, *Canada Remapped*, 43.
251. Reid, *Canada Remapped*, 47.
252. Reid, *Canada Remapped*, 47.
253. Reid, *Canada Remapped*, 46.
254. Jockel, *Security to the North*, 184.
255. Jockel, *Security to the North*, 184.
256. Jockel, *Security to the North*, 184.
257. Jockel, *Security to the North*, 185.
258. Jockel, *Security to the North*, 185.
259. Jockel, *Security to the North*, 186.
260. Jockel, *Security to the North*, 186.
261. Jockel, *Security to the North*, 186.
262. Jockel, *Security to the North*, 186–87.
263. Jockel, *Security to the North*, 187.
264. Jockel, *Security to the North*, 197–98.
265. Carly Weeks, "Harper Wants to Recognize Québec as Nation within a United Canada," *Canwest News Service*, November 22, 2006.
266. Andrea Mandel-Campbell, "Who Controls Canada's Arctic? Spies, Submarines, and Foreign Ships May Signal That Our Claim to the North Is Melting," *The Walrus*, January 2005, http://www.walrusmagazine.com/articles/2005.01-national-affairs-Arctic-global-warming/.
267. Mandel-Campbell, "Who Controls Canada's Arctic?"
268. Mandel-Campbell, "Who Controls Canada's Arctic?"
269. Mandel-Campbell, "Who Controls Canada's Arctic?"
270. See Frances Widdowson and Albert Howard, *Disrobing the Aboriginal Industry: The Deception Behind Indigenous Cultural Preservation: How Aboriginal Deprivation Is Maintained by a Self-serving "Industry" of Lawyers and Consultants* (Toronto: McGill-Queens University Press, 2008). This work was selected as one of five books in Canada as a finalist for the prestigious 2009 Donner Prize, though it was not the eventual winner. Nonetheless, their work has transformed the debate in Canada on how best to address the issue of indigenous sovereignty, and shined a much-needed light on the problem of the inherent corrupting influence of what they effectively dub the "Aboriginal industry." In a review of their controversial book in the *National Post*, Kevin Libin wrote: "In their book, published by McGill-Queen's University Press, they identify the main culprits as the primarily non-native agents such as lawyers, consultants and anthropologists who thrive on our segregated policy approach to First Nations people. The tens of billions of dollars a year channeled to reserves and Canada's North from governments and industrialists, they argue, attracts mercenaries in swarms, manipulating Natives to inflate land claim grievances, demand industry payoffs and pressure politicians for more funding with few strings attached. . . . 'When you break down the romantic mythology, you find yourself immediately being accused of being anti-native people. But this whole thing came out of the fact that we looked at this and we said Native people are getting screwed over here,' Mr. Howard says." Kevin Libin, "Leftist Couple's Stance on Aboriginals Leaves Them in the Cold," *National Post*, October 31, 2008, http://mqup.mcgill.ca/extra.php?id=860.

271. Marika Kemeny, "Thomas Berger Discusses Northern Challenges at Glendon's Annual John Holmes Lecture," *Glendon News*, April 3, 2009, http://monglendon.yorku.ca/monglendon.nsf/.

272. Kemeny, "Thomas Berger Discusses Northern Challenges."

273. Mandel-Campbell, "Who Controls Canada's Arctic?"

274. Mandel-Campbell, "Who Controls Canada's Arctic?"

275. Inuit Circumpolar Council, "Circumpolar Inuit Declaration on Sovereignty in the Arctic," Section 4.3, April 28, 2009.

276. Inuit Circumpolar Council Press Release, "Circumpolar Inuit Launch Declaration on Arctic Sovereignty," Tromsø, Norway, April 28, 2009.

277. Inuit Circumpolar Council Press Release, "Circumpolar Inuit Launch Declaration on Arctic Sovereignty."

Chapter Three

1. Capt. Alec Scott, *Canada: A Failing State? The Canadian Forces' Role of Pride and Influence in Canada's North*, as Presented to the Aboriginals and the Canadian Military: Past, Present, Future Conference, Canadian Defence Academy, Kingston, Ontario, June 21–22, 2006.

2. Scott, *Canada: A Failing State?*

3. Scott, *Canada: A Failing State?*

4. Scott, *Canada: A Failing State?*

5. Scott, *Canada: A Failing State?*

6. Scott, *Canada: A Failing State?*

7. Scott, *Canada: A Failing State?*

8. Scott, *Canada: A Failing State?*

9. Scott, *Canada: A Failing State?*

10. Scott, *Canada: A Failing State?*

11. Scott, *Canada: A Failing State?*

12. Scott, *Canada: A Failing State?*

13. Scott, *Canada: A Failing State?*

14. Scott, *Canada: A Failing State?*

15. Scott, *Canada: A Failing State?*

16. Scott, *Canada: A Failing State?*

17. Scott, *Canada: A Failing State?*

18. Scott, *Canada: A Failing State?*

19. Scott, *Canada: A Failing State?*

20. Scott, *Canada: A Failing State?*

21. Scott, *Canada: A Failing State?*

22. Scott, *Canada: A Failing State?*

23. Scott, *Canada: A Failing State?*

24. Scott, *Canada: A Failing State?*

25. Scott, *Canada: A Failing State?*

26. Scott, *Canada: A Failing State?*

27. Scott, *Canada: A Failing State?*

28. Scott, *Canada: A Failing State?*

29. Scott, *Canada: A Failing State?*

30. *Native Americans in the Military*. Available online at: http://www.hud.gov/offices/pih/ih/codetalk/onap/veterans.cfm.

31. *Native Americans in the Military*. Available online at: http://www.hud.gov/offices/pih/ih/codetalk/onap/veterans.cfm.

32. Barry Zellen, "Sovereignty and Freedom in the Inupiaq Homeland: An Interview with General John Schaeffer, Alaska National Guard," *The Sourdough*, September 1, 1992. Also cited by Barry Zellen in Arctic Security Project Report, Part 3, Center for Contemporary Conflict, Naval Postgraduate School, http://www.ccc.nps.navy.mil/events/recent/2009-OnThinIce-Part3.asp.

33. GlobalSecurity.org, "Alaska Army National Guard," *GlobalSecurity*.org, http://www.globalsecurity.org/military/agency/army/arng-ak.htm.

34. Charles Etok Edwardsen, Jr., "Attributes of Original Sovereignty: A Memorandum from the Kasigluk Elders Conference," Kasigluk, Alaska, September 19, 1991. Edwardsen also observed: "Today, the territorial reaches of the Constitution of the United States of America are in question by the Inuit of the Republic of the Arctic." In his analysis, he noted that the U.S. government "has desired to characterize itself as the 'Apostle of Democracy' for the world. However, the most recent developments in the Soviet Union, and the recognition of independence for the Baltic Republics by President Gorbachev on September 2, 1991 may surpass the United States' claim to democratic leadership. By way of a historical comparison, the annexation of Alaska from the Russians to the United States is just as illegal as the secret protocol between Molotov of the USSR and Ribbentrop of Germany's Third Reich. There, Eastern Europe was carved into the familiar spheres of influence; Estonia, Lithuania, and Latvia fell into the Soviet Union . . . and [were] annexed by the USSR in August 1940. This Soviet annexation has never been recognized by the United States."

35. Charles Etok Edwardsen, Jr., "Science and the Indigenous Arctic," Center for World Indigenous Studies, June 15, 1993.

36. Edwardsen, Jr., "Science and the Indigenous Arctic."

37. Edwardsen, Jr., "Science and the Indigenous Arctic."

38. Edwardsen, Jr., "Science and the Indigenous Arctic."

39. Barents Observer, "Indigenous Peoples Agree on 'Bovanenkovskoe,'" *Barents Observer*, April 24, 2008.

40. See: Paul Brown, "Melting Ice Cap Brings Diamond Hunters and Hopes of Independence to Greenland," *The Guardian*, October 4, 2007; Krista Mahr, "Greenland to World: 'Keep Out!'" *Time*, September 21, 2007; Colin Woodard, "As a Land Thaws, So Do Greenland's Aspirations for Independence," *The Christian Science Monitor*, October 16, 2007.

41. Details on the sizes of the world's largest islands are from "Islands of the World," *WorldAtlas.com*.

42. Population statistics provided by *Wikipedia*, the online encyclopedia.

43. Colin Woodard, "As a Land Thaws, So Do Greenland's Aspirations for Independence," *The Christian Science Monitor*, October 16, 2007.

44. Woodard, "As a Land Thaws."

45. Brown, "Melting Ice Cap."

46. Brown, "Melting Ice Cap."

47. Brown, "Melting Ice Cap."

48. Brian Cathcart, "The Greening of Greenland," *News Statesman*, September 13, 2007.

49. Roger Boyes, "Global Warming Could Help Greenland to Independence," *The Times*, May 7, 2008.

50. Boyes, "Global Warming Could Help Greenland."

51. Boyes, "Global Warming Could Help Greenland."
52. Mahr, "Greenland to World."
53. Mahr, "Greenland to World."
54. Mahr, "Greenland to World."
55. Mahr, "Greenland to World."
56. Christian Wienberg, "Denmark, Greenland Divide," *Bloomberg*, June 13, 2008.
57. Wienberg, "Denmark, Greenland Divide."
58. Wienberg, "Denmark, Greenland Divide."
59. Wienberg, "Denmark, Greenland Divide."
60. Wienberg, "Denmark, Greenland Divide."
61. Woodard, "As a Land Thaws."
62. Woodard, "As a Land Thaws."
63. Woodard, "As a Land Thaws."
64. Brown, "Melting Ice Cap."
65. Mahr, "Greenland to World."
66. Mahr, "Greenland to World."
67. "Statement by the Department of State on the U.S.-Danish Agreement on Greenland, April 10, 1941," U.S. Department of State, Publication 1983, *Peace and War: United States Foreign Policy, 1931-1941* (Washington, D.C.: U.S., Government Printing Office, 1943), 641-47.
68. "Statement by the Department of State," April 10, 1941.
69. "Statement by the Department of State," April 10, 1941.
70. "Statement by the Department of State," April 10, 1941.
71. Article IX, Agreement on the Defense of Greenland between the United States and the Kingdom of Denmark, April 9, 1941.
72. Exchange of Notes Between the Secretary of State and the Minister of Denmark, U.S. Department of State, Washington, DC, April 7, 1941.
73. See: *Defense of Greenland: Agreement Between the United States and the Kingdom of Denmark*, April 27, 1951. Online at: http://denmark.usembassy.gov/1951-agreement.html. Signed in Copenhagen in duplicate in the English and Danish languages, both texts being equally authentic, this twenty-seventh day of April, 1951, by the undersigned duly authorized representatives of the Government of the United States of America and the Government of the Kingdom of Denmark.
74. Article I, Defense of Greenland: Agreement between the United States and the Kingdom of Denmark, April 27, 1951. Online at: http://denmark.usembassy.gov/1951-agreement.html
75. Article VI, Defense of Greenland: Agreement between the United States and the Kingdom of Denmark, April 27, 1951. Online at: http://denmark.usembassy.gov/1951-agreement.html.
76. "History Made in Southern Greenland," Archives 2003-2004, Denmark.dk. Online at: http://www.denmark.dk/en/servicemenu/News/FocusOn/Archives2003-2004/HistoryMadeInSouthernGreenland.htm.
77. "History Made in Southern Greenland."
78. "History Made in Southern Greenland."
79. Alan Cowell, "Greenland Vote Favors Independence," *New York Times*, November 26, 2008.
80. Cowell, "Greenland Vote Favors Independence."
81. Cowell, "Greenland Vote Favors Independence."

82. "Canadian Inuit Leader Salutes Greenland Vote for Self Rule," *AFP*, November 26, 2008.

83. Press Release: "ITK President Acknowledges Importance of Greenland Vote on Enhanced Self-Rule," Inuit Tapiriit Kanatami, November 27, 2008.

84. Press Release: "ITK President Acknowledges Importance of Greenland Vote."

85. Associated Press, "Warfare Course Shows Canadian Military Still Struggling in Arctic," *Associated Press*, June 22, 2008.

86. Associated Press, "Warfare course shows Canadian Military Still Struggling."

87. Honderich, *Arctic Imperative*, 89.

88. Honderich, *Arctic Imperative*, 90.

89. Am Johal, "Rabble Exclusive: Interview with Michael Byers," *Rabble.ca*, July 16, 2008. Online at: http://www.rabble.ca/rabble_interview.shtml?x=73486.

90. Fred Chartrand, "PM Starts Fight for North," *Canadian Press*, August 10, 2007. Online at: http://www.thestar.com/News/article/245117.

91. Clare Kines, "Of Ships and Sovereignty," *The House and Other Arctic Musings*, August 10, 2007.

92. Kines, "Of Ships and Sovereignty."

93. Kines, "Of Ships and Sovereignty."

94. Kines, "Of Ships and Sovereignty."

95. ICC Press Release. "ICC Chair, Sheila Watt-Cloutier, to Receive Three Honours," May 9, 2006.

96. Mary Simon, "Sovereignty from the North: An Inuit Leader Says Canada Is Asleep at the Post in the Arctic," *The Walrus*, November 2007. Online at: http://www.walrusmagazine.com/articles/2007.11-arctic-canada/3/.

97. Mary Simon, "Sovereignty from the North."

98. Mary Simon, "Sovereignty from the North."

99. Mary Simon, "Sovereignty from the North." Simon believes that 2007's "crisis caused by Russia planting its flag at the North Pole is somewhat different from past episodes, and it holds important messages for Canada. Russia hasn't strayed into Canadian territory to plant a flag. They have acted first in a contest of interests to demarcate their claims to continental shelf margins. Indeed, Russia acted some time ago, in 2001, by filing a claim with the United Nations, as permitted by the UN Convention on the Law of the Sea (UNCLOS)." She thus asks, "What has Canada been doing since 2001? The federal government has a plan to act by 2013, as required under UNCLOS, but too often it substitutes press releases for action. In recent interviews, the lead scientist for Canada on this file concedes that the country will be in trouble with its claims if ice conditions hamper scientific studies in the Arctic basin over the next five years. Again Canada is playing catch-up while Russia's objectives are clear."

100. Mary Simon, "Sovereignty from the North."

101. Mary Simon, "Sovereignty from the North."

102. Barry Zellen, "Risks and Promises in the New North," *The Globe and Mail*, May 28, 1992.

103. Thomas R. Berger, *Nunavut Land Claims Agreement Implementation Contract Negotiations for the Second Planning Period 2003-2013: Conciliator's Final Report—The Nunavut Project*, March 1, 2006. Online at: http://www.cda-acd.forces.gc.ca/aborig_conference_autoch/engraph/docs/canada.pdf.

104. Berger, *Conciliator's Final Report*, 60.

105. Berger, *Conciliator's Final Report*, 61.

106. Berger, *Conciliator's Final Report*, 61.

107. Berger, *Conciliator's Final Report*, 61.

108. Berger, *Conciliator's Final Report*, 65.

109. Berger, *Conciliator's Final Report*, 65.

110. Berger, *Conciliator's Final Report*, 65.

111. Berger, *Conciliator's Final Report*, 65–66.

112. Prime Minister Stephen Harper, *Throne Speech: Strong Leadership, A Better Canada*, October 16, 2007. Harper also reiterated his commitment to the defense and security of the North: "Our Government will build a world-class Arctic research station that will be on the cutting edge of Arctic issues, including environmental science and resource development. This station will be built by Canadians, in Canada's Arctic, and it will be there to serve the world. As part of asserting sovereignty in the Arctic, our Government will complete comprehensive mapping of Canada's Arctic seabed. Never before has this part of Canada's ocean floor been fully mapped. Defending our sovereignty in the North also demands that we maintain the capacity to act. New Arctic patrol ships and expanded aerial surveillance will guard Canada's Far North and the Northwest Passage. As well, the size and capabilities of the Arctic Rangers will be expanded to better patrol our vast Arctic territory. Ensuring our capacity to defend Canada's sovereignty is at the heart of the Government's efforts to rebuild the Canadian Forces. Canada's men and women in uniform risk their lives for their country, and deserve the equipment and training required for a first-class, modern military. Our Government will modernize Canada's military to provide effective surveillance and protection for all of our country, cooperate in the defence of North America, and meet our responsibilities abroad to the United Nations and our allies. Further, recognizing the important role that the Reserves play in this modernization, our Government will work with the provinces and territories to bring forward a comprehensive plan to modernize reservist reinstatement policies. . . . Rebuilding our capabilities and standing up for our sovereignty have sent a clear message to the world: Canada is back as a credible player on the international stage."

113. Prime Minister Stephen Harper, *Throne Speech: Strong Leadership, A Better Canada.*, October 16, 2007.

114. Inuit Tapiriit Kanatami Press Release, "Throne Speech Opens Doors—Creates Opportunities," October 16, 2007.

115. ITK Press Release, "Throne Speech Opens Doors."

116. ITK Press Release, "ITK President Encouraged."

117. ITK Press Release, "ITK President Encouraged."

118. ITK Press Release, "ITK President Encouraged."

119. ITK Press Release, "ITK President Mary Simon Launches Cross Canada Speaking Tour: 'Inuit and the Canadian Arctic: Sovereignty Begins at Home,'" October 23, 2007.

120. ITK Press Release, "ITK President Mary Simon Launches Cross Canada Speaking Tour."

121. Berger, *Conciliator's Final Report*, 61–62.

122. Berger, *Conciliator's Final Report*, 61–62.

123. Berger, *Conciliator's Final Report*, 61–62.

124. Berger, *Conciliator's Final Report*, 62.

125. Berger, *Conciliator's Final Report*, 62.

126. Berger, *Conciliator's Final Report*, 62.

127. Press Release, National Snow and Ice Data Center (NSIDC), October 1, 2007.

128. Berger, *Conciliator's Final Report*, 62.

129. Berger, *Conciliator's Final Report*, 62–63.

130. Berger, *Conciliator's Final Report*, 63.

131. Berger, *Conciliator's Final Report*, 63.

132. Berger, *Conciliator's Final Report*, 63.

133. Berger, *Conciliator's Final Report*, 63–64.

134. Berger, *Conciliator's Final Report*, 64.

135. Berger, *Conciliator's Final Report*, 64.

136. Berger, *Conciliator's Final Report*, 64.

137. Jim Bell, "Ottawa Needs Policy on Aboriginal Relocations," *Nunatsiaq News*, October 15, 1999.

138. Bell, "Ottawa Needs Policy on Aboriginal Relocations."

139. Bell, "Ottawa Needs Policy on Aboriginal Relocations."

140. Michael Byers, "Mr. Harper, Apologize to the 'High Arctic Exiles': Not Only Is This the Right Thing to Do, but It Would Help Cement Canada's Northern Claims," *The Globe and Mail*, June 12, 2008.

141. Byers, "Mr. Harper, Apologize to the 'High Arctic Exiles'."

142. Byers, "Mr. Harper, Apologize to the 'High Arctic Exiles'."

143. Byers, "Mr. Harper, Apologize to the 'High Arctic Exiles'."

144. Byers, "Mr. Harper, Apologize to the 'High Arctic Exiles'."

145. Byers, "Mr. Harper, Apologize to the 'High Arctic Exiles'."

146. Byers, "Mr. Harper, Apologize to the 'High Arctic Exiles'."

147. Michael R. Marrus, "Official Apologies and the Quest for Historical Justice," Controversies in Global Politics and Societies, Munk Centre for International Studies, University of Toronto, 2006, 2.

148. Marrus, "Official Apologies and the Quest for Historical Justice," 4.

149. Marrus, "Official Apologies and the Quest for Historical Justice," 3.

150. Marrus, "Official Apologies and the Quest for Historical Justice," 5.

151. Marrus, "Official Apologies and the Quest for Historical Justice," 40.

152. Marrus, "Official Apologies and the Quest for Historical Justice," 40.

153. Inuit Circumpolar Council, *Circumpolar Inuit Declaration on Arctic Sovereignty*, 4.1, April 28, 2009.

154. ICC, *Circumpolar Inuit Declaration on Arctic Sovereignty*, 4.1.

155. Inuit Circumpolar Council Press Release, "Arctic Sovereignty Begins with Inuit: Circumpolar Inuit Commit to Development of 'Inuit Declaration on Sovereignty in the Arctic,'" Ottawa, Ontario, November 10, 2008.

156. ICC Press Release, "Arctic Sovereignty Begins with Inuit."

157. ICC, *Circumpolar Inuit Declaration on Arctic Sovereignty*, 1.1.

158. ICC, *Circumpolar Inuit Declaration on Arctic Sovereignty*, 1.2.

159. ICC, *Circumpolar Inuit Declaration on Arctic Sovereignty*, 1.3.

160. ICC, *Circumpolar Inuit Declaration on Arctic Sovereignty*, 1.3.

161. ICC, *Circumpolar Inuit Declaration on Arctic Sovereignty*, 1.4.

162. ICC, *Circumpolar Inuit Declaration on Arctic Sovereignty*, 1.4.

163. ICC, *Circumpolar Inuit Declaration on Arctic Sovereignty*, 1.5.

164. ICC, *Circumpolar Inuit Declaration on Arctic Sovereignty*, 1.6.

165. ICC, *Circumpolar Inuit Declaration on Arctic Sovereignty*, 1.7.

166. ICC, *Circumpolar Inuit Declaration on Arctic Sovereignty*, 1.8.

167. ICC, *Circumpolar Inuit Declaration on Arctic Sovereignty*, 1.8.

168. ICC, *Circumpolar Inuit Declaration on Arctic Sovereignty*, 2.1.

169. ICC, *Circumpolar Inuit Declaration on Arctic Sovereignty*, 2.1.

170. ICC, *Circumpolar Inuit Declaration on Arctic Sovereignty*, 2.1.
171. ICC, *Circumpolar Inuit Declaration on Arctic Sovereignty*, 2.2.
172. ICC, *Circumpolar Inuit Declaration on Arctic Sovereignty*, 2.3.
173. ICC, *Circumpolar Inuit Declaration on Arctic Sovereignty*, 2.4.
174. ICC, *Circumpolar Inuit Declaration on Arctic Sovereignty*, 2.5.
175. ICC, *Circumpolar Inuit Declaration on Arctic Sovereignty*, 2.6.
176. ICC, *Circumpolar Inuit Declaration on Arctic Sovereignty*, 3.1.
177. ICC, *Circumpolar Inuit Declaration on Arctic Sovereignty*, 3.2.
178. ICC, *Circumpolar Inuit Declaration on Arctic Sovereignty*, 3.3.
179. ICC, *Circumpolar Inuit Declaration on Arctic Sovereignty*, 3.4.
180. ICC, *Circumpolar Inuit Declaration on Arctic Sovereignty*, 3.5.
181. ICC, *Circumpolar Inuit Declaration on Arctic Sovereignty*, 3.6.
182. ICC, *Circumpolar Inuit Declaration on Arctic Sovereignty*, 3.6.
183. ICC, *Circumpolar Inuit Declaration on Arctic Sovereignty*, 3.7.
184. ICC, *Circumpolar Inuit Declaration on Arctic Sovereignty*, 3.8.
185. ICC, *Circumpolar Inuit Declaration on Arctic Sovereignty*, 3.9.
186. ICC, *Circumpolar Inuit Declaration on Arctic Sovereignty*, 3.10.
187. ICC, *Circumpolar Inuit Declaration on Arctic Sovereignty*, 3.10.
188. ICC, *Circumpolar Inuit Declaration on Arctic Sovereignty*, 3.11.
189. ICC, *Circumpolar Inuit Declaration on Arctic Sovereignty*, 3.12.
190. ICC, *Circumpolar Inuit Declaration on Arctic Sovereignty*, 3.13.
191. ICC, *Circumpolar Inuit Declaration on Arctic Sovereignty*, 4.2.
192. ICC, *Circumpolar Inuit Declaration on Arctic Sovereignty*, 4.2.
193. ICC, *Circumpolar Inuit Declaration on Arctic Sovereignty*, 4.3.
194. ICC, *Circumpolar Inuit Declaration on Arctic Sovereignty*, 4.3.
195. Ariel Cohen, Lajos F. Szaszdi, and Jim Dolbow, "The New Cold War: Reviving the U.S. Presence in the Arctic," Heritage Foundation Backgrounder No. 2202, October 30, 2008.
196. Cohen, Szaszdi, and Dolbow, "The New Cold War."
197. Cohen, Szaszdi, and Dolbow, "The New Cold War."
198. Oran Young, *Arctic Politics: Conflict and Cooperation in the Circumpolar North* (Hanover: University Press of New England, 1992), 176, 189.
199. Young, *Arctic Politics*, 176, 189.
200. Young, *Arctic Politics*, 245.
201. Young, *Arctic Politics*, 245.
202. Young, *Arctic Politics*, 246.
203. John Bird, "Feds Tried to Bypass Inuit on Polar Bears: Canada Wanted to Offer Europe a Partial Ban on Exports without Consulting Inuit," *Nunatsiaq News*, November 28, 2008.
204. Bird, "Feds Tried to Bypass Inuit on Polar Bears."
205. Bird, "Feds Tried to Bypass Inuit on Polar Bears."
206. Bird, "Feds Tried to Bypass Inuit on Polar Bears."
207. Carnaghan and Goody, *Canadian Arctic Sovereignty*, 1.
208. Carnaghan and Goody, *Canadian Arctic Sovereignty*, 1–2. The Government of Canada has been active in developing an increasingly holistic approach to Arctic sovereignty, as reflected in its 2008 integrated northern strategy, and its reformulated 2009 northern strategy. See: Office of the Prime Minister, *Northern Strategy—Backgrounder*, Government of Canada, Ottawa, Ontario, March 10, 2008, which observes that the "Government supports a vision of a new North that realizes its full social and economic poten-

tial and secures its future, for the benefit of all Canadians," and that its "integrated North-ern Strategy supports this vision by focusing on four integrated priorities: economic and social development, governance, environmental protection, and sovereignty." Available online at: http://pm.gc.ca/eng/media.asp?id=2016. Also see: Department of Indian and Northern Affairs, *Federal Government's Northern Strategy Delivers for All Canadians— Ministers Highlight Progress Towards Canada's Northern Vision*, Government of Canada, Ottawa, Ontario, July 26, 2009, which observes: "Canada's Northern Strategy: Our North, Our Heritage, Our Future—provides a comprehensive explanation of the Northern Strategy and its four pillars of exercising Canada's Arctic sovereignty, protecting the North's environmental heritage, promoting social and economic development, and im-proving and devolving northern governance." Available online at: http://www.ainc-inac.gc.ca/ai/mr/nr/m-a2009/nr000000417-eng.asp.

Bibliography

Aboriginal Rights Coalition of British Columbia. "The Sparrow Case." Aboriginal Rights
Coalition of British Columbia. Online at: http://arcbc.tripod.com/sparrow.htm.
AFN Press Release. "Assembly of First Nations National Chief Demands that Federal
Government Immediately Repudiate and Remove Reference to First Nations from
Military's Terror Manual List." Assembly of First Nations Press Release. Ottawa,
Ontario, April 1, 2007.
AFP, "Canadian Inuit Leader Salutes Greenland Vote for Self Rule," AFP, November 26,
2008.
———. "Stop Stealing Our Land, Inuits Say, as Arctic Resources Race Heats Up." *AFP*,
June 16, 2008.
———. "U.S. Negroponte to Attend Arctic Conference in Greenland." *AFP*, May 22,
2008.
Agreement to Amend and Supplement the 1951 Agreement on the Defense of Greenland,
August 10, 2004.
Agreement on the Defense of Greenland between the United States and the Kingdom of
Denmark, April 9, 1941.
Agreement on the Defense of Greenland between the United States and the Kingdom of
Denmark, April 27, 1951.
Alaska Federation of Natives. *1991: Making It Work: A Guide to Public Law 100-241,
1987 Amendments to the Alaska Native Claims Settlement Act.* Alaska Federation of
Natives. Anchorage, Alaska. Reissued in PDF format in October 2001 by Sealaska
Corporation.
———. *Subsistence Chronology, A Short History of Subsistence Policy in Alaska Since
Statehood*, rev. ed. Alaska Federation of Natives, Anchorage, Alaska, 1998.
———. *The Trust Responsibility in Alaska: An Analysis of Congressional Authority to
Legislate on Behalf of the Alaska Natives.* Alaska Federation of Natives, Inc., Febru-
ary 18, 2007.
Alaska History and Cultural Studies, Inc. "Alaska's Cultures: Military in Alaska." Alaska
History and Cultural Studies Website. Online at:
http://www.akhistorycourse.org/articles/article.php?artID=446.
Alaska Native Claims Settlement Act Resource Center. Online at:
http://www.lbblawyers.com/ancsa.htm.

Alaska State Senate. *Senate Bill No. 443: "The Governor's Bill on Subsistence."* Juneau, AK: State of Alaska, 1992.

Allagui, Slim. "Arctic Powers Upbeat as Greenland Summit Opens." *AFP*, May 28, 2008.

Alunik, Dennis. "Court Battle Looms as IRC Seeks to Guarantee Access." *Tusaayaksat*, November 13, 1991, 2.

Alvarez, Sloan, and Associates Ltd. *Mineral Guide to the Inuvialuit Settlement Region.* March 2000.

Amagoalik, John. "What Price Nunavut? . . . The Amount of Effort it Took to Make Progress Took its Toll on Inuit Leaders." *Nunavut99.* Iqaluit, Nunavut: Nortext Multimedia and Nunavut Tunngavik Incorporated, 1999. Online at: http://www.nunavut.com/nunavut99/english/index.html.

Anchorage Daily News Editorial Board. "Rejected Subsistence Compromise Cracks Up." *Anchorage Daily News*, March 30, 1992.

ANCSA at 30. A retrospective on ANCSA published by LitSite Alaska, a web portal promoting literacy, cultural diversity, and wellbeing in Alaska, presents interviews with the "original participants reflecting upon the 30 years since the passage of the Alaska Native Claims Settlement Act," conducted by Sharon McConnell, executive director of Blueberry Productions, Inc., and Ronald Spatz, project director of LitSite Alaska. Online at: http://litsite.alaska.edu/aktraditions/ancsa/.

Archinald, Janet, Robert D. Arnold, Margie Bauman, Nancy Yaw Davis, Robert A. Frederick, Paul Gaskin, John Havelock, Gary Holthaus, Chris McNeil, Thomas Richards, Jr., Howard Rock, and Rosita Worl. *Alaska Native Land Claims.* Anchorage, AK: Alaska Native Foundation, 1976.

Arctic-Caribou.com. "NTI Think They Know the Answers." *Arctic-Caribou.com.* Online at: http://www.arctic-caribou.com/news_july06.html.

———. "Pro-Uranium Position Elicits Grave Concerns." *Arctic-Caribou.com*, the website of the Beverly and Qamanirjuaq Caribou Management Board. Online at: http://www.arctic-caribou.com/news_july06.html.

Arctic Circle Magazine. "Beaufort Blues Again." March/April 1991.

Arctic Coastal Zone Management Program, No. 3. Barrow, Alaska: March/April 1977. Online at: http://www.ebenhopson.com/czm/1977cz/MarApr1977/index.html.

Arctic Policy Review. "Berger Launches ANCSA Hearings: Focus on Native Sovereignty." *Arctic Policy Review*, June 1984, http://www.alaskool.org /projects/ancsa/berger1984/ANRC_Berger.html.

———. "Judge Thomas Berger Appointed Head of ICC-ANCSA Review Commission: Stirs International Attention." *Arctic Policy Review*, October/November 1983.

Arctic Region Map: Political, 1995. From the Perry-Castañeda Library Map Collection, Polar Regions and Oceans Maps Section, University of Texas. Online at: http://www.lib.utexas.edu/maps/islands_oceans_poles/arctic_region_pol_95.jpg.

Armstrong, Fred, Jr. "An Alaska Native's Perspective." *Endangered Species Bulletin* 24, No. 2 (March/April 1999): 17

Arnold, Elizabeth. "Alaska: Polar Bear Isn't Endangered." *NPR*, February 12, 2008, http://www.npr.org/templates/story/story.php?storyId=18913804.

Assembly of First Nations. "AFN National Chief Acknowledges 25th Anniversary of Section 35 of Canada's 1982 Constitution as a Victory for First Peoples but a Vision Yet to be Realized." Assembly of First Nations Press Release. Ottawa: Assembly of First Nations, April 17, 2007.

———. "Assembly of First Nations National Chief Demands that Federal Government Immediately Repudiate and Remove Reference to First Nations from Military's Terror Manual List." Assembly of First Nations Press Release. Ottawa: Assembly of First Nations, April 1, 2007.

Associated Press. "Mule Deer, Cougars Reported in Alaska." *Associated Press*, August 11, 2005.

———. "Russia's Message from the North Pole: We're a Force to Be Reckoned With." *International Herald Tribune*, August 7, 2007.

———. "Warfare Course Shows Canadian Military Still Struggling in Arctic." *Associated Press*, June 22, 2008.

Atkinson Charitable Foundation. "Veteran Arctic Journalist, Ed Struzik, Wins Fellowship." Atkinson Charitable Foundation Press Release, June 23, 2006:

Attali, Jacques. "An Age of Yugoslavias." *Harper's*, January 1993.

Aubin, Mario, Sergeant, Canadian Rangers, Department of National Defence. Interview with author. Yellowknife, NWT. January 1991.

Baker, Stacy. "Why We Apologize Too Much, and How to Stop." *Fitness Magazine.*

Bailey, Sue. "Protest Leader Willing to Talk." *Canadian Press*, June 29, 2007. Online at: http://www.thestar.com/News/article/230878.

Banks, Michael. "Systems Analysis and the Study of Regions." *International Studies Quarterly* 13, No. 4, Special Issue on International Subsystems (December, 1969): 335–360.

Barents Observer. "Indigenous Peoples Agree on 'Bovanenkovskoe,'" *Barents Observer*, April 24, 2008.

Barrett, Vice Admiral Thomas J., USCG (Ret.), Deputy Secretary of Transportation. Remarks to the MARAD Arctic Transportation Conference. Washington, D.C. June 5, 2008.

Baskin, Leonid M., Lyudmila S. Bogoslovskaya, Kjell Danell, Anne Gunn, David R. Klein, David B. Irons, Gary P. Kofinas, Kit M. Kovacs, Margarita Magomedova, Rosa H. Meehan, Don E. Russell, Patrick Valkenburg. "Management and Conservation of Wildlife in a Changing Arctic Environment." *Arctic Climate Impact Assessment* (ACIA), 2005, 597–648.

BBC News. "Russia Plants Flag under N. Pole." *BBC News*, August 2, 2007.

Beaufort-Mackenzie Mineral Development Area (BMMDA) Website. A regional information project coordinated by NWT Department of Industry, Tourism and Investment's Minerals, Oil and Gas Division, the Joint Secretariat-Inuvialuit Renewable Resource Committees, and the Inuvialuit Land Corporation, Yellowknife, NWT, http://www.bmmda.nt.ca/.

Beaufort Sea Steering Committee. *A Report to the Minister of Indian Affairs and Northern Development Regarding Issues Arising from the Environmental Impact Review Board Reviews of the Isserk and Kulluk Drilling Program Applications.* Vancouver: Beaufort Sea Steering Committee, 1991.

Belanger-Fontaine, Suzanne, Director of Environment. As presented to the *Aboriginal Human Resources and Contaminated Sites: Identifying and Creating New Opportunities* conference on February 1, 2005.

Bell, Jim. "Berger Report: Dead on Arrival." *Nunatsiaq News*, June 22, 2007. Online at: http://www.nunatsiaq.com/opinionEditorial/editorial.html.

———. "Leona Makes a Good Point." *Nunatsiaq News*, March 14, 2008.

———. "Ottawa Needs Policy on Aboriginal Relocations." *Nunatsiaq Nerws*, October 15, 1999, http://www.nunatsiaq.com/archives/nunavut991030/editorial.html.

———. "The Quiet Revolution." *Arctic Circle Magazine* 2, No. 4 (January/February 1992): 12–21.

Bellinger, John B. "Treaty on Ice." *New York Times*, June 23, 2008.

Berger, Thomas R. "Letter to the Minister of Indian Affairs and Northern Development." *Conciliator's Final Report: Nunavut Land Claims Agreement Implementation Planning Contract Negotiations for the Second Planning Period.* Vancouver, March 1, 2006, http://www.ainc-inac.gc.ca/pr/agr/nu/lca/index_e.html.

————. "The North as Frontier and Homeland." *The Arctic: Choices for Peace and Security—A Public Inquiry.* West Vancouver: Gordon Soules Book Publishers, 1989, 37–44.

————. *Northern Frontier, Northern Homeland,* revised edition. Vancouver: Douglas and McIntyre, 1988.

————. *Village Journey: The Report of the Alaska Native Review Commission.* New York: Hill and Wang, 1985.

Berk, Michael. "The Arctic Bridge: Churchill, Man., Is the Key to Linking Afghans with the World," *Financial Post,* November 27, 2007, http://www.financialpost.com/money/rrsp/Story.html?id=125273.

Berry, Mary Clay. *The Alaska Pipeline: The Politics of Oil and Native Land Claims.* Bloomington: University of Indiana Press, 1975.

Bevan, Scott. "Arctic Ice Cap Could Melt by 2070, Russia Warns."*Australian Broadcasting Corporation,* July 1, 2008.

Bird, John. "Feds Tried to Bypass Inuit on Polar Bears: Canada Wanted to Offer Europe a Partial Ban on Exports without Consulting Inuit." *Nunatsiaq News,* November 28, 2008.

Black, Richard. "Inuit Sue U.S. over Climate Policy." *BBC News,* December 8, 2005.

Blanchfield, Mike, and Randy Boswell, "Bush Asserts Power Over Arctic," *Canwest News Service,* as published by *The Calgary Herald,* January 13, 2009, http://www.calgaryherald.com/opinion/Bush+asserts+power+over+Arctic/1170484/story.html.

Blatchford, Edgar. Presentation to the ICC General Assembly. Inuvik, NWT, July 1992.

Block, Walter. "Beaufort Oil." *Fraser Forum,* September 1990, 27.

Blondin-Andrew, Ethel. "Remarks to the First Session of the 38th Parliament, The Parliament of Canada." Ottawa, Ontario, October 6, 2005. Online at: http://www2.parl.gc.ca/HousePublications/Publication.aspx?Language=E&Mode=1&Parl=38&Ses=1&DocId=2020650.

Borgerson, Scott G. "An Ice-Cold War." *New York Times,* August 8, 2007.

Boswell, Randy. "Canada Draws Line in the Ice over Arctic Seabed." *Canwest News Service,* June 30, 2007.

————. "Canadian Expedition Seeks to Prove Claim on Underwater Ridge." *Canwest News Service,* February 15, 2008.

————. "Conference Could Mark Start of an Arctic Power Struggle." *Canwest News Service,* May 29, 2008.

————. "Russian General Fires Arctic Warning." *Canwest News Service,* June 24, 2008.

————. "U.S. and Canada on Collision Course over Arctic Rights: U.S. Official." *Canwest News Service,* February 12, 2008.

Bouchard, Chad. "Bali Roadmap Officially Kicks Off New Round of Climate Change Negotiations." *Voice of America News,* December 17, 2007.

Bowermaster, Jon. "The Last Front of the Cold War." *The Atlantic,* November 1993.

Boyes, Roger. "Global Warming Could Help Greenland to Independence." *The Times,* May 7, 2008.

Boyle, Pat. "BSSC Issues Recommendations." *Arctic Petroleum Review* 14, No. 1 (Summer 1991): 5–6, 10.

————. "Of Land Claims and Northern Development." *Arctic Petroleum Review* 14, No. 1 (Summer 1991): 3–5.

Breslauer, George W. "On Collaborative Competition." In George W. Breslauer, ed., *Soviet Strategy in the Middle East.* Boston: Unwin Hyman, 1990.

————. "Soviet Policy in the Middle East, 1967–1972: Unalterable Antagonism or Collaborative Competition?" In Alexander L. George, ed., *Managing U.S.-Soviet Rivalry: Problems of Crisis Prevention.* Boulder: Westview Press, 1983.

Brodie, Bernard. *Strategy in the Missile Age.* Princeton: Princeton University Press, 1959.

Brody, Hugh. *The People's Land: Eskimos and Whites in the Eastern Arctic.* Harmondsworth, UK: Penguin, 1975.

Brown, Dee. *Bury My Heart at Wounded Knee: An Indian History of the American West.* New York: Bantam Books, 1972.

Brown, Paul. "Melting Ice Cap Brings Diamond Hunters and Hopes of Independence to Greenland." *The Guardian*, October 4, 2007.

Bull, Hedley. *The Anarchical Society: A Study of Order in World Politics.* New York: Columbia University Press, 1977.

Bunting, Glenn F. "Navy Warms up to Idea of Presence in Cold Bering Sea." *Los Angeles Times*, August 31, 1986.

Burgess, Tom. "Tension in the Bering Sea: In Icy little Adak, Two Superpowers are Eye to Eye." *San Diego Union*, November 22, 1987.

————. "Alaska: Navy Jet Feints at USSR Told: Mock Attack Called Response to Soviet Flights; Tactics and Tensions in the Bering Sea." *San Diego Union*, November 22, 1987.

Bush, George W. 2003 State of the Union Address. Washington, D.C.: The White House, January 28, 2003, http://www.whitehouse.gov/news/releases/2003/01/20030128-19.html.

Byers, Michael. "Mr. Harper, Apologize to the 'High Arctic Exiles'; Not Only Is This the Right Thing to Do, but It Would Help Cement Canada's Northern Claims." *The Globe and Mail*, June 12, 2008.

Byers, R. B. and Michael Slack, eds. *Strategy and the Arctic.* Toronto: Canadian Institute of Strategic Studies, 1986.

Cairns, Alan C. *Citizens Plus.* Vancouver: UBC Press, 2000.

Caldwell, Nathaniel French, Jr. *Arctic Leverage: Canadian Sovereignty and Security.* Westport: Praeger, 1990.

Campbell, Kim. Former Prime Minister of Canada. Interview with author. Cambridge, MA, January 1994.

Canada Command. "CF Arctic Operation Practices Assistance to RCMP and Response to a Major Airline Disaster." Canada Command Press Release, April 16, 2007. Online at: http://www.dnd.ca/site/newsroom/view_news_e.asp?id=2255.

Canadian Arctic Resources Committee. *Aboriginal Self-Government and Constitutional Reform.* Ottawa: Canadian Arctic Resource Committee, 1988.

————. "The Soviet North." *Northern Perspectives* 16, No. 4 (July/August 1988), http://www.carc.org/pubs/v16no4/index.html.

Canadian Boreal Initiative. "Dehcho First Nations and Conservation Groups Seek Solution to Implement Land Use Plan in Advance of Mackenzie Pipeline." *Canadian Boreal Initiative*, Calgary, Alberta, April 4, 2007.

Canadian Environmental Assessment Agency. "Backgrounder: Joint Review Panel for the Mackenzie Gas Project." Canadian Environmental Assessment Agency Website. Online at: http://www.ceaa.gc.ca/010/0001/0001/0020/bg040818_e.htm.

Canadian Navy. "Operations and Exercises" section of the *Canadian Navy Website*. Online at: http://www.navy.dnd.ca/cms_operations/operations_e.asp?id=460.

Canadian Peace Alliance. *Transformation Moment: A Canadian Vision of Common Security: The Report of the Citizens' Inquiry into Peace and Security*. Ottawa: Project Ploughshares and the Canadian Peace Alliance, March 1992.

Canadian Press. "Canadian Scientists Test New Electronic Surveillance of Northwest Passage." *Canadian Press*, July 13, 2008.

———. "New Arctic Army Facility, Navy Port Support Battle for the North." *Canadian Press*, August 10, 2007.

———. "Rogue Mohawk Protesters Warn of More Barricades; Busy Ontario Road Opens." *Canadian Press*, June 29, 2007. Online at: http://www.edmontonsun.com/News/Canada/2007/06/29/pf-4301029.html.

Carmichael, Fred. *From the Chair: Fred Carmichael Shares His Thoughts about the Pipeline*. Aboriginal Pipeline Group Website. Online at: http://www.mvapg.com/page/page/2501879.htm.

Carnaghan, Matthew, and Allison Goody. *Canadian Arctic Sovereignty*, Political and Social Affairs Division, Parliamentary Information and Research Service, Library of Parliament, Ottawa, Ontario, January 26, 2006.

Carns, Teresa W. "A Picture of Rural Justice: Alaska Judicial Council Studies." *Alaska Justice Forum*, 1993, http://justice.uaa.alaska.edu /forum/10/3fall1993/a_rural.html.

Case, David S. "Village Home Rule—A Practical Approach to Alaska Native Land and Governance." *Alaska Native News 3*, No. 5 (February 1985): 17–20.

Cassidy, Frank, ed. *Aboriginal Self-Determination: Proceedings of a Conference Held September 30–October 3, 1990*. Halifax: Oolichan Books/Institute for Research on Public Policy, 1991.

Cassidy, Frank, and Dale Norman. *After Native Claims?* Lantzville, BC: Oolichan Books/Institute for Research on Public Policy, 1988.

Cathcart, Brian. "The Greening of Greenland." *News Statesman*, September 13, 2007.

Cattaneo, Claudia. "Inuvik Prosperity on Ice: Residents Await the Mackenzie Valley Pipeline Boom with Impatience . . . and Growing Resentment." *Financial Post*, February 4, 2006.

CBC Ideas. "The Northern Front." *CBC Ideas*, October 1985.

CBC News. "Highway Blockade May Not be the Last, Mohawk Activist Warns." June 29, 2007.

———. "Manitoba Chief Calls for National Day of Rail Blockades." *CBC News*, May 23, 2007, http://www.cbc.ca/canada/manitoba/story/2007/05/23/aboriginal-conference.html.

———. "Manitoba Chief Calls Off Blockade Plans." *CBC News*, June 21, 2007. Online at: http://www.cbc.ca/canada/story/2007/06/21/aboriginal-day.html.

———."U.S. Polar Bear Decision Condemned in North." *CBC News*, May 15, 2008.

CBC Television Archives, "Dempster Highway Opens 'Road to Resources' across Arctic." *CBC News*, Aug. 18, 1979. Online at: http://archives.cbc.ca/IDC-1-73-2346-13552-10/on_this_day/politics_economy/twt.

Center for Arms Control, Energy and Environmental Studies. "Collision of Two U.S. Nuclear Powered Submarines on March 19, 1998." Center for Arms Control, Energy and Environmental Studies at MIPT. April 8, 1998.

Center for War, Peace and the News Media. "Russia and the 'Near Abroad.'" Working Paper 14. New York: Center for War, Peace and the News Media, April 1994.

Chamberlain, J. E. "Ted." *The Harrowing of Eden: White Attitudes Toward Native Americans.* New York: Seabury, 1975.
———. "Sovereignty, Sovereignty, Sovereignty." *Alaska Native News* 3, No. 2 (November 1984): 24–28.
Chanton, J. P., F. S. Chapin, III, D. Verbyla, K. M. Walter, S. A. Zimov. "Methane Bubbling from Siberian Thaw Lakes as a Positive Feedback to Climate Warming," *Nature* 443 (September 7, 2006): 71–75.
Chapin, F. S., III, M. C. Chapin, S. P. Davidov, S. F. Prosiannikov, I. P. Semiletov, S. Trumbore, S. Tyler, Y. V. Voropaev, and S. A. Zimov. "North Siberian Lakes: A Methane Source Fueled by Pleistocene Carbon." *Science* 277, No. 5327 (1997): 800–802.
Chapin, F. S., III, E. A. G. Schuur, and S. A. Zimov. "Permafrost and the Global Carbon Budget." *Science* 312 (2006): 1612–13.
Charron, Andrea. "The Northwest Passage Shipping Channel: Is Canada's Sovereignty Really Floating Away?" War Studies Programme. Royal Military College of Canada, Kingston, Ontario. Presented to the CDAI-CDFAI 7th Annual Graduate Student Symposium, RMC, October 29–30, 2004.
Chartrand, Fred. "PM Starts Fight for North." *Canadian Press*, August 10, 2007. Online at: http://www.thestar.com/News/article/245117.
Chronicle Herald Op-Ed Editors. "Arctic Sovereignty: No More Northern Lite." *Chronicle Herald*, Halifax, Nova Scotia, January 15, 2009, http://thechronicleherald.ca/Editorial/1100831.html.
Churchill Gateway Development Corporation. "Port of Churchill Welcomes First-Ever Ship From Russia." October 17, 2007, http://www.marketwire.com/press-release/Churchill-Gateway-Development-Corporation-782085.html.
Churchill, Winston. "Sinews of Peace." Westminster College, Fulton, Missouri. March 5, 1946.
Clark, Joe. "Charlottetown 10 Years On: From Activism to Incrementalism." *Policy Options* 24, No. 1 (December 2002/January 2003): 59–61. Online at: http://www.irpp.org/po/archive/dec02/clark.pdf.
———. *Constitution and Democracy: Ten Years after the Charlottetown Accord.* October 25, 2002.
———. *Sovereignty in an Interdependent World.* Speech at Carleton University, Ottawa. October 18, 1988.
———. "Statement on Sovereignty to the House of Commons," Ottawa, Ontario, Canada, September 10, 1985. As presented on page "Appendix: Statement on Sovereignty." In Franklyn Griffiths, ed., *Politics of the Northwest Passage.* Montreal: McGill-Queens, 1987, 269.
Clausewitz, Carl von. *On War.* Edited and translated by Michael Howard and Peter Paret. Princeton: Princeton University Press, 1976.
Clearwater, John. *"Just Dummies": Cruise Missile Testing in Canada.* Calgary: University of Calgary Press, 2006.
Cloe, John Haile, and Michael Monaghan. *Top Cover for America: The Air Force in Alaska 1920-1983.* Missoula, Montana: Anchorage Chapter—Air Force Association with Pictorial Histories Publishing, Co., 1984.
CN Rail. "CN Halts Rail Operations, Embargoes All Traffic in Toronto-Montreal Corridor, Following Illegal Blockade of Rail Line." CN Rail Press Release, June 29, 2007. Online at: http://www.marketwire.com/mw/release.do?id=747305.

Coates, Ken, P. Whitney Lackenbauer, Greg Poelzer, Bill Morrison, *Arctic Front: Defending Canada in the Far North.* Markham, Ontario: Thomas Allen Publishers, 2008.

———. *Canada's Colonies: A History of the Yukon and Northwest Territories.* Toronto: James Lorimer and Co., 1985.

———. *North to Alaska: Fifty Years on the World's Most Remarkable Highway.* Toronto: McClelland and Stewart, 1992.

Cohen, Ariel. Telephone interview conducted by the author, August 14, 2007.

Cohen, Ariel, Lajos F. Szaszdi, and Jim Dolbow. "The New Cold War: Reviving the U.S. Presence in the Arctic." Heritage Foundation Backgrounder #2202, October 30, 2008.

Cohen, Stan. *The Forgotten War,* I and II. Missoula, Montana: Pictorial Histories Publishing Company, 1988.

Cole, Charles. *The Balkanization of Alaska.* A speech delivered in Barrow, Alaska, February 1, 1992.

———. *The Native Sovereignty Challenge.* A speech delivered in Juneau, February 20, 1992.

Commission for Constitutional Development, "How Can We Live Together?" *The Commission for Constitutional Development.* Yellowknife: NWT Legislative Assembly, 1991.

———. *Working Toward a Common Future.* The Report of the Commission for Constitutional Development of the Western NWT, also known as the Western Constitutional Forum. Yellowknife, NWT, April 1992.

Commission on Rural Governance and Empowerment. *Commission on Rural Governance and Empowerment Final Report.* Juneau, June 1999.

Common Ground. "Winners Named for Cartledge and Calder Awards." *Common Ground* 8, No. 2 (January/February 1997).

Communications and Electronics Branch of Canada's Department of National Defence Website. A partial history of Arctic military operations, of which a significant portion were related to communications and surveillance, is presented. See Ch. 6, "The Cold War Period and United Nations Service," and Ch. 7, "Toward a New World (Dis)Order." Online at: http://www.commelec.forces.gc.ca/.

Condon, Richard. "Canadian Inuit Land Claims and Economic Development." *Alaska Native News* 1, No. 11: 10–12, 37; and *Alaska Native News* 1, No. 12: 16–18, 40.

Conference of First Peoples and the Constitution. *Report of the Conference of First Peoples and the Constitution.* Ottawa, March 31, 1992.

Connor, Steve. "Exclusive: Scientists Warn that There May Be No Ice at North Pole this Summer; Polar Scientists Reveal Dramatic New Evidence of Climate Change." *The Independent,* June 27, 2008.

Consensus Report on the Constitution: The Charlottetown Accord, Final Text. Intergovernmental Affairs Division of the Privy Council of Canada, Ottawa, August 28, 1992.

Constitutional Development Steering Committee. *The Western Arctic Regional Government: Inuvialuit and Gwich'in Proposal for Reshaping Government in the Western Arctic.* Member Group Research Reports. Constitutional Development Steering Committee, Government of the Northwest Territories, Yellowknife, NWT, 1994.

Contenta, Sandro. "Indian Summer." *The Toronto Star,* June 2, 2007. Online at: http://www.thestar.com/article/220686.

Cook, Bradley. "Russian Army Trains for Arctic Combat to Defend Resource Claim." *Bloomberg*, June 24, 2008.

Coulombe, Pierre. "The End of Canadian Dualism?" *Canadian Parliamentary Review* 15, No. 4 (1992). Online at: http://www.parl.gc.ca/Infoparl/english/issue. htm?param=143&art=948.

Cowell, Alan. "Greenland Vote Favors Independence." *New York Times*, November 26, 2008.

Cowper, Steve. *Administrative Order No. 123.* Office of the Governor, Juneau, September 10, 1990, http://www.gov.state.ak.us/admin-orders/123.html.

CTV News Staff. "Young Natives Becoming Desperate: Fontaine." *CTV News*, May 16, 2007.

Cumming, Peter S., and Neil H. Mickenberg. *Native Rights in Canada.* Toronto: The Indian Eskimo Association of Canada in association with General Publishing Co. Ltd., 1972.

Dacks, Gurston. *Devolution and Constitutional Development in the Canadian North.* Ottawa: Carleton University Press, 1990.

Dahl, Jens, Jack Hicks, and Peter Jull, eds. *Nunavut: Inuit Regain Control of Their Lands and Their Lives.* Copenhagen: International Work Group for Indigenous Affairs, 2000.

Danish Prime Minister's Office. "The Greenland Home Rule Arrangement." Danish Prime Minister's Office website, http://www.stm.dk/.

Darnton, John. "Spanish Stirred by 'War' over a Fish They Don't Eat." *New York Times*, April 15, 1995.

Dehcho First Nations. "Army General Tells Dehcho Leader No Pressure Intended." Dehcho First Nations Press Release. Fort Simpson, NWT, April 16, 2007.

———. "Dehcho Refuse To Join Mackenzie Valley Review Boards." Dehcho First Nations Press Release. Fort Simpson, NWT, March 19, 2007.

———. "Troops At Fort Simpson Will Not Be Welcomed." Dehcho First Nations Press Release. Fort Simpson, NWT, April 13, 2007.

Deutsch, Karl W. *Nationalism and Social Communication: An Inquiry into the Foundations of Nationality.* 2nd ed. Cambridge, MA: MIT Press, 1966.

Diadem Resources Ltd. "Franklin Diamond Project." Online at: http://diademresources.com/projects/franklin.html.

Dixon, Karol. "Indian Country in Alaska: A Rhetorical Analysis." *Cultural Survival Quarterly* 27, No. 3 (September 15, 2003), http://www.cs.org/publications/csq/csq-article.cfm?id=1686.

Dosman, Edgar J. *The National Interest: Politics of Northern Development, 1968-75.* Toronto: McClelland and Stewart, 1975.

Dougherty, James E., and Robert L. Pfaltzgraff, Jr. *Contending Theories of International Relations.* 3rd ed. New York: Harper and Row, 1990.

Doward, Jamie, Robin McKie, and Tom Parfitt. "Russia Leads Race for North Pole Oil." *The Observer*, July 29, 2007.

DuBay, William. "Alaska Natives and Municipal Governments." *Alaska Native News.* 3, No. 5 (February 1985).

Dwyer, John B. "Remembering the Alaska Scouts." *American Thinker*, November 12, 2005.

Eccleston, Paul. "Marine Life is Destroyed by Acid Environment." *BBC*, June 8, 2008.

Echohawk, John E. "From the Director's Desk." *Justice Newsletter*, Native American Rights Foundation, Spring 1997.

————. "From the Director's Desk." *Justice Newsletter*, Native American Rights Foundation, Spring 1999.

Eckel, Mike. "Russia Defends North Pole Flag-Planting." *Associated Press*, August 8, 2007.

Economist. "Not-So-Secret War: America Foils a Coup Plot against One of its Former Enemies." *The Economist*, June 7, 2007.

Edwardsen, Charles Etok, Jr. "Attributes of Original Sovereignty: A Memorandum from the Kasigluk Elders Conference." Kasigluk, Alaska, September 19, 1991.

————. "Science and the Indigenous Arctic." Center for World Indigenous Studies, June 15, 1993.

Enbridge Inc. "First Mackenzie Delta Natural Gas Flows in Inuvik, NWT." Enbridge Inc. Press Release. Calgary, Alberta, September 10, 1999.

Encyclopedia.com. "European Parliament Supports Specific Aid for Arctic Agriculture." European Report. *Encyclopedia.com*, March 13, 1999.

Epstein, Howard E. Telephone interview conducted by the author, June 9, 2008, and June 12, 2008.

Fairbanks News-Miner. "Weird Wildlife Reportedly Wandering into Interior." *Fairbanks News-Miner*, August 8, 2005.

Farnsworth, Clyde H. "Canada and Spain Face Off Over Fishing Zone." *New York Times*, March 12, 1995.

Federal Field Committee for Development Planning in Alaska Archives. Consortium Library of the University of Alaska, Anchorage and Alaska Pacific University, http://consortiumlibrary.org/archives/CollectionsList/CollectionDescriptions/USCto USN/USFFLDCT.wpd.html.

Fenge, Terry. "Environment Security in the Arctic." *Nunatsiaq News*, November 25, 1994,10.

————. "Who's Minding the Arctic?" *The Globe and Mail*, November 3, 1994, A19.

Fettweis, Christopher J. "Sir Halford Mackinder, Geopolitics, and Policymaking in the 21st Century." *Parameters* (Summer 2000): 58–71.

Financial Post. "War Unlocks Our Last Frontier," April 3, 1941.

Florendo, Leonora. "Time For New Corporate Leaders." Presentation to the Alaska Native Review Commission, in *Alaska Native News Magazine* 3, No. 5 (February 1985).

Foot, Richard, and Randy Boswell. "Russians Plant a Flag Right Under Our Frosty Feet." *National Post*, August 2, 2007.

Foxwell, David, and Mark Hewish. "Dipping into Deeper Waters: New Airborne Sonars." *International Defence Review*, January 1992.

Fraser, Whit. "The Polar Sea Controversy." *CBC News*, July 29, 1985.

Freeman, Milton M. R., Eleanor E. Wein, and Darren E. Keith. *Recovering Rights: Bowhead Whales and Inuvialuit Subsistence in the Western Canadian Arctic*. Edmonton, Alberta: Canadian Circumpolar Institute, University of Alberta, 1992.

Frolov, Vladimir. "The Coming Conflict in the Arctic: Russia and the U.S. Square off over Arctic Energy Reserves." *Russia Profile*, July 17, 2007.

————. E-mail interview conducted by the author, July 26, 2007.

Fukuyama, Francis. "The End of History?" *The National Interest* (Summer 1989).

————. *The End of History and the Last Man*. New York: Free Press, 1992.

Garfield, Brian. *The Thousand Mile War: World War II in Alaska and the Aleutians*. Fairbanks: University of Alaska Press, 1995.

Gedney, Larry. "Billy Mitchell: Alaska Pioneer." *Alaska Science Forum*, January 13, 1986.

Georgia. "Arctic Diary: Father Didier Translates 'Gavamint.'" *Arctic Circle Magazine* 2, No. 4 (January/February 1992): 44.

Gessell, Paul. "Spanish Envoy Tackles Tobin, Canada on Internet." *Ottawa Citizen*, March 27, 1996.

Gilligan, Ian. "Neanderthal Extinction and Modern Human Behaviour: The Role of Climate Change and Clothing," *World Archaeology* 39, No. 4. (2007): 499–514.

Gladwell, Malcolm. *The Tipping Point: How Little Things Can Make a Big Difference.* Boston: Little Brown, 2000.

Glantz, Michael H. "Oh! What a Lovely Climate Change: Global Warming's Winners and Losers." *Fragilecologies.com*, August 21, 2007. Available online at: http://www.fragilecologies.com/aug21_07.html.

Glenny, Misha. *The Fall of Yugoslavia.* London and New York: Penguin Books, 1992.

GlobalSecurity.org. "Alaska Army National Guard." *GlobalSecurity.*org, http://www.globalsecurity.org/military/agency/army/arng-ak.htm.

Globe and Mail Editorial Board. "For Aboriginal Self-Government in a Constitutional Context." *The Globe and Mail*, January 1993.

Gore, Al. *The Assault on Reason: How the Politics of Fear, Secrecy, and Blind Faith Subvert Wise Decision Making, Degrade Our Democracy, and Put Our Country and Our World in Peril.* New York: Penguin Press, 2007.

———. *An Inconvenient Truth: The Planetary Emergency of Global Warming and What We Can Do About It.* New York: Rodale Books, 2006.

———. "Nobel Lecture—Nobel Peace Prize 2007." Nobel Foundation Website, December 10, 2007, http://nobelprize.org/nobel_prizes/peace/laureates/2007/gore-lecture_en.html.

Government of Canada. Ottawa, Ontario. *Constitution Act of 1982.* Section 25. Available online at: http://laws.justice.gc.ca/en/const/annex_e.html.

———. Ottawa, Ontario. Department of Indian Affairs and Northern Development. *Agreement Between The Inuit of the Nunavut Settlement Area and Her Majesty The Queen in Right of Canada,* 1993.

———. Ottawa, Ontario. Department of Indian Affairs and Northern Development. *Agreement-in-Principle Between the Inuit of the Nunavut Settlement Area and Her Majesty in Right of Canada,* 1990.

———. Ottawa, Ontario. Department of Indian Affairs and Northern Development. *Dene/Métis Agreement-in-Principle,* 1988.

———. Ottawa, Ontario. Department of Indian Affairs and Northern Development. *Inuvialuit Land Rights Settlement Agreement-in-Principle,* October 31, 1978.

———. Ottawa, Ontario. Department of Indian Affairs and Northern Development. "Message from the Ministers." *The Government of Canada's Approach to Implementation of the Inherent Right and the Negotiation of Aboriginal Self-Government,* 1995. Available online at: http://www.ainc-inac.gc.ca/pr/pub/sg/plcy_e.html.

———. Ottawa, Ontario. Department of Indian Affairs and Northern Development. "Part I: Policy Framework." *The Government of Canada's Approach to Implementation of the Inherent Right and the Negotiation of Aboriginal Self-Government,* 1995. Online at: http://www.ainc-inac.gc.ca/pr/pub/sg/plcy_e.html#PartI.

———. Ottawa, Ontario. Department of Indian Affairs and Northern Development. "Part II: Various Approaches to Self-Government." *The Government of Canada's Approach to Implementation of the Inherent Right and the Negotiation of Aboriginal Self-Government,* 1995, http://www.ainc-inac.gc.ca/pr/pub/sg/plcy_e.html#PartII.

————. Ottawa, Ontario. Department of Indian Affairs and Northern Development. "Proposed Pipeline Route." *NWT Plain Talk on Land and Self-Government*, Fall 2004.

————. Ottawa, Ontario. Department of Indian Affairs and Northern Development. *The Western Arctic Claim: The Inuvialuit Final Agreement*, March 27, 1984.

————. Ottawa, Ontario. Department of Indian and Northern Affairs. *Backgrounder: Inuvialuit/Gwich'in Self-Government Agreement-In-Principle*. 2003.

————. Ottawa, Ontario. Department of Indian and Northern Affairs. *Backgrounder on the Gwich'in (Dene/Métis) Comprehensive Land Claim Agreement*. Online at: http://www.ainc-inac.gc.ca/pr/info/info22_e.html.

————. Ottawa, Ontario. Department of Indian and Northern Affairs. *Comprehensive Land Claim Agreement Between Her Majesty the Queen in Right of Canada and the Gwich'in as Represented by the Gwich'in Tribal Council*.

————. Ottawa, Ontario. Department of Indian and Northern Affairs. *Federal Policy Guide: Aboriginal Self-Government—The Government of Canada's Approach to Implementation of the Inherent Right and the Negotiation of Aboriginal Self-Government*. Online: http://www.ainc-inac.gc.ca/pr/pub/sg/plcy_e.html.

————. Ottawa, Ontario. Department of Indian and Northern Affairs. *Frequently Asked Questions: Inuvialuit/Gwich'in Self-Government Agreement-In-Principle*, 2003. Online at: http://www.ainc-inac.gc.ca/nr/prs/j-a2003/02285bbk_e.html.

————. Ottawa, Ontario. Department of Indian and Northern Affairs. *Government of Canada's Approach to Implementation of the Inherent Right and the Negotiation of Aboriginal Self-Government*, 1995. Available online at: http://www.ainc-inac.gc.ca/pr/pub/sg/plcy_e.html.

————. Ottawa, Ontario. Department of Indian and Northern Affairs. *A Guide to the Inuvialuit Settlement Region for Mineral Prospectors and Developers*. Prepared by Alvarez, Sloan and Associates Ltd., March, 2000. Online at: http://nwt-tno.inac-ainc.gc.ca/mpf/refs/guidediand.htm.

————. Ottawa, Ontario. Department of Indian and Northern Affairs. *Gwich'in and Inuvialuit Self-Government Agreement-in-Principle Signed*. Press Release, Inuvik, NWT, April 16, 2003. Online at: http://www.ainc-inac.gc.ca/nr/prs/j-a2003/2-02285_e.html.

————. Ottawa, Ontario. Department of Indian and Northern Affairs. "John Amagoalik—Politician." *Aboriginal People Profiles*. Online at: www.ainc-inac.gc.ca/ks/3101_e.html.

————. Ottawa, Ontario. Department of Indian and Northern Affairs. "Message from the Ministers," *The Government of Canada's Approach to Implementation of the Inherent Right and the Negotiation of Aboriginal Self-Government*, 1995.

————. Ottawa, Ontario. Department of Indian and Northern Affairs. "Part I: Policy Framework." *The Government of Canada's Approach to Implementation of the Inherent Right and the Negotiation of Aboriginal Self-Government*, 1995.

————. Ottawa, Ontario. Department of Indian and Northern Affairs. "Part II: Various Approaches to Self-Government." *The Government of Canada's Approach to Implementation of the Inherent Right and the Negotiation of Aboriginal Self-Government*, 1995.

————. Ottawa, Ontario. Department of Indian and Northern Affairs. *Treaty No. 8*, June 21, 1899.

————. Ottawa, Ontario. Department of Indian and Northern Affairs. *Treaty No. 11*, June 27, 1921.

————. Ottawa, Ontario. Department of National Defence. *Backgrounder: The DEW Line Cleanup Project.* Online at: http://www.rmc.ca/academic/gradrech /esg/dlcu_e.html.

————. Ottawa, Ontario. Department of National Defence. *Backgrounder on the Exercise NARWHAL Series.* Available online at: http://www.dnd.ca/site/newsroom/view_news_e.asp?id=2254.

————. Ottawa, Ontario. Department of National Defence. *Backgrounder on the Northern Rangers.*

————. Ottawa, Ontario. Department of National Defence. *Canadian Defence Policy 1992*, April 1992.

————. Ottawa, Ontario. Department of National Defence. *Canadian Defence Policy 2005.*

————. Ottawa, Ontario. Department of National Defence. *CF Arctic Operation Practices Assistance to RCMP and Response to a Major Airline Disaster.* Canada Command Press Release, April 16, 2007. Online at: http://www.dnd.ca/site/newsroom/ view_news_e.asp?id=2255.

————. Ottawa, Ontario. Department of National Defence. *Challenge and Commitment: A Defence Policy for Canada*, June 1987.

————. Ottawa, Ontario. Department of National Defence. *Learning from the Canadian Rangers*, May 29, 2007, http://www.army.forces.gc.ca/LF/English/ 6_1_1.asp?id=1950.

————. Ottawa, Ontario. Department of National Defence. *NAADM Backgrounder.*

————. Ottawa, Ontario. Department of National Defence. *Planning Guide to Northern Operations.*

————. Ottawa, Ontario. Department of National Defence. *White Paper on Defence 1994.*

————. Ottawa, Ontario. Intergovernmental Affairs Division of the Privy Council of Canada. "Unity and Diversity." *Consensus Report on the Constitution: The Charlottetown Accord*, Final Text, August 28, 1992.

————. Ottawa, Ontario. Special Joint Committee of the Senate and of the House of Commons on Canada's International Relations. *Independence and Internationalism*, June 1986. In particular, see: Chapter 10, "A Northern Dimension for Canada's Foreign Policy," 127–135.

————. Ottawa, Ontario. Statistics Canada. *Highlights of the Statistics Canada Presentation to the Royal Commission on Aboriginal Peoples.* Statistics Canada, Government of Canada, Ottawa, Ontario, October 1991.

Government of the Northwest Territories. Yellowknife, NWT. Department of Environment and Natural Resources. "Muskox Harvest Levels." Wildlife Division Website. Online at: http://www.nwtwildlife.com/NWTwildlife/muskox/harvest.htm.

————. Yellowknife, NWT. *Military Activity in the North and the Establishment of a Circumpolar Zone of Peace and Security.* November 1990.

————. Yellowknife, NWT. *NWT Discussion Paper on Military Activity in the North.* November 1, 1991.

Government of Nunavut. "Balanced Approach for Uranium Mining in Nunavut." Press Release, Government of Nunavut. Iqaluit, Nunavut. June 4, 2007. Online at: http://www.gov.nu.ca/Nunavut/English/news/2007/june/june4.pdf.

Grant, Shelagh. "Arctic Wilderness—and Other Mythologies." *Journal of Canadian Studies* (Summer 1998).

————. *Sovereignty and Security? Government Policy in the Canadian North, 1936–1950.* Vancouver: University of British Columbia Press, 1988.

Greenwald, Jeff. "The Unrepresented Nations and Peoples Organization: Diplomacy's Cutting Edge." *Whole Earth Review*, Winter 1992.

Griffiths, Franklyn. "Beyond the Arctic Sublime." Chapter 12. Franklyn Griffiths, ed. *Politics of the Northwest Passage*. Montreal: McGill-Queens, 1987, 241–268.

———, ed. *Politics of the Northwest Passage*. Montreal: McGill-Queens, 1987.

Grima, Adrian. "The Oka Crisis." *Geocities*, September 11, 1995. Online at: http://www.geocities.com/adriangrima/oka.htm.

Groh, Clifford John, II. *Oil, Money, Land and Power: Passage of the Alaska Native Claims Settlement Act of 1971*. Cambridge, MA: Harvard University/Harvard College Honors Thesis, 1976.

Gruben, Ethel-Jean. "Inuvialuit Want a Voice." *News North*, April 17, 2006. Online at: http://mostlywater.org/node/4820.

Gwertzman, Bernard. "Gwertzman Asks the Experts: Medvedev Trying to Carve Out New Role as President to Help Modernize Nation: An interview with Stephen R. Sestanovich, George F. Kennan Senior Fellow for Russian and Eurasian Studies." Council on Foreign Relations Website, July 2, 2008.

Haas, Ernst. *Beyond the Nation State: Functionalism and International Organization*. Stanford: Stanford University Press, 1964.

Haas, Michael. "International Subsystems: Stability and Polarity." *American Political Science Review* 64, No. 1 (March, 1970): 98–123.

Haglund, David G., and Joel J. Sokolsky, eds. *The U.S.-Canada Security Relationship: The Politics, Strategy, and Technology of Defense*. Boulder: Westview Press, 1989.

Hamilton, Alexander. "The Federalist No. 9: The Utility of the Union as a Safeguard Against Domestic Faction and Insurrection." *Independent Journal*, November 21, 1787.

Hanes, Allison. "Native Blockades Snarl Traffic across Ontario." *National Post*, June 30, 2007.

Hardaker, Bernadette. Interview with Senator Davey Steuart, Chief Federal Land Claims Negotiator on "Mackenzie Morning." *CBC North Radio*, June 8, 1982.

Harden, Blaine. "After '89 Oil Spill, Waves of Money Roll In." *Washington Post*, March 28, 2003.

Harlow, John. "Polar Bears Set to join U.S. At-Risk List." *Times Online*, February 17, 2008, http://www.timesonline.co.uk/tol/news/environment/article3382278.ece.

Harper, Stephen, Prime Minister of Canada. "Prime Minister Harper Announced New Arctic Offshore Patrol Ships," July 9, 2007.

———. *Throne Speech: Strong Leadership, A Better Canada*. October 16, 2007.

Harwood, Lois A., and Thomas G. Smith. "Whales of the Inuvialuit Settlement Region in Canada's Western Arctic: An Overview and Outlook." *Arctic* 55, Supp. 1 (2002): 77–93. Online at: http://pubs.aina.ucalgary.ca/arctic/Arctic55-S-77.pdf.

Haworth, William. Comments to Barry Zellen. "We Should Warm to the Idea of Melting Poles." *The Globe and Mail*, April 28, 2008.

Haycox, Stephen W. *Alaska: An American Colony*. Seattle: University of Washington Press.

Haydon, Peter T. "The Strategic Importance of the Arctic: Understanding the Military Issues." *Canadian Defence Quarterly* 17, No. 4 (Spring 1988).

Haygood, Will. "The Lie at the Top of the World." *Boston Globe*, August 9, 1992.

Hayward, Dan. "Gorbachev's Murmansk Initiative: New Prospects for Arms Control in the Arctic?" *Northern Perspectives* 16, No. 4 (July/August 1988), http://www.carc.org/pubs/v16no4/4.htm.

Heartland Institute website, http://www.heartland.org/NewYork08/newyork08.cfm.

Hickel, Walter J. *Administrative Order No. 125.* Office of the Governor, Juneau, Alaska, July 1, 1991. Online at: http://gov.state.ak.us/admin-orders/125.html.

———. *Crisis in the Commons: The Alaska Solution.* Oakland, CA: ICS Press, 2002.

———. "The Day of the Arctic Has Come." *Reader's Digest,* June 1973.

Hills, Mark. "Wild Arctic Muskox Harvest on Banks Island Brings Employment to the Inuit of the North." *Restaurant News,* December 1997. Online at: http://www.hillsfoods.com/article1.html.

Hoff, Don, Jr. "Perpetuate Tribes Not Corporations." *Stories in the News (Sitnews.us),* Ketchikan, Alaska, April 22, 2007.

Hoffmann, Stanley. *Duties Beyond Borders: On the Limits and Possibilities of Ethical International Politics.* Syracuse, NY: Syracuse University Press, 1981.

Homer-Dixon, Thomas F. *Environment, Scarcity, and Violence.* Princeton: Princeton University Press, 1999.

Honderich, John. *Arctic Imperative: Is Canada Losing the North?* Toronto: University of Toronto Press, 1987.

Howard, Brian Clark. "50% Chance North Pole Will Be Ice-Free This Summer." *The Daily Green,* June 27, 2008.

Howard, Michael. "Turkey Warns of Plans to Invade Northern Iraq." *The Guardian,* June 30, 2007. Online at: http://www.guardian.co.uk/Iraq/Story/0,,2115285,00.html.

Huebert, Rob. "Arctic Security: Different Threats and Different Responses: A Discussion Paper." Department of Political Science, Centre for Military and Strategic Studies, University of Calgary, presented at the 3rd NRF Open Meeting in Yellowknife and Rae Edzo, Canada, September 15–18, 2004.

———. "Renaissance in Canadian Arctic Security." *Canadian Military Journal,* Winter 2005–2006.

———. Telephone interview conducted by the author, August 14, 2007.

Huebert, Rob, and Brooks B. Yeager. *A New Sea.* Oslo: World Wildlife Fund, January 2008, http://assets.panda.org/downloads/a_new_sea_jan08_final_11jan08.pdf.

Hughes, Wesley G. "Geologist Sees Methane 'Doomsday.'" *San Bernardino Sun,* June 7, 2008.

Hurlburt, W. H., ed. *The Arctic: Choices for Peace and Security—A Public Inquiry.* West Vancouver: Gordon Soules Book Publishers, 1989.

Hurley, James Ross. "The Canadian Constitutional Debate: From the Death of the Meech Lake Accord of 1987 to the 1992 Referendum." Revised text of a paper presented at the 1992 Conference of the Association of Canadian Studies in Australia and New Zealand, Wellington, New Zealand. December 16, 1992. Available in the *The Constitutional File and the Unity File* on the website of the Intergovernmental Affairs Division of the Government of Canada's Privy Council Office. Online at: http://www.pco-bcp.gc.ca/aia/default.asp?Language=E&Page=consfile.

Hurtig, Mel, ed. *The True North Strong and Free?* West Vancouver: Gordon Soules Book Publishers, 1987.

Ilulissat Declaration. Arctic Ocean Conference, Ilulissat, Greenland. May 28, 2008.

Imperial Oil. "Mackenzie Gas Project Proponents Ready to Proceed to Public Hearings." Imperial Oil Press Release, Calgary, Alberta, November 23, 2005.

Indianz.com. "Senator Says Natives Threaten State of Alaska." *Indianz.com,* October 7, 2003.

Indigenous Studies Program. "Agreements, Treaties and Negotiated Settlements Project (ATNS) of the Indigenous Studies Program." The University of Melbourne. Online at: http://www.atns.net.au/agreement.asp?EntityID =2097.

————. "White Paper on Indian Policy." *Agreements, Treaties and Negotiated Settlements (ATNS) Project*. Indigenous Studies Program, University of Melbourne, Australia. Online at: http://www.atns.net.au/agreement.asp ?EntityID=1936.

Interim Report on the Constitutional Commission of the Western NWT. Government of the Northwest Territories. Yellowknife, NWT, February 1992.

Inuit Circumpolar Conference. *ICC Self Government Workshop*. Inuvik, NWT, July 1992.

————. *Principles and Elements for a Comprehensive Arctic Policy*. Ottawa, Ontario, 1992.

Inuit Circumpolar Council Press Release. "Arctic Sovereignty Begins with Inuit: Circumpolar Inuit Commit to Development of 'Inuit Declaration on Sovereignty in the Arctic.'" Ottawa, Ontario, November 10, 2008.

————. "Canadian Inuit Call for Direct Say on Arctic Sovereignty." June 2, 2008.

————. "Circumpolar Inuit Declaration on Sovereignty in the Arctic." Tromsø, Norway, April 28, 2009.

————. "Circumpolar Inuit Launch Declaration on Arctic Sovereignty." Tromsø, Norway, April 28, 2009.

————. "ICC Chair, Sheila Watt-Cloutier, to Receive Three Honours." May 9, 2006.

————. "Inuit Leader Reminds Foreign Ministers: Much of the Arctic Belongs to all Inuit; Pan-Inuit Sovereignty Summit to Convene in November." Ilulissat, Greenland, November 29, 2008.

Inuit Cultural Institute. *Uqaqta*. Eskimo Point, Nunavut: Inuit Cultural Institute, July 1986.

Inuit Tapiriit Kanatami. "ITK President Acknowledges Importance of Greenland Vote on Enhanced Self-Rule." Inuit Tapiriit Kanatami, November 27, 2008.

————. "ITK President Mary Simon Underlines Urgency of Action to Intervene in European Plans to Impose Bans on the Import of Canadian Seal Pelts." Inuit Tapiriit Kanatami, Ottawa, Ontario, March 30, 2007. Online at: http://www.itk.ca/media/2007/press-archive-20070330.php.

————. "Mary Simon's First Speech as ITK President at the Inuit Circumpolar General Assembly in Barrow, Alaska." Inuit Tapiriit Kanatami Speech, Barrow, Alaska, July 10, 2006.

————. "New ITK President Mary Simon Tells International Conference Canadian Inuit Need to Take Tougher Approach in Dealing with Governments." Inuit Tapiriit Kanatami Press Release, Barrow, Alaska, July 10, 2006.

————. "Nunavut and the West." *Nunavut Newsletter* 11, No. 2. ITC, 1992, 26.

————. *Political Development in Nunavut*. 1979.

————. "Strong Inuit Presence at UN Climate Change Conference UNFCCC COP-13 in Bali." Inuit Tapiriit Kanatami Press Release, November 30, 2007.

————. "Throne Speech Opens Doors—Creates Opportunities." Inuit Tapiriit Kanatami Press Release, October 16, 2007.

Inuvialuit Final Agreement Implementation Coordinating Committee. *Annual Report 1999-2000: Inuvialuit Final Agreement Implementation Coordinating Committee*. Online at: http://www.ainc-inac.gc.ca/pr/agr/inu/inuv_e.pdf.

————. "Appendix 1: Map of the Inuvialuit Settlement Region." *Annual Report 1999-2000: Inuvialuit Final Agreement Implementation Coordinating Committee*. Department of Indian Affairs and Northern Development, Ottawa, 2000.

Inuvialuit Regional Corporation/Tungavik Federation of Nunavut Joint Press Release, June 1992.

Inuvialuit Workshop on Constitutional Development and Community Government. Inuvi-aluit Regional Corporation, Inuvik, NWT, November 1991.

Ipellie, Alootook. "Thirsty for Life: A Nomad Learns to Write and Draw." In John Moss, ed., *Echoing Silence: Essays on Arctic Narrative.* Ottawa: University of Ottawa Press, 1997.

Itschenko, Victor. "The Mission Syndrome." *NEDAA: Your Eye on the Yukon.* White-horse, Yukon: Northern Native Broadcasting, 1988.

Izenberg, Dafna. "The Conscience of Nunavut." *Ryerson Review of Journalism*, Summer 2005. Online at: http://www.rrj.ca/issue/2005/summer/566/.

Jaeger, Lisa. *Tribal Court Development: Alaska Tribes.* Fairbanks, Alaska: Tanana Chiefs Conference, Inc., 2002. Online at: http://thorpe.ou.edu/AKtribalct /index.html.

Jockel, Joseph T. *Security to the North: Canada-U.S. Defense Relations in the 1990s.* East Lansing: Michigan State University Press, 1991.

Johal, Am. "Rabble Exclusive: Interview with Michael Byers." *Rabble.ca*, July 16, 2008. Online at: http://www.rabble.ca/rabble_interview.shtml?x=73486.

Johnson, Carl H. "A Comity of Errors: Why John v. Baker is Only a Tentative First Step in the Right Direction." *Alaska Law Journal* 17, No. 1 (June 2001): 1–58.

Johnson, Evans. "Soviet Troops Hold Five Oil-Rich Islands in the Arctic Despite Com-peting U.S. Claim." *Washington Times*, November 24, 1987.

Joint Review Panel for the Mackenzie Gas Project Website. About Section. Online at: http://www.jointreviewpanel.ca/about.html.

——.FAQ Section. Online at: http://www.jointreviewpanel.ca/faq.html

Joint Secretariat. *Co-management in the Western Arctic and Yukon North Slope: The Inuvialuit Final Agreement.* An information brochure published by the Joint Secre-tariat, Inuvik, NWT.

Jorgensen, Joseph G. *Oil Age Eskimos.* Berkeley and Los Angeles: University of Califor-nia Press, 1990.

Kaiser, Karl. "The Interaction of Regional Subsystems: Some Preliminary Notes on Re-current Patterns and the Role of Superpowers." *World Politics* 21, No. 1 (October, 1968): 84–107.

Keenan, Steve. Email interview conducted by the author, August 11, 2007.

Keeping, Janet M. *The Inuvialuit Final Agreement.* Calgary, Alberta: The Canadian Insti-tute of Resource Law, 1989.

Keohane, Robert O., ed. *Neorealism and Its Critics.* New York: Columbia University Press, 1986.

Kemeny, Marika. "Thomas Berger Discusses Northern Challenges at Glendon's Annual John Holmes Lecture." *Glendon News*, April 3, 2009, http://monglendon.yorku.ca/monglendon.nsf/.

Kilner, James. "Russian Expedition Sets Off to Conquer the Arctic." *ABC News*, July 24, 2007.

Kines, Clare. "Of Ships and Sovereignty." *The House and Other Arctic Musings.* August 10, 2007.

Kirby, Alex. "Russia's Growing Nuclear Dustbin." *BBC*, March 3, 1999.

Kirton John, and Don Munton. "The Manhattan Voyages and Their Aftermath." Chapter 4. Franklyn Griffiths, ed., *Politics of the Northwest Passage.* Montreal: McGill-Queens, 1987, 67–97.

Kitka, Julie. Testimony to the Alaska State Senate Judiciary Committee, April 1992.

Klare, Michael. E-mail interview conducted by the author, May 1, 2007.

Knowles, Tony. "Administrative Order No. 174." Office of the Governor, State of Alaska, Juneau, Alaska, February 20, 1998. Online at: http://www.gov.state.ak.us/admin-orders/174.html.

———. "Alaska Solutions for Safe, Healthy, Rural Communities." Online at: http://www.tonyknowles.com/issues/rural/index.php.

Koring, Paul. "Russians Hope to Show Potential of 'Arctic bridge.'" *Globe and Mail*, July 22, 2008. *Kurdish Aspect*. Online at: http://www.kurdishaspect.com/index.html.

Labonté, Capt. Joanna. "The North Honours Our Veterans." *The Maple Leaf*, October 26, 2005. Available online at: http://www.forces.gc.ca/site/community /mapleleaf/vol_8/vol8_37/837_16.pdf.

Labrador Inuit Land Claims Agreement (Land Claims Agreement Between the Inuit of Labrador and Her Majesty the Queen in Right of Newfoundland and Labrador and Her Majesty the Queen in Right of Canada), 2005, http://www.ainc-inac.gc.ca/al/ldc/ccl/fagr/labi/labi-eng.pdf.

Lackenbauer, P. Whitney. *Battlegrounds: The Canadian Military and Aboriginal Lands.* Vancouver: UBC Press, 2007.

———. "The Canadian Rangers: A 'Postmodern' Militia that Works." *Canadian Military Journal* 6, No. 4 (Winter 2005–06): 49–60.

Lackenbauer, P. Whitney, Matthew J. Farish, and Jennifer Arthur-Lackenbauer. *The Distant Early Warning (DEW) Line: A Bibliography and Documentary Resource List Prepared for the Arctic Institute of North America*. Arctic Institute of North America, October 2005, 6–7.

Lackenbauer, P. Whitney, R. Scott Sheffield, and Craig Leslie Mantle, *Aboriginal Peoples and Military Participation: Canadian and International Perspectives*. Winnipeg: Canadian Defence Academy Press, 2007.

Lamb, David. "Superpower Strategies Focus on Alaska: Military Activity Accelerates, Especially Along Aleutians." *Los Angeles Times*, September 25, 1987.

Lamb, John, ed. *Proceedings of a Conference on "A Northern Foreign Policy for Canada."* Ottawa: Canadian Polar Commission and the Canadian Centre for Global Security, October 1994.

Larly, S. J. "Review of *A Frozen Hell: The Russo-Finnish Winter War Of 1939-40* by William R. Trotter." Chapel Hill, NC: Algonquin Books, 2000. Online at: http://www.ralphmag.org/winter-warZJ.html.

Lee, James. "Cruise Missile Testing in Canada: The Post–Cold War Debate." Political and Social Affairs Division, Parliamentary Research Branch, Depository Services Program. Government of Canada, January 21, 1994.

Lennie, John, and Beverly Lennie. Letter to Prime Minister Trudeau. May 7, 1984.

Levy, John. "I.R.A. Power: Its Sources and Its Consequences." *Alaska Native News* 1, No. 11 (October 1983): 21–23.

Libin, Kevin. "Leftist Couple's Stance on Aboriginals Leaves Them in the Cold." *National Post*, October 31, 2008, http://mqup.mcgill.ca/extra.php?id=860.

Liddell Hart, B. H. *Strategy: The Indirect Approach.* New York: Frederick Praeger, Inc., 1954.

Lincoln, Abraham. "The Gettysburg Address." Gettysburg, PA, November 19, 1863.

Linden, Ronald H. "The Security Bind in East Europe." *International Studies Quarterly* (June 1982): 155–89.

Linden, Sidney B. "Commissioner's Statement: Public Release of Report." *Report of the Ipperwash Inquiry*. Government of Ontario, May 31, 2007. Online at: http://www .ipperwashinquiry.ca/report/index.html.

Lynas, Mark. *Six Degrees: Our Future on a Hotter Planet.* Washington: National Geographic, 2008.

MacIsaac, David. "Voices from the Central Blue: The Air Power Theorists." In Peter Paret and Gordon A. Craig, eds., *Makers of Modern Strategy: From Machiavelli to the Nuclear Age.* Princeton: Princeton University Press, 1986.

Mackenzie Gas Project Website. Online at: http://www.mackenziegasproject.com/whoWeAre/APG/APG.htm.

Mackenzie, Richard. "Apache Attack." *Air Force Magazine* 74, No. 10 (October 1991).

Mackinder, Halford John, *Democratic Ideals and Reality: A Study in the Politics of Reconstruction.* London: Constable and Co. Ltd., 1919.

———. "Round World and the Peace." *Foreign Affairs,* 1943.

Madison, James. "The Federalist No. 10: The Utility of the Union as a Safeguard Against Domestic Faction and Insurrection, continued." *Daily Advertiser,* November 22, 1787. Available online at http://www.constitution.org/fed/federa09.htm, and http://www.constitution.org/fed/federa10.htm.

Mahr, Krista. "Greenland to World: 'Keep Out!'" *Time,* September 21, 2007.

Management Concepts Group. "Alaska Natives and Municipal Governments." *Tribal Government in Alaska.*

Mandel-Campbell, Andrea. "Spies, Submarines, and Foreign Ships May Signal That Our Claim to the North is Melting." *The Walrus,* January 2005, http://www.walrusmagazine.com/print/2005.01-national-affairs-Arctic-global-warming/.

The Maple Leaf. "New Deep Water Facility to Support Arctic Offshore Patrol Ships." *The Maple Leaf* 10, No. 25 (September 5, 2007): 10.

Marrus, Michael R. "Official Apologies and the Quest for Historical Justice." Controversies in Global Politics and Societies, Munk Centre for International Studies, University of Toronto, 2006.

Marston, Marvin "Muktuk." *Men of the Tundra: Eskimos at War.* New York: October House, Inc., 1969.

Mayell, Hillary. "Climate Change Killed Neandertals, Study Says." National Geographic News, February 9, 2004.

Mayer, Paul. *Mayer Report on Nunavut Devolution.* Department of Indian and Northern Affairs, Government of Canada, Ottawa, Ontario, June 2007. Online at: http://www.ainc-inac.gc.ca/nr/prs/m-a2007/2-2891-m_rprt-eng.pdf.

McBeath, Gerald, Thomas Morehouse, and Linda Leask. *Alaska's Urban and Rural Government.* Fairbanks, AK: Institute of Social and Economic Research and Department of Political Science, University of Alaska, 1983.

McCaslin, John. "U.S. to Resume Talks with Soviets over Five Islands." *Washington Times,* March 2, 1988.

McClanahan, Alexandra J. "Alaska Native Claims Settlement Act (ANCSA)." *LitSite Alaska.* Online at: http://litsite.alaska.edu/aktraditions/ancsa.html.

McCormack, Sean. Daily Press Briefing, U.S. Department of State, Washington, D.C., January 13, 2009, http://2001-2009.state.gov/r/pa/prs/dpb/2009/jan/113781.htm.

McCullum, Hugh. "News Analysis Mackenzie Gas Project May 31, 2007 (June 8 UPDATE)." Dehcho First Nations News Analysis. Online at: http://www.dehchofirstnations.com/documents/press/07_06_08_analysis_mccullum_mgp_update.pdf.

McGrath, Melanie. *The Long Exile: A Tale of Inuit Betrayal and Survival in the High Arctic.* New York: Knopf, 2007.

McLaughlin, Kim. "Arctic Claimants Say They Will Obey U.N. Rules." *Reuters*, May 29, 2008.

McRae, D. M. "The Negotiation of Article 234." Chapter 5 in Franklyn Griffiths, ed. *Politics of the Northwest Passage.* Montreal: McGill-Queens, 1987, 98–114.

Mehta, Aalok. "North Pole May Be Ice Free for First Time This Summer." *National Geographic News*, June 20, 2008.

Member Group Research Reports. *Constitutional Development Steering Committee.* Government of the Northwest Territories, Yellowknife, NWT, August 1994.

Merritt, John. "Has Glasnost Come Knocking?" *Northern Perspectives*, Special Edition, October 1987.

Merritt, John, and Terry Fenge, eds. *Nunavut: Political Choices and Manifest Destiny.* Ottawa: Canadian Arctic Resources Committee, 1989.

Mertz, Douglas K. "A Primer on Alaska Native Sovereignty." 1991. Online at: http://www.alaska.net/~dkmertz/natlaw.htm.

Miasnikov, Eugene. "Submarine Collision Off Murmansk: A Look from Afar." *DACS Breakthroughs Magazine.* Defense and Arms Control Studies Program at M.I.T., Winter 1992/1993 II, No. 2, 19–24. Reprinted in *The Submarine Review* (April 1993): 6–14. Online at: http://www.armscontrol.ru/subs/collisions/db080693.htm.

Minogue, Sara. "Uranium Rush Floods Western Nunavut; Huge Jump in Price, Demand Has Juniors Racing to Stake Claims." *Nunatsiaq News*, April 28, 2006. Online at: http://www.nunatsiaq.com/archives/60428/news/nunavut/60428_05.html.

Mitchell, Don. "Alaska News Nightly." *Alaska Public Radio*, October 15, 2003, www.narf.org/cases/alaska/downloads/transcript%20of%20aprn%2010.15.pdf.

Montgomery, John D., ed. *International Dimensions of Land Reform.* Boulder: Westview, 1984.

Montgomery, Shannon. "All Companies Needed to Make Mackenzie Pipeline Viable, Says Partner." *Canadian Press*, June 8, 2007.

Moore, John. "A Primitivist Primer." *Eco-Action.org.* Online at: http://www.eco-action.org/dt/primer.html.

Morrison, Alex, ed. *Divided We Fall: The National Security Implications of Canadian Constitutional Issues.* Toronto: Canadian Institute of Strategic Studies, 1991.

Mottola, Kari, ed. *The Arctic Challenge: Nordic and Canadian Approaches to Security and Cooperation in an Emerging International Region.* Boulder: Westview Press, 1988.

Munro, John. *In All Fairness—a Native Claims Policy.* Department of Indian and Northern Affairs, December 16, 1981. Available online at: http://www.brandonu.ca/Library/cjns/2.1/policy.pdf.

Murkowski, Lisa. Speech to the Arctic Transportation Conference. U.S. Maritime Administration, Washington, D.C., June 5, 2008.

Murphy, Michael. "Review of *Citizens Plus.*" *Canadian Review of Sociology* 25, No. 4 (Fall 2000): 517.

Naske, Claus-M., and Herman E. Slotnick. *Alaska, a History of the 49th State*, Second Edition. Norman: University of Oklahoma Press, 1987.

National Park Service. Aleutian World War II National Historic Area Website. Online at: http://www.nps.gov/archive/aleu/AleutInternmentAndRestitution.htm.

Native American Rights Fund. "Alaska Native Subsistence." *Justice Newsletter*, Spring 1999.

———. "Indian Country in Alaska—The Venetie Decision." *Justice Newsletter*, Spring 1997.

————. "The Preservation of Tribal Existence." *Justice Newsletter*, Winter 1998.

National Oceanic and Atmospheric Administration. "UNH-NOAA Ocean Mapping Expedition Yields New Insights into Arctic Depths." NOAA Press Release, February 12, 2008.

National Security Presidential Directive and Homeland Security Presidential Directive: Arctic Region Policy, January 9, 2009, http://fas.org/irp/offdocs/nspd/nspd-66.htm.

National Snow and Ice Data Center. "Permafrost Threatened by Rapid Retreat of Arctic Sea Ice, NCAR/NSIDC Study Finds." NSIDC Press Release, June 10, 2008.

Newmark, Russell. *Study Tour to Northern Alaska by Inuvialuit Representatives.* Inuvik, NWT: Inuvialuit Regional Corporation, October 1991.

New York Times Editorial Board. "Sack the General to Save the Strategy." *New York Times*, September 18, 1990.

Noah, Timothy. "Meet Mr. 'Shock and Awe'—Harlan Ullman Says They're Doing It Wrong." *Slate.com*, April 1, 2003.

Norris, Frank. *Alaska Subsistence: A National Park Service Management History.* Anchorage: Alaska Support Office, National Park Service, U.S. Department of the Interior, 2002.

North Slope Borough. *The Arctic Coastal Zone Management Program.* No. 3. Barrow, AK: March/April 1977. Available online at: http://www.ebenhopson.com/czm/1977cz/MarApr1977/index.html.

Norwegian Nobel Committee. "The Nobel Peace Price for 2007." *Nobel Foundation Website*, October 12, 2007.

Nowak, David. "Russian Ships to Patrol Arctic Again." *Time*, July 14, 2008.

Nunavut: A Report on Land Claims from the Tungavik Federation of Nunavut. Ottawa: Tungavik Federation of Nunavut, 10, No. 2 (July 1991).

————. Ottawa: Tungavik Federation of Nunavut, 10, No. 3 (August/September 1991).

Nunavut Land Claims Agreement (Agreement Between the Inuit of The Nunavut Settlement Area and Her Majesty the Queen in Right of Canada), 1993, http://www.ainc-inac.gc.ca/al/ldc/ccl/fagr/nuna/nla/nunav-eng.pdf.

Nunavut Land Claim Agreement in Plain Language. Ottawa: Tungavik Federation of Nunavut, 1992.

NWT Power Corporation. "Inuvik Gas Project Signals New Era for NWT Power Corporation." NWT Power Corporation Press Release. Inuvik, NWT, September 10, 1999.

O'Brien, Karen L., and Robin M. Leichenko. "Winners and Losers in the Context of Global Change." *Annals of the Association of American Geographers* 93, No. 1 (2003).

Office of the Attorney General of the State of Alaska. *Sovereignty Overview for the State Judiciary Committee.* February 1992.

Offley, Edward. *Pen & Sword: A Journalist's Guide to Covering the Military.* Oak Park, IL: Marion Street Press, 2001, 223.

Olson, Rod, Frank Geddes, and Ross Hastings. *Northern Ecology and Resource Management.* Edmonton: University of Alberta Press, 1984.

Olynyk, John, and Keith Bergner. *Update on Land Claims and Devolution in the Yukon and the Northwest Territories.* Lawson Lundell Barristers and Solicitors, September 2002, presented at the 4th Annual Far North Oil and Gas Conference, September 30–October 1, 2002. Online at: http://www.lawtech.ca/resources/updateonlandclaims-oct02.pdf.

O'Neill, Dan. *The Firecracker Boys.* New York: St. Martin's Press, 1994.

O'Neill, Katherine. "Harper Plays Down Threat to Arctic Sovereignty." *The Globe and Mail*, January 14, 2009.

On the Surface. "What is Maritime Strategy?" *On the Surface*, October 16, 1987.

Osherenko, Gail, and Oran Young. *The Age of the Arctic: Hot Conflicts and Cold Realities*. Cambridge: Cambridge University Press, 1989.

Ostreng, Willy. "The Militarization and Security Concept of the Arctic." *The Arctic: Choices for Peace and Security—A Public Inquiry*. West Vancouver: Gordon Soules Book Publishers, 1989, 113–126.

Parekh, Bhikhu, and Thomas Pantham, eds. *Political Discourse: Explorations in Indian and Western Political Thought*. New Delhi: Sage, 1987.

Paret, Peter, and Gordon A. Craig, eds. *Makers of Modern Strategy: from Machiavelli to the Nuclear Age*. Princeton: Princeton University Press, 1986.

Paris, Roland. "Human Security: Paradigm Shift or Hot Air?" In Michael E. Brown, Owen R. Cote, Jr., Sean M. Lynn-Jones, and Steven E. Miller, eds. *New Global Dangers: Changing Dimensions of International Security*. Cambridge, MA: MIT Press, 2004, 249–64.

Parliament of Canada. "Map 1–Nunavut." *Nunavut Fisheries: Quota Allocations and Benefits: A Report of the Standing Senate Committee on Fisheries and Oceans*. Parliament of Canada, Ottawa, Ontario. April 2004. Online at: http://www.parl.gc.ca/37/3/parlbus/commbus/senate/com-e/fish-e/rep-e/rep04apr04-e.htm.

PBS. "Timeline: Alaska Pipeline Chronology." *American Experience. PBS*. Online at: http://www.pbs.org/wgbh/amex/pipeline/timeline/index.html.

Penner, Robert. "Is Canada a Silent Nuclear Power?" *The True North Strong and Free?* West Vancouver: Gordon Soules, 1987, 55–70.

Perin, Marshall. *CBC Western Arctic Radio News*. October 22, 1982.

Petersen, Charles C. "Soviet Military Objectives in the Arctic Theater." *Naval War College Review*, Autumn 1987.

Popkov, Yuri. *Peoples of the North of Russia: History and Problems of Modern Development*. Novosibirsk: Institute of History, Philology and Philosophy of the Russian Academy of Sciences in Novosibirsk, 1991.

Posner, Eric. "The New Race for the Arctic." *Wall Street Journal*, August 3, 2007.

Potter, Jean. *Alaska Under Arms*. New York: The Macmillan Company, 1942.

Prime Minister's Office of Canada. "Prime Minister Harper Announces Major Reforms to Address the Backlog of Aboriginal Treaty Claims." PMO Press Release, June 12, 2007.

———. "Prime Minister Stephen Harper Announces New Arctic Offshore Patrol Ships." PMO Press Release, July 9, 2007, Esquimalt, British Columbia.

Pullen, Thomas C. "That Polar Icebreaker." *Northern Perspectives* 14, No. 4 (September/October 1986).

———. "What Price Canadian Sovereignty?" *Naval Institute Proceedings* 113 (1987): 66–72.

Purver, Ronald G. "Arms Control Proposals for the Arctic: A Survey and Critique." In Kari Mottola, ed., *The Arctic Challenge: Nordic and Canadian Approaches to Security and Cooperation in an Emerging International Region*. Boulder: Westview Press, 1988, 183–219.

———. "Implications of Change in the Soviet Union for Arctic Security." Canadian Institute for International Peace and Security Working Paper, Ottawa, Ontario, 1991.

———. "The Strategic Importance of the Arctic Region." In R. B. Byers and Michael Slack, eds., *Strategy and the Arctic*. Toronto: Canadian Institute of Strategic Studies, 1986.

Quinn, Daniel. *Ishmael*. New York: Bantam Books, 1991. A website on Quinn's work and ideas can be found online at: http://www.ishmael.com/welcome.cfm.

Reed, Maureen G. "Environmental Assessment and Aboriginal Claims: Implementation of the Inuvialuit Final Agreement." Canadian Environmental Assessment Research Council (CEARC), April 1990, 1.

Reid, Scott. *Canada Remapped: How the Partition of Québec Will Reshape the Nation*. Vancouver: Pulp Press, 1992.

Reuters, "MacKay Mocks Russia's '15th Century' Arctic Claim." *Reuters*, August 2, 2007.

Revkin, Andrew C. "Ice Retreat Prompts Bush Shift in Arctic Policy." Dot.Earth Blog, *New York Times*, January 13, 2009. Available online at http://dotearth.blogs.nytimes.com/2009/01/13/in-parting-move-bush-sets-arctic-priorities/.

———. "A New Middle Stance Emerges in Debate over Climate." *New York Times*, January 1, 2007.

———. *The North Pole Was Here: Puzzles and Perils at the Top of the World*. New York: Kingfisher, 2006.

———. "A Tempered View of Greenland's Gushing Drainpipes." Dot Earth, *New York Times*, July 3, 2008.

———. "What's Really Up With North Pole Sea Ice?" *The New York Times*, June 27, 2008.

Reynolds, Jerry. "Eklutna Class II Gaming Hopes Bring Backlash for Alaska Natives." *Indian Country Today*, May 18, 2007. Available online at: http://www.chiefezi.net/article20070518-1.htm.

Richards, Thomas, Jr. "Organization Hirelings Have Too Much Leeway." *The Tundra Times*, June 30, 1971, as reprinted in *A Scrapbook History*, 55.

Richstone, Jeff. "Arctic Sovereignty: The Search for Substance." *Northern Perspectives* 14, No. 4 (September/October 1986).

Riewe, Rick. "The Demise of the Great White North: Environmental Impacts on the Circumpolar Aboriginal Peoples." *Information North* 18, No. 4 (1992): 1–7.

Roach, John. "Grizzly-Polar Bear Hybrid Found—But What Does It Mean?" *National Geographic News*, May 16, 2006.

Robertson, Gordon. "The Human Foundation for Peace and Security in the Arctic." *The Arctic: Choices for Peace and Security—A Public Inquiry*. West Vancouver: Gordon Soules Book Publishers, 1989, 87–92.

———. *Northern Provinces: A Mistaken Goal*. Montreal: The Institute for Research on Public Policy, 1985.

———. "Nunavut and the International Arctic." *Northern Perspectives* 15, No. 2. (May/June 1987).

Robinson, Michael, and Lloyd Binder. "The Inuvialuit Final Agreement and Resource Use Conflict: Co-Management in the Western Arctic and Final Decisions in Ottawa." *Growing Demands on a Shrinking Heritage: Managing Resource-Use Conflicts*. Calgary, Alberta: Canadian Institute of Resource Law, 1992.

Rogers, J. David. "J. David Rogers' Military Service, NAS Adak in Aleutian Islands." Online at: http://web.mst.edu/~rogersda/military_service/adak.htm.

Rohmer, Richard H. *The Arctic Imperative: An Overview of the Energy Crisis*. Toronto: McClelland and Stewart, 1974.

Rolling Stone Magazine. "Warriors & Heroes: Twenty-Five Leaders Who Are Fighting to Stave Off the Planetwide Catastrophe." *Rolling Stone Magazine*, November 3, 2005.

Rowley, Graham. "An Arctic Affair." In John Moss, ed., *Echoing Silence: Essays on Arctic Narrative*. Ottawa: University of Ottawa Press, 1997.

Royal Commission on Aboriginal Peoples. *The Right of Aboriginal Self-Government and the Constitution: A Commentary*. Ottawa: Royal Commission on Aboriginal Peoples, January 1991.

———. "Volume 1: Looking Forward, Looking Back." *The Report on the Royal Commission on Aboriginal Peoples*. Ottawa, Ontario, October 1996.

———. "Word from Commissioners." *Report on the Royal Commission on Aboriginal Peoples*. Ottawa, Ontario, October 1996.

Rozell, Ned. "Ice Fog a Product of Temperature, Topography, Dogs." Article #1319. *Alaska Science Forum*, January 8, 1997. Online at: http://www.gi.alaska.edu/ScienceForum/ASF13/1319.html.

Ryan, David. "Muskox Harvest Returns: 300 Tags for Commercial Hunt Mean 30 to 35 Jobs." *News North*, March 6, 2006.

Sapadin, Linda. *Master Your Fears: How to Triumph Over Your Worries and Get On with Your Life*. Boston: Wiley, 2004.

Saunders, A. "Beaufort Blues Again." *Arctic Circle Magazine* (March/April 1991): 14–23.

Schaeffer, John, former Adjutant General of the Alaska National Guard, Commissioner of the Department of Military and Veterans Affairs, and president of the Alaska Federation of Natives, Presentation to the ICC General Assembly, July 1992, Inuvik, NWT.

Schelling, Thomas C. *Micromotives and Macrobehavior*. New York: Norton, 1978.

Scott, Capt Alec. *Canada: A Failing State? The Canadian Forces' Role of Pride and Influence in Canada's North*. Presented to Aboriginals and the Canadian Military: Past, Present, Future Conference, Canadian Defence Academy, Kingston, Ontario, June 21–22, 2006.

Scott, Norval. "Northern Rights: U.S., Canada to Chart Path for Arctic Future; Icebreakers Head North to Map out Area Long in Dispute." *The Globe and Mail*, July 2, 2008.

Seward, William H. "The Destiny of America." Speech at the dedication of Capital University, at Columbus, Ohio, September 14, 1853.

Shukman, David. "Diary: Siberia and Climate Change." *BBC*, September 12, 2006.

Simon, Mary. "Security, Peace and the Native Peoples of the Arctic." *The Arctic: Choices for Peace and Security—A Public Inquiry*. West Vancouver: Gordon Soules Book Publishers, 1989, 31–36.

———. "Sovereignty from the North." *The Walrus*, November 2007. Online at: http://www.walrusmagazine.com/articles/2007.11-arctic-canada/3/.

Simpson, Erika. "Redefining Security." *The McNaughton Papers* 1. Toronto: Canadian Institute for Strategic Studies, March 1991, 57–75.

Sokolsky, Joel J. *Defending Canada: U.S.-Canadian Defense Policies*. New York: Priority Press, 1989.

Solovyov, Dmitry. "Mammoth Dung, Prehistoric Goo May Speed Warming." *Reuters*, September 17, 2007.

Standlea, David M. *Oil, Globalization, and the War for the Arctic Refuge*. Albany: State University of New York Press, 2006.

Steeves, John. *CBC Western Arctic Radio News*, November 2, 1981.

Stitt, Peter. "Kurdish Defences." *Kurdishaspect.com*, June 30, 2007, http://www.kurdishaspect.com/doc063007PS.html.

Stoneman, Steven. "United States Strategic Bombing." 390th Memorial Museum Foundation. Online at: http://www.390th.org/research/Stories/usbombing.htm.

Stoneman-McNichol, Jane. *On Blue Ice: The Inuvik Adventure*. Inuvik, NWT: Outcrop Ltd., 1983.

Strohmeyer, John. *Extreme Conditions: Big Oil and the Transformation of Alaska*. New York: Simon and Schuster, 1993.

Struzik, Ed. "The End of Arctic." *Equinox*, November/December 1992, 76–91.

Subsistence Management Information Site, http://www.subsistmgtinfo.org/basics.htm.

Summers, Harry G., Jr. *On Strategy: A Critical Analysis of the Vietnam War*. Novato, CA: Presidio Press, 1982.

———. *On Strategy II: A Critical Analysis of the Gulf War*. New York: Dell Publishing, 1992.

Supreme Court of Canada. "Sparrow Decision." *Judgments of the Supreme Court of Canada*, May 31, 1990. Online at: http://scc.lexum.umontreal.ca/en/1990/1990rcs1-1075/1990rcs1-1075.html.

Sykes, Jim. *Holding Our Ground: A Radio Documentary Series Featuring Alaska Natives*. Western Media Concepts, Anchorage, Alaska, 1985/1986. Online at: http://ankn.uaf.edu/curriculum/ANCSA/HoldingOurGround/.

Taylor, Glenn. "Former IRC Chair Under Investigation." *Inuvik Drum*, August 15, 1997.

Thomas, Brodie. "How Does Your Garden Grow?" *Inuvik Drum*, May 29, 2008.

Thompson, William R. "The Regional Subsystem: A Conceptual Explication and a Propositional Inventory." *International Studies Quarterly* 17, No. 1 (March 1973): 89–117.

Time Magazine. "Land of Beauty & Swat." June 9, 1958.

———. "Seward's Ice Box: A Review of *Lord of Alaska: Baranov and the Russian Adventure* by Hector Chevigny and *Alaska Under Arms* by Jean Potter." October 12, 1942. Online at: http://www.time.com/time/magazine/article/0,9171,851551-2,00.html.

———. "Thaw in the Ice Curtain." June 27, 1988.

Todorov, Tzvetan. *The Conquest of America*. Translated by Richard Howard. New York: Harper and Row, 1984.

Toronto AM 640. "UPDATE: 401 Closed as Mohawk Protest Begins." *640Toronto.com*, June 28, 2007.

Treaty of Cession (Treaty Concerning the Cession of the Russian Possessions in North America by his Majesty the Emperor of all the Russias to the United States of America). Concluded March 30, 1867; Ratified by the United States May 28, 1867; Exchanged June 20, 1867; Proclaimed by the United States June 20, 1867. Text of the Treaty is available online at: http://explorenorth.com/library/yafeatures/bl-Alaska1867.htm.

Tucker, Chris M. *Environmentalism and Environmental Change as it Affects Canadian Defence Policy and Operations*. Ottawa: Department of National Defence, 1992.

Tyler, Patrick E. "Soviets' Secret Nuclear Dumping Causes Worry for Arctic Waters." *New York Times*, May 4, 1992.

Ullman, Harlan K., and James P. Wade, *Shock and Awe: Achieving Rapid Dominance*. Washington: National Defense University, 1996.

United Nations Development Program. "New Dimensions of Human Security." In the *United Nations Development Program, Human Development Report 1994*. Oxford: Oxford University Press, 1994, 22–40. Available online at: http://www.undp.org/hdro/hdrs/1994/english/94ch2.pdf.

United Nations Environment Programme. "Adaptation to Climate Change Key Challenge for Arctic Peoples and Arctic Economy; Thawing Permafrost, Melting Sea Ice and Significant Changes in Natural Resources Demands Comprehensive Sustainable Development Plan." United Nations Environment Programme Press Release, April 10, 2007.

United States Central Intelligence Agency. *Polar Regions Atlas*. London: Jones and Bartlett Publishers International, 1985.

United States Congress. *Alaska Native Claims Settlement Act*. Public Law 92-203, December 18, 1971. Online at: http://www.lbblawyers.com/ancsatoc.htm#top.

————. *Public Law 100-241, 101 Stat. 1789: Alaska Native Claims Settlement Act Amendments of 1987; Congressional Findings and Declaration of Policy*. February 3, 1988. Online at: http://www.lbblawyers.com/87amtoc.htm.

————. *Public Law 96-487: Alaska National Interest Lands Conservation Act*. Washington, D.C., December 2, 1980. Online at: http://alaska.fws.gov/asm/anilca/toc.html.

United States Department of the Interior. Office of the Secretary. "Secretary Kempthorne Announces Decision to Protect Polar Bears under Endangered Species Act Rule Will Allow Continuation of Vital Energy Production in Alaska," May 14, 2008.

————. *Report to Congress on the Impact of Potential Crude Oil Spills in the Arctic Ocean on Alaskan Natives, Oil Pollution Act of 1990*. Sec. 8302. January 23, 1990.

United States Department of State and the Government of Denmark. Exchange of Notes Between the Secretary of State and the Minister of Denmark, U.S. Department of State, Washington, D.C., April 7, 1941.

United States Department of State Press Release. "Taken Question: Office of the Spokesman." Daily Press Briefing, Washington, D.C., January 13, 2009, http://2001-2009.state.gov/r/pa/prs/ps/2009/01/113934.htm.

University of the Arctic. "Thematic Network in Arctic Agriculture and Nature Use—the Northern Agriculture PhD Network." University of the Arctic Website. Online at: http://www.uarctic.org/singleArticle.aspx?m=280&amid=1142.

UN Works for People and Planet. "Threatened by Global Warming: Polar Bear." Online: http://www.un.org/works/environment/animalplanet/polarbear.html.

Vano, Gerard S. *Canada: The Strategic and Military Pawn*. Westport: Praeger, 1988.

Van Meurs, Pedro. *"Ten Years IFA"—Successes and Failures, A Report Card*. December 1993.

VF Project Team. "VF-24 Fighting Renegades Command History." Online at: http://www.topedge.com/panels/aircraft/sites/vf24/comhist.html.

Vmyths.com. "NSA Printer Virus (1991)." *Vmyths.com: Truth About Computer Security Hysteria*, July 24, 2000.

Wagner, Gary William. "Implementing the Environmental Assessment Provisions of a Comprehensive Aboriginal Land Rights Settlement." Master's Thesis, Department of Environment and Resource Studies, University of Waterloo, 1996.

Waltz, Kenneth. *Man, the State, and War*. New York: Columbia University Press, 1954.

————. "Political Structures." In Robert O. Keohane, ed., *Neorealism and Its Critics*. New York: Columbia University Press, 1986.

————. *Theory of International Politics*. Reading, MA: Addison-Wesley, 1979.

Washington Times. "Mock Bombing Raids of Soviet Base Halted." *Washington Times*, November 25, 1987.

————. "Soviet, US Submarines, Aircraft Wage Arctic Cold War." *Washington Times*, November 16, 1987.

————. "Soviets Shadow Navy Drill in Aleutians." *Washington Times,* November 18, 1987.

Watt-Cloutier, Sheila. "Nobel Prize Nominee Testifies About Global Warming: Inuit Leader Sheila Watt-Cloutier's Testimony Before the Inter-American Commission on Human Rights Put Spotlight on Climate Change and Indigenous Peoples." March 1, 2007. Online at: http://www.earthjustice.org/news/press/007/nobel-prize-nominee-testifies-about-global-warming.html.

Weaver, R. Kent. *The Collapse of Canada?* Washington, D.C.: Brookings Institution Press, April 1992.

Weeks, Carly. "Harper Wants to Recognize Québec as Nation within a United Canada." *CanWest News Service,* November 22, 2006.

Weigley, Russell F. *The American Way of War: A History of U.S. Military. Strategy and Policy.* Bloomington: Indiana University Press, 1973.

Whittington, Michael S. *Native Economic Development Corporations: Political and Economic Change in Canada's North, Canadian Arctic Resources Committee Policy Paper 4.* Ottawa: Canadian Arctic Resources Committee, July 1986.

Widdowson, Frances. "The Inherent Right of Unethical Governance." Presented to the Annual Meeting of the Canadian Political Science Association at York University, Toronto, Ontario, on June 1-3, 2006.

Widdowson, Frances, and Albert Howard. *Disrobing the Aboriginal Industry: The Deception Behind Indigenous Cultural Preservation; How Aboriginal Deprivation is Maintained by a Self-Serving "Industry" of Lawyers and Consultants.* Toronto: McGill-Queen's University Press, 2008.

Wickwire, James. "Alaska Natives and Their Land: Will They Keep It?" *Alaska Native Magazine 5,* No. 4 (April 1987).

Wienberg, Christian. "Arctic Countries Agree to Uphold Sea Law in North Pole Claims." *Bloomberg,* May 29, 2008.

Wikipedia. "Alaska v. Native Village of Venetie Tribal Government." *Wikipedia.org,* http://en.wikipedia.org/wiki/Alaska_v._Native_Village_of_Venetie_Tribal _Government.

————. "Bennett Island." *Wikipedia.org,* http://en.wikipedia.org/wiki/Bennett_Island.

————. "DEW Line." *Wikipedia.org,* http://en.wikipedia.org/wiki/DEW_Line.

————. "Gulf of Sidra." *Wikipedia,* http://en.wikipedia.org/wiki/Gulf_of_Sidra.

————. "Fourth World." *Wikipedia.org,* http://en.wikipedia.org/wiki/Fourth-World.

————. "Holocene." *Wikipedia.org,* http://en.wikipedia.org/wiki/Holocene.

————. "Ice Age." *Wikipedia.org,* http://en.wikipedia.org/wiki/Ice_Age.

————. "Interbreeding of Cro-Magnon and Neanderthal." *Wikipedia.org,* http://en.wikipedia.org/wiki/Interbreeding_of_Cro-Magnon_and_Neanderthal.

————. "Politics of Québec." *Wikipedia.org,* http://en.wikipedia.org /wiki/Politics_of_Québec."

————. "2007 United Nations Climate Change Conference." *Wikipedia.* Online at: http://en.wikipedia.org/wiki/2007_United_Nations_Climate_Change_Conference.

Wilson, Larry S. "Links to Military & Radar Related Sites." *Larry's Homepage. Online* at: http://www.lswilson.ca/page4.htm.

Woodard, Colin. "As a Land Thaws, So Do Greenland's Aspirations for Independence." *The Christian Science Monitor,* October 16, 2007.

Woodhead, Robert. Comments responding to Barry Zellen. "We Should Warm to the Idea of Melting Poles." *The Globe and Mail,* April 28, 2008.

Woods Hole Research Center. "The Kyoto Protocol." The "Warming Earth" section of the Woods Hole Research Center website (WHRC.org). Online at: http://www.whrc.org/resources/online_publications/warming_earth/kyoto.htm.

Worl, Riccardo. "Inupiat Self Government." *Alaska Native Magazine* 5, No. 7 (October 1987).

———. "The 1991 Time Bomb Defused." *Alaska Native Magazine* 6, No. 1 (June 1988).

Worl, Rosita. "Models of Sovereignty and Survival in Alaska." *Cultural Survival Quarterly* 27, No. 3 (September 15, 2003). Available online at: http://www.cs.org/publications/csq/csq-article.cfm?id=1692.

———. "A Political History of the North Slope Borough." *Alaska Native News Magazine* 3, No. 5 (February 1985).

WorldAtlas.com. "Islands of the World." *WorldAtlas.com.*

York, Geoffrey, and Loreen Pindera. *People of the Pines: The Warriors and the Legacy of Oka.* Toronto: Little, Brown and Co., 1991.

Young, Oran R. "The Age of the Arctic." *Foreign Policy* 61 (Winter 1985-86): 160–179.

———. *Arctic Politics: Conflict and Cooperation in the Circumpolar North.* Hanover, NH: Dartmouth University Press, 1992.

———. *Creating Regimes: Arctic Accords and International Governance.* Ithaca: Cornell University Press, 1998.

———. "Governing the Arctic: From Cold War Theater to Mosaic of Cooperation, *Global Governance: A Review of Multilateralism and International Organizations* 11 (2005): 9–15.

———. *Resource Management at the International Level: The Case of the North Pacific.* London: Frances Pinter; New York: Nichols, 1977.

Young, Oran R., and Gail Osherenko. *The Age of the Arctic: Hot Conflicts and Cold Realities.* Cambridge: Cambridge University Press, 1989.

———, eds. *Polar Politics: Creating International Environmental Regimes.* Ithaca: Cornell University Press, 1993.

Zaritsky, John. "Romeo and Juliet in Sarajevo." *PBS Front Line*, May 10, 1994. Produced by Virginia Storring, and written and edited by John Zaritsky. Online at: http://www.pbs.org/wgbh/pages/frontline/programs/transcripts/1217.html.

Zellen, Barry. "Amoco lays off Inuvialuit Staff: Questions Remain." *Tusaayaksat*, August 12, 1991, 4–5.

———. "Cold Front Rising: As Climate Change Thins Polar Ice, a New Race for Arctic Resources Begins." *Strategic Insights* 7, No. 1 (February 2008).

———. "Congratulations Bowhead Hunters." *Tusaayaksat*, October 7, 1991, 6–7.

———. "DIZ Group May Have To 'Dizzolve,' Lacks Support." *Tusaayaksat*, February 10, 1992, 10.

———. "Fisheries' Spokesman Ayles Says Bowhead Hunt Is Legal." *Tusaayaksat*, August 28, 1991, 6.

———. "44 Inupiat Visit Western Arctic; Lobby for ANWR Development." *Tusaayaksat*, December 6, 1991, 6–7.

———. "Gruben Foils Rangers' Invasion." *Tusaayaksat*, January 31, 1991, 7.

———. "Gwich'in Assembly Endorses Claim." *Tusaayaksat*, August 12, 1991, 6.

———. "Gwich'in Claim Cedes Aboriginal Rights." *Tusaayaksat*, August 12, 1991, 15.

———, ed. *The Inuvialuit Bowhead Harvest of 1991: A Pictorial History and Analysis.* Inuvik, NT: Inuvialuit Communications Society, 1992.

———. "Inuvialuit Get Bowhead License: Feds Defend IFA." *Tusaayaksat*, August 12, 1991, 2.

———. "Inuvialuit Propose Regional Government for the ISR." *Tusaayaksat*, December 6, 1991, 8–9.

———. "Inuvialuit Say Yes, but Canada Says No." *Tusaayaksat*, October 31, 1992, 2–3.

———. "Inuvialuit Seek Solution to Gwich'in Land Overlap." *Tusaayaksat*, October 21, 1991, 5, 8.

———. "IRC Holds AGM in Tuk; Re-elects Gruben Chief." *Tusaayaksat*, February 10, 1991, 16.

———. "A Look at Controversial 'Chapter Three.'" *Tusaayaksat*, August 12, 1991, 16.

———. "Lots of Info at IRC AGM." *Tusaayaksat*, February 10, 1991, 18.

———. "One Arctic, One Future?" *Arctic Circle Magazine*, September 1992.

———. "Risks and Promises in the New North." *Globe and Mail*, May 28, 1993.

———. "Sovereignty and Freedom in the Inupiaq Homeland: An Interview with General John Schaeffer, Alaska National Guard." *The Sourdough*, September 1, 1992.

———. "Toward a Post-Arctic World." *Strategic Insights* 8, No. 1 (January 2009), http://www.ccc.nps.navy.mil/si/2008/Dec/zellenDec08.asp.

———. "Two Views on ANWR; IRC Considers a Position." *Tusaayaksat*, July 10, 1991, 20.

———. "Vuntut Gwich'in Chief Roger Kaye on ANWR." *Tusaayaksat*, July 10, 1991, 20

———. "We Should Warm to Idea of Melting Poles," *Globe and Mail*, April 28, 2008, http://www.theglobeandmail.com/servlet/story/RTGAM.20080428.wcomment0428/ BNStory/specialComment/home

Zur, Ofer. "Psychology of Victimhood: Reflections on a Culture of Victims and How Psychotherapy Fuels the Victim Industry." The Zur Institute. Online at: http://www.zurinstitute.com/victimhood.html.

Index

About the Author

Barry S. Zellen is a specialist on Arctic politics and history. He lived in the Canadian Arctic from 1988–2000, where he managed several indigenous language media properties sponsored by the Northern Native Broadcast Access Program (NNBAP), a program at the Government of Canada's Department of Canadian Heritage. Zellen has been the homeland security and counterterrorism correspondent for *Intersec* since 2001, and since 2004, he has been editor of *Strategic Insights*, the quarterly journal published by the Center for Contemporary Conflict at the Naval Postgraduate School, where he directs the Arctic Security Project, a long-term research project exploring the transformation of the polar region. Zellen was educated at Harvard, where he earned his B.A. in Government in 1984, and U.C. Berkeley, where he earned his M.A. in Political Science in 1985. He has received research fellowships and grants from the MacArthur Foundation, the Institute on Global Conflict and Cooperation, and the Canadian Institute for International Peace and Security, and has taught at Wesleyan University, the Center for Northern Studies, and Arctic College. Zellen is also author of *Breaking the Ice: From Land Claims to Tribal Sovereignty in the Arctic*, published by Lexington Books in 2008.

Breinigsville, PA USA
12 March 2010
234097BV00002B/1/P